Energy, Environment and Transitional Green Growth in China

Ruizhi Pang · Xuejie Bai
Knox Lovell
Editors

Energy, Environment and Transitional Green Growth in China

 Springer

Editors
Ruizhi Pang
College of Economic and Social
  Development
Nankai University
Tianjin
China

Knox Lovell
School of Economics
University of Queensland
Brisbane, QLD
Australia

Xuejie Bai
College of Economic and Social
  Development
Nankai University
Tianjin
China

ISBN 978-981-10-7918-4   ISBN 978-981-10-7919-1   (eBook)
https://doi.org/10.1007/978-981-10-7919-1

Library of Congress Control Number: 2018931445

Printed on acid-free paper

This Springer imprint is published by the registered company Springer Nature Singapore Pte Ltd.
part of Springer Nature
The registered company address is: 152 Beach Road, #21-01/04 Gateway East, Singapore 189721,
Singapore

Contents

Part I The Expert Overviews

1 Editors' Introduction 3
Xuejie Bai, Knox Lovell and Ruizhi Pang

2 Composite Indicators for Sustainability Assessment:
Methodological Developments 15
P. Zhou and L. P. Zhang

3 Pollution Meets Efficiency: Multi-equation Modelling of
Generation of Pollution and Related Efficiency Measures 37
Finn R. Førsund

4 Environmental Productivity Growth in Consumer Durables 81
Xun Zhou

Part II Studies in Energy and Environment

5 Revisiting Reasons for Ten Years of Power Shortages
in China 111
Hui-Xian Wang, Hong-Zhou Li, Tao Zou and Yuki Tamai

6 Allocation Schemes and Efficiencies of China's Carbon
and Sulfur Emissions 139
Zhongqi Deng, Ruizhi Pang and Yu Fan

7 Carbon Productivity and Carbon Shadow Price in China's
Power Industry: An Endogenous Directional Distance
Function Approach 161
Yujiao Xian and Ke Wang

8 The Context-Dependent Total-Factor Energy Efficiency
of China's Regions 177
Jin-Li Hu and Tzu-Pu Chang

9   Was Economic Growth in China Environmentally Friendly?
    A Case Study of the Chinese Manufacturing Sector 189
    Sung Ko Li and Xinju He

10 Environmental and Energy Efficiencies Using the Stochastic
    Frontier Cost Function Type 209
    Sangmok Kang

11 Evaluating Performance of New Energy—Evidence
    from OECD 223
    Ching-cheng Lu, Jin-chi Hsieh, Yung-ho Chiu and Zhen-sheng Lin

Part III   Studies in Transitional Green Growth

12 Factor Price Distortion, Technological Innovation Pattern
    and the Biased Technological Progress of Industry in China:
    An Empirical Analysis Based on Mediating Effect Model 247
    Xuejie Bai and Shuang Li

13 Environmental Innovation and Green Transformation of
    Economic Growth Pattern: Evidence from China 277
    Xie Rong-hui

14 Study of Regional Efficiency in China: Perspectives
    of FDI and Green Development 289
    Yang Li, Chao-Ling Guo, Xiaoying Guo and Yu-Hsuan Liao

15 Emissions Cost and Value-Added Benefit of Exports in China:
    An Analysis Based on a Global Input-Output Model 307
    Wencheng Zhang and Rui Wei

Part I
The Expert Overviews

Chapter 1
Editors' Introduction

Xuejie Bai, Knox Lovell and Ruizhi Pang

1 Background

1.1 Background for the Volume

The transitional growth experience China is undergoing, with its emphasis on reducing the energy intensity of the economy while maintaining satisfactory rates of economic growth, is one of the most important research topics concerned with the performance of China's economy. The Nankai research group on efficiency and productivity, located in the College of Economic and Social Development at Nankai University, is one of the first research teams engaged in the study of the efficiency and green productivity growth of China's economy. Since 2006 the Nankai research group, which includes scholars in industrial economics, regional economics and green logistics, has achieved fruitful research outcomes. A measurement framework for China's green growth experience has been proposed, including an appropriate GDP growth rate and measures of energy saving, low pollution and low carbon emissions. Such green growth can be achieved through economic reform and innovation oriented to improve China's efficiency and productivity, inclusive of its economic resources and its energy use and composition, and its conventional GDP and its emissions and other environmental impacts. In addition to these efforts, the Nankai research group has formed strong partnerships with scholars overseas who are interested in the transitional growth performance of China's economy.

X. Bai · R. Pang (✉)
Nankai University, Tianjin, China
e-mail: prz0525@nankai.edu.cn

K. Lovell
University of Queensland, Brisbane, Australia

© Springer Nature Singapore Pte Ltd. 2018
R. Pang et al. (eds.), *Energy, Environment and Transitional Green Growth in China*, https://doi.org/10.1007/978-981-10-7919-1_1

The Nankai research group has actively participated in a range of international conferences related to economic development. It hosted the Conference on Industrial Development and Industrial Efficiency across the Taiwan Strait in 2008, 2010, and 2013. In addition, several members of the Nankai research group participated and delivered presentations at the Asia-Pacific Productivity Conference (APPC) in 2006, 2008, 2010 and 2014, and the European Workshop on Efficiency and Productivity Analysis (EWEPA) in 2007 and 2009. A wide range of topics related to the measurement and estimation of efficiency and productivity, and their roles as important drivers of economic and industrial development, were the focus of academic discussions.

In July of 2015, Professor Knox Lovell (University of Queensland, Australia), Professor Robin Sickles (Rice University, USA), Professor Cliff Huang (Vanderbilt University, USA) and Professor Tsutan Fu (Soochow University, Taiwan), were invited by Nankai University to host a workshop for advanced research methodology in the fields of efficiency and productivity, further internationalizing the fields of the study at the Nankai research group. In July of 2016, with the support of Professor Knox Lovell, Professor Cliff Huang and Professor Tsutan Fu, the Nankai research group successfully hosted APPC2016, the first Asian-Pacific Productivity Conference hosted in China. APPC2016 was attended by over 120 scholars and experts from more than 20 countries around the world, including Australia, USA, Canada, England, Germany, Italy, Japan, South Korea, Malaysia, Thailand, Hong Kong and Taiwan. Since it was the first APPC to take place in China, it attracted many participants from Chinese universities, and the main topics were selected to focus on the efficiency, productivity and green composition of China's economic growth.

We believe the focus of efficiency and productivity, including the green component of both, of China's economic growth experience is not only important to the economic development of China as it transitions from one growth model to another, but also in light of China's sheer economic size, to the long-term health of world economic development. Considering that APPC2016 was the first such event held in China, as the host, we feel obligated to continue the study of China's economic development. This is the background of this collection of research. In addition, the Centre for Efficiency and Productivity (CEP) in Nankai University has been newly established, and we consider this monograph to be a good gift for CEP with the website http://cep.nankai.edu.cn.

1.2 Background on China's Economic Growth Model and Its Transition

Between 1978, the year when China started its economic reform and 2008, China experienced nearly 30 years of uninterrupted high-speed economic growth, which was regarded by many as "the Chinese miracle." However, accompanying the fast economic growth was a huge consumption of energy, depletion of natural resources, and continuous deterioration of the ecosystem. For approximately the first decade of the 21st century China's domestic economic policy continued to emphasise energy-intensive rapid growth based on capital investment and expansion of heavy industry and exports. During this decade China's GDP grew by roughly 10% per year, primary energy consumption increased proportionately, and carbon dioxide emissions grew by about 8% per year (see Figs. 1.1, 1.2 and 1.3 for the post-1978 history). At about 2007 China became the world's largest contributor to global greenhouse gas emissions. (Sources: Chinese Statistics Yearbook, 1980–2016, Chinese Energy Statistics Yearbook, 2009–2015, and Chinese Environment Statistics Yearbook, 2009–2015).

Beginning in 2008 the world economy declined sharply as a result of the global financial crises initiated by the subprime mortgage crisis in the US, before recovering only recently. With this background, China's development model of reliance on heavy industry, exports and capital investment met with serious challenges. The subsequent decline in exports and downward trend in capital investment both contributed to a significant slowdown in China's economic growth. Both of the changes that have taken place globally and domestically constitute an opportunity for China to transform its growth model from a rapid growth energy- and resources-intensive economy driven by investment and exports to a slower growth energy- and resources-saving economy driven largely by domestic consumption. The transition can be enhanced by raising the efficiency and productivity of resources, energy and management.

Beginning with the 12th Five Year Plan (2011–2015), China's domestic economic policy transitioned to a "New Normal" approach to economic development involving slower growth with an emphasis on domestic services and consumption and reduced energy intensity. Economic growth has slowed to 7–8% per year, and the growth in primary energy consumption and greenhouse gas emissions has slowed dramatically. The energy intensity and carbon intensity of GDP have both

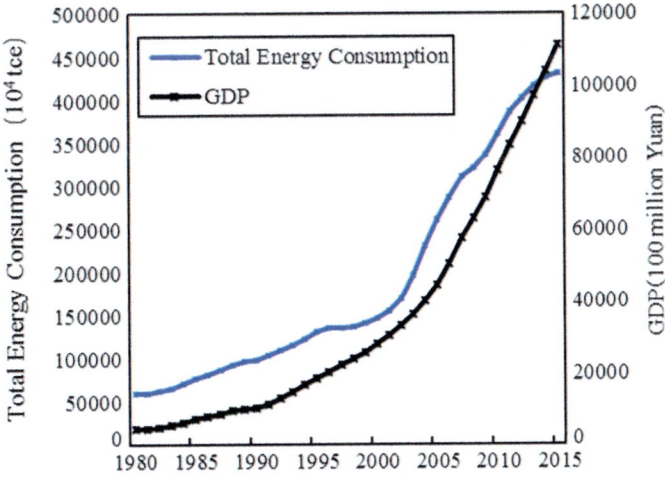

Fig. 1.1 Energy consumption and GDP

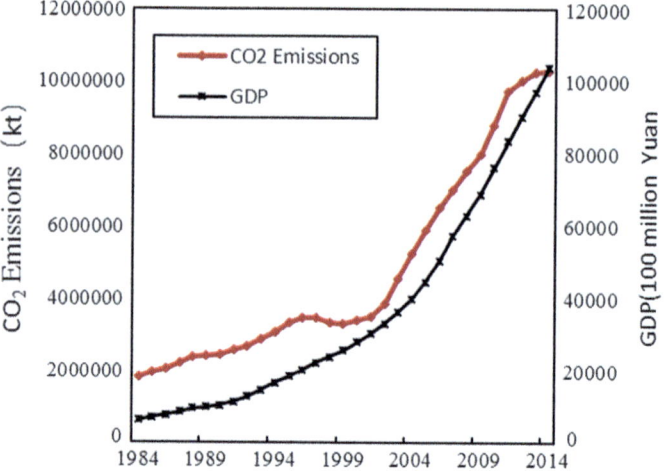

Fig. 1.2 CO₂ emissions and GDP

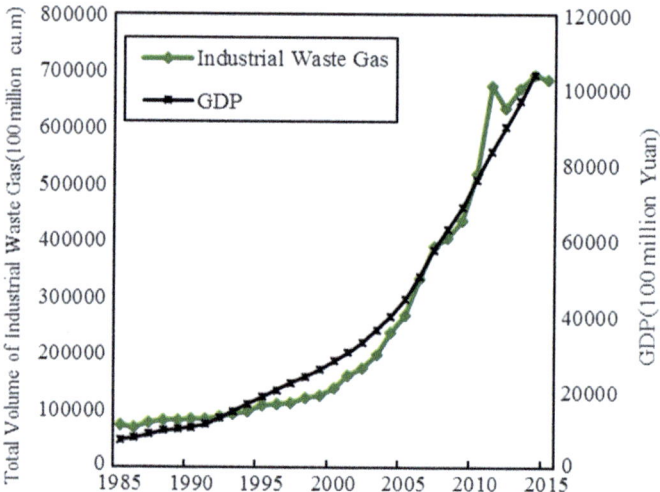

Fig. 1.3 Industrial waste gas and GDP

declined. The trends can be seen from international comparisons with other countries depicted in Figs. 1.4, 1.5 and Table 1.1. (Sources: The World Bank, https://data.worldbank.org/indicator) In 1995 China's energy intensity was 14. 23 MJ/$GDP (2011 PPP), nearly 2.7 times that of Japan and 1.7 times that of the U.S. By 2014 China's energy intensity had declined to 8.68, just 1.8 times that of Japan and 1.3 times that of the U.S. China's relative energy efficiency increased substantially, although its absolute efficiency is still not high. As for its CO_2 emissions intensity, China also experienced a big decline from 1.07 kg/$GDP

(2011 PPP) in 1995 to 0.59 kg/$GDP (2011 PPP) in 2014, decreasing nearly 50% of that in 1995. Hu (2016) surveys the environmental objectives and impacts of the five most recent five year plans, concluding with the 12th Five Year Plan.

An important driver of these domestic changes has been an increased role for market mechanisms in the allocation of resources. Market-based environmental policies such as environmental subsidies and taxes and emissions trading schemes have been implemented in an effort to meet environmental targets as efficiently and cost-effectively as possible, as emphasised by Wang et al. (2015, 2017), Zhang (2015) and Gu et al. (2016), among others. Part of the impetus for the enactment of market-based policies is a growing awareness by Chinese citizens of the adverse impacts of air, water and land pollution on human health and prosperity (Yang and Feng 2017) and an acknowledgement that road transport is a major source of air pollution (Kishimoto et al. 2017).

The recent history is chronicled in great detail, with policy recommendations, in a pair of reports issued by the China Council for International Cooperation on Environment and Development (CCICED), "Evaluation and Prospects for a Green Transition Process in China" and "Progress in Environment and Development Policies in China and Impact of CCICED's Policy Recommendations", available at the link provided at the end of this chapter.

From the first year of 13th Five Year Plan (2016–2020), China has enacted very restrictive environmental protection policies, and thousands of industrial plants and coal-fired boilers that failed to meet the new emissions targets are obliged to close down. The serious problem of air pollution in the Beijing-Tianjin-Hebei area has been addressed, in part by implementation of the aforementioned emissions trading scheme. Air pollution originating in road transport is to be reduced by removing millions of high-emission vehicles and by greatly expanding the electric vehicle market. By the end of the plan, the energy intensity of GDP is to be reduced by 15% from 2015 levels, and the carbon intensity of GDP is to be reduced by 18%, principally through a shift in the energy mix away from fossil fuels and toward renewables. Consequently, and also due to slower planned economic growth,

Fig. 1.4 International comparison of energy intensity

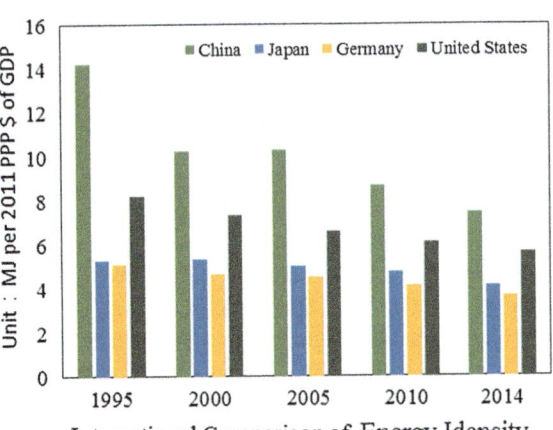

International Comparison of Energy Idensity

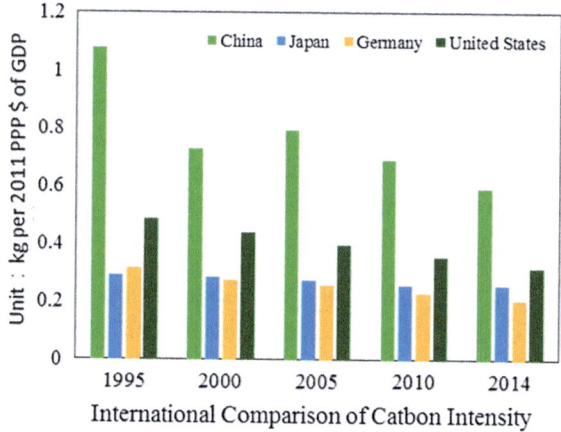

Fig. 1.5 International comparison of carbon intensity

Table 1.1 International comparison of energy intensity and carbon intensity

Year	Energy intensity unit: MJ/GDP ($2011 PPP)				Carbon intensity unit: kg/GDP ($2011 PPP)			
	China	Japan	Germany	The U.S.	China	Japan	Germany	The U.S.
1995	14.23	5.28	5.10	8.23	1.07	0.29	0.31	0.49
2000	10.23	5.31	4.64	7.34	0.73	0.28	0.27	0.44
2005	10.28	5.02	4.51	6.60	0.79	0.27	0.26	0.39
2010	8.68	4.74	4.12	6.07	0.69	0.26	0.23	0.35
2014	7.43	4.09	3.63	5.63	0.59	0.26	0.20	0.32

greenhouse gas emissions are to be reduced by 18% from 2015 levels. This provides a strong indication of the intention of China's central government to adjust its economic growth model. Seligsohn and Hsu (2016) survey the intended impacts of the 13th Five Year Plan on the environment.

In conjunction with its greener domestic economic policy, China has modified its international approach to climate change and global warming. At the Paris Conference of the Parties in 2015 China committed to peaking its total greenhouse gas emissions by around 2030, reducing the carbon intensity of GDP by about two-thirds from its 2005 level, reducing the share of fossil fuels in primary energy consumption, and increasing its forest coverage (Center for Climate and Energy Solutions 2015). China has also begun playing a constructive role in international climate negotiations. China was an early signatory to the Paris Agreement in April 2016, it ratified the Agreement in September 2016 and the Agreement entered into force in November 2016. China's involvement on the international front is summarised by Gao (2016) and updated frequently on the China Climate Change Info-Net (http://en.ccchina.gov.cn/index.aspx).

With this background, we expect this volume to contribute to a continuing chronicling of the development of China's economy during the green transition period, and also to spur additional policy-relevant research into economic growth patterns that are both economically productive and environmentally friendly.

2 Part I: The Expert Overviews

The three chapters in Part I provide authoritative, and frequently opinionated, surveys of and original contributions to three important research areas directly related to a simultaneous analysis of economic and environmental performance. In Chap. 2 Zhou analyses the construction of meaningful composite indicators and the properties they should satisfy, with an emphasis on indicators of environmental sustainability. In Chap. 3 Førsund provides a wide-ranging treatment of the construction of meaningful analytical models of joint production that generate environmental externalities and that satisfy the materials balance condition. In Chap. 4 Zhou shows how to analyse environmental performance, not of widely studied production activities but of rarely studied but equally important consumption activities.

2.1 Chapter 2

Against a backdrop of the causes and consequences of global warming and climate change, Zhou and Zhang summarise recent state-of-the-art methodological developments underlying the construction of meaningful composite indicators. The authors pay special attention to the development of indicators created for the assessment of sustainable development and their subsequent use in policy analysis and decision making. Underlying the concept of sustainable development are climate change, environmental pollution and natural resource depletion.

Many such composite indicators exist, three of the most popular being the Ecological Footprint, the Environmental Sustainability Index and the Environmental Performance Index. The objective of each is to aggregate numerous diverse individual component indicators having different units of measurement and different ranges or scales into a single coherent aggregate composite indicator. Aggregation requires assigning weights to each component indicator that reflect their relative importance. The authors develop and evaluate alternative aggregation procedures, which they categorize as exogenous methods (in which weights are determined prior to the construction of the composite indicator, either arbitrarily or by expert judgement), endogenous methods (in which weights are determined simultaneously with the construction of the composite indicator by the behaviour of the individual component indicators themselves) and hybrid methods. After evaluating the strengths and weaknesses of alternative methods, the authors provide a menu of challenges for future work on composite sustainability indicators, and an extensive, up-to-date list of references spanning a number of disciplines.

2.2 Chapter 3

Førsund also uses global warming and climate change to motivate an investigation into the modelling of production activities that combine primary inputs with materials inputs to produce intended outputs and also generate unintended by-products, or residuals. A prominent example involves the use of fossil fuels to generate electricity and also carbon dioxide emissions that contribute to global warming.

A meaningful joint production model must incorporate four sets of variables: service inputs, such as capital and labour; materials inputs, such as coal and gas; intended outputs, such as electricity and steel; and unintended by-products, such as ground- and surface-water pollution and greenhouse gas emissions. The model must include two sets of equations: one for the production of the intended outputs and the other for the generation of the unintended by-products. The two sets of equations are not independent, but linked, since changes in inputs must generate changes in both intended outputs and unintended by-products. The model must satisfy a number of properties, the most important being the materials balance condition, which states that mass contained in the materials inputs cannot disappear during the production process, but must appear either in the intended outputs or the unintended by-products. Until recently this condition was ignored in much of the economics and operations research literature devoted to the measurement of environmental efficiency and productivity.

Førsund considers the measurement of efficiency, overall and environmental, within the complete model, by converting equations to weak inequalities, and he also considers alternative approaches to regulation of the unintended by-products. Throughout he incorporates a rich history of thought on the topics he considers, and his list of references ranges from Jevons, Pigou and Frisch up to the present day.

2.3 Chapter 4

Whereas Førsund examines the generation of unintended by-products of production activities, Zhou examines an equally widespread phenomenon that for some reason, the data constraint perhaps, has rarely been studied: the generation of unintended by-products of consumption activities. The problem of consumer-driven externalities was examined most prominently by Pigou and Coase, but the problem has been largely ignored in the environmental performance literature. A prominent example, which Zhou studies empirically, is driving a car, a consumption activity that combines resources and energy to provide transportation services and residual air pollution. This activity, which might be called joint consumption in parallel with the joint production activity studied by Førsund, is of increasing concern in China and elsewhere.

The concept of productivity change, the ratio of an index of output quantities to an index of input quantities, is widely studied, at the aggregate economy level, at the industry level, and at the level of individual firms or plants. The concept has been generalised to incorporate unintended by-products, which has led to a variety of environmental productivity indices. Zhou applies the concept of an environmental productivity index to the consumption of passenger car services. In his simplified model, engine power and curb weight combine to jointly produce transportation services and carbon dioxide emissions. Using data from Finland, he finds environmental productivity growth of over 3% per year since the turn of the century. He attributes virtually all environmental productivity growth to improvements in technology, as manufacturers have produced more environmentally friendly cars.

The real value of Zhou's contribution lies not productivity developments in Finnish automobiles however, but in three areas: (i) highlighting a phenomenon, environmental productivity change in consumer durables, that deserves further research; (ii) emphasising the need for more data on the environmental impacts of consumption activities; and (iii) developing an analytical framework capable of supporting empirical work in the area. As a final thought, Zhou's work may usefully be related to the "home production" literature associated with Gary Becker, recipient of the 1992 Nobel Prize in Economic Sciences.

3 Part II: Studies in Energy and Environment

Chapters 5–11 explore a wide range of topics concerning energy utilization and its environmental impacts. Five chapters discuss China's experience, and the two chapters that examine the experiences of OECD countries are likely to have insights of relevance to China's experience. Chapters 5–9 all use Chinese provincial data to explore a variety of issues related to energy use. Chapters 10 and 11 also explore energy use, but with aggregate data from OECD countries.

In Chap. 5 Li, Wang, Zou and Tamayi search for the sources of a decade of serious power shortages in China. One obvious potential source is waste, or operational inefficiency, which they reject, using both parametric and non-parametric methods. They also reject underinvestment as a source. They finally settle on a sort of market failure hypothesis brought on by a gap between the market price of coal and the government-imposed price of electricity, which induced management to reduce capacity utilisation, leading to power shortages.

In Chap. 6 Deng, Pang and Fan, and in Chap. 7 Xian and Wang, use different analytical frameworks to examine alternative aspects of the same problem: uncovering the relationship linking fossil fuel use and greenhouse gas emissions across Chinese provinces. The first team uses a zero sum gain version of data envelopment analysis to contrast actual emissions with exogenous administrative emissions reduction targets embodied in the 11th Five Year Plan and endogenous emissions reduction targets generated by their analytical framework. Unsurprisingly, they find large differences between the two allocation schemes, which they attribute to the inefficiency of the administrative targets. The second team examines a measure of environmental productivity change and its components, and trends in the shadow price of CO_2 emissions, in a framework in which inputs, including coal equivalents, produce electricity and CO_2 emissions. They find productivity decline, except in the western region, and a doubling of the shadow price of CO_2, with wide variation across regions. Both studies provide a basis for optimism. Inefficient administrative allocation schemes can be improved, and regional variation in shadow prices allow for efficiency-enhancing reallocation, as may happen when China's new emissions trading scheme gets underway.

In Chap. 8 Hu and Chang compare total efficiency and energy efficiency across China's provinces, using a context-dependent analytical framework in which inputs, including coal equivalents, produce GDP and SO_{-2} emissions. Total efficiency treats all inputs as variable, while energy efficiency treats all inputs except coal equivalents as quasi-fixed. The authors find inter-regional variation in both types of efficiency, but the nature of the variation differs geographically, with efficient provinces by one efficiency measure tending to be inefficient by the other. In Chap. 9 Li and He ask whether Chinese economic growth has been environmentally friendly, examining trends in the environmental performance of Chinese cities rather than provinces. In their analytical framework inputs, including energy, produce gross output and three undesirable by-products, waste dust emission, waste gas and waste water. In one exercise they maximise the desirable output, and in the other they minimise the three by-products. The authors find an upward trend through time in the average efficiency of producing the desirable output, and a somewhat less pronounced upward trend through time in the average efficiency of reducing the three waste by-products. They also find wide geographic dispersion in both efficiency measures. They discuss these findings and more against a background of China's 12th Five Year Plan aimed at enhancing green economic growth.

In Chap. 10 Kang uses a stochastic cost frontier framework in a creative manner, as a way of investigating the abilities of OECD countries to maximise environmental efficiency, by attempting to minimise CO_2 emissions, given desirable outputs and inputs, one of which is fossil fuel use. A second stage is devoted to the estimation of energy efficiency, as the ratio of minimum fossil fuel use to actual fossil fuel use, controlling for other inputs and outputs. Results indicate considerable inefficiency of both types. In Chap. 11 Lu, Hsieh, Chiu and Lin use a meta-frontier framework based on dynamic data envelopment analysis to investigate the use of new forms of green energy, by estimating green energy efficiency and green energy performance of OECD countries. In their model new energy is one of three inputs used to generate CO_2 emissions and a carry-over output, total revenue. The main finding is a wide variation in green energy efficiency between the top-ten and bottom-ten countries. Once again it is possible to draw an optimistic conclusion from both studies: there is much room for improvement in energy usage performance.

4 Part III: Studies in Transitional Growth

Chapters 12–15 use a wide range of empirical techniques to explore a similarly wide range of topics related to China's transitional growth experience, with emphasis on its environmental impacts. Chapters 12 and 13 take different approaches to the analysis of the crucial role of environmental innovation as a driver of the magnitude and structure of economic growth. Chapters 14 and 15 explore the roles of two dimensions of international trade, the regional allocation of foreign direct investment *into* China and the emissions embodied in exports *from* China.

In Chap. 12 Bai and Li find that technical progress has been biased in a capital-using direction in Chinese industry. While they do not incorporate an energy input or an environmental by-product, depending on complementarities between future capital investment and energy usage, their findings have potential implications for the environmental nature of transitional growth in Chinese industry and for the desirability of market-oriented reforms. In Chap. 13 Xie divides innovation into green and traditional components and examines the impacts of each type of innovation on a creative indicator of the greenness of economic growth apparently introduced by Xie et al. (2017). The finding that green innovation is a driver of both the magnitude and the green-ness of economic growth is perhaps unsurprising, but the finding that traditional innovation does not have a positive impact is surprising, and receives an interesting explanation.

In Chap. 14 Li, Guo, Guo and Liao examine the impacts of foreign direct investment from two sources, overseas and non-overseas Chinese regions, on the sustainable development of Chinese regions, in which "sustainable" encompasses three dimensions, economic, environmental and social. Selection of proxies for the three dimensions is creative, and the findings suggest that the regional pattern of both sources of foreign direct investment has been suboptimal from a sustainability perspective. In Chap. 15 Zhang and Wei reverse directions and analyse Chinese exports from both economic and environmental perspectives. They do so by calculating the domestic value added and emissions content of Chinese exports. They find an increase in the value added of exports combined with a reduction in the pollution intensity of value added exports, implying an improvement in the environmental efficiency of export production. They also conduct a decomposition analysis of gaps in the pollution intensity of value added exports between China and other large economies, which they attribute largely to a combination of a dirtier domestic production technology and a cleaner export structure.

Some Useful References and Links

Center for Climate and Energy Solutions (2015), "China's Contribution to the Paris Climate Agreement," https://www.c2es.org/site/assets/uploads/2015/07/chinas-contribution-paris-climate-agreement.pdf

Gao, Yun (2016), "China's Response to Climate Change Issues after Paris Climate Change Conference," *Advances in Climate Change Research* 7, 235–40

Gu, A., F. Teng and X. Feng (2016), "Effects of Pollution Control Measures on Carbon Emissions Reduction in China: Evidence from the 11th and 12th Five-Year Plans," *Climate Policy* http://dx.doi.org/10.1080/14693062.2016.1258629

Hu, A.-G. (2016), "The Five-Year Plan: A New Tool for Energy Saving and Emissions Reduction in China," *Advances in Climate Change Research* 7, 222–28

Kishimoto, P. N., V. J. Karpus, M. Zhong, E. Saikawa, Xu. Zhang and Xi. Zhang (2017), "The Impact of Coordinated Policies on Air Pollution Emissions from Road Transportation in China," *Transportation Research Part D* 54, 30–49

Seligsohn, D., and A. Hsu (2016), "How China's 13th Five-Year Plan Addresses Energy and the Environment," http://www.chinafile.com/reporting-opinion/environment/how-chinas-13th-five-year-plan-addresses-energy-and-environment

Wang, C., Y. Yang and J. Zhang (2015), "China's Sectoral Strategies in Energy Conservation and Carbon Mitigation," *Climate Policy* 15 (sup 1), S60–S80

Wang, P., L. Liu and T. Wu (2017), "A Review of China's Climate Governance: State, Market and Civil Society," *Climate Policy* https://doi.org/10.1080/14693062.2017.1331903

Xie, R. H., Y. J. Yuan and J. J. Huang (2017), "Different Types of Environmental Regulations and Heterogeneous Influence on "Green" Productivity: Evidence from China," *Ecological Economics* 132, 104–12

Yang, X., and F. Teng (2017), "Air Quality Benefit of China's Mitigation Target to Peak its Emission by 2030," *Climate Policy* http://dx.doi.org/10.1080/14693062.2016.1244762

Zhang, Z. (2015), "Carbon Emissions Trading in China: The Evolution from Pilots to a Nationwide Scheme," *Climate Policy* 15 (sup 1), S104–S126

China Climate Change Info-Net http://en.ccchina.gov.cn/index.aspx

China Council for International Cooperation on Environment and Development www.cciced.net

The Tsinghua-MIT China Energy and Climate Project https://globalchange.mit.edu/research/research-projects/china-energy-and-climate-project-cecp

Policy Research Center for Environment and Economy (PRCEE) www.greengrowthknowledge.org

Center for Energy & Environmental Policy Research, BIT. http://www.ceep.net.cn/index.htm

Center for Energy & Environmental Policy Research, http://www.ceep.cas.cn/

Energy Research Institute of National Development and Reform Commission, http://www.eri.org.cn/jgsz.php?aid=231&cid=61

China Center of Energy Economics Research at XMU, http://cceer.xmu.edu.cn/main.htm

Academy of Chinese Energy Strategy, http://www.cup.edu.cn/aces/

Chapter 2
Composite Indicators for Sustainability Assessment: Methodological Developments

P. Zhou and L. P. Zhang

1 Introduction

The intensive alteration to the natural environment by human beings has been posing challenges to the natural and socio-economic systems (Munda and Saisana 2011). Global warming causes a huge economic loss to agriculture sector of some countries including China in the past decade (Chen et al. 2016). Air pollution has severe negative health effects, especially for those vulnerable people such as the elderly, infant and child (He et al. 2016). Some pollution reduction mandates by central and local governments also triggered severe unintended consequences. For example, due to the effect "polluting thy neighbor", the most downstream county of a province in China has up to 20% more water polluting activities than other counterparts since 2001 (Cai et al. 2016). Undoubtedly, problems resulted from climate change, environmental pollution, depletion of natural resources and others have been threatening the development of our society (Tilman et al. 2002). A rising concern has been voiced in scientific community and policy circles on how human beings should interact with nature, and how they are responsible for future generations in a sustainable way (Baumgärtner and Quaas 2010). Indeed, there are so many efforts and initiatives towards sustainable development in our society. However, whether those activities are adequate for pursuing sustainable development is still questionable (Sala et al. 2015). To provide a scientific basis for fighting with climate change and avoiding unanticipated consequence, the status of sustainability should be evaluated in a solid and reliable manner to assess whether the

P. Zhou (✉) · L. P. Zhang
College of Economics and Management, Nanjing University of Aeronautics
and Astronautics, 29 Jiangjun Avenue, Nanjing, China
e-mail: cemzp@nuaa.edu.cn

P. Zhou
School of Economics and Management, China University of Petroleum,
No. 66 Changjiang West Road, Qingdao, China

© Springer Nature Singapore Pte Ltd. 2018
R. Pang et al. (eds.), *Energy, Environment and Transitional Green Growth in China*, https://doi.org/10.1007/978-981-10-7919-1_2

target of "meet the needs of the present without compromising the ability of future generations to meet their own needs" has gradually been realized (WCDE 1987).

Theoretically, sustainability is a multi-dimension (e.g. economic, social and ecological) concept encompassing internal relationships between different dimensions, which brings difficulty in sustainability assessment (Mayer 2008). In addition, the issues such as multi-interpretation in concept, the determination of boundaries and measurability, also cause a rising concern on the reliability of sustainability assessment (Hák et al. 2012). Different methods have been introduced into sustainability assessment, e.g. indicators, product-based assessment, and integrated assessment (Ness et al. 2007). The indicator approach, owing to some desirable properties like simplicity, quantifiability and timely indentification of the trends, has acquired compelling attention in the literature of environmental and ecological economics (Díaz-Balteiro and Romero 2004). At the end of last century, the United Nations suggested to develop indicators for sustainable development to provide an analytical foundation for policy analysis and decision making at different levels (UNCED 1992). Since then, various indicators have been developed, e.g. Ecological Footprint (Wackernagel and Rees 1998), Environmental Sustainability Index (Esty et al. 2005), Human Development Index (UNDP 2014), Environmental Policy Stringency Index (Botta and Kozluk 2014), World Energy Trilemma Index (WEC 2016), Oxford Sustainability Index (OCC 2016), and Environmental Performance Index (Hsu et al. 2016). According to Zhou and Ang (2008), the existing sustainability indicators may broadly be grouped into non-composite and composite indicators. Non-composite indicators are usually in the form of a set of indicators or an integrated indicator. The approach of composite indicators aims to aggregate various indicators into a single real-valued score to represent an entity's sustainable performance. As Nardo et al. (2008) argued, composite indicators can reduce the visible size of indicators and are easier to interpret than a set of individual indicators. Hence, composite indicators have recently gained much popularity in sustainability assessment. Hereafter we refer to composite indicators for sustainability assessment as composite sustainability indicators (CSI) for convenience purpose.

The reliability of a CSI heavily depends on the underlying methods which are used for constructing the CSI. In the past decades, scholars have contributed to developing alternative methods for constructing CSI. See, for example, van den Bergh and Veen-Groot (2001), Cherchye and Kuosmanen (2004), Díaz-Balteiro and Romero (2004), Munda (2005), Despotis (2005a, b), Zhou et al. (2007) and Zanella et al. (2015). In parallel, Ebert and Welsch (2004) showed how to construct a meaningful environmental index from the social choice perspective. Zhou et al. (2006a) proposed an information loss criterion for comparing different aggregation functions. More recently, Pollesch and Dale (2015, 2016) investigated on the application of aggregation theory and normalization methods to sustainability assessment. Zhou et al. (2017) further looked through the meaningfulness of composite environmental indices and showed that a cardinally meaningful composite indicator can be constructed by nonparametric frontier approach. Several scholars have also reviewed past CSI studies with emphasis on their theoretical and conceptual developments, e.g. Parris and Kates (2003), Ness et al. (2007) and Mori and Christodoulou (2012). As pointed out by Mayer (2008), the identification of bias introduced by method choice plays a significant role in improving the utility of CSI for supporting policy making. The study by Böhringer and Jochem (2007) highlights the significance of scientifically sound methods for normalization, weighting and aggregation in building meaningful CSI. The purpose of this chapter is to provide a systematic literature review of the methodological developments in constructing CSI. It is expected that such a review provides not only a sketch of the mainstream methods with their strengths and weaknesses but also useful insights on the choice of an appropriate method for constructing CSI in various application scenarios.

The rest of this chapter is organized as follows. Section 2 provides a description of the framework on CSI construction. Section 3 summarizes the most popular or promising methods in constructing CSI. In Sect. 4, we discuss the influential factors and principles in method choice at the stages of normalization and aggregation. The last section concludes this study with discussions on potential future research topics.

2   Generic Procedure of Constructing CSI

The construction of CSI starts from the determination of a set of indicators for the entities whose sustainable performance is to be evaluated. The given information may be represented by a performance matrix X as shown in Eq. (1) that deals with m entities and n indicators.

$$X = \begin{bmatrix} x_{11} & \cdots & x_{1n} \\ \vdots & \ddots & \vdots \\ x_{m1} & \cdots & x_{mn} \end{bmatrix} \quad (m, n \geq 2) \tag{1}$$

$$W = \begin{bmatrix} w_1 & \cdots & w_n \end{bmatrix}$$

In Eq. (1), x_{ij} refers to the performance value of entity i pertinent to indicator j, and W is a weight vector in which w_j denotes the weight assigned to indicator j. The indicators for sustainability performance evaluation are usually measured by different units. In order to aggregate individual indicators into CSI, some aggregation methods require each indicator to be dimensionless by certain transformation function, i.e. $V = v(X)$. We assume that the performance matrix after normalization is denoted by

$$V = \begin{bmatrix} v_{11} & \cdots & v_{1n} \\ \vdots & \ddots & \vdots \\ v_{m1} & \cdots & v_{mn} \end{bmatrix} \quad (m, n \geq 2) \tag{2}$$

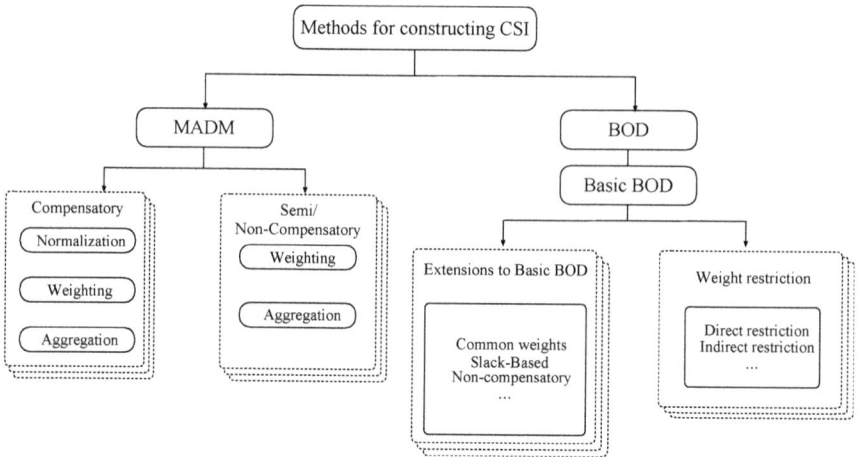

Fig. 1 Classification of the methods for constructing CSI

Once the weight vector W is determined, different aggregation techniques might be used to combine individual indicators into real-valued CSI. In general, the aggregation techniques aim to:

Seek a function $r_i = f_1(X(\text{or } V), W)$ for providing sustainable performance rankings of entities, and/or

Seek a function $u_i = f_2(X(\text{or } V), W)$ for providing sustainable performance index for each entity.

As described above, the construction of CSI from a set of pre-defined indicators mainly involves the normalization of indicators, the assignment of indicator weights and the search for an appropriate aggregation function. In literature, various methods have been used for these three steps, which might broadly be classified into two categories. One is based on multi-attribute decision making (MADM), and the other is based on benefit of the doubt (BOD) that is a data envelopment analysis (DEA)-like approach (see Fig. 1). Although BOD methods in the broad sense can be attributed to MADM, they are different from each other in several aspects. For example, by MADM, a set of common weights are shared by each entity. However, BOD methods often aim to find a different set of weights which are most favorable for each entity. Besides, CSI based on BOD methods may not require normalization.

3 MADM Methods

MADM is a well-established methodology with the aim to make choice under multiple conflict criteria be more explicit, rational and efficient (Yoon and Hwang 1995). MADM methods can be involved in all procedure of constructing CSI. In the followings, we shall describe the steps with focus on the methods used. It starts from normalization followed by data aggregation, by which the importance of indicator weighting is highlighted and discussed.

3.1 Normalization Methods

The underlying indicators for assessing sustainability are generally in different measurable units, and different indicators have distinct ranges or scales (Mayer 2008). As such, normalization procedure is often taken for making underlying indicators comparable (Nardo et al. 2008). The commonly used normalization methods in constructing CSI may be categorized into three categories, namely, standard deviation from the mean (i.e. z-score), distance from a reference, and distance from best and worst performers (i.e. re-scaling). Table 1 provides a description of the three normalization methods.

Z-score is used to statistically measure the relationship between the value of a sustainable indicator and the mean of the values of the sustainable indicator system. It has an average of zero, indicating that it can avoid introducing aggregation distortions stemming from the differences in indicator means (Freudenberg 2003). The positive (negative) value indicates that it is above (below) the mean by how many standard deviations. Z-score transforms the original variables into a common scale. These desirable characteristics make it be frequently used in normalization, see Floridi et al. (2011).

Distance to a reference aims to normalize the underlying indicators by measuring the distance of an entity to a reference point. When the sustainable indicators are ratio-scale and the distance to a reference method is used for normalization, the CSI derived from the simple additive weighting aggregation function are found to be meaningful (Ebert and Welsch 2004). In operation, the method of distance to a reference needs to first determine the reference point, which could be the leader of the entities (Zhou et al. 2006a) or an external benchmark (Nardo et al. 2008). A popular practice in application is to use the base time as a reference so that the sustainability performance of entities could be dynamically monitored. Examples of such studies can be found in Kang (2002), Kang et al. (2002), Krajnc and Glavič (2005) and

Table 1 The commonly used normalized methods

Method	Formula	Notes
Z-score	$v_{ij} = \frac{(x_{ij} - \bar{x}_j)}{\sigma_j}$	$\bar{x}_j$ and σ_j are the mean and standard deviation of the value of indicator x_{ij}, respectively. v_{ij} is the normalized value of indicator x_{ij}
Distance to a reference	$v_{ij} = \frac{x_{ij}}{x_{ij}^r}$	x_{ij}^r is the value of reference indicators
Re-scaling	$v_{ij} = \frac{x_{ij} - \min_i x_{ij}}{\max_i x_{ij} - \min_i x_{ij}}$	$\max_i x_{ij}$ and $\min_i x_{ij}$ are the maximum and the minimum values of indicator x_{ij} across all entities

Cherchye et al. (2007a). In the circumstance, it is also possible to make meaningful comparison over time when panel data is involved (Cherchye et al. 2007a).

Re-scaling method attempts to re-scale the original indicators to dimensionless range [0, 1] by using the global maximum and minimum. One well-known example is the Human Development Index. Other examples using the re-scaling method can be found in Neumayer (2001), Díaz-Balteiro and Romero (2004), Hajkowicz (2006), Gómez-Limón and Riesgo (2009), and Gómez-Limón and Sanchez-Fernandez (2010).

3.2 Aggregation Methods

The aggregation process implies the search for an appropriate function that can incorporate multiple indicators into a single composite indicator. In the literature, there are many aggregation functions available for use. Most of them can be represented by the following equation:

$$
CI_i = \begin{cases} \left[\displaystyle\sum_{j=1}^{n} w_j \left(v_{ij}\right)^{\beta} \right]^{\frac{1}{\beta}} & \text{for} \quad \beta \neq 0 \\ \displaystyle\prod_{j=1}^{n} v_{ij}^{w_j} & \text{for} \quad \beta = 0 \end{cases}
\tag{3}
$$

When the parameter β is assigned to different values, the aggregation function will collapse to different forms. It should be pointed out that the values of β have an impact on the trade-offs between different indicators. More discussions can be found in Decancq and Lugo (2013). Table 2 shows several aggregation functions which are often used in constructing CSI.

Table 2 Several popular aggregation methods

Function name	Formula
Simple additive weighting	$CI_i = \displaystyle\sum_{j=1}^{n} w_j v_{ij}$ when $\beta = 1$
Weighted product	$CI_i = \displaystyle\prod_{j=1}^{n} v_{ij}^{w_j}$ when $\beta = 0$
Weighted displaced ideal	$CI_i = (1 - \lambda) \cdot \min w_j v_{ij} + \lambda \displaystyle\sum_{j=1}^{n} w_j v_{ij}$ (λ is the compensatory parameter that ranges from 0 to 1)
Social multi-criterion evaluation method	$CI_i = \sum e_{jk}$ $\left(e_{jk} = \displaystyle\sum_{i=1}^{m} w_i \left(P_{jk}\right) + \frac{1}{2} w_i \left(I_{jk}\right)\right)$

3.2.1 Simple Additive Weighting

When the parameter $\beta = 1$, Eq. (3) reduces to the simple additive weighting (hereafter referred to as SAW). In the context of constructing CSI, the simple additive weighting might be the most commonly used aggregation function, e.g. Kang (2002), Kang et al. (2002), Krajnc and Glavič (2005), Esty et al. (2005), Hajkowicz (2006), Singh et al. (2009), Murillo et al. (2015), and Global Warming Potential (IPCC 2001). The SAW method is easy to understand and can visualize the relative contribution of each indicator to the CSI. Since the assumption of preferentially independent relationship between indicators may not be satisfied in practice, statistical techniques such as principal component analysis (PCA) and factor analysis (FA) are often applied before aggregation (Grupp and Schubert 2010). Additionally, the use of SAW allows for the full substitutability between the indicators so that the weights imply trade-offs, which is inconsistent with the meaning of importance coefficients quoted by many earlier studies (Munda and Nardo 2009). From a practical point of view, this characteristic of the SAW method is not desirable since it violates the spirit of sustainable development (Ayres et al. 1998).

3.2.2 Weighted Product Method

With the parameter $\beta = 0$, Eq. (3) is referred to as weighted product (WP) method. Although WP method is not widely applied in constructing CSI, it has attracted much attention owing to its several desirable characteristics, e.g. semi-compensatory property (Nardo et al. 2008), meaningfulness for ratio-scale indicators (Ebert and Welsch 2004; Böhringer and Jochem 2007), and less information loss (Zhou and Ang 2009). In application, WP method has been used for constructing HDI to replace SAW method by the United Nations Development Programme, which could be affected by these earlier studies as discussed by Tofallis (2013).

Due to the exponent property, WP method requires that all ratings are greater than one (Yoon and Hwang 1995). The relative contribution by each individual indicator to the CSI is not visualized as that in SAW. Furthermore, the results usually do not have a numerical upper bound. The former problem can be solved by multiplied by 10^l. The later problem, Yoon and Hwang (1995) suggested to compute the distance between each entity and the ideal entity as follows:

$$R_i = \frac{\prod_{j=1}^{n} v_{ij}^{w_j}}{\prod_{j=1}^{n} \left(v_{ij}^{*}\right)^{w_j}} \quad (i = 1, \ldots, m) \tag{4}$$

where v_{ij}^{*} is the best value for the jth indicators. It is clear that $0 \leq R_i \leq 1$, in which 1 (0) indicates the most (least) sustainable entity.

3.2.3 Weighted Displaced Ideal

Weighted displaced ideal (WDI) method is on the basis of the ideal solution theory that aims to calculate the distance between the normalized value of each entity and the "ideal" entity (Zeleny and Cochrane 1981). This concept has further been generalized by Díaz-Balteiro and Romero (2004) which can provide solutions of "total compensability" among the sustainable indicators and "total non-compensability" of the indicators, as well as a compromise set of solutions between these two extreme cases. By setting $\beta \rightarrow +\infty$, Eq. (3) is transformed to the form $CI_i = \min w_j v_{ij}$, in which substitutability between indicators are prohibited. To reach a balanced evaluation, Díaz-Balteiro and Romero (2004) introduced a parameter λ representing the degree of substitutability between indicators. When $\lambda = 0$, non-compensatory between indicators is assumed. When $\lambda = 1$, the WDI method will be simplified as the SAW method which assumes full compensability. For $0 < \lambda < 1$, partial compensation between indicators will be allowed. This aggregation function is also attracted an increasing attention, e.g. Zhou et al. (2006a), Zhou and Ang (2009), Gómez-Limón and Riesgo (2009), Blancas et al. (2010), Gómez-Limón and Sanchez-Fernandez (2010), and Pollesch and Dale (2015).

3.2.4 Social Multi-criterion Evaluation Method

Social multi-criteria evaluation (SMCE) method, introduced by Munda (2005), is a non-compensatory technique to provide rankings of the entities based on a Condorcet-type of aggregation procedure. SMCE aims to improve the quality of composite indicators by overcoming two technical weaknesses: independence between indicators and the meaningfulness of weights (Munda and Nardo 2003). Once the weights are determined, SMCE undergoes two steps to obtain the overall sustainability rankings. At first, an outranking matrix is built by pair-wise comparison. Elements $(e_{jk}(j \neq k))$ in the matrix is the score of the sum of the weights for corresponding indicators under the condition of indicator j performing better than indicator k. A half of the weight will be added if the relationship between indicator j and k is indifference. Such process can be expressed by

$$e_{jk} = \sum_{i=1}^{m} \left(w_i \left(P_{jk} \right) + \frac{1}{2} w_i \left(I_{jk} \right) \right) \tag{5}$$

where $P_{jk}(I_{jk})$ indicates preference (indifference) relationship. In this step, $n(n-1)$ pair-wise combinations need to be compared. The second step is to sum up the relevant scores for a complete pre-order of entities. For instance, to rank three entities (e.g. E1, E2, and E3), all possible permutations of these entities are E1E2E3, E1E3E2, E2E1E3, E2E3E1, E3E1E2, and E3E2E1. Then the value of each permutation can be calculated. The one with the highest score is used to determine the ranking of the entities.

Compared with the aggregation methods described above, SMCE requires a large amount of computation, especially in the second step. The information including in the final results might also be limited. Nevertheless, SMCE provides a novel framework for assessing sustainability. When CSIs are derived from SMCE, their underlying subjective aspect only comes from the determination of indicator's weight. This property decreases the uncertainty in constructing CSI and also relieves some burden in sensitivity analysis. Besides, SMCE is a totally non-compensatory aggregation method which may better reflect the concept of strong sustainability.

3.3 Weighting Methods

From the previous section, it is clear that there is close relationship between the indicator weights and data aggregation. The existing weighting methods could be partitioned into three categories: exogenous (or called normative) methods, endogenous (or called data-driven) methods, and hybrid methods. The main difference between the three categories lies in the degree of value judgement of decision-makers or experts involved in determining the weights. Exogenous methods, mainly dependent on the value judgement of decision-makers or experts are determined by participatory methods. Endogenous methods on the other hand mainly rely on the data distribution, tending to let data "speak". Hybrid methods attempt to balance the exogenous and endogenous methods.

3.3.1 Exogenous Methods

Equal weighting, arbitrary weighting, and analytic hierarchy process (AHP) are three frequently used exogenous methods. See, for example, Ecological Footprint, Hope et al. (1992) and Murillo et al. (2015) for equal weighting, Kang (2002), Kang et al. (2002) and Krajnc and Glavič (2005) for AHP. Equal weights are usually applied in the circumstance of the absence of comprehensive understanding for the entity. With the improvement of data collection techniques and the extensive research on sustainability, equal weights have gradually been abandoned in constructing CSI. AHP and other methods like budget allocation processes and conjoint analysis are heavily dependent on a thorough understanding about how each entity works. The challenge in the application of these exogenous methods is the choice of appropriate experts (Decancq and Lugo 2013). Once this problem is properly handled, the reliability of the exogenous methods would significantly increase. It should be noted that exogenous methods are ex ante approaches, which makes performance comparison across time and space be feasible.

3.3.2 Endogenous Methods

Statistical weighting and BOD methods are two major endogenous families in determining the weights for constructing CSI. Statistical weighting methods are based on statistical properties of the data, e.g. PCA, FA, and regression analysis (RA). PCA is basically a multivariate statistical technique to summarize the data. FA is based on the assumption that some observed indicators rely on a certain number of unobserved factors. Although the basic assumption of these two methods is distinct, in practice, one usually does not distinguish the difference. Once the principal components are extracted, the factor loading matrix and eigenvalues of the associate principal components can be calculated. The weights of indicators then equal to the ratio of squared factor loadings to the corresponding eigenvalues. The technical details can be found in Gómez-Limón and Riesgo (2009). Despite their statistical soundness, the meaning of the weights estimated by PCA or FA fails in accordance with the original meaning, i.e. importance, since these two methods measure the overlapping information between two or more correlated indicators (Shen et al. 2013). RA approach determines weight by multiple regression or linear programming and assumes that individual indicator relies on the sum of an observed variable and an error term. Thus, the RA approach is usually defined as unobserved components model or observed derived weight method (Nardo et al. 2008).

3.3.3 Hybrid Methods

In addition to assess sustainability, one valuable characteristic of CSI is to compare among all entities so that decision makers can detect the gap and then take actions to improve sustainability performance. From this perspective, endogenous methods somewhat fail to perform this function. Exogenous methods do not suffer the issue since they do not rely on the data distribution. However, exogenous methods depend on the value judgments that might be affected by different expert panels. As mentioned by Decancq and Lugo (2013), expert groups might be underrepresented or simply uninformed resulting in a skewed weighting scheme.

Hybrid methods are proposed to combine exogenous methods with endogenous methods. Decancq and Lugo (2013) listed two hybrid methods, namely stated preference weight and hedonic weights. Stated preference weight, instead of imposing weights by expert panel, is directly based on individual opinions. Hedonic weights also rely on the individual self-reported preference. After obtaining the preference matrix, weights can be estimated by a linear regression. An example of hybrid weighting methods is the BOD model with weight restrictions that can be determined by experts.

4 BOD Methods

Two problems in constructing CSI by MADM models are the information loss caused by normalization (Zanella et al. 2015) and the subjectivity in determining the weights. Fixed weight stemming from MADM models has been controverted with argument that different cultural and social settings value individual weighting framework in different ways (Cherchye et al. 2008).

Alternatively, as suggested by Lovell et al. (1995) and Lovell (1995), linear programming models can be used to construct the 'best practice' frontier for the entities. The linear programming approach for constructing CSI is usually defined as benefit of the doubt (BOD). BOD roots in DEA which was originally proposed for evaluating the relative efficiency of a homogeneous set of entities which use multiple inputs to produce multiple outputs. In DEA, the weights of inputs and outputs can be endogenously determined by raw data without using price information. In methodology, CSI based on BOD borrow the idea of DEA for the purpose of weighting and aggregation.

4.1 Basic BOD Model

For each of entities, the basic BOD model explores its most favorable weights (Cherchye et al. 2007b). It can be formulated as follows:

$$
\begin{aligned}
CI_i &= \max \sum_{j=1}^{n} w_i x_{ij} \\
s.t. &\sum_{j=1}^{m} w_i x_{ik} \le 1 \quad k = 1, \ldots, n \\
&w_j \ge 0
\end{aligned}
\tag{6}
$$

Model (6) is equivalent to the input oriented DEA model with the assumption of constant returns to scale and a dummy input for all the evaluated entities. It provides the optimal aggregated performance values for all entities by solving the model n times. Different from the MADM models, the weight assignment based on BOD adheres to a posterior weighting scheme and the weights of the individual indicators weight may differ between entities. Model (6) holds several desirable properties, such as normalization-free and the invariance with respect to ratio scale transformations (Athanassoglou 2015). Normalization-free can avoid the information loss caused by data transformation. Invariance allows practitioners to aggregate individual indicators into a meaningful composite indicator (Ebert and Welsch 2004). In essence, model (6) measures how far the evaluated entity is from the best practice entity under most favorable weights (Zhou et al. 2007).

Model (6) has been used in many application contexts. The earliest literature may date back to Mahlberg and Obersteiner (2001) who introduced model (6) to reassess HDI. Despotis (2005a, b) used an extension to model (6) to reevaluate HDI. It is worth pointing out that Cherchye and his collaborators applied the model in several backgrounds including sustainable development (Cherchye and Kuosmanen 2004), internal market (Cherchye et al. 2007a) and technology achievement (Cherchye et al. 2008).

4.2 Weight Restriction in Basic BOD Model

The BOD model brings new perspective for constructing CSI, while it also suffers from some shortcomings. For example, model (6) assumes that the weights are nonnegative. It is possible that all the weights are assigned to a single indicator which may not be expected since all the selected indicators are theoretically importance and thus need to be considered (Zhou et al. 2007). Besides, it could open up the debate on the CSI's credibility and acceptability. To overcome the problems, it is appropriate to restrict weights in certain ways. A straightforward way is to introduce non-Archimedean infinitesimal variable ε into the model, e.g. Despotis (2005a, b) and Kao (2010). With such modification, however, it is still possible to diagnose an entity well performing even if it is only superior with respect to one indicator but performs poorly with respect to the remaining indicators (Mahlberg and Obersteiner 2001). Hence, further restrictions on weights usually are considered in practice.

Broadly speaking, weight restriction could be classified into two categories, i.e. direct restriction and indirect restriction (Allen et al. 1997). Direct restriction on weights could be formulated in the forms of Eqs. (7) and (8) which are respectively termed as "Type I Assurance Regions" and "Type II Assurance Regions" by Thompson et al. (1990). The Greek letters in Eqs. (7) and (8) are specified by decision makers to reflect their preference regarding the relative importance of indicators. w' could be the combination of weights. The use of direct restriction on weights can be found in Mahlberg and Obersteiner (2001), Cherchye and Kuosmanen (2004), and Cherchye et al. (2007b). Indirect restrictions on weights could be formulated as the form of Eq. (9) which was originally proposed by Wong and Beasley (1990). ϕ and φ also indicate the preference of decision-makers. Rather than restricting actual weights, Eq. (9) places lower and upper bounds on the relative contribution of each indicator to the entity's aggregate performance value. This restriction method has been adopted in many previous studies, e.g. Zhou et al. (2007, 2010), Cherchye et al. (2008), Zanella et al. (2015) and Athanassoglou (2015).

$$\alpha_j \leq \frac{w_j}{w_{j+1}} \leq \beta_j \tag{7}$$

$$\lambda w' \leq \kappa w_j \leq \gamma w' \tag{8}$$

$$\phi_j \leq \frac{w_j x_{ij}}{\sum_{j=1}^{n} w_j x_{ij}} \leq \varphi_j \tag{9}$$

The above restrictions cannot only overcome the problem aforementioned but also introduce "valued judgment" to incorporate prior views or information in assessing the performance of entities. The prior information can be incorporated via the determination of boundaries by MADM method such as AHP, BAP and the social surveys, e.g. Cherchye et al. (2008). Direct restriction usually incorporates information of marginal rates of substitution between indicators which is sensitive to the units of measurement (Allen et al. 1997). Consequently, it is often difficult to specify meaningful substitution in real-life applications (Zanella et al. 2015). In contrast, indirect restriction method holds the desirable property of ratio-scale invariance (Cherchye et al. 2008; Zhou et al. 2007). This is particularly compelling in the case of constructing environmental performance index (Ebert and Welsch 2004). Furthermore, as Cherchye et al. (2008) discussed, Eq. (9) can be expressed as pie share constraints which are pure numbers and can be easily grasped by decision makers. Nevertheless, the meaning of Eq. (9) is not so straightforward since the implied restrictions on weights are entity-specific. Hence, Wong and Beasley (1990) suggested several modifications. One of the modifications, i.e. replacing x_{ij} with $\sum_{j=1}^{n} \frac{x_{ij}}{n}$ in Eq. (9), which represents the level of the ith indicator of the "average" entity, has also been applied in constructing composite indicators, e.g. Zanella et al. (2015).

4.3 Extensions of Basic BOD Model

Due to its striking properties, BOD model has been extended to solve various problems in constructing CSI, e.g. hierarchy problem, compensability, comparability, etc.

The basic BOD model usually treats all the indicators at the same level and thus leaves out the information of the hierarchical structure of indicators. This hierarchy problem might be unrealistic due to the fact that multiple layer indicator framework is constructed in order to evaluate the increasing complicated sustainable performance in a more comprehensive way. According to Becker (2005), frameworks are mostly hierarchical extending from broad categories of data and information to detailed measures. To overcome this limitation, Shen et al. (2013) improved the basic BOD model to fit the property of hierarchical indicator system by specifying weights in each category of each layer. More straightforwardly, in the situation of multiple hierarchical indicator framework, the basic BOD model is first used to determine the "best practice" performance of certain layer indicators. Then the aggregation of higher layer indicators can be done by MADM methods. See, for example, Kao et al. (2008).

In addition, due to the linear characteristic of its objective function, BOD also faces the compensatory issue as discussed earlier. Munda and Nardo (2009) suggested that it is compulsory to construct non-compensatory composite indicators so that weights are theoretical consistent with the meaning of importance. To relax the compensatory characteristic, Zhou et al. (2010) combined the WP aggregation method with basic BOD model to construct a multiplicative optimization approach with semi-compensatory characteristic to reach a compromise solution. Pakkar (2014) proposed a similar model for constructing Technology Achievement Index. Fusco (2015) introduced directional penalties to enhance the non-compensatory characteristic of basic BOD model to take into account the preference structure among indicators. Generally, the methods take similar perspective, i.e. imposing more penalties upon the indicators with worse performance.

The basic BOD model on the basis of conventional DEA technique distinguishes efficient and inefficient entities in the DEA terminology, and is not suitable for ranking the performance of entities (Kao 2010). The main strength of basic DEA models is to recognize the inefficient entities. Hence, many studies have been devoted to improve the comparability of basic BOD model under the framework of composite indicators. For example, from an opposite perspective of Model (6), Zhou et al. (2007) proposed a model to seek the "worst" set of weights for each entity, and use an adjusting parameter to combine the "best practice" and the "worst practice" to form composite indicators. Several studies have adopted this model to construct composite indicators in various contexts, e.g. Domínguez-Serrano and Blancas (2011), Rogge (2012), and Blancard and Hoarau (2013). Athanassoglou (2015) further improved the worst-case of basic BOD model for constructing composite indicators.

Besides, the concept of common-weight is also applied to enhance the comparability of basic BOD model. Its basic idea is that every entity need to use the same benchmark for calculating the performance score. Despotis (2005a, b) initially introduced the concept of common-weight, in which basic BOD model is firstly used to determine most favorable weights for entities and then a goal programming model is developed to discriminate entities with the same performance score. Dong et al. (2015) used similar two-stage method to measure farm sustainability. Kao et al. (2008) proposed a similar two-stage model for evaluating the national competitiveness. Kao (2010) combined the concept of common-weights with Malmquist productivity index. Built upon Zhou et al. (2007), Hatefi and Torabi (2010) also proposed a common-weights MCDA-DEA approach in which the common-weights are calculated in one step. Tofallis (2013) also used two-stage model to seek a common set of weights to apply to all entities. More recently, Hatefi and Torabi (2016) further analyzed how to improve the composite indicators of inefficient entities on the basis of a slack analysis framework.

BOD methods are flexible and systematic for constructing CSI. In recent years, conventional DEA models are also used to establish composite indicators, e.g. environmental performance index (EPI). Application of conventional DEA models to construct EPI might begin with the establishment of environmental production technology (Zhou and Ang 2008). Then an EPI can be constructed by different types of DEA models with different properties. See, for example, Zaim et al. (2001), Zhou et al. (2006b), Zhou and Ang (2008), Blancard and Hoarau (2013), and Wang (2015). More recently, Zhou et al. (2017) evaluated previous studies and showed that the range adjusted DEA model can generate a cardinally meaningful composite index.

5 The CSI Robustness and Beyond

5.1 Selection Principle

So far, we have examined three methodological aspects pertinent to CSI construction. Besides, two additional issues have often been questioned, i.e. comparability and meaningfulness. Comparability is mainly caused by the incommensurability of indicators' measurement units. Martinez-Alier et al. (1998) theoretically showed that the incommensurability does not imply incomparability but weak comparability, which means that there is a good potential for applying multi-indicator evaluation methods (e.g. MADM and BOD) to sustainability assessment. Although the above argument provides theoretical comparability foundation, sustainability assessment still faces the difference and ambiguity caused by measurement units, which may make CSI meaningfulness.

Ebert and Welsch (2004) first discussed how to construct a meaningful environmental index, which has been used as a criterion for investigating whether an environmental or sustainable index is meaningful or not by Böhringer and Jochem (2007) and Singh et al. (2009). Meaningful CSI indicates that the preference orderings does not vary with different scale of underlying indicators. Ebert and Welsch (2004) classified different scales into four categories according to the concept of comparability (measurability) of scales: interval-scale non-comparability, interval-scale full comparability, ratio-scale non-comparability, and ratio-scale full comparability. If interval-scaled indicators are full comparable, the arithmetic mean aggregation function satisfies continuous, strongly monotone, and separable properties and thus can generate a meaningful index. If ratio-scaled indicators are non-comparable, geometric mean aggregation function is recommended. Table 3 provides a summary of different cases. It should be pointed out that it is impossible to construct meaningful CSI when there exist indicators with distinct measurement scales (Böhringer and Jochem 2007; Ebert and Welsch 2004). More recently, Pollesch and Dale (2015) investigated aggregation functions for six different scales of indicators in constructing an appropriate meaningful CSI. Zhou et al. (2017) generalized the meaningfulness concept by Ebert and Welsch (2004) and showed how to construct a cardinally meaningful index.

In addition to scales, many other factors can have impact on the selection of aggregation function in constructing CSI, e.g. interactive phenomena between indicators, the types of weight, and the assumption of sustainability. When there are interactive phenomena between indicators, some preliminary treatments should be firstly conducted to eliminate those interactive relationships. However, as Mayer

Table 3 Aggregation rules for indicators by Ebert and Welsch via Böhringer and Jochem (2007)

	Non-comparable	Full comparable
Interval scale	Dictatorial ordering	Arithmetic mean
Ratio scale	Geometric mean	Any homothetic function

(2008) stated, without a clear understanding of interactive relationship between indicators and how those relationships influence the results, it is hard for decision makers to formulate policy with the aim to increase economic equity, environmental improvement, and further increase possibilities for long-term sustainability. Hence, those aggregation methods taking interaction into consideration, e.g. Choquet integral with fuzzy measure, might be a good choice. The types of weight can also have impact on the application of aggregation function. For example, weights, no matter on which weighting methods, can be classified into two categories: ordinal and cardinal ones. Ordinal weights usually cannot be handled well by compensatory aggregation methods. In this situation, non-compensatory approach may be an appropriate choice. In addition, the assumption of sustainability theoretically determines the choice of aggregation algorithm (Munda 2005). There are usually two economic paradigms of sustainability: weak sustainability and strong sustainability (Dietz and Neumayer 2007; Neumayer 2013). From weak sustainability perspective, natural capital is considered to be substitutable. In this view, those compensatory aggregation algorithms might be suitable. From the perspective of strong sustainability, natural capital is regarded as non-substitutable. Then, the non-compensatory or semi-compensatory aggregation schemes may be more appropriate.

In general, we may summarize the procedure for selecting an appropriate approach to constructing CSI as follows. First and most importantly, economic paradigms (weak or strong sustainability) should be clearly defined, based on which either compensatory or non-compensatory aggregation scheme can be determined. The indicator framework following the definition of different paradigms can also be established. With the premise of indicator framework, practitioners can check the scales of indicators and assign weight for each indicator. Once indicator framework show the property of the same measurement scales, the procedure can continue. Otherwise, indicators with different scales should be replaced by other proxy indicators with the same scale. Additionally, there are two other factors that should be considered, namely interactive phenomena between indicators and hierarchical structure. If practitioners decide to model the interactive relationship between indicators, the way for assigning weights to indicators might be different on which the selection of aggregation scheme will directly be influenced.

5.2 Uncertainty and Sensitivity Analysis

It must be acknowledged that each method has its own merits. However, as Booysen (2002) discussed, every element of methods used to construct composite indicators cannot escape from criticism. The disagreements originate from many facets, and one main source is the robustness of CSI. Theoretically, different combinations of methods can be used to construct CSI which implies that it is possible to derive very different results.

Two alternative approaches are used in constructing CSI to increase their robustness. One is to ensure the transparency of the whole construction process. This requires vivid statement of the models including those important aspects, such as mathematical and descriptive properties. In addition, the way by which such models are used and integrated in a decision process still needs to be elaborated clearly. The other approach is to assess the uncertainties by sensitivity analysis. Sensitivity analysis can answer the question why those entities with similar sustainable performance get distinct rankings, and can also be used to globally analyze the variation in CSI when different aspects vary over a reasonable range of possibilities (Saisana et al. 2005; Munda and Saisana 2011). For instance, Zhou et al. (2010) compared different rankings of entities obtained by a large set of randomly chosen weighting schemes. Munda and Saisana (2011) analyzed the stability of sustainability rankings by different aggregation rule while keeping the weights of indicators unchanged.

Keeping transparency and conducting sensitivity analysis are posterior uncertainty analysis. Correspondingly, there are also a priori uncertainty analysis methods, e.g. the Shannon-Spearman measure (SSM) developed by Zhou et al. (2006a, b) and Zhou and Ang (2009). SSM is based on the concept of information loss in the process of aggregating underlying indicators into a composite index. Intuitively, methods with smaller SSM, i.e. less loss of information, may be regarded as better ones. Methods with zero SSM are deemed inheriting full information, and thus are regarded as perfect model. In this sense, SSM might be another approach for uncertainty evaluation of CSI.

5.3 Beyond Rankings

Although CSI intuitively provides the index values and ranking results, as emphasized by Nardo et al. (2008) and Grupp and Schubert (2010), it can be a means of initiating discussion to facilitate communication between different stakeholders. The influential CSI can draw the attention from policy makers towards the importance of sustainable development. Its intuitive construction also provides opportunity to uncover the debate for the public, instead of excluding them straightaway. Besides, CSI may help to stir policy competition about best practice in sustainable development policies and become a useful monitoring tool to avoid unintended consequence caused by unsuitable policies. The process of constructing CSI also provides the possibility of further analyzing the questions. For example, where is the strength? Which aspect of the entity should be improved? What is the real contribution of certain indicators to CSI? The information hidden in the CSI can be visually exhibited with the help of spider diagrams or radar charts, by which the strengths and weaknesses can be easily and intuitively represented. The correlation analysis between underlying indicators and the values of CSI can illustrate the contribution of each indicator, and then help identify the priority of improvement.

6 Conclusions

This chapter provides a state-of-the-art review of CSI construction with focus on the methodological developments. We firstly introduce the general structure of CSI construction. Then, we classify the methods for constructing CSI into two groups, i.e. MADM and BOD. In MADM, methods for normalization, weighting and aggregation together with their pros and cons are respectively discussed. It is found that z-score normalization scheme, hybrid weighting methods and compensatory/ semi-compensatory aggregation functions are most commonly used in application. Non-compensatory aggregation scheme has received increasing attention by some recent studies. In BOD, the basic BOD model, weight restriction and other extensions are described. A new trend is that analysts tend to incorporate various MADM methods into BOD to construct CSI. Finally, we investigate the principles for selecting appropriate aggregation methods in constructing CSI. Uncertainty and sensitivity analysis have also been discussed in order to establish CSI with robustness.

CSI has evolved as a popular tool for the purpose of monitoring sustainability performance and providing valuable information for supporting policy analysis and decision making. However, various challenges still exist, e.g. the conceptual issue of sustainability, dimensional diversity, data availability and so on. The widely accepted definition of sustainability includes the impacts on the next generation, which implies that it is important to incorporate the influence of time and geographical factor. When taking geographical factors into account, practitioners may also need to consider entities' different culture and development patterns. There is also a rising concern on how to construct a meaningful CSI from both theoretical and methodological perspectives, as the existing CSIs seldom satisfy the axiomatic requirements of the meaningfulness definition. In this sense, further efforts are still required to improving the meaningfulness and robustness of existing CSIs.

Acknowledgements We are grateful to the financial support provided by the National Natural Science Foundation of China (nos. 71273005 & 71573119) and the Funding of Jiangsu Innovation Program for Graduate Education (KYZZ16_0159).

References

Allen, R., Athanassopoulos, A., Dyson, R.G., Thanassoulis, E., 1997. Weights restrictions and value judgements in data envelopment analysis: Evolution, development and future directions. Annals of Operations Research 73, 13–34.

Athanassoglou, S., 2015. Revisiting worst-case DEA for composite Indicators. Social Indicators Research 128(3), 1259–1272.

Ayres, R.U., van den Bergh, J.C.J.M., Gowdy, J., 1998. Viewpoint: Weak versus strong sustainability. Tinbergen Institute Discussion Paper (No. 98-103/3).

Baumgärtner, S. Quaas, M., 2010. What is sustainability economics? Ecological Economics 69(3), pp. 445–450.

Becker, J., 2005. Measuring progress towards sustainable development: An ecological framework for selecting indicators. Local Environment 10, 87–101.

Blancard, S., Hoarau, J.-F., 2013. A new sustainable human development indicator for small island developing states: A reappraisal from data envelopment analysis. Economic Modelling 30, 623–635.

Blancas, F. J., Caballero, R., González, M., Lozano-Oyola, M., Pérez, F. 2010. Goal programming synthetic indicators: An application for sustainable tourism in Andalusian coastal counties. Ecological Economics 69(11), 2158–2172.

Booysen, F., 2002. An overview and evaluation of composite indices of development. Social Indicators Research 59, 115–151.

Botta, E., Kozluk, T. 2014. Measuring environmental policy stringency in OECD countries: A composite index approach. OECD Economics Department Working Papers, No. 1177, OECD Publishing, Paris.

Böhringer, C., Jochem, P.E., 2007. Measuring the immeasurable—A survey of sustainability indices. Ecological Economics 63, 1–8.

Cai, H., Chen, Y., Gong, Q., 2016. Polluting thy neighbor: Unintended consequences of China's pollution reduction mandates. Journal of Environmental Economics and Management 76, 86–104.

Chen, S., Chen, X., Xu, J., 2016. Impacts of climate change on agriculture: Evidence from China. Journal of Environmental Economics and Management 76, 105–124.

Cherchye, L., Kuosmanen, T., 2004. Benchmarking sustainable development: A synthetic meta-index approach. Research Paper, UNU-WIDER, United Nations University.

Cherchye, L., Lovell, C.K., Moesen, W., Van Puyenbroeck, T., 2007a. One market, one number? A composite indicator assessment of EU internal market dynamics. European Economic Review 51, 749–779.

Cherchye, L., Moesen, W., Rogge, N., Van Puyenbroeck, T., 2007b. An introduction to 'benefit of the doubt' composite indicators. Social Indicators Research 82, 111–145.

Cherchye, L., Moesen, W., Rogge, N., Van Puyenbroeck, T., Saisana, M., Saltelli, A., Liska, R., Tarantola, S., 2008. Creating composite indicators with DEA and robustness analysis: The case of the Technology Achievement Index. Journal of the Operational Research Society 59, 239–251.

Decancq, K., Lugo, M.A., 2013. Weights in multidimensional indices of wellbeing: An overview. Econometric Reviews 32, 7–34.

Despotis, D., 2005a. Measuring human development via Data Envelopment Analysis: The case of Asia and the Pacific. Omega 33, 385–390.

Despotis, D., 2005b. A reassessment of the Human Development Index via Data Envelopment Analysis. Journal of the Operational Research Society 56, 969–980.

Díaz-Balteiro, L., Romero, C., 2004. In search of a natural systems sustainability index. Ecological Economics 49, 401–405.

Dietz, S., Neumayer, E., 2007. Weak and strong sustainability in the SEEA: Concepts and measurement. Ecological Economics 61, 617–626.

Domínguez-Serrano, M., Blancas, F.J., 2011. A gender wellbeing composite indicator: The best-worst global evaluation approach. Social Indicators Research 102, 477–496.

Dong, F., Mitchell, P.D., Colquhoun, J., 2015. Measuring farm sustainability using data envelope analysis with principal components: The case of Wisconsin cranberry. Journal of Environmental Management 147, 175–183.

Ebert, U., Welsch, H., 2004. Meaningful environmental indices: A social choice approach. Journal of Environmental Economics and Management 47, 270–283.

Esty, D.C., Levy, M., Srebotnjak, T., De Sherbinin, A., 2005. Environmental sustainability index: benchmarking national environmental stewardship. New Haven: Yale Center for Environmental Law & Policy.

Floridi, M., Pagni, S., Falorni, S., Luzzati, T., 2011. An exercise in composite indicators construction: Assessing the sustainability of Italian regions. Ecological Economics 70, 1440–1447.

Freudenberg, M. 2003. Composite indicators of country performance: A critical assessment, OECD Science, Technology and Industry Working Papers, No. 2003/16, OECD Publishing, Paris.

Fusco, E., 2015. Enhancing non-compensatory composite indicators: A directional proposal. European Journal of Operational Research 242, 620–630.

Gómez-Limón, J.A., Riesgo, L., 2009. Alternative approaches to the construction of a composite indicator of agricultural sustainability: An application to irrigated agriculture in the Duero basin in Spain. Journal of Environmental Management 90, 3345–3362.

Gómez-Limón, J.A., Sanchez-Fernandez, G., 2010. Empirical evaluation of agricultural sustainability using composite indicators. Ecological Economics 69, 1062–1075.

Grupp, H., Schubert, T., 2010. Review and new evidence on composite innovation indicators for evaluating national performance. Research Policy 39, 67–78.

Hák, T., Moldan, B., Dahl, A.L., 2012. Sustainability indicators: A scientific assessment. Island Press.

Hajkowicz, S., 2006. Multi-attributed environmental index construction. Ecological Economics 57, 122–139.

Hatefi, S., Torabi, S., 2010. A common weight MCDA–DEA approach to construct composite indicators. Ecological Economics 70, 114–120.

Hatefi, S.M. and Torabi, S.A., 2016. A slack analysis framework for improving composite indicators with applications to human development and sustainable energy indices. Econometric Reviews.

He, G., Fan, M., Zhou, M., 2016. The effect of air pollution on mortality in China: Evidence from the 2008 Beijing Olympic Games. Journal of Environmental Economics and Management 79, 18–39.

Hope, C., Parker, J., Peake, S., 1992. A pilot environmental index for the UK in the 1980s. Energy Policy 20, 335–343.

Hsu, A., de Sherbinin, A. C., Esty, D., Levy, M., 2016. Environmental Performance Index. New Haven, CT: Yale University. Available: www.epi.yale.edu.

Intergovernmental Panel on Climate Change (IPCC), 2001. Climate Change 2001: The Scientific Basis. Intergovernmental Panel on Climate Change, Cambridge University Press, Cambridge, UK.

Kang, S.M., 2002. A sensitivity analysis of the Korean composite environmental index. Ecological Economics 43, 159–174.

Kang, S.M., Kim, M.S., Lee, M., 2002. The trends of composite environmental indices in Korea. Journal of Environmental Management 64, 199–206.

Kao, C., 2010. Malmquist productivity index based on common-weights DEA: The case of Taiwan forests after reorganization. Omega 38, 484–491.

Kao, C., Wu, W.-Y., Hsieh, W.-J., Wang, T.-Y., Lin, C., Chen, L.-H., 2008. Measuring the national competitiveness of Southeast Asian countries. European Journal of Operational Research 187, 613–628.

Krajnc, D., Glavič, P., 2005. A model for integrated assessment of sustainable development. Resources, Conservation and Recycling 43, 189–208.

Lovell, C.A.K., 1995. Measuring the macroeconomic performance of the Taiwanese economy. International Journal of Production Economics 39, 165–178.

Lovell, C.A.K., Pastor, J.T., Turner, J.A., 1995. Measuring macroeconomic performance in the OECD: A comparison of European and non-European countries. European Journal of Operational Research 87, 507–518.

Mahlberg, B., Obersteiner, M., 2001. Remeasuring the HDI by Data Envelopement Analysis. Available at SSRN 1999372.

Martinez-Alier, J., Munda, G., O'Neill, J., 1998. Weak comparability of values as a foundation for ecological economics. Ecological Economics 26, 277–286.

Mayer, A.L., 2008. Strengths and weaknesses of common sustainability indices for multidimensional systems. Environment International 34, 277–291.

Mori, K., Christodoulou, A., 2012. Review of sustainability indices and indicators: Towards a new City Sustainability Index (CSI). Environmental Impact Assessment Review 32, 94–106.

Munda, G., 2005. Measuring sustainability: A multi-criterion framework. Environment, Development and Sustainability 7, 117–134.

Munda, G., Nardo, M., 2003. On the methodological foundations of composite indicators used for ranking countries. Ispra, Italy: Joint Research Centre of the European Communities.

Munda, G., Nardo, M., 2009. Noncompensatory/nonlinear composite indicators for ranking countries: A defensible setting. Applied Economics 41, 1513–1523.

Munda, G., Saisana, M., 2011. Methodological considerations on regional sustainability assessment based on multicriteria and sensitivity analysis. Regional Studies 45, 261–276.

Murillo, J., Romaní, J., Suriñach, J., 2015. The business excellence attraction composite index (BEACI) in small areas. Design and application to the municipalities of the Barcelona province. Applied Economics 47, 161–179.

Nardo, M., Saisana, M., Saltelli, A., Tarantola, S., Giovannini, E., Hoffmann, A., 2008. Handbook on constructing composite indicators: Methodology and User guide. OECD publishing.

Ness, B., Urbel-Piirsalu, E., Anderberg, S., & Olsson, L. 2007. Categorising tools for sustainability assessment. Ecological Economics 60(3), 498–508.

Neumayer, E., 2001. The human development index and sustainability—A constructive proposal. Ecological Economics 39, 101–114.

Neumayer, E., 2013. Weak versus strong sustainability: Exploring the limits of two opposing paradigms. Edward Elgar Publishing.

Oxford City Council (OCC), 2016. Oxford Sustainability Index Report 2016. https://www.oxford. gov.uk/downloads/file/2655/oxford_sustainability_index_2016.

Pakkar, M.S., 2014. Using Data Envelopment Analysis and Analytic Hierarchy Process to construct composite indicators. Journal of Applied Operational Research 6, 174–187.

Parris, T.M., Kates, R.W., 2003. Characterizing and measuring sustainable development. Annual Review of Environment and Resources 28, 559–586.

Pollesch, N., Dale, V., 2015. Applications of aggregation theory to sustainability assessment. Ecological Economics 114, 117–127.

Pollesch, N., Dale, V., 2016. Normalization in sustainability assessment: Methods and implications. Ecological Economics 130, 195–208.

Rogge, N., 2012. Undesirable specialization in the construction of composite policy indicators: The Environmental Performance Index. Ecological Indicators 23, 143–154.

Saisana, M., Tarantola, S., Saltelli, A., 2005. Uncertainty and sensitivity techniques as tools for the analysis and validation of composite indicators. Journal of the Royal Statistical Society A 168, 1–17.

Sala, S., Ciuffo, B., Nijkamp, P., 2015. A systemic framework for sustainability assessment. Ecological Economics 119, 314–325.

Shen, Y., Hermans, E., Brijs, T., Wets, G., 2013. Data Envelopment Analysis for composite indicators: A multiple layer model. Social Indicators Research 114, 739–756.

Singh, R.K., Murty, H., Gupta, S., Dikshit, A., 2009. An overview of sustainability assessment methodologies. Ecological Indicators 9, 189–212.

Thompson, R.G., Langemeier, L.N., Lee, C.-T., Lee, E., Thrall, R.M., 1990. The role of multiplier bounds in efficiency analysis with application to Kansas farming. Journal of Econometrics 46, 93–108.

Tilman, D., Cassman, K.G., Matson, P.A., Naylor, R., Polasky, S., 2002. Agricultural sustainability and intensive production practices. Nature 418, 671–677.

Tofallis, C., 2013. An automatic-democratic approach to weight setting for the new Human Development Index. Journal of Population Economics 26, 1325–1345.

UNCED, 1992. Rio declaration on environment and development. Report of the United Nations Conference on Environment and Development.

UNDP (United Nations Development Programme). 2014. Human development report - Sustaining human progress: Reducing vulnerabilities and building resilience. New York.

van den Bergh, J.C.J.M., van Veen-Groot, D.B., 2001. Constructing aggregate environmental-economic indicators: A comparison of 12 OECD countries. Environmental Economics and Policy Studies 4(1), 1–16.

Wackernagel, M., & Rees, W. 1998. Our ecological footprint: reducing human impact on the earth (No. 9). New Society Publishers.

Wang, H., 2015. A generalized MCDA–DEA (Multi-Criterion Decision Analysis–Data Envelopment Analysis) approach to construct slacks-based composite indicator. Energy 80, 114–122.

Wong, Y.-H., Beasley, J., 1990. Restricting weight flexibility in Data Envelopment Analysis. Journal of the Operational Research Society 41(9), 829–835.

Yoon, K.P., Hwang, C.-L., 1995. Multiple attribute decision making: An introduction. Sage publications.

World Commission on Environment Development (WCED), 1987. Our common future. Oxford University Press.

World Energy Council (WEC), 2016. World Energy Trilemma Index: Benchmarking the sustainability of national energy systems. https://trilemma.worldenergy.org/reports/main/2016/2016%20Energy%20Trilemma%20Index.pdf.

Zaim, O., Färe, R., Grosskopf, S., 2001. An economic approach to achievement and improvement indexes. Social Indicators Research 56(1), 91–118.

Zanella, A., Camanho, A.S., Dias, T.G., 2015. Undesirable outputs and weighting schemes in composite indicators based on Data Envelopment Analysis. European Journal of Operational Research 245, 517–530.

Zeleny, M., Cochrane, J.L., 1981. Multiple criteria decision making. Mcgraw-Hill.

Zhou, P., Ang, B. W. 2008. Indicators for assessing sustainability performance. In: Handbook of Performability Engineering (905–918). Springer London.

Zhou, P., Ang, B., 2009. Comparing MCDA aggregation methods in constructing composite indicators using the Shannon-Spearman measure. Social Indicators Research 94, 83–96.

Zhou, P., Ang, B., Poh, K., 2006a. Comparing aggregating methods for constructing the composite environmental index: An objective measure. Ecological Economics 59, 305–311.

Zhou, P., Ang, B. W., Poh, K. L. 2006b. Slacks-based efficiency measures for modeling environmental performance. Ecological Economics 60(1), 111–118.

Zhou, P., Ang, B., Poh, K., 2007. A mathematical programming approach to constructing composite indicators. Ecological Economics 62, 291–297.

Zhou, P., Ang, B., Zhou, D., 2010. Weighting and aggregation in composite indicator construction: a multiplicative optimization approach. Social Indicators Research 96, 169–181.

Zhou, P., Delmas, M.A., Kohli, A., 2017. Constructing meaningful environmental indices: A nonparametric frontier approach. Journal of Environmental Economics and Management 85, 21–34.

Chapter 3
Pollution Meets Efficiency: Multi-equation Modelling of Generation of Pollution and Related Efficiency Measures

Finn R. Førsund

1 Introduction

Pointing out the importance of the materials balance principle Ayres and Kneese (1969); Kneese et al. (1970) signalled the start of a new more realistic way of modelling the interaction between human activities of consumption and production and the discharge of residuals to the environment that can be polluting. The concept of (negative) externalities had been used before in the literature to analyse pollution. However, somewhat innocent examples like vibrations from a confectionary's machines disturbing a doctor having a consulting room next door (Coase 1959, p. 26), sparks from a locomotive causing forest fire, and smoke from a factory chimney dirtying washing hanging out to dry (Pigou 1920), were used. The materials balance principle underlined the pervasiveness of generation of residuals caused by using material resources and the unavoidability of their generation, invoking the two thermodynamic laws. The same principle holds for energy inputs. Energy residuals are heat and noise. As to energy production, like charcoal or electricity, the second law of thermodynamics tells us that all energy contained in primary inputs cannot be fully utilised in the energy outputs due to the entropy created (Baumgärtner and de Swaan Arons 2003).

We now face threats of global warming due to emission of greenhouse cases, increasing urban health problems mainly due to emissions from the transport sector, problems due to increased acidity of lakes and oceans from burning fuel like coal and oil for thermal electricity production, and residential heating and cooking. The capacity of Nature to absorb emissions from human activities have long since been exhausted, and the exponential accumulation of certain substances in the environment may result in the necessity of a drastic future cut in carbon-based energy use if global disasters are to be avoided. A necessary international cooperation to reduce

F. R. Førsund (✉)
Department of Economics, University of Oslo, Oslo, Norway
e-mail: finn.forsund@econ.uio.no

© Springer Nature Singapore Pte Ltd. 2018
R. Pang et al. (eds.), *Energy, Environment and Transitional Green Growth in China*, https://doi.org/10.1007/978-981-10-7919-1_3

the emission of global pollutants started with the Kyoto Protocol in 1997, and the Paris Agreement in 2016 is the last effort of the United Nations. To achieve results reliable modelling is needed at all levels of aggregation, also at the micro level studied in this chapter.

The purpose of the chapter is to develop a way to model the generation of residuals in production (or consumption[1]) activities when producing intended outputs that complies with the materials balance. A distinction is made between an efficient production of desirable outputs for given resources and inefficient operations facilitating measuring both efficiency in producing desirable outputs and efficiency in generating residuals. The dominating single equation model in empirical studies comprising resources and two types of output; desirable and undesirable, is shown not to comply with the materials balance and efficiency properties of the production relations, both in the cases of strong (free) disposability of outputs and inputs and weak disposability for desirable- and undesirable outputs together. It is demonstrated in the chapter that separating production relations for desirable outputs and undesirable ones is in theoretical compliance with both the materials balance and efficiency of production relations.

The chapter is organised as follows. Section 2 states the general model blocks of environmental economics limited to a static analysis, the definition of the materials balance, and provides a brief non-technical overview of recent developments concerning the joint generation of desirable and undesirable outputs in the case of inefficiency. Section 3 discusses the concept of joint production and the Frisch classification scheme. It is demonstrated that a single functional representation of frontier technology relying on a trade-off between desirable and undesirable outputs for given resources does not satisfy the materials balance. In Sect. 4 the multi-equation model based on a special case of multiple output production set out in Frisch (1965) satisfying the materials balance, is introduced and discussed. End-of-pipe abatement is introduced in Sect. 5, and the impact of regulating the emission of pollutants studied. Inefficiency is discussed in Sect. 6. The assumption of weak disposability that has dominated efficiency studies of joint desirable and undesirable outputs is scrutinised and found to violate the materials balance principle and efficiency assumptions of production relations. Section 7 introduces efficiency measures that can be estimated for a non-parametric multi-equation production model. Section 8 concludes.

2 Environmental Economics

Concerns about the environment have old roots in economics, as indicated in Sect. 1. We will focus on the modelling of relationships after the introduction of the materials balance principle in Ayres and Kneese (1969).

---

[1]Xun Zhou studies environmental productivity growth in consumer durables in this volume.

2.1 Environmental Economics Post Externality Models

The need for sound modelling of the interaction between human activities and Nature is obvious for the understanding of how to deal with the problems in a way that is most effective in utilising the trade-offs between intended man-made goods and the environmental qualities. Within the strand of research of environmental economics the main model elements to capture are [see Førsund 1985, 2011; Førsund and Strøm 1988; Perman et al. 2011 (first edition 1996)]:

(a) The generation of residuals in production and consumption and discharge to receptors.
(b) The natural processes taking place in the environment as reactions to discharge of residuals, like transformation of residuals by diluting, decaying, decomposing, and transportation between and among receptors.
(c) Defining the environmental services "produced" by the environmental medium and establishing the impact on these of ambient concentrations of residuals.
(d) Evaluating the preferences attached to changes in environmental services, including the time perspective (of the "present generation").

The materials balance, based on the first and second thermodynamic laws, tells us that production activities using material inputs and energy will also generate material or energy residuals. Therefore production activities represent joint production; at least one desirable output is produced and at least one residual is generated simultaneously.

The receiving bodies of Nature, the environmental receptors, play a decisive role in the economic analysis of pollution. The view common in environmental economics is that the receptors provide man with two types of services: residual disposal services and environmental services. The former type relates to the inherent generation of residuals by the materials-processing economy of an industrialised society, and the last type is an omnivorous category of recreation activities like sport fishing, boating, skiing, etc., amenity services, aesthetic values, including the intrinsic value of Nature, and the provision of extraction possibilities from mineral deposits, water, air, etc.

A residual is defined as a pollutant if the corresponding disposal service of receptors negatively affects, quantitatively or qualitatively, the raw materials and recreation services "produced" by the receptors (points (c) and (d) above). The discharge of residuals does not of necessity generate pollution. The natural environment has an assimilative capacity. Owing to dilution, decay, decomposition, chemical transformation, etc. occurring in nature, there are certain threshold values of ambient residual concentrations that must be exceeded before harmful effects appear.

A general equilibrium analysis must show the trade-offs open to rational decisions. However, this chapter will only focus on the first point (a) above. (Dynamic problems caused by accumulating residuals in the environment will thus not be covered.)

Significant sources for change as regards point (a) are

(i)   The scale of the activities and the output mix among activities
(ii) The input mix in an activity
(iii) Process technologies of production and consumption
(iv) The product characteristics, including durability
(v)   Modification[2] of primary residuals ("end-of-pipe" treatment)
(vi) Recycling of residuals
(vii) The location of activities.

We will assume that changes in process technologies [option (iii)] are rather modest and short-term measures (done within a year), that the products remain the same [option (iv)] and that recycling of waste materials [option (vi)] is internal only. The last option (vii) is not useful for global pollutants, but for local or regional pollutants like e.g. acid rain or pollutants emitted to air causing localised health effects.

2.2   The Materials Balance

The materials balance concerns the first step (a) above in Sect. 2.1 in environmental economics modelling.[3] We will simplify and use production activity to cover economic activity. It is the mass of material inputs that appears in the materials balance relation, and it is therefore convenient to operate with two classes of inputs; material inputs (tangible raw materials) x_M and non-material inputs x_S that we will call service inputs (Ayres and Kneese 1969, p. 289). These inputs are not "used up" or transformed in the production process. The materials balance tells us that mass contained in material inputs x_M cannot disappear, but must be contained in either the products y or end up as residuals z. All three types of variables are in general vectors. The residuals are discharged to the natural environment [step (b) in Sect. 2.1]. The variables must be expressed in the same unit of measurement in the materials balance relation. Weight of mass is a natural unit of measurement. The weight of the different inputs can then be summed over the number of material inputs and the same can be done with outputs and residuals:

---

[2]As observed in Ayres and Kneese (1969, p. 283) abatement does not "destroy residuals but only alter their form". Following Russell and Spofford (1972), the concept of "modification" should be used instead of waste treatment or purification to underline the conservation of mass. The mass of residuals does not physically disappear by waste treatment or purification.

[3]The materials balance is quite seldom mentioned in papers published in operational research journals or papers written by researchers from that field. In a recent survey article (Sueyoshi et al. 2017) based on 693 papers using data envelopment analysis within energy and environment, materials balance is never mentioned once.

$$\sum_{j=1}^{n_M} a_{jk}x_{Mj} \equiv \sum_{i=1}^{m} b_{ik}y_i + c_k z_k \quad (k = 1, \ldots, K),$$

$$\sum_{k=1}^{K}\sum_{j=1}^{n_M} a_{jk}x_{Mj} \equiv \sum_{k=1}^{K}\sum_{i=1}^{m} b_{ik}y_i + \sum_{k=1}^{K} c_k z_k \tag{1}$$

There are n_M inputs containing mass (there are n_S service inputs and $n_M + n_S = n$ inputs), m outputs y and K residuals z. The weights a_{jk}, b_{ik}, c_k convert the unit of measurements commonly used for the variables (piece, area, length, etc.) into weight. (The parameters a_{jk} are also called emission coefficients.) The first line in (1) shows the mass balance for one type of substance (k) (see Baumgärtner and de Swaan Arons 2003, footnote 5, p. 121), while the second line shows the total mass balance for the production unit. One issue is the creation of residuals during the production process also containing materials provided free by nature; like oxygen for combustion processes, oxygen used to decompose organic waste discharged to water (biological oxygen demand, BOD), nitrogen oxides created during combustion processes, and water for pulp and paper that adds to the weight of residuals discharged to the environment. Such substances must either be added to the left-hand side as material inputs—and then contained in the residuals z—or we can focus on the actual materials in inputs and redefine z accordingly, like calculating the carbon content in weight for all three types of variables and not measure residuals as CO_2 or CO, etc.

For each production unit we have an *accounting identity* for the use of materials contained in the input x_M. It follows from Eq. (1) that the residuals cannot exceed the material content of inputs measured in the same unit; $c_k z_k \leq \sum_{j=1}^{n_M} a_{jk}x_{Mj}$ ($k = 1, \ldots, K$). The materials can be part of the intended goods y or contained in the residuals z. The relation holds as an identity meaning that it must hold for any accurately measured observation, being efficient or inefficient. The relation should not be regarded a production function, but serves as a restriction on specifications of these (more on this later in Sect. 4.3).

The materials balance is valid at a real-life micro level. If production relations are specified at a sufficiently detailed level, we do not have to worry about the materials balance being fulfilled. However, as expressed in Frisch (1965, p. 14): "If we go into details we shall find that the number of circumstances which in one way or another can influence a production result is endless." He mentions both gravity and molecular forces, and continues: "No analysis, however completely it is carried out, can include all these things at once. In undertaking a production analysis we must therefore *select* certain factors whose effect we wish to consider more closely." It is unavoidable to simplify, but this must be based on a good engineering understanding of the activity in question, and following the principle of Ockham's razor. The specification may then not satisfy the materials balance accurately, but we should be satisfied if our specification is "accurate enough", and especially avoid specifying relations that cannot in principle conform to the materials balance principle.

2.3   Literature on Modelling Production of Goods and Generation of Waste

This subsection is an overview of main modelling issues occurring after the seminal paper Ayres and Kneese (1969) was published that will be brief and not show the formal models. However, the key models and issues will be treated in detail in later sections.

The formal model in Ayres and Kneese (1969) is basically an input-output model covering the complete flow of materials between production and consumption and discharge to the natural environment, formulated as a static general equilibrium exercise in the spirit of Walras-Cassel. The use of linear relationships with fixed coefficients served their purpose of demonstrating the pervasiveness of residuals generation, but lacked flexibility regarding technology.

More conventional input-output models including pollutants were formulated by Leontief (1970); Leontief and Ford (1972). An abatement sector dealing with pollutants was introduced. The fixed input-output coefficients were extended to include fixed emission coefficients for various pollutants calculated as emissions per unit of output. Recognising the role of material inputs, fixed coefficients related to outputs were assumed, and also that there were fixed coefficients in production in general, as there are in the standard input-output model. Førsund and Strøm (1974) introduced extensive input-output emission coefficients for Norway in a multi-sector model of economic growth (Johansen 1960) to predict the time paths of discharge of a large number of pollutants, following the economic growth of sectors. Based on data for Norway, the costs of obtaining a "greener" mix of final deliveries for a given amount of primary inputs were shown in Førsund and Strøm (1976); Førsund (1985), the last paper also providing a survey of input-output models including residuals.

A more flexible modelling of production was formulated in Førsund (1972) based on a special formulation of joint production in Frisch (1965) termed factorially determined multi-output production.[4] This model is the main model of this chapter and will be extensively treated in Sect. 4. Suffice it to say that the main idea is that inputs generate simultaneously both intended outputs and unintended ones in the form of waste or residuals, in accordance with the materials balance principle. It is assumed that each output has its own production function in the same set of inputs.[5] This model was extended in Førsund (1973) to include end-of-pipe abatement of residuals.

---

[4]This type of model but without reference to Frisch (1965) was used in Mäler (1974). His book was written when the author was a visiting scholar at Resources for the Future (RFF) invited for a year by Allen V. Kneese.

[5]This model applied with explicit reference to Frisch (1965) to production of both desirable and undesirable outputs, was, to the best of our knowledge, first used in Førsund (1972, 1973) and developed further in Førsund (1998, 2009, 2018).

Baumol and Oates (1988) (first published in 1975) introduced a transformation function in desirable and undesirable outputs and inputs.[6] However, the possibility of allocating given resources to produce a different mix of outputs that was a consequence of the formulation was not discussed. To overcome the inherent problem of allocating zero resources to produce undesirable outputs, residuals were treated as inputs without any discussion. It will be pointed out in Sects. 3.3 and 4.3 that this procedure is counter to the materials balance.

The use of a Baumol and Oates type of transformation function is widely adopted in the environmental economics literature. In the well-reputed textbook of Perman et al. (2011, p. 25) the assumption of using residuals as inputs is defended, based on their production function (2.3) for firm i: $Q_i = f_i(L_i, K_i, M_i)$ where Q_i is the desirable output, L_i labour, K_i capital and M_i residuals:

> Equation (2.3) may appear strange at first sight as it treats waste flows as an input into production. However, this is a reasonable way of proceeding given that reduction in wastes will mean reductions in output for given levels of the other inputs, as other inputs have to be diverted to the task of reducing wastes.

Cropper and Oates (1992, p. 678) are adopting the same type of arguments. However, such a diversion of inputs may be relevant in a macro setting, but not in a setting of a single firm. A marginal productivity is calculated for an input keeping all other inputs constant. However, if production is efficient then output cannot increase by increasing a residual because the other inputs are constant, so the materials balance rules out both an increase in output and an increase in residuals. The residuals are generated by material inputs, and thus cannot itself be treated as an input.

The Ecological Economics journal started publishing in 1989. Joint production is regarded as a fundamental part of ecological economics. As Baumgärtner et al. (2001, p. 365) state, "the concept of joint production should be considered as one of the conceptual foundations of ecological economics". Joint production will be discussed in Sect. 3.

Pethig (2003, 2006) follow up the general equilibrium approach of Ayres and Kneese (1969). However, the materials balance is used as a part of the production relations. This usage is criticised in Sect. 4.3.

The papers reviewed so far did not discuss inefficiency of operations. The production relations were based on efficient utilisation of inputs. Within the axiomatic approach to measuring inefficiency, Färe et al. (1986, 1989) were the first empirical papers to introduce generation of residuals, or bads as these outputs were called, together with desirable outputs, or goods. Then environmental efficiency could be measured. Especially the 1989 paper spawned a large number of papers (623 citations

---

[6]A production possibility set was also introduced using the transformation relation such that the value of the transformation function is zero for efficient utilisation of resources and less than zero for inefficient operations, but no inefficiency issues were discussed. The solutions to the optimisation problems were based on the production of desirable outputs being efficient.

in SSCI per 25.01.2018).[7] The 1986 paper was somewhat peculiar assuming a technology with strong disposability of the bads before the introduction of regulation of residuals, and then assuming weak disposability of the bads after the introduction of the policy. (Shephard (1970) introduced the concept weak disposability that will be discussed in Sect. 6.) It is rather questionable if imposing a regulation can change the nature of technology in such a way (see Sect. 5 where abatement is introduced without any change in the production technology). The opportunity cost of regulation is measured as the relative loss of outputs based on the two sets of different hypothetical *frontier* values given the inputs of the observations.

Färe et al. (1989) introduced a hyperbolic efficiency measure expanding the goods with a common scalar and contracting the bads with the inverse of the scalar to project an inefficient observation to a reference point on the frontier. This was done in order to credit producers for "their provision of desirable outputs and penalize them for their provision of undesirable outputs" (Färe et al. 1989, p. 90). A problem with this procedure is the arbitrariness of using a scalar and its inverse only, there is no obvious rational for this and no argument is offered. The problem is that the common scalar implies an arbitrary trade-off between goods and bads confounding the efficiency analysis as such.[8] The assumptions that goods and bads are jointly weakly disposable, but that goods alone are strongly disposable, are also made without any explanation. (The criticism of the single equation model and weak disposability is presented in Sects. 3.3, 4.3 and 6.)[9]

The use of a directional distance function instead of a radial one to discriminate between goods and bads were introduced in Chung et al. (1997), and the approach has become popular.[10] However, it is based on a single-equation model and assuming weak disposability. An expansion factor for outputs that enters additively for goods but is subtracted for the bads when identifying frontier points (footnote 8 also applies here) is estimated. "Rewarding" the production of the good and "punishing" the production of the bad with the same factor is just an implicit relative evaluation of these outputs that is quite arbitrary. Preferences have to be involved (see point (d) in Sect. 2.1). In addition the choice of direction to the frontier will influence the measures.

Consequences on efficiency of introducing environmental regulation was put forward in Porter (1991); Porter and van der Linde (1995), and called The Porter hypothesis in the literature.[11] It is based on the existence of inefficiency, but the

---

[7]Chinese researchers have written several such papers, see e.g. Wang et al. (2012, 2017a, b); Xie et al. (2017); Zhao et al. (2015) for recent applications to Chinese data.

[8]In Førsund (2017), it is argued that desirable and undesirable outputs must be measured in the same unit in order to perform a trade-off, cf. point (d) in Sect. 2.1. This can be done by introducing a damage function, as also used in Førsund (2017, 2018).

[9]Førsund (1998) was the first to criticise both the assumption of bads as inputs and the weak disposability assumption. However, the first submission to a journal of the paper was rejected, and an improved version Førsund (2009) published first 11 years later.

[10]However, problems with translation properties are pointed out in Aparicio et al. (2016), and infeasibility problems pointed out in Arabi et al. (2015).

[11]The text below builds on Førsund (2017), Chapter 8.5.

approach is different from the axiom-based measures of efficiency, being purely empirically based. The hypothesis is that substantive environmental regulation giving flexibility of firms' choice of abatement techniques may induce firms to innovate to such a degree that profit increases. Such regulation represents a win-win situation. It is stated that the pessimistic view stems from considering a static situation only, but that the pressure of environmental regulation induces a dynamic process of change representing retooling, process improvement and technical change, which more than offsets the abatement costs. However, Porter and van der Linde do not present any formal mechanism supporting the cost-offset hypothesis, but refer to a few examples of successful adaptation and technical change. The Porter hypothesis and attempts to model the positive dynamics, empirical studies and critique of the hypothesis (e.g. Palmer et al. 1995), are extensively reviewed in Brännlund and Lundgren (2009), Lanoie et al. (2011), Ambec et al. (2013). These three references provide long lists of references to the literature on the Porter hypothesis.

Porter and van der Linde suggest two different dynamic effects. A neat illustration of the story told in Porter and van den Linde (1995) of the increased efficiency effect and the shift in technology effect, is presented in Brännlund and Lundgren (2009), connecting the Porter hypothesis to the efficiency literature. First, assuming that there is inefficiency in utilisation of resources before the introduction of environmental regulation, this inefficiency is reduced or even removed after regulation has been introduced. Second, the regulation induces new technology to be developed, shifting the production function outwards. This is set out in Fig. 1. In the space of the desirable output (q in the original figure) and emissions z the pre-regulation position of the firm is at the inefficient point C below the initial frontier production function $f_0(z)$. The efficient point A on the frontier shows the production the firm could have had corresponding to emission z^0. After introducing regulation, the firm improves its efficiency and reduces the emissions down to the regulated amount, z^R, and increases output from q^0 to q^R at point B on the initial frontier. Then there is a shift of the frontier due to innovation after introducing regulation to $f_R(z)$ where the point E is the efficient point for the level z^R of the

Fig. 1 The Porter hypothesis. *Source* Brännlund and Lundgren (2009, p. 83)

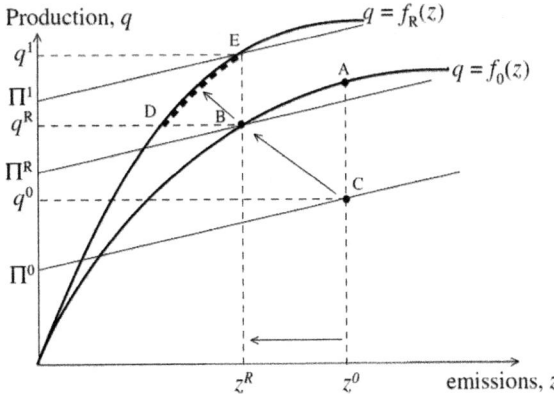

reduced emission. The firm continues to reduce emissions and increase output q, and profit Π moving towards the new frontier.

In a series of eight more or less overlapping papers published in the period 2010–2013 (see Førsund (2018) for the list of these references and evaluations), Sueyoshi with co-authors actually employed the Frisch (1965) factorially determined multi-output model with both good and bad outputs being functions of the same inputs (see e.g. models 4 and 5 in Sueyoshi and Goto 2010, p. 5905), using non-parametric DEA models for empirical applications mainly to the energy sector. This is as formulated for frontier models in Førsund (1972, 1973, 2009). No explanation is given for the choice of this type of model (and the references above are not given). Sueyoshi et al. developed separate efficiency measures for desirable and undesirable outputs, but emphasis was put on unified measures by solving for the combined production possibility sets.

The multi-equation model of Førsund (2009) is followed up in Murty et al. (2012) using a model called the by-production approach.[12] In the theoretical model with abatement, the first relation is a transformation relation between a desirable output, an abatement output and two types of resources; one pollution generating and the other not. The second relation has the pollution (or residual) as a function of the polluting input (positive impact) and the abatement output (negative impact). The production possibility set is formed by the intersection of the two sets based on these relations. Efficiency measures for the two types of output separately and a form of aggregated measure were developed for non-parametric DEA models.[13] Førsund (2018) argues against the usefulness of aggregate measures for policy purposes.

The abatement activity is only indirectly treated in a non-transparent way in Murty et al. (2012), maybe due to reflecting process changes. In Førsund (2018) it is pointed out that it is difficult to get data for process changes and resources consumed in such activities. Instead an end-of-pipe abatement facility is explicitly modelled there, separate efficiency measures for desirable outputs and residuals efficiency are developed, and also a measure for abatement efficiency.

Murty and Russell (2018)[14] show that the multi-equation by-product model in Murty et al. (2012) (with abatement) has an axiomatic foundation supporting such models, reconciling the abstract axiomatic characterization of an emission-generating technology in Murty (2015) with the empirically oriented by-production technology formulated by Murty et al. (2012).

---

[12]The name is meant to point to the production of both desirable goods and residuals. However, the name is not according to the classical economist, calling by-products commercial outputs, but with less value than other goods. Their word for residuals was waste, see next Sect. 3.1.

[13]Dakpo et al. (2016) review weak disposability models and the by-production model. Hampf (2018) reviews single equation models only, and has several critical remarks to the typical Färe et al. models of desirable and undesirable outputs.

[14]Førsund (2018), Murty and Russell (2018) and Hampf (2018) are forthcoming in a special issue 'Good modelling of bad outputs' of *Empirical Economics*, see Kumbhakar and Malikov (2018).

3 Joint Production

The materials balance forcefully establishes that any production involving material inputs results in two types of outputs; desirable and undesirable. Therefore, a joint output model must be used in order to model such type of production.

3.1 The Historical Background

Most of the current textbooks, at least on a lower level, dealing with production theory assume a single output being produced by two or more inputs. However, this choice of modelling is not based on any empirical evidence that this is the dominating form of production. On the contrary, joint production seems to be the general rule in practice. As pointed out in Kurz (1986, pp. 1–2):

> The view "that these cases of joint production, far from being 'some peculiar cases', form the general rule, to which it is difficult to point out any clear or important exception", has been advocated already one century ago by W.S. Jevons.

Kurz (1986) reviews how a number of classical and early neoclassical economists, among them Adam Smith, Karl Marx, von Thünen, Longfield, Mill, von Mangoldt, Jevons, and Marshall, treat joint production. The examples used by these economists were mainly drawn from agriculture; like raising sheep yielding wool and mutton, animal rearing yields meat and hides, growing wheat yields grain and straw, and forestry yields timber and firewood, etc.

A standard textbook way to represent a multiple-output multiple input production relation is to use a single implicit functional representation:

$$F(y,x) = 0, F'_y > 0, F'_x < 0 \tag{2}$$

$F(.)$ is commonly called the transformation function. y and x are vectors of outputs and inputs, respectively. The signing of partial derivatives identify outputs and inputs. We assume that $F(.)$ is continuous, but not necessarily differentiable at all points.

There is a clear distinction between inefficient and efficient operation. The production possibility set corresponding to (2) can be written

$$F(y,x) \leq 0, \tag{3}$$

and contains in principle all feasible production plans. An engineer will probably not waste his time mapping inefficient ways of producing; a blueprint of technology represents efficient operations. The production function concept (2) is attached to efficient operations that are on the border of the set. In the efficiency literature the efficient way of producing is termed the frontier function (or best practice as used in

Farrell 1957) due to the factual observations used to estimate the frontier function. Strongly inefficient observations are found in the interior of the set.

The concept of disposability is expressed by assuming that for a feasible point, an increase of the x-vector for constant outputs leaves the new point inside the production set, and a decrease of the output vector y for constant inputs leaves the new point inside the set. On the frontier, we see from (2) that an (infinitesimal) increase in an input leads to the interior of the set, as will a decrease in an output.[15] The monotonicity expressed by the partial derivatives in (2) corresponds to the free (strong) disposability of outputs and inputs of the set (3). The production possibility set allows observations to be located in the interior of the set, so such a set is therefore a natural starting point for analysing inefficiency. We will return to this point later in Sect. 6.

According to Kurz (1986, p. 16) Karl Marx researched production technologies extensively and in addition to agriculture examples had many other examples of joint production, like mining, forestry, paper manufacturing, the chemical industries, the textile industries, mechanical engineering, etc. Marx divided products into a main desired product, and one or several by-products that may or may not be useful, and that, at any rate, are of secondary economic interest. He was especially concerned by waste and stated (according to Kurz 1986, p. 16): "The so-called *waste* plays an important role in almost every industry." True to form Marx called waste *excretions of production*. Furthermore, Marx stated that the "excretions of production" should be reduced to a minimum, and the immediate utilisation should be increased to a maximum of all raw- and auxiliary materials required in production. This sounds very modern!

Jevons introduced the distinction between commodities and discommodities, the last category could cause inconvenience or harm (Jevons 1965, p. 58), and he pointed out that discommodities could have negative value. He used as an example of discommodity waste from a chemical plant fouling the water downstream (Jevons 1965, p. 202).

The classical and neoclassical economists focused much of the discussion of joint production on the problem of unique determination of the output prices. There is a problem of determining the share of costs due to joint outputs. It was often assumed that market forces would lead to as many equations as outputs, and that a unique set of prices could be determined.

There is one more recent definition of joint production in the literature (Pasinetti 1980) that has some following based on Sraffa (1960) that should be mentioned. Considering time as periods, capital is entered as an input at the start of a period, and defined as an output at the end of the period. This type of joint production is not the type of joint production that we are concerned with in this chapter and will be disregarded in our classification.

---

[15]To say that inputs and outputs can be disposed of by throwing them away (Shephard 1970, p. 14) is not in accordance with economic use of inputs and outputs.

3.2 Frisch on Joint Production

The materials balance tells us that desirable and undesirable outputs are produced jointly. Therefore the modelling of joint production is essential within environmental economics. Joint production takes place when the production unit in question produces more than one output. According to Frisch (1965), who has a comprehensive discussion and classification of joint production, joint production implies that there is a technical connection between products; because there are certain inputs either which *can* be used or on technical grounds *must* be used jointly, or because there are inputs that can be used alternatively for one product or the other.[16] In The New Palgrave, producing outputs by separate production processes is also classified as joint production; there is a choice how to allocate a given amount of inputs to outputs. This is a typical situation in international trade when countries are considered as production units. In Chambers (1988); Kohli (1983); Nadiri (1987, p. 1028) this is called non-joint production.[17] In the two first references, a main example is how production is modelled in the international trade literature.

We will use the Frisch (1965) classification below.[18] Two main forms of joint production are suggested:

(i) Inputs can be used to produce different outputs within the same general production technology. Examples in Frisch (1965) are that a piece of agricultural land can be used alternatively to grow different crops, and that a wood cutting machine tool can be used to produce different types of wood articles. The producer has a freedom of choice as to the mix of products he wants to produce. Frisch calls this *assorted production.*

(ii) The technical process is such that it is impossible to produce one product without at the same time producing one or more other products; using coal as input gas, coke, and tar are produced, and raising sheep results in wool and mutton.

---

[16]According to Kurz (1986, p. 25), Mangoldt's definition is about the same as the one of Frisch: "pure joint production (or joint production in the technical sense) and what may be called competing, alternative or rival (Edgeworth) production which derives from the fact that a firm's (given) productive equipment may be used for several purposes."

[17]Using non-jointness when defining joint production seems a little awkward; sounding almost like a contradiction. Nadiri (1987, p. 1028) claims that absence of non-jointness is a crucial test of joint production, in spite of including non-jointness as part of the definition of joint production: "Joint production includes two cases: (1) when there are multiple products, each produced under separate production processes—i.e. the production function is non-joint [...]". He uses the term "intrinsic jointness" when there is jointness in a technical sense.

[18]There are unfortunately few references to Frisch (1965) about joint production, neither Chambers (1988); Kohli (1983), nor Nadiri (1987) refer to Frisch. It seems appropriate to make his take on joint production better known.

The connection between outputs demands, according to Frisch (1965, p. 269), that production laws cannot be studied separately for each product, but must be considered simultaneously for all connected products. In order to catch the engineering complexities of multioutput production Frisch (1965) generalised various possibilities by introducing a system of μ equations between m outputs y and n inputs x[19]:

$$F^i(y_1, \ldots, y_m, x_1, \ldots, x_n) = 0, \quad i = 1, \ldots, \mu \tag{4}$$

These relations are frontier ones in our terminology. Corresponding production possibility sets will be

$$F^i(y_1, \ldots, y_m, x_1, \ldots, x_n) \leq 0, \quad i = 1, \ldots, \mu \tag{5}$$

The two classes (i) and (ii) above are special cases of (4). The production possibility set for the system of Eq. (4) will be the intersection of the production possibility sets (5) for each equation (see Chambers 1988, p. 290).

Frisch (1965) introduced the concept of degree of assortment α that tells us the limits for reallocating inputs on outputs, $\alpha = m - \mu$. If we have only a single relation in (4), i.e. $\mu = 1$—as in (2)—then the degree of assortment is maximal; $\alpha^{max} = m - 1$. If there is no assortment, i.e., there is no choice of output mix given the inputs, then $\alpha^{min} = m - \mu = m - m = 0$. There are as many equations μ as there is products m.

An important case is $m \geq \mu$; the degree of assortment is non-negative as assumed above. However, in the system (4) there may be more relations than products so the case $m < \mu$ cannot be excluded. If this is the case then there are one or more pure product bands independent of factors. Frisch (1965) calls the number of such equations for the degree of coupling κ. This is not determined by m, n, μ, but is expressed by the greatest number of equations in (4) that do not contain any of the inputs when transforming the equations in such a way that as many of them as possible are free from inputs (Frisch 1965, pp. 278–279). The band (or coupling) between outputs is expressed by:

$$F^c(y_1, \ldots, y_m) = 0, c \in C \tag{6}$$

where C is the set of relations between outputs only of the μ equations in (4). In the classical literature on joint production, it was often assumed a fixed relation between outputs, e.g. the quantity of wool bears a fixed relation to the quantity of mutton (Frisch 1965, p. 271).

---

[19]In a very readable book, Whitcomb (1972) discusses the connection between externalities and joint production. He refers both to Frisch (1965) and specifies a variant of the system (4), and to Ayres and Kneese (1969), but does not use the materials balance explicitly in his analysis.

There may also be pure factor bands between inputs, i.e. relations between inputs independent of outputs:

$$F^b(x_1, \ldots, x_n) = 0, \quad b \in B \tag{7}$$

where B is the set of relations between inputs only of the μ equations in (4), e.g. a chemical process where inputs must be applied in fixed proportions.

The efficient border of the production possibility set (3) is specified as a single functional relationship in (2). This is commonly done, but we see that the system of Eq. (4) is much more general. However, it may be problematic to impose convexity assumptions on the general specification of the intersection of μ technology sets (5).

An important special case of the system (4) is that the equations can be solved with respect to the m products (cf. the concern of the classical economists mentioned in Sect. 3.1), and where the m ensuing production functions are single valued. This is the case of *Factorially determined multi-output production* (Frisch 1965, p. 270)[20,21]:

$$y_i = f_i(x_1, \ldots, x_n), \quad i = 1, \ldots, m \tag{8}$$

The same set of inputs appears in all separate production functions. Both the degree of coupling and the degree of assortment are zero. The products are separable, but the ratios between outputs are not fixed, but change with input mix. The mix of wool and mutton depends on the breed of sheep and maybe feeding, and the mix of eggs and poultry meat depends on the feeding.

Within this case, there are important sub-cases. Frisch (1965, p. 275) claims that necessary and sufficient condition for coupled (joint) products in the case of factorially determined multi-output production functions is that there exist a functional relationship $F(y_1, \ldots, y_m) = 0$, independent of inputs. One way of obtaining a fixed ratio between outputs is:

$$y_i = c_i f(x_1, \ldots, x_n) \Rightarrow \frac{y_i}{y_j} = \frac{c_i}{c_j}, \quad i, j = 1, \ldots, m, \quad i \neq j \tag{9}$$

where the c's are constants. The technology is the same for all outputs except for a scaling constant c_i implying a fixed ratio between the outputs. An example of coupled products is refining of crude oil and the distillates emerging from the same process.

---

[20]Kohli (1983) introduces this case in his Definition 4 on p. 213 and calls it "non-joint in input prices". This seems a little peculiar name since there are no input prices appearing in the definition (however, duality results use shadow prices). He has no reference to Frisch (1965) that introduced this type of relation decades before.

[21]Chambers (1988, p. 289) calls the factorially determined functions for generalised fixed coefficients technologies.

There may be more complex couplings than (9). The ratios between products may be a function of the quantities of outputs, but the degree of assortment is still zero. A complete coupling occurs when isoquants in the input space coincide, and substitution regions are identical (see Frisch 1965, p. 273 for an illustration). The relation between outputs for the same isoquant is independent of input quantities.

3.3   Restrictions on Production Models

Going back to classical or neoclassical economists concerned with joint production in Sect. 3.1, the three categories of outputs specified were main products, by-products and waste products. By-products (the alternative spelling 'bi-products' is used in Frisch 1965, p. 11) are commercial products of more minor economic importance than the main products. Waste products without economic value to the producer are termed residuals in this chapter.

In the influential textbook by Baumol and Oates (1988, first edition 1975) the essence of their model can be captured by specifying a single transformation relation as the border of the set and the production possibility set as follows (more based on externalities modelling than referring to the materials balance)[22]:

$$
\begin{aligned}
F(y, z, x) &= 0, F'y, F'z > 0, F'x < 0 \\
F(y, z, x) &\leq 0
\end{aligned}
\tag{10}
$$

Notice that with the sign conventions for the partial derivatives all variables exhibit strong (free) disposability. However, the question is if this relation can function as the efficient border of the production possibility set as relation (2) does for the set (3). As the first relation in (10) stands it has a maximal degree of assortment according to the scheme of Frisch (1965), meaning that all the inputs can be reallocated to produce the desirable products y and no resources used to produce the undesirable products z, unless more conditions are specified. However, this goes against the fact that the residual z is not a result of choice as is the case with the desirable outputs, but is physically linked to the material inputs used in the production of desirable outputs. Baumol and Oates may have been aware of this problem, because without telling the reader they assume that the z variables function *as if* they are inputs. The formal Pareto-optimal results when they maximise the utility of one consumer for a given input vector x, under the condition that all other consumers' utilities shall not be lower than given levels, then apparently seems to make sense. However, this cannot be done because as we see from the materials balance (1), the material content is distributed on products y and residuals z. Residuals cannot be

---

[22]The assortment property is not discussed in Baumol and Oates (1988, Chap. 4). The materials balance principle is not mentioned in the book.

reduced in (10) for given x because the transformation function is by definition efficient, in the sense that it is constructed by maximising outputs y for given inputs x, neglecting residuals z because they are undesirable outputs. The maximal possible amount of raw materials is already extracted from x to produce desirable outputs y, and this amount cannot then be increased for a given x vector.

The conjecture is that a single transformation relation cannot work without specifying restrictions on the degree of assortment. However, even more serious is the combination of the materials balance and the efficiency assumption that the transformation function is based on. The combination of these two factors implies that we cannot operate with a functional trade-off between a desirable output and a residual. The option to reallocate inputs between desirable goods and residuals is simply not available. The residuals are generated simultaneously with desirable outputs by using material inputs. Some sort of separation between modelling of production relations for the desirable and undesirable output is needed. This point will be developed further in Section 6.

4 Multi-equation Models for Desirable and Undesirable Outputs

To make a useful model is an art. As quoted in Sect. 2.1 Ragnar Frisch was fully aware of the need for simplification. He introduced the term 'model world' in Frisch (2010, pp. 31–32):

> The observational world itself, taken as a whole in its infinite complexity and with its infinite mass of detail, is impossible to grasp. […] In order to create points where the mind can get a grip, we make an intellectual trick: in our mind we create a little *model world* of our own, a model world that is not too complicated to be overlooked, and which is equipped with points where the mind can get a grip, so that we can find our way without getting confused. And then we analyse this little model world instead of the real world. […] It shall picture those indefinable things in the real world which we may call 'essentials' […]

Part of the 'essentials' is that the model should satisfy the materials balance and efficiency properties of the production relations. A solution to the problems is to employ the Frisch (1965) scheme of factorially determined multi-output production in the previous Sect. 3.2 as in (8), introducing residuals as outputs in the same way as desirable outputs. The adoption of a multi-equation model instead of a single-equation one is crucial for satisfying theoretically the materials balance and efficiency conditions. More specifically, as stated in the previous subsection, there cannot be any functional trade-off between desirable and undesirable outputs for given resources.

4.1   The Frisch Multi-equation Model

As stated previously, residuals are generated simultaneously with the desirable products and stem from the raw materials employed as inputs. It seems important to satisfy these physical realities arising from use of material inputs in any sound modelling of the interaction of economic activity and generation of pollutants. The model from the production theory of Frisch (1965) presented in Sect. 3.2 of product separability, the factorially determined multi-output model, seems tailor-made for capturing the physical process of generation of residuals simultaneously with desirable outputs. Single-output production functions for each undesirable residual are added to the single-output functions for desirable goods[23]:

$$y = f(x_M, x_S), f'_{x_M}, f'_{x_S} > 0, \quad f''_{x_M}, f''_{x_S} < 0$$
$$z = g(x_M, x_S), g'_{x_M} > 0, g'_{x_S} \leq 0, \quad g''_{x_M}, g''_{x_S} > 0 \tag{11}$$

To keep the model as simple as possible we consider a single desirable output y (or the good for short) that is the purpose of the production activity, and a single residual or undesirable output z (a pollutant or a bad for short). Two types of inputs only are also specified following Ayres and Kneese (1969); material inputs x_M and non-material inputs, or service inputs x_S. Generalising to multi-output and multi-pollutants can be done just by adding more equations, one for each variable, keeping the same inputs (their number can easily be expanded too) as arguments in all relations (see Førsund 2009).

In the previous Sect. 3.3, it was stated that the model must have a certain property of separability. The model (11) satisfies this property because the production of desirable outputs is not influenced by undesirable outputs, and vice versa for the production of undesirable outputs.[24]

It should be stressed that the two relations in (11) do not represent physically separate technologies. It is the analyst that simplifies a complex technology of simultaneous transformations to the two relations. Changes in inputs generate simultaneously both the intended and unintended outputs. Generation of residuals cannot be controlled independently, but follows from the use of the inputs needed for production of the intended outputs.

---

[23]Leontief type models with fixed coefficients are not considered.

[24]The Frisch model of factorially determined multi-output equations is not the only model having the sufficient separability properties.

The material inputs are *essential* in the sense that we will have no production neither of material goods nor bads if $x_M = 0$[25,26]:

$$y = f(0, x_S) = 0, z = g(0, x_S) = 0 \tag{12}$$

The function $f(.)$ is defined by maximising y for given inputs, and the function $g(.)$ is defined by minimising z for given inputs. They are both frontier functions. The partial productivities in the good output production have the standard properties of positive but decreasing values. The signing of partial derivatives of the residuals function may be more unconventional. It seems reasonable to assume positive but increasing marginal productivity of the material input, and negative but decreasing marginal productivity of the service input. The positive partial productivity of service inputs x_S in the desirable output production function and the negative sign in the residuals generation function can be explained by the fact that more of a service input improve the utilisation of the given raw materials through better process control, fewer rejects and increased internal recycling of waste materials.[27] The negative partial derivative of service inputs in the residuals function mirrors the positive sign in the output function. If y is non-material (e.g. electricity) then $b_k = 0$ in (1) and $g'_{x_S} = 0$ implying that the residual has the same mass but that the output is increased when x_S increases. The residuals generation function may degenerate to a fixed relation between residuals and raw materials similar to Leontief technologies, but then we will have a Leontief relation for the good y also.

4.2   Substitution Possibilities

There will in general be substitution possibilities between material and service inputs. The rate of substitution evaluated at a point on an isoquant for y in (11) is $(-f'_{x_M}/f'_{x_S}) < 0$ in the interior of the substitution region (this is a Frisch concept for the economic region; i.e. all marginal productivities in goods production are positive). This is the amount of the service input that has to be increased if the material input is reduced with one unit, keeping output y constant. Considering several material inputs there may be substitution possibilities between them also,

---

[25]One or more service inputs may also be essential, but the point is that residuals are in general an unavoidable feature using material inputs in production. Although $y = f(x_M, 0) = 0$ we may have $z = g(x_M, 0) > 0$; e.g. as in a fully automated thermal electricity-generating plant running in a spinning mode (the energy stored by spinning is then not considered an output).

[26]In Murty and Russell (2018, p. 15) x_M is called jointly essential with z, it is rather obvious that z cannot be zero for $x_M > 0$, however, Rødseth (2017a) covers the possibilities with the concepts output- and input essentiality.

[27]Cf. the famous chocolate production example in Frisch (1935), discussed in Førsund (1999), of substitution between labour and cocoa fat due to more intensive recycling of rejects not filling the forms the more labour and less cocoa fat that are employed producing the same amount of chocolate.

Fig. 2 Isoquants for the production of y and z

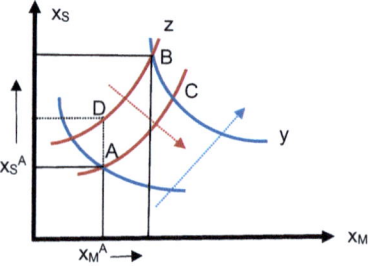

e.g. between coal and natural gas, that will keep the output constant, but decrease the generation of bads if the marginal contribution of gas to creation of bads is smaller than the marginal contribution of coal.

There is also substitution between the two types of inputs in the residuals-generating function. The marginal rate of substitution is positive, $(-g'_{x_M}/g'_{x_S}) > 0$ in the interior of the substitution region for bads due to the marginal productivity of service inputs being negative in this case. The necessary increase in the service input to keep a constant level of the residual when the material input increases with one unit, is increasing following the signing of the partial derivatives in (11). This implies a special form of isoquants in the factor space and the direction of increasing residual level compared with a standard isoquant map for the output, as seen in Fig. 2. (The substitution regions, the borders of which have zero marginal productivities, are not shown.) The isoquants for the two outputs can be shown in the same diagram because the arguments in the functions are the same. The level of the residual z is increasing moving South-East (red isoquants) in the direction of the broken red arrow, while the level of the intended (desirable) good y is increasing moving North-East (blue isoquants) in the direction of the broken blue arrow. Going from point A to point B in input space, increasing both the material and service inputs, but changing the mix markedly towards the service input, we see that the production of the residual z has decreased while the production of output y has increased. Reducing the service input but increasing the material input going from point B to point C, keeping the same level of the desirable output, the level of the undesirable output increases. All points of the type (x_S^A, x_M^A) in input space generating points (y^A, z^A) in output space are frontier points.

There are obviously limits to substitution between material and service input keeping the same desirable output.[28] Moving along the y isoquant from point A in a North-West direction there is a limit to the amount of raw materials that can be extracted from the material input and keeping the output constant, i.e. there is a limit on how much the residual generation can be reduced. The lower limit of the residual is reached at the border of the substitution region for the good output

---

[28]Continuing the chocolate example in footnote 27: when so much labour is employed so that all the defect chocolates re-circulated to the production cannot be increased any more employing more labour, based on a given mass of raw material with a minimum of cocoa fat for the required taste.

isoquant in question. (This is not illustrated in the figure.) Another angle on this lower limit is keeping the material input constant at the level x_M^A at point A, and then see how much residuals can be reduced increasing the service input from x_S^A. Let us say point D will be the point with the minimum generation of residuals z, but then the good output has also increased. Point D is then on the border of the substitution region (zero marginal productivity for service input) for the isoquant for the new level of good output. The minimum level of residual generation depends typically on the level of both types of inputs, as does the level of maximal good output.

Obviously, there must also be upper bounds on emission generation for given amounts of emission-generating inputs; residuals cannot exceed the material inputs measured in mass units [see the discussion of (1)]. Since minimum levels are the crucial variables in the analysis upper bounds will not be specified explicitly for convenience (following Murty and Russell 2018).

In addition to the two ways of reducing generation of residuals by input substitutions there is the obvious way of reducing the production of desirable products by scaling down the use of both inputs. However, this may be often the most expensive way to reduce residuals generation (Rødseth 2013).

4.3 The Materials Balance and the Multi-equation Model

Model (11) is a theoretical one, our model world, and as such can be compatible with the materials balance. A theoretical model that is not compatible with the materials balance is obviously inferior to a model that does comply. Notice that the materials balance (1) is a physical law and should not be regarded as a separate part of the production relations (11). The observations of y and z generated by inputs x_M and x_S through the $f(.)$ and $g(.)$ functions must satisfy the materials balance. Thus, this identity constrains what kind of production relations to specify, but does not give any specific information as to the nature of the technology. It should be born in mind that the system (11) of production functions is a long way from describing physical engineering relations in real life details. As is standard in economics, the relations are extreme simplifications, but containing the essential features necessary for the analyses we want to do in our model world. As stated in Sect. 2.2 the materials balance is functioning on a much more detailed level of aggregation, especially when representing the residuals discharged to the environment and the part of residuals that are due to physical/chemical processes of combustion. It will be difficult to get data on the level necessary to control the materials balance numerically.[29]

---

[29]A practical use of the materials balance is the estimation of emission coefficients, e.g. when coal is used in thermal electricity generation, assuming a specific physical composition of coal and optimal running of the process. Then, because the complete contents of coal end up as residuals, knowledge of the combustion process allows the emission coefficients concerning the substances actually discharged to the external environment to be calculated.

It may be the case that the materials balance principle is taken a little too literally or philosophically in ecological economics doing practical modelling (Baumgärtner et al. 2001; Lauwers 2009). It should be born in mind that the materials balance, as an identity for all kinds of processes using material inputs, cannot give any information about a specific technology at hand, but only give some restrictions on what kind of relations to specify. A restriction mentioned in Pethig (2003) is that the Cobb–Douglas function cannot be used because of the extreme substitution possibility between inputs. A problem in Pethig (2003, 2006) is the use of the materials balance in specifying the residuals generation function by just inserting for z in the materials balance identity (1). It is rather difficult to believe that such a relation can properly represent any specific technology.

How can we then know that the frontier relations (11) comply with the materials balance principle? The short answer is that we cannot know this until we have accurate observations, but due to the requirement of details, this will be quite difficult to carry out. However, what we do know from the results of Section 3 is that there cannot be what we can call a direct functional basis for a trade-off between goods y and bads z.[30] In Fig. 2 we have no trade-off between y and z for given x; i.e. at point A the output levels y and z are given for the input levels x_M^A and x_S^A at A. To change the mix between y and z always requires changing input mixes and levels.

5 End-of-Pipe Abatement and Regulation

5.1 End-of-Pipe

We will add an independent abatement process to the multi-equation model (11). End-of-pipe abatement often consists of a facility separated from the production activity. Other abatement options in the short run is to retool the processes and do small-scale changes. These options are alternatives to integrated technological process solutions. However, it is often rather difficult to identify such activities distinct from the general process activity and to identify the inputs involved. It is easier to do this with a stand-alone abatement facility in terms of inputs used and outputs produced. Add-on abatement requires that we make a clear distinction between primary pollutants z from the production process and pollutants z^D actually discharged to the environment. Primary pollutants can then be regarded as an input to the abatement process. In addition to inputs like labour, capital, and energy, other inputs like absorbing substances, chemicals and specialised capital, may have to be used in order to convert part of the primary pollutants z into abated pollutants z^a as outputs creating

---

[30]This trade-off should not be confused with a correlation between y and z depending on indirect effects. Increasing x_M in (11) will lead to increases in both y and z, thus we have a positive correlation, increasing x_S will increase y but decrease z (if y contains materials), and thus we have a negative correlation.

less harm (usually no harm at all is assumed in applications) than the primary ones (Førsund 2009)[31] In the long run there may be a choice between end-of-pipe abatement and large-scale investment in new technology integrating production processes and abatement. The time horizon for environmental improvement, uncertainty about what can be achieved by new technology, and uncertainty about the future regulatory regime may determine the choice between these two options.

Expressing the abated residuals as outputs we formulate the following abatement production function (see also Førsund 1973; Pethig 2006; Färe et al. 2013; Hampf 2014; Førsund 2009, the last paper provides a generalisation to more than one primary residual, and the introduction of new types of abatement outputs with detrimental environmental effects)[32]:

$$\delta z^a = zA\left(x_M^a, x_S^a\right), A'_{x_S}, A'_{x_S} > 0, \frac{\delta z^a}{z} \in [0, 1]$$
$$z^D = z - \delta z^a \geq 0$$
(13)

The abatement activity receives the primary residual z appearing in (11) and uses resources x_M^a, x_S^a to modify z into another form z^a that by assumption (for convenience) can be disposed of without social or private costs. In order to express the residual variables in the same unit, we can convert abatement residuals z^a, typically given another form than the primary residual, into units of primary residual applying a conversion coefficient δ. The theoretical feasible range of modification is from zero to one. In practice 0.95 seems to be the upper limit, e.g. for flue-gas desulphurisation. The partial productivities in the abatement production function are assumed positive. Increases in the abatement inputs contribute to an increase in the relative share of abated amount and an absolute increase for a given amount of primary residual.

To make sense of the abatement function (13) it is assumed that the amount of abatement inputs determines the capacity to treat the primary residual generated by the production system (11). It may be more realistic that capital equipment determines a physical capacity to treat the primary residual. However, we do not want to introduce an analysis of investing in abatement capacity. We let the amount of current inputs in (13) determine the abated amount and assume that the maximal relative abatement level that realistically exists will not be reached for economic reasons (e.g. due to sufficiently decreasing marginal productivities of the inputs).

The second equation defines the amount of residual z^D that is actually emitted to the environment. It is often called the secondary residual in the environmental economics literature, but also controlled emission is used. One may think of the

---

[31]Modification and recycling of residuals using factorially determined multioutput production functions was introduced already in Førsund (1973).

[32]Hampf (2014) has a similar specification of the abatement function with primary residuals as input together with a stage-specific amount of non-polluting abatement inputs (same as similar inputs in the production of the good output in stage 1), a shared input of the two stages, and part of the output from stage 1 as an input. The abated amount is the single output, and the secondary residual emitted to the environment is residually calculated as in Førsund (2009, 2018).

secondary pollutant as an output, but it is more to the point (and analytically more convenient) to regard the secondary pollutant to be determined residually.[33] It is assumed that the secondary residual has the same form as the primary residual, e.g. measured in CO_2, or SO_2, or in carbon and sulphur, or in the form determined by the combustion process or production process in general. It is typically the case that at least all gaseous residuals cannot be dealt with completely and modified to harmless substances, so $z > \delta z^a \Rightarrow z^D > 0$. The partial productivities in the abatement production function are assumed positive. Increases in the abatement inputs contribute to an increase in the relative share of abated amount and an absolute increase for a given amount of primary residual. Given the amount of the primary residual from the production stage, and knowing the rate of abatement A, both the absolute amounts of the two abatement outputs can be calculated: $\delta z^a = Az$, $z^D = (1 - A)z$.

The multiplicative decomposition of primary pollutants and the relative abatement part facilitates focussing on the latter as the endogenous variable of the end-of-pipe abatement activity. It may be assumed that the function $A(.)$ is concave.

Usually abatement is represented by a cost function in the environmental economics textbooks (Førsund and Strøm 1988; Perman et al. 2011, see also Rødseth and Romstad (2014, p. 119) for a non-parametric application to US electricity generation regulating sulphur emissions). The main advantage is simplification (see Førsund 2017), but the details of a physical abatement production function (13) are then hidden. Here it is chosen to focus on the relative amount of primary residual that is modified to other forms, e.g. from gas to solid waste. We can also say that there are two outputs generated by the abatement activity; the harmless abatement residual z^a and the remaining amount of the primary residual in its original form.

Applying the materials balance principle to (13) the abatement activity will add to the total mass of residuals if material inputs are used; the material factors and primary pollutants are now inputs to a production process and the mass is distributed on the output z^a and the secondary pollutant z^D. The total mass of residuals has increased, but the point is that abatement means less mass of the harmful residual; $z^D < z$.

In the environmental efficiency literature, the resources of a firm are often regarded as given, and then increased abatement will imply fewer resources to produce the intended output and thereby decreasing the generation of primary pollutants (see e.g. Martin 1986; Färe et al. 2013). To do this requires an explicit restriction to be imposed on the availability of inputs (done only in Färe et al. 2013). However, this problem is created by the analyst and does not necessarily reflect decisions of a firm having access to markets for inputs to given prices. If it is assumed that abatement is a separate identifiable activity, as e.g. end-of-pipe, and

---

[33]The abatement stage in Färe et al. (2013, p. 112) does not, somewhat awkwardly, show the use of the abated amount explicitly, neither in the definition of their production possibility set (16) nor in their model Eqs. (18), (19) and (20). In Pethig (2006, p. 189) the primary residual seems to be the output of abatement.

inputs are sourced in markets, there is no reason to assume that abatement resources are taken from the production inputs of a firm. Thus, abatement does not influence the output directly, but increases the cost of production and may then indirectly reduce output and production inputs. It is closer to reality at the micro level not to consider a common resource pool for the production unit, but to regard the activities (11) and (13) as separate "profit centres".

We recommend to follow this approach and thus avoid constructed trade-offs not embedded in technology. The abatement inputs therefore have a super-index "a" to indicate abatement inputs. It may also be the case that there are specific types of abatement inputs, e.g. chemicals and capital equipment, not used in the production process itself. In the case of thermal electricity generation, it is quite usual that abatement activities require electricity as an input. Carbon capture and storage may draw as much as 20% of the gross production of electricity. However, this electricity can be formally regarded as a bought input so (13) may still be used.

5.2 Imposing a Constraint on Emission

Environmental regulatory agencies typically prefer direct regulation and not indirect economic instrument.[34] The most common type of direct regulation is to impose an upper limit on discharge of harmful residuals on firms. In order to predict how a firm reacts to direct regulation it is necessary that the firm acts rationally, commonly interpreted as meaning in a private economic sense. It is then standard to assume that the firm starts out being technically efficient and not to be inefficient as was the case discussing the Porter hypothesis in Sect. 2.3.

For simplicity, we consider a single undesirable output only. An environment agency may impose an upper limit z_R^D on the amount emitted from a firm during a specific time period; $z^D \leq z_R^D$. The firm's optimisation problem, cast as a profit maximisation problem, becomes

$$\text{Max}\, py - \sum_{j=M,S} q_j x_j - \sum_{j=M,S} q_j^a x_j^a$$

s.t.

$$y = f(x_M, x_S)$$
$$z = g(x_M, x_S)$$
$$\delta z^a = zA(x_M^a, x_S^a) \tag{14}$$
$$z^D = z - \delta z^a$$
$$z^D \leq z_R^D$$

----

[34]See Zhao et al. (2015), Xie et al. (2017) for studies of types of command-and-control and market-based environmental regulation in China.

The optimisation problem may be written more compactly as

$$\text{Max } pf(x_M, x_S) - \sum_{j=M,S} q_j x_j - \sum_{j=M,S} q_j^a x_j^a$$

s.t.   (15)

$$g(x_M, x_S)(1 - A(x_M^a, x_S^a)) \leq z_R^D$$

The necessary first-order conditions are:

$$pf_{x_j}' - q_j - \lambda g_{x_j}'(1 - A) = 0, j = M, S$$
$$- q_j^a + \lambda z A_{x_j}' = 0, j = M, S$$ (16)

Here λ is the shadow price on the emission constraint. Assuming that the constraint is binding the shadow price shows the gain in profit of marginally relaxing the constraint.

Without the regulation on discharge of residuals, the standard first-order condition is $pf_{x_j}' = q_j, j = M, S$; the value of the marginal productivity of a factor is equal to the factor price. With regulation binding the unit factor cost will increase for the material input but decrease for the service input, thus leading to a substitution between the factors. However, total costs will go up leading to reduced output. If abatement is used this means that abatement is cheaper than reducing discharge of residuals by only reducing production of the good, and reduction of output will then not be so great as without abatement.

6   Allowing for Inefficient Operations

6.1   Defining Inefficiency

In view of the importance of the materials balance for how to specify a technology based on using material inputs, it might be of interest to expand on the meaning of inefficiency. Inefficiency arises in general when the potential engineering or blue-print technology, the frontier for short, is not achieved when transforming inputs into outputs, assuming that this is feasible.[35] For given desirable outputs too much resource of raw materials and service inputs are used. For a given amount of inputs containing physical mass it means that at the frontier more outputs could have been produced. In terms of the materials balance (1) the implication is that the

---

[35]In the case of the presence of embodied technology or vintage capital, a distinction should be made between efficient utilisation of the mix of existing technologies and the most modern technology (Førsund 2010).

amount of residuals z for constant inputs x_M at inefficient operation will be reduced if the frontier is achieved, assuming that intended output y contains materials. Inefficiency in the use of service inputs means that with better organisation of the activities more output could be produced if the frontier is realised for constant x_S. The materials balance also holds for inefficient observations (as pointed out in Sect. 2.2). It is the amount of residuals and outputs that have potentials for change, while the a, b, c coefficients and the inputs in Eq. (1) remain the same. The combustion process may be less efficient in converting the raw material into heat, and a different mix of combustion substances may be produced than at efficient operation, e.g., for thermal electricity production based on coal, the mix of substances CO_2, CO, particles, NO_x and ash may differ between inefficient and efficient operations.

Another source of inefficiency is the occurrence of rejects and unintended waste of raw materials, e.g., producing tables of wood, residuals consists of pieces of wood of different sizes from rejects and down to chips and sawdust. The ways of improving the use of raw materials and thereby reducing the amount of residuals are more or less of the same nature as factors explaining substitution possibilities between material and service inputs in Sect. 4.2.

There is another type of problem in the efficiency strand of research not often mentioned concerning the behaviour of (or the management of) firms. It is difficult to assume, as in standard production theory using frontier functions only, that inefficient firms can optimise in the usual sense of obtaining maximal profit or minimising costs, as modelled in the previous Sect. 5.2. There is no production function formulated for inefficient firms in non-parametric analyses. Introducing behaviour in non-parametric DEA models for a unit it is assumed that frontier technology is used. However, in the real world all firms, also inefficient ones, have to react to e.g. environmental regulation. If firms do know the frontier, how come they end up being inefficient? To appeal to randomness only is not so satisfying. [See e.g. Førsund (2010) for a review of reasons for inefficiency.] When efficiency is estimated the observations are usually taken as given and no behavioural action on the part of the units is assumed to take place. It is the analyst that creates an optimisation problem when calculating efficiency measures. This may be a reason for the lack of pursuing policy instruments in the literature addressing inefficiency when both desirable and undesirable outputs are produced. In the environmental economics literature not addressing efficiency issues the design of policy instruments, playing on giving firms incentives to change behaviour, is of paramount interest, as exemplified in Sect. 5.2. However, the assumptions in the inefficiency literature reviewed in Sect. 2.3 are made for measuring efficiency, and are not suitable for developing policy instruments applied to all units in an industry. We saw this in Färe et al. (1986) making introduction of regulation of emissions change the form of the production possibility set for all units and not addressing the reactions of each individual unit to the regulation. If economic behaviour is assumed in the efficiency literature, then the unit in question operates on the frontier.

6.2   The Production Possibility Set

The general production possibility set allowing for inefficiency including both desirable and undesirable outputs is:

$$T = \{(y, z, x) | y \geq 0 \text{ and } z \geq 0 \text{ can be produced by } x \geq 0\} \quad (17)$$

Such a definition covers the possibility of both efficient and inefficient operations. The border of the production possibility set is commonly referred to as the frontier and expresses efficient operation. This frontier corresponds to the transformation relation (2) in neoclassical production theory used in Sect. 3.

The technology set (17) can equivalently be represented by the output set

$$P(x) = \{(y, z) | x \geq 0 \text{ can produce } y \geq 0 \text{ and } z \geq 0\} \quad (18)$$

In the case of desirable outputs it is obvious that efficient use of resources implies that maximal amount of these outputs are produced for given resources. Concerning undesirable outputs these are automatically kept at a minimum given the maximisation of desirable outputs.

6.3   Weak Disposability

In order to operate the single equation model (10) with undesirable outputs avoiding the zero solution for residuals pointed out in Sect. 3.3, restrictions must be placed on the production possibility set.[36] This has typically been done in the axiomatic efficiency literature by imposing weak disposability, a mathematical concept introduced by Shephard (1970), defined as

$$\text{If } (y, z) \in P(x), \text{ then } (\theta y, \theta z) \in P(x) \text{ for } 0 \leq \theta \leq 1 \quad (19)$$

This means that along the frontier desirable and undesirable outputs must change with the same proportionality factor (segment-specific in the case of a non-parametric frontier). No economic or engineering reasoning for this restriction is given in Shephard (1970), but it may resemble the assumption of fixed input-output coefficients in input-output models including pollution, as in the fixed coefficient model of Ayres and Kneese (1969) reviewed in Sect. 2.3 that is backed up by economic reasoning and empirical findings.

---

[36]In Färe et al. (2013, p. 110) it is stated: "which [without a restriction] as pointed out by Førsund (2009) would give us a [...] nonsensical result that zero bads can be achieved at no costs [...]".

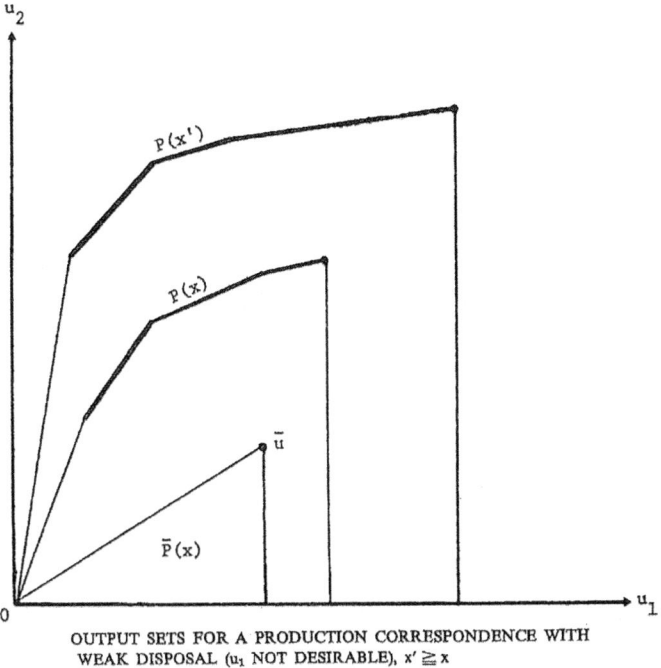

OUTPUT SETS FOR A PRODUCTION CORRESPONDENCE WITH
WEAK DISPOSAL (u_1 NOT DESIRABLE), $x' \geqq x$

Fig. 3 Illustration of weak disposability. *Source* Shephard (1970, p. 188)

Illustrations of weak disposability for output sets, taken from the first illustration of weak disposability of desirable and undesirable outputs in Shephard (1970), are presented in Fig. 3.

The desirable output is u_2 and the undesirable is u_1. The trade-off contours for two levels of inputs are shown together with the Leontief (1970) case of a fixed relationship between the two outputs as indicated by the ray $0\bar{u}$.[37] The contour curves starting from the origin (thinner lines are not part of the efficient frontier according to Shephard) secure the condition of inevitability of positive undesirables when desirable output is positive, termed the null-jointness condition in Shephard and Färe (1974).[38]

---

[37]Notice that using input-output type of models does not support the assumption of weak disposability, as is made clear in Fig. 3; the input-output assumption means that there is only a *single* ratio between the good and the bad, not many as illustrated by the two other trade-off curves. However, notice that the Leontief assumption is valid for the point $\bar{u}$ only. Furthermore, weak disposability is not a case of Frisch (1965) output couplings as in Eq. (6).

[38]Note that Shephard (1970, p. 187) was aware of the fact that production relations need not be of a single-equation type: "It is useful to reiterate at this point that the foregoing assumptions for the production correspondence do not exclude the technology being composed of several processes (or sub-technologies) which are to be jointly planned, as well as situations where joint outputs are inherently involved."

An explanation of the simultaneous reduction of desirable and undesirable outputs along a trade-off curve often used is that inputs are reallocated to abatement of pollutants.[39] However, it seems rather difficult to both have constant inputs along the curve and to take some inputs away to be used in another activity. If abatement is to take place it must be introduced explicitly, and show the connection between input use and abatement.

A problem with the approach of Shephard to overcome the problem of strong disposability of the residual is the coupling between desirable and undesirable outputs. The situation is that the couplings are between raw materials and the outputs, and take place simultaneously. Specifically, the single-equation model using distance functions cannot capture this fact. The popular use of the directional distance function (Chung et al. 1997):

$$\vec{D}_o(x, y, b; g_y, -g_b) = \max\left\{\beta : (y + \beta g_y, b - \beta g_b) \in P(x), \vec{D}_o(x, y, b; g_y, -g_b) \geq 0\right\},$$

where $(g_y, -gb)$ is the directional vector and $P(x)$ is the output production set (18), has the problem that assuming differentiability, as is often done (Färe et al. 2013), then $(\partial\vec{D}_o(x, y, z; g_y, -g_b)/\partial z)/(\partial\vec{D}_o(x, y, z; g_y, -g_b)/\partial y)$ is the rate of transformation between the good and the bad for given inputs. This ratio is used for estimating shadow price of the residual (Färe et al. 2013), and the trade-off curve is illustrated in numerous papers by Färe et al. (2013) and authors of similar models. However, such a trade-off is not compatible with the material balance.[40]

6.4   Recent Attempts to Improve the Single-Equation Model

In Rødseth (2017a) there are interesting attempts to reconcile the type of efficiency model used in Chung et al. (1997) based on directional distance functions with the materials balance, extending the model with abatement and also some new axioms. (The new model is applied in Rødseth 2016.) However, the model remains a single-equation one. Such a model is based on a trade-off between desirable and undesirable outputs for given inputs at the frontier. As shown previously a single-equation model building on such a trade-off is not compatible with the materials balance. Rødseth (2016) introduces a way to satisfy the materials balance when identifying the reference point for an inefficient observation on the frontier using a special directional vector called weak g-disposability by keeping the materials balance identity for a fixed input vector when projecting the observation

---

[39]Färe et al. (2008, p. 561) state: [...] "disposal of bad outputs is costly—at the margin, it requires diversion of inputs to 'clean up' bad outputs" [...].

[40]A peculiarity with the trade-off in Färe et al. (2013) is that the trade-off occurs with the output for final consumption and the secondary pollutants from the abatement stage, and not between the total output of the good (electricity) and the generation of pollutants in the production stage. However, it is the last trade-off that is the functional trade-off that goes against the materials balance principle in the single-equation model of the production stage.

to the frontier. However, the single equation model is based on a trade-off at the frontier between y and z, implying that the materials balance is not fulfilled. The materials balance, that is an accounting identity, cannot in general be used as a production technology. As explained in Sect. 4.3 (see also Førsund 2018, pp. 77–78), the materials balance expressed by Eq. (1) is an accounting identity and cannot explain how residuals are created within a production process. However, introducing axioms of jointness of inputs and outputs are improvements over the assumption of null jointness of the desirable and undesirable outputs.

The new model in Rødseth (2017a) is implemented empirically in Hampf (2018) and compared with Färe et al. models applied to the same data. However, choosing the best model based on empirical applications is not the approach recommended in Sect. 4. Theory should come first.

Abatement is introduced in Rødseth (2014, 2016, 2017b). However, abatement as a production activity is not modelled explicitly. In Färe et al. (2013) explicit end-of-pipe abatement is added to the production of desirable and undesirable outputs. Inputs to abatement come from a given resource pool by reallocation, and in addition abatement receives part of desirable output as input together with primary pollutants. However, the two distinct production activities are lumped together using a directional distance function with final delivery of desirable outputs, secondary undesirable outputs, and total "source" resources.[41]

A similar two-stage approach is also developed in Hampf (2014). The distinct production activities are as the first stage producing desirable and undesirable outputs, and intermediate desirable output used as input in the abatement production, and at the second stage producing abatement outputs using undesirable output from the first stage as input together with non-polluting inputs and a commonly shared input. A restriction in the form of a material balance is introduced in the first stage, so no production relation proper is used for the undesirable output. The modelling of the production activities of desirable and undesirable outputs remain a single equation that does not satisfy the materials balance.

It should be emphasised that the arguments as formulated in Sect. 3.3 are not only concerning weak disposability, but also strong disposability. It was demonstrated how also strong disposability fails. The point is that single-equation models when material inputs are involved, cannot fulfil the materials balance and efficiency conditions for the frontier relations because a trade-off between intended and unintended outputs violates the materials balance and the efficiency properties of the frontier. There must be a clear disentanglement between the modelling of the production of desirable and undesirable outputs.[42] It is the single-equation approach

---

[41]A material balance restriction is mentioned, but not implemented in the empirical model. Weak disposability is assumed.

[42]This is also the message in Murty and Russell (2018, p. 18) stating: […] "the complex real-world trade-offs among inputs and outputs in these technologies cannot be captured by a single functional relation. For example, it is impossible for a single function to capture, simultaneously, the positive relations between emissions and emission-causing inputs and the positive relations between emissions and intended outputs."

that is at fault, not specifically the imposition of weak disposability. The crucial feature of the Frisch-inspired two-equation model Eq. (11) in Sect. 4 is just the separate frontier functions for goods and bads.

The single equation model has apparently been successfully applied in the numerous empirical studies found in the literature. The data have seemingly allowed the model to be estimated. However, the ease of obtaining estimates of efficiency does not guarantee that the results are correct. Unfortunately, at the level of abstraction of such models the risk is that a 'false frontier'[43] is estimated, i.e., the data fit a model that goes against the physical law of materials balance principle, and against a fundamental efficiency requirement of a frontier production function.[44]

7 Efficiency Measures and Their Estimation in the Multi-equation Model

7.1 The Production Possibility Sets of the Factorially Determined Multi-equation Model

The multi-equation frontier model (11) with add-on abatement (13) can be straightforwardly extended to include inefficient operations. It remains to show how such a model can be implement empirically. The multi-equation model with abatement allowing inefficiency can be set up using inequalities [with the partial derivatives of the functions as given in (11) and (13)]:

$$
\begin{aligned}
y &\leq f(x_M, x_S) \\
z &\geq g(x_M, x_S) \\
\delta z^a / z &\leq A(x_M^a, x_S^a)
\end{aligned}
\tag{20}
$$

Following Murty et al. (2012) the production possibility sets can formally be written:

$$
\begin{aligned}
T_1 &= \{(x_M, x_S, y) \,|\, y \leq f(x_M, x_S) \text{ and } y \geq 0, x_M \geq 0, x_S \geq 0\} \\
T_2 &= \{(x_M, x_S, z) \,|\, z \geq g(x_M, x_S) \text{ and } z \geq 0, x_M \geq 0, x_S \geq 0\} \\
T_3 &= \{(x_M^a, x_S^a, z, z^a) \,|\, \delta z^a \leq z A(x_M^a, x_S^a), z^a \geq 0, z \geq 0, x_M^a \geq 0, x_S^a \geq 0\}
\end{aligned}
\tag{21}
$$

---

[43]This apt expression is due to Barnum et al. (2017).

[44]Dakpo et al. (2016, p. 356) argue that all the different models introduced should be estimated for comparison. As mentioned previously this is also the approach in Hampf (2018). However, in light of the risk of estimation a 'false model', one cannot identify the "best" model in such a way. The only way is to choose the theoretically best model.

The functions $f(.)$, $g(.)$ and $A(.)$ represent the frontier technologies. For given inputs the realised amount of the desirable output may be less than the potential, the primary pollutant may be greater than the potential, and the relative share of abated primary residuals may be less than the potential at each frontier technology, respectively.

7.2   The Multi-equation By-Product Model

The by-product model in Murty et al. (2012, p. 122) with abatement (also used in Murty and Russell 2018) has two frontier relations:

$$f(x_M, x_S, y, y^a) = 0$$
$$z^D = g(x_M, y^a) \tag{22}$$

(The notation in Model (11) is used.) The variable y^a is called abatement output, but its functional role is somewhat unclear. The partial derivative of the goods in the first relation is assumed positive and the partial derivatives for the inputs are assumed negative. In the second residual-generating equation the partial derivative of the polluting input is assumed positive and the partial derivative of the abatement output negative. The undesirable output z^D is the secondary residual, i.e. the residuals actually emitted to the environment, see Eq. (13). We notice that the residual z^D does not appear in the first relation, and that the desirable good does not appear in the second relation, thus the generation of emissions seems to be independent of intended-output production and usage of non-emission-causing inputs. (This is in accordance of the definition of the emission-generating technology of Murty et al. (2012) as shown in Murty and Russell 2018, p. 19, Theorem 1.)

The two production possibility sets can be written:

$$T_1 = \{(x_M, x_s, y, y^a, z^D) \in R_+^5 \,| f(x_M, x_S, y, y^a) \leq 0\}$$
$$T_2 = \{(x_M, x_s, y, y^a, z^D,) \in R_+^5 \,| z^D \geq g(x_M, y^a)\} \tag{23}$$

The technology set T for the total activity is the intersection of the two subsets; $T = T_1 \cap T_2$. Murty and Russell (2018) combine Murty et al. (2012) and Murty (2015) to make the case for an axiomatic foundation for the multi-equation model.

Comparing the frontier models (21) and (23) we see that the Murty et al. (2012) model does not conform to the factorially determined multi-output format regarding the residuals-generating relation by specifying the secondary residual as output and materials inputs and abatement output as inputs.[45] How abatement takes place is

---

[45]The multi-equation model in Serra et al. (2014) is based on the development in Førsund (2008) (an improved version of this working paper is Førsund 2009) and Murty et al. (2012). Both polluting and non-polluting inputs are specified to produce residuals emitted to the environment [see their Eq. (3)], i.e. no abatement is taking place.

then rather hidden. End-of-pipe abatement is ruled out, so there must then be some internal adjustment of technology or recycling of raw materials (cf. the chocolate production example in footnote 27). A problem excluding the non-polluting input in the residuals-generating function is that reducing the residual by input substitution, as explained in Sect. 4.2 (see Fig. 2), is not reflected in the specification of the residuals relation. However, more seriously, as explained in Sect. 4.1, positive marginal productivity as assumed in the first relation in (22), i.e. increasing x_S partially increasing y is usually obtained by utilising raw material better. This then implies less residuals for constant x_M, but the second relation states that only change in x_M can influence the generation of residuals and not changes in x_S. This seems a drawback and goes against knowledge about substitution (cf. footnote 27).

The Frisch scheme of joint production separating outputs and having the same set of inputs as arguments in all production functions is a well-argued scheme, and is especially so in our case of simultaneous production of both goods and bads, because it is just the inputs that are used producing a desirable output that also generates the nondesirable outputs.

In accordance with theorems in Murty and Russell (2018) a strategy for efficiency measures is to introduce separate measures for each of the different activities. Then the Farrell (1957) technical measures of efficiency may be used (these are equivalent to distance functions), giving us three types of measures based on relative distance from best-practice frontiers: desirable output efficiency E_y, primary residual efficiency E_z, and abatement efficiency E_A, all three measures restricted to be between zero and one. Efficiency measures can in general be either input oriented or output-oriented. In our setting output orientation is a natural choice.

7.3   The Efficiency Measures

Concerning the estimation of the unknown frontiers a non-parametric DEA model, build up as a polyhedral set, assuming standard axioms such as compactness, convexity and monotonicity, can be applied to estimate the efficiency measures based on the estimate of the best practice frontier that the data at hand can give us. However, forming the residual production possibility set is not quite standard due to the negative sign of the derivative of the service input.

In the three DEA optimisation problems below for unit i among N units in total, variable returns to scale functions are specified (for simplicity a single output and two inputs are specified):

$$1/E_{y_i} = \text{Max}_{\lambda,\theta}\theta$$

s.t.

$$\sum_{j=1}^{N} \lambda_j y_j \geq \theta y_i,$$

$$\sum_{j=1}^{N} \lambda_j x_{kj} \leq x_{ki}, k \in M, S \tag{24}$$

$$\sum_{j=1}^{N} \lambda_j = 1, \lambda_j \geq 0, \theta \geq 0$$

The optimal solution of the weighted sum of observed outputs and inputs of the efficient units spanning the frontier are the output and input values at the frontier segment for the radial projection of observations (y_i, x_i), (z_i, x_i). As to disposability decreasing good output for given inputs, and increasing input for given good output leaves us in the interior of the production possibility set.

Remember that we have assumed that the function $g(.)$ is convex when formulating the primary residuals efficiency measure:

$$E_{z_i} = \text{Min}_{\lambda',\varphi}\varphi$$

s.t.

$$\sum_{j=1}^{N} \lambda'_j z_j \leq \varphi z_i,$$

$$\sum_{j=1}^{N} \lambda'_j x_{kj} \geq x_{ki}, k \in M, S \tag{25}$$

$$\sum_{j=1}^{N} \lambda'_j = 1, \lambda_j \geq 0, \varphi \geq 0$$

As to disposability increasing bad output for given inputs, and decreasing input for given bad output leaves us in the interior of the production possibility set. For the two first frontier production relations in theoretical models in (20), a unit that is on the frontier for the intended output, will also be residual-efficient because of the combined effect of the materials balance and the efficiency assumptions of the functions. (All points on isoquants illustrated in Fig. 2 are by definition efficient.) However, the estimation of the border of a polyhedral set based on observations implies typically a negative bias of the frontier technology compared with the unknown theoretical model. It may then be the case that best practice points spanning the set may not be efficient within the true unknown technologies (20). A best practice unit in the problem (24) in desirable output production may not be efficient in undesirable output production in the problem (25), and vice versa.

The materials balance identity is not specified for the efficiency problems above. It holds for the two problems together, not (24) and (25) separately, but only if the polyhedral model is the true theoretical model. The concern with the materials balance estimating a non-parametric frontier using DEA is then that projections to the frontier in problems in (24) and (25) of inefficient points may not satisfy the relevant materials balance conditions. The projection points for inefficient observations within the N units are:

$$\sum_{j=1}^{N} \lambda_j y_j, \sum_{j=1}^{N} \lambda_j x_{kj}, k \in M, S$$

$$\sum_{j=1}^{N} \lambda'_j z_j, \sum_{j=1}^{N} \lambda'_j x_{kj}, k \in M, S \tag{26}$$

These points are not observations, but constructs of the analyst. Assuming projection points being on efficient faces, i.e. all the inequalities in (24) and (25) hold as equalities, it may be tempting to say that the materials balance restriction for the frontier projection of unit i is

$$a \sum_{j=1}^{N} \lambda_j x_{Mj} \equiv b \sum_{j=1}^{N} \lambda_j y_j + c \sum_{j=1}^{N} \lambda'_j z_j \Rightarrow a x_{Mi} = b\theta y_i + c\varphi z_i, \quad i = 1, \ldots, N \tag{27}$$

However, this is only correct if the border of the estimated polyhedral set is the true frontier. The materials balance condition in (27) can be checked by inserting the optimal solution for the projected residuals point solving (25) and the solution for the desirable output solving (24) into (27), thus exposing difference between the left-hand and right-hand of (27). (Notice that we must have $\sum_{j=1}^{N} \lambda_j x_{Mj} = \sum_{j=1}^{N} \lambda'_j x_{Mj}$ by definition.)

The expansion of y_i ($\theta \geq 1$) must be counteracted by the reduction in z_i ($0 \leq \varphi \leq 1$). However, without imposing this restriction on projection points on the frontier there may be no guarantee that this is fulfilled. It may be a problem that the frontier output projection points come from two different models, while the inputs are the same. Regarding weakly efficient faces there will be slacks on constraints yielding zero shadow prices. However, the set of these units may be different between the models. Material inputs with zero shadow prices not impacting the efficiency scores must also be counted in the materials balance.

Imposing a materials balance constraint on projection points as in Rødseth (2017a) in the single-equation model is not straightforward in the multi-equation model. However, given the possibility of biased estimation using DEA it may not be desirable to force the materials balance condition upon synthetic projection points possibly changing the estimates of efficiency scores.

In the non-parametric estimation model for abatement efficiency the observed amount of primary residual for unit i is now given from the production stage and not appearing in the model determining the frontier relative degree of abatement due to the assumption of multiplicative decomposition of the abatement function in the first relation in (13)[46]:

$$1/E_{A_i} = \text{Max}_{\lambda'',\phi} \, \phi$$

s.t.

$$\sum_{j=1}^{N} \lambda_j'' A_j \geq \phi A_i$$

$$\sum_{j=1}^{N} \lambda_j'' x_{kj}^a \leq x_i^a, k \in M, S \qquad (28)$$

$$\sum_{j=1}^{N} \lambda_j'' = 1, \lambda_j'' \geq 0, \phi \geq 0$$

Once we have the solution for the relative abatement the absolute amounts of abatement residuals and secondary residuals for a projection of an inefficient unit to the frontier can be calculated. As to disposability decreasing the degree of purification for given inputs, and increasing input for given degree of purification leaves us in the interior of the production possibility set.

For the materials balance to hold in the models in (20) the relations must be a "good" representation of the production relations (see Sect. 2.2). A problem is that it is quite difficult to verify the goodness. One may doubt that the piecewise linear frontiers, or the faceted structure of the borders of the production possibility sets, meet a goodness criterion. There is also the problem of the variables with zero shadow prices generating faces not of full dimension regarding forming projection points of inefficient observations on the frontier. However, forming the materials balance all variables containing mass must be counted, also for units with zero shadow prices.

The term environmental efficiency or eco-efficiency is used somewhat differently in the literature and is not used in the efficiency measures introduced above. One reason for this is that one would expect that environmental efficiency has something to do with what happens within the environment in terms of degradation of environmental qualities, cf. points (c) and (d) in Sect. 2.1. However, the most common notion of environmental efficiency is showing the potential relative reduction in emission of residuals. The so called unified approach in Sueyoshi and Goto (2010) and the measure for the set T used in Murty et al. (2012) have the drawbacks that they show measures for the aggregate level and hide the individual results as in (24) and (25).

However, for policy purposes the individual measures above provide most valuable information for designing specific direct regulations or indirect economic instruments.

---

[46]Hampf (2014) also solves separate optimisation problems for the production stage and the abatement stage, but this is done by minimising the weighted emissions in the two stages.

8 Conclusions

The introduction of the materials balance in the environmental economics literature (Ayres and Kneese 1969) heralded a new approach to modelling the interactions between the production of desirable outputs and the natural environment. The materials balance tells us that mass (and energy) in an economic activity cannot disappear, but only takes on different forms. Surveying the use of the materials balance 30 years after Ayres and Kneese (1969) pioneered the concept within environmental economics, Pethig (2003), from a standpoint of ecological economics, complains that the materials balance has not been used to the extent it warrants.

However, the position in this chapter (supported by Murty et al. 2012; Murty and Russell 2018) is that the materials balance is important when picking the model to use. However, the materials balance is an accounting identity and cannot give information about specific technologies explaining the transformation of resources to desirable and undesirable outputs, so an active use of the materials balance condition may not be necessary if the right model is picked. In addition, at the aggregation level the models are usually formulated on, it may be difficult to represent all the physical quantities involved. Data accuracy and availability are also important factors.

In production activities involving material inputs, the simultaneous generation of desirable outputs and residuals as undesirable outputs, the latter turning up as pollutants in the natural environment, must be captured in a sufficiently realistic way. Classical and neoclassical economists were concerned with production of waste and have many interesting observations that should be utilised. In the efficiency literature the last decades, the most popular approach to empirical efficiency studies of simultaneous production of 'goods' and 'bads' has been to apply a single-equation model. To assume a mathematical property of weak disposability of the production possibility set allowing for inefficient observations, has then been seen necessary. This property blocks the maximal assortment case of using all resources on desirable outputs resulting in zero emission of residuals.

However, a main result of the chapter is that a functional trade-off between desirable and undesirable outputs, as implied by the weak disposability model, is not theoretically compatible with the materials balance and efficiency in resource utilisation. Notice that it was shown in Sect. 3.4 that also strong disposability of outputs is not compatible with this trade-off. But more importantly, this implies further that it is the format of a single equation model to tackle efficiency measurement when producing both desirable and undesirable outputs using material inputs, which is at fault, not weak disposability as such. The main message of the chapter is that the single-equation model, which has been almost exclusively used in the literature about inefficiency when dealing with material-based bads, is not able to conform to the materials balance and efficiency requirements on frontier relations. A multi-equation model is required separating production relations of desirable and undesirable outputs.

A multi-equation model, based on 'classical' joint production theory, that theoretically satisfies the materials balance and frontier efficiency requirements, is developed in the chapter, and shown to function well both in an efficient and in an inefficient world. It is also straightforward to understand the mechanisms of the model without mathematical knowledge necessary to relate to rather complex axiomatic approaches.

The model proposed in the chapter can straightforwardly be extended to cover abatement efforts of the end-of-pipe type.

The single-equation models based on weak disposability have had a good run for decades. However, as happens with technologies when experiencing technical progress in an economy also happens to models: they become outmoded and should then substituted with better ones; the multi-equation models. As Ragnar Frisch expresses it: [...] "we disregard a model world as soon as we get upon the idea of another model world which 'smells' better" (Frisch 2010, p. 33).

It was conjectured that single-equation models cannot comply with the materials balance, and furthermore that a specific type of a multi-equation model can obey the materials balance. Further research will be focussed on substantiating more formally this conjecture.

Other research tasks are implementing empirically the type of multi-equation models including abatement proposed in this chapter. More challenging are introducing dynamics not only involving embodied technologies, but also dynamic analyses of how inefficiencies are reduced due to pressure of environmental regulation, i.e. tackling the Porter hypothesis in a dynamic framework.

As underlined in the chapter generation of residuals occurs when material inputs are used. Typical industries studied in the environmental efficiency literature are thermal generation of electricity and pulp and paper. In addition, we have material throughput industries such as oil refineries, other chemicals, steel and iron, aluminium, and other energy-intensive industries, as well as food processing and cement. A common feature for all these industries is that much of the key technologies are embodied in the capital equipment.

The pace of technical progress depends on investments in new technology. A consequence is that care must be exercised when having observations for several vintages of plants when using DEA to estimate the best practice frontiers. The risk is great for estimating a 'false frontier', in the sense that there may be a mix of plants of different vintages spanning out the frontier. An efficiency measure may then give a false picture of obtainable improvement (Førsund 2010; Belu 2015, point to some related problems). Developing more appropriate models for tackling vintage structures when studying environmental efficiency is a challenge for future research.[47]

---

[47]Hampf and Rødseth (2015) find that most of the efficiency differences in U.S. power plants measured by electricity generation using coal can be explained by the age of plants.

Acknowledgment The chapter is based on a presentation at the 2016 Asia-Pacific Productivity Conference, Nankai University, Tianjin, China, 7–10 July, and building largely on the work in progress for Førsund (2017, 2018). I am indebted to Benjamin Hampf, Robert Russell, Kenneth Løvold Rødseth, Victor V. Podinovski and an anonymous reviewer for challenging and constructive comments improving the chapter.

References

Ambec S, Coheny MA, Elgiez S, and Lanoie P (2013) The Porter hypothesis at 20: can environmental regulation enhance innovation and competitiveness? Review of Environmental Economics and Policy 7(1), 2–22

Arabi B, Munisamy S and Emrouznejad A (2015) A new slacks-based measure of Malmquist–Luenberger index in the presence of undesirable outputs. Omega 51 (March), 29–37, http://dx.doi.org/10.1016/j.omega.2014.08.006

Aparicio J, Pastor JT and Vidal F (2016) The directional distance function and the translation invariance property. Omega 58 (January), 1–3, http://dx.doi.org/10.1016/j.omega.2015.04.012

Ayres RU and Kneese AV (1969) Production, consumption and externalities. American Economic Review 59(7), 282–297

Barnum D, Coupet J, Gleason J, McWilliams A and Parhankangas A (2017) Impact of input substitution and output transformation on data envelopment analysis decisions. Applied Economics 49(15), 1543–1556. Published online 24 August 2016. http://dx.doi.org/10.1080/00036846.2016.1221042

Baumgärtner S, Dyckhoff H, Faber M, Proops J, and Schiller J (2001) The concept of joint production and ecological economics. Ecological Economics 36(3), 365–372

Baumgärtner S and de Swaan Arons J (2003) Necessity and inefficiency in the generation of waste: a thermodynamic analysis. Journal of Industrial Ecology 7(2), 113–123

Baumol WJ and Oates W (1988) The theory of environmental policy (second edition). Cambridge: Cambridge University Press (first edition 1975, Washington: Prentice Hall)

Belu C (2015) Are distance measures effective at measuring efficiency? DEA meets the vintage model. Journal of Productivity Analysis 43(3), 237–248

Brännlund R and Lundgren T (2009) Environmental policy without cost? A review of the Porter hypothesis. International Review of Environmental and Resource Economics 3(1), 75–117

Chambers RG (1988) Applied production analysis. Cambridge: Cambridge University Press

Chung YH, Färe R and Grosskopf S (1997) Productivity and undesirable outputs: a directional distance function approach. Journal of Environmental Management 51(3), 229–240

Coase R (1959) The federal communications commission. Journal of Law and Economics 2 (October), 1–40

Cropper ML and Oates WE (1992). Environmental economics: a survey. Journal of Economic Literature 30(2), 675–740

Dakpo KH, Jeanneaux P, Latruffe L (2016) Modelling pollution-generating technologies in performance benchmarking: recent developments, limits and future prospects in the nonparametric framework. European Journal of Operational Research 250(2), 347–359

Färe R, Grosskopf S, and. Pasurka C (1986) Effects on relative efficiency in electric power generation due to environmental controls. Resources and Energy 8(2), 167–184

Färe R, Grosskopf S and Margaritis D (2008) Efficiency and productivity: Malmquist and more. In Fried HO, Lovell CAK and Schmidt SS (eds.) The measurement of Productive Efficiency and Productivity Growth, Chapter 5, 522–622, New York: Oxford University Press

Färe R, Grosskopf S and Pasurka C (2013) Joint production of good and bad outputs with a network application. In: Shogren J (ed.) Encyclopedia of energy, natural resources and environmental economics. Vol 2, pp. 109–118. Amsterdam: Elsevier

Färe R, Grosskopf S, Lovell CAK and Pasurka C (1989). Multilateral productivity comparisons when some outputs are undesirable: a nonparametric approach. Review of Economics and Statistics 71(1), 90–98

Farrell MJ (1957) The measurement of productive efficiency of production. Journal of the Royal Statistical Society, Series A, 120(III), 253–281

Frisch R (1935) The principle of substitution. An example of its application in the chocolate industry. Nordisk Tidskrift for Teknisk Økonomi 1(September), 12 – 27

Frisch R (1965). Theory of production. Dordrecht: D. Reidel

Frisch R (2010) A dynamic approach to economic theory. The Yale lectures by Ragnar Frisch, 1930. Bjerkholt O and Qin D (eds.), Routledge Studies in the History of Economics. London and New York: Routledge

Førsund FR (1972) Allocation in Space and Environmental Pollution. Swedish Journal of Economics 74(1), 19–34

Førsund FR (1973) Externalities, environmental pollution and allocation in space: a general equilibrium approach. Regional and Urban Economics 3(1), 3–32

Førsund FR (1985) Input-output models, national economic models, and the environment. In: Handbook of natural resource and energy economics, vol. I. Kneese AV and Sweeney JL (eds.). Chapter 8, pp. 325–341. Amsterdam: Elsevier Science Publishers BV

Førsund FR (1998) Pollution modelling and multiple-output production theory. Discussion Paper # D-37/1998, Department of Economics and Social Sciences, Agricultural University of Norway (Re-printed as Memorandum No 10/2016 Department of Economics University of Oslo, available on the internet.)

Førsund FR (1999) On the contribution of Ragnar Frisch to production theory. Rivista Internazionale di Scienze Economiche e Commerciali (International Review of Economics and Business) 46(1), 1–34

Førsund FR (2008) Good Modelling of Bad Outputs: Pollution and Multiple-Output Production. Memorandum No 30/2008 Department of Economics, University of Oslo

Førsund FR (2009) Good Modelling of Bad Outputs: Pollution and Multiple-Output Production," International Review of Environmental and Resource Economics 3(1), 1–38

Førsund FR (2010) Dynamic efficiency measurement. Indian Economic Review 45(2), 125–159. Also published as Chapter 4 (pp. 187–219) in Ray SC, Kumbhakar SC, Dua P (eds.) (2015) Benchmarking for performance evaluation. A frontier production approach. https://doi.org/10. 1007/978-81-322-2253-8_4. New Delhi- Heidelberg-New York-Dordrecht-London: Springer

Førsund FR (2011) Industrial ecology: reflections of an environmental economist. In Batabyal AA and Nijkamp P (eds.). Research tools in natural resource and environmental economics. Chapter 14, pp. 423–455. Singapore: World Scientific

Førsund FR (2017) Productivity measurement and the environment. In: The Oxford handbook of productivity analysis, Grifell-Tatje E, Lovell CAK, Sickles R (eds.), Chapter 8. Forthcoming. Oxford: Oxford University Press

Førsund FR (2018) Multi-equation modelling of desirable and undesirable outputs satisfying the materials balance. Empirical Economics. 54(1), 67–99. https://doi.org/10.1007/s00181-016-1219-9

Førsund FR and Strøm S (1974) Industrial structure, growth and residuals flows. In Rothenberg J and Heggie IG (eds.). The management of water quality and the environment. Chapter 2, pp. 21–69. International Economic Association Series. London: MacMillan

Førsund FR and Strøm S (1976) The generation of residual flows in Norway: an input-output Approach. Journal of Environmental Economics and Management 3(2), 129–141

Førsund FR and Strøm S (1988) Environmental economics and management: pollution and natural resources. London: Croom Helm. (Also re-published in the series Routledge Revivals, 2011. Abingdon-New York: Routledge.)

Hampf B (2014) Separating environmental efficiency into production and abatement efficiency: A nonparametric model with application to US power plants. Journal of Productivity Analysis 41(3), 457–473

Hampf B (2018) Measuring inefficiency in the presence of bad outputs: does the disposability assumption matter? Empirical Economics. 54(1), 101–127. https://doi.org/10.1007/s00181-016-1204-3

Hampf B and Rødseth KL (2015) Carbon dioxide emission standards for U.S. power plants: an efficiency analysis perspective. Energy Economics 50(1), 140–153

Jevons WS (1965) The theory of political economy (first published 1871, reprinted 1965). New York: Augustus M. Kelley

Johansen L (1960) A multi-sectoral study of economic growth. Amsterdam: North-Holland Publishing Company

Kneese AV, Ayres RU and d'Arge RC (1970) Economics and the environment. A materials balance approach. Resources for the Future, Washington. Baltimore: Johns Hopkins Press

Kohli U (1983) Non-joint technologies. The Review of Economic Studies 50(1), 209–219

Kumbhakar SC and Malikov E (2018) Good modeling of bad outputs: editors' introduction. Empirical Economics. 54(1), 1–6. https://doi.org/10.1007/s00181-017-1231-8

Kurz HD (1986). Classical and early neoclassical economists on joint production, Metroeconomica 38(1), 1–37

Lanoie P, Laurent-Lucchetti J, Johnstone N, and Ambec S (2011) Environmental policy, innovation and performance: new insights on the Porter hypothesis. Journal of Economics and Management Strategy 20(3), 803–842

Lauwers L (2009) Justifying the incorporation of the materials balance principle into frontier-based eco-efficiency models. Ecological Economics 68(8), 1605–1614

Leontief W (1970) Environmental repercussions and the economic structure: an input-output approach. The Review of Economics and Statistics 52(3), 262–271

Leontief W and Ford D (1972) Air pollution and the economic structure: empirical results of input – output computations. In Brody A and Carter A (eds.). Input – output techniques, pp. 9–30. Amsterdam-London: North-Holland

Mäler K-G (1974) Environmental Economics: A Theoretical Inquiry. Baltimore: The Johns Hopkins Press

Martin RE (1986) Externality regulation and the monopoly firm. Journal of Public Economics 29 (3), 347–362

Murty S (2015) On the properties of an emission-generating technology and its parametric representation. Economic Theory 60(2), 243–282

Murty S and Russell RR (2018) Modeling emission-generating technologies: reconciliation of axiomatic and by-production approaches. Empirical Economics. 54(1), 7–30. https://doi.org/10.1007/s00181-016-1183-4

Murty S, Russell RR and Levkoff SB (2012) On modelling pollution-generating technologies. Journal of Environmental Economics and Management 64(1), 117–135

Nadiri I (1987) joint production. In: The new Palgrave. A dictionary of economics. Eatwell J, Milgate M, Newman P (eds.). Vol 2 (E to J), pp. 1028–1030. London, New York, Tokyo: Macmillan

Palmer K, Oates WE, and Portney PR (1995) Tightening environmental standards: the benefit-cost or the no-cost paradigm? Journal of Economic Perspectives 9(4), 119–132

Pasinetti LL (1980) Introductory note: joint production. In: Essays on the theory of joint production, Pasinetti LL (ed.). London and Basingstoke: Macmillan.

Perman R, Ma Y, Common M, Maddison D and McGilvray J (2011) Natural resources and environmental economics (4th edition). Harlow: Pearson Education Limited (First edition 1996, Longman Group Limited)

Pethig R (2003) The 'materials balance' approach to pollution: its origin, implications and acceptance. University of Siegen, Economics Discussion paper No. 105-03, 2003

Pethig R (2006) Non-linear production, abatement, pollution and materials balance reconsidered. Journal of Environmental Economics and Management 51(2), 185–204

Pigou AC (1920) The economics of welfare. London: Macmillan

Porter ME (1991) America's green strategy. Scientific American 264(4), 168

Porter ME and van der Linde C (1995) Toward a new conception of the environment-competitiveness relationship. Journal of Economic Perspectives 9(4), 97–118

Russell CS and Spofford WO Jr (1972) A quantitative framework for residuals management decisions. In: Kneese AV and Bower BT (eds.). Environmental quality analysis: theory and method in the social sciences, pp. 115–179. Baltimore-London: The Johns Hopkins Press

Rødseth KL (2013) Capturing the least costly way of reducing pollution: A shadow price approach. Ecological Economics 92(August), 16–24

Rødseth KL (2014) Efficiency measurement when producers control pollutants: a non-parametric approach. Journal of Productivity Analysis 42(2), 211–223 (https://doi.org/10.1007/s11123-014-0382-2)

Rødseth KL (2016) Environmental efficiency measurement and the materials balance condition reconsidered. European Journal of Operational Research 250(1), 342–346, https://doi.org/10.1016/j.ejor.2015.10.061

Rødseth KL (2017a) Axioms of a polluting technology: a materials balance approach. Environment and Resource Economics. 67(1), 1–22. https://doi.org/10.1007/s10640-015-9974-1

Rødseth KL (2017b) Environmental regulations and allocative efficiency: application to coal-to-gas substitution in the U.S. electricity sector. Journal of Productivity Analysis 47(2), 129–142, https://doi.org/10.1007/s11123-017-0495-5

Rødseth KL and Romstad E (2014) Environmental regulations, producer responses, and secondary benefits: carbon dioxide reductions under the acid rain program. Environmental Resource Economics 59(1), p. 111–135, https://doi.org/10.1007/s10640-013-9720-5

Serra T, Chambers RG and Oude Lansink A (2014) Measuring technical and environmental efficiency in a state-contingent technology. European Journal of Operational Research 236(3), 706–717

Shephard RW (1970) Theory of Cost and Production Functions. Princeton NJ: Princeton University Press

Shephard RW and Färe R (1974) The law of diminishing returns. Zeitschrift für Nationalökonomie 34(1–2), 69–90

Sraffa P (1960) Production of commodities by means of commodities. Cambridge: Cambridge University Press

Sueyoshi T and Goto M (2010) Should the US clean air act include CO2 emission control? Examination by data envelopment analysis. Energy Policy 38(10), 5902–5911

Sueyoshi T, Yuana Y and Goto M (2017) A literature study for DEA applied to energy and environment. Energy Economics 62(February), 104–124

Wang K, Wei Y-M and Zhang X (2012) A comparative analysis of China's regional energy and emission performance: which is the better way to deal with undesirable outputs? Energy Policy 46 (July), 574–584, https://doi.org/10.1016/j.enpol.2012.04.038

Wang K, Wei Y-M and Huang Z (2017a) Environmental efficiency and abatement efficiency measurements of China's thermal power industry: a data envelopment analysis based materials balance approach. European Journal of Operational Research, online 27 April 2017 http://dx.doi.org/10.1016/j.ejor.2017.04.053

Wang H, Anga BW, Wang QW and Zhou P (2017b) Measuring energy performance with sectoral heterogeneity: a non-parametric frontier approach. Energy Economics 62 (February), 70–78

Whitcomb DK (1972) Externalities and welfare. New York and London: Columbia University Press

Xie R-h, Yuan Y-i, and Huang J-j (2017) Different types of environmental regulations and heterogeneous influence on "green" productivity: evidence from China. Ecological Economics 132 (February), 104–112

Zhao X, Yin H and Zhao Y (2015) Impact of environmental regulations on the efficiency and CO_2 emissions of power plants in China. Applied Energy 149(1 July), 238–247

Chapter 4
Environmental Productivity Growth in Consumer Durables

Xun Zhou

1 Introduction

Environmental productivity[1] refers to the ratio of an aggregate measure of economic outputs (goods and services) to that of environmental costs (i.e., energy and resources used, pollutants and wastes emitted during production) (Arabi et al. 2014; Kuosmanen 2013; OECD 2011).[2] Growth in environmental productivity would thus be necessary for production units to increase economic outputs while mitigating environmental pressure. In recent decades, a large number of studies on environmental productivity have appeared across various sub-disciplines of economics (e.g., energy economics, environmental economics, ecological economics, agricultural economics, production economics, mathematical economics, econometrics, etc.), as well as in other related disciplines such as operations research, management science, engineering, and public administration. In these studies, production units of interest are usually *plants* or *firms* [e.g., paper and pulp mills in (Chung et al. 1997; Färe et al. 1989); power plants in (Arabi et al. 2017; Song et al. 2017; Yu et al. 2017b; Zhang and Choi 2013); iron and steel enterprises in (He et al. 2013); automobile manufacturers in (Du et al. 2017); airlines in (Liu et al. 2017)], *sectors* or *industries* [e.g., agriculture in (Kuosmanen 2013; Lin and Fei 2015); transportation in (Yu et al. 2017a; Zhang et al. 2015); manufacturing industries in (Emrouznejad and Yang 2016; Shao and Wang 2016; Yao et al. 2016; Yu et al.

---

[1]Similar notions include environmentally sensitive productivity, green total-factor productivity, environmental performance, and various forms of eco-efficiency.
[2]Alternative interpretations of environmental productivity exist: In addition to environmental costs, economic inputs (such as capital, labor) may also be included in the denominator.

X. Zhou (✉)
Aalto University School of Business, 00100 Helsinki, Finland
e-mail: xun.zhou@aalto.fi

© Springer Nature Singapore Pte Ltd. 2018
R. Pang et al. (eds.), *Energy, Environment and Transitional Green Growth in China*, https://doi.org/10.1007/978-981-10-7919-1_4

2016)], *regions* [e.g., (Du et al. 2017; Sueyoshi et al. 2017; Zhang et al. 2011)], and *countries* [e.g., (Aparicio et al. 2017; Shen et al. 2017; Zhou et al. 2010)]. To our knowledge, however, only one previous study by Kortelainen and Kuosmanen (2007) considers environmental performance of consumer durables. This is somewhat surprising because, during their use phase, consumer durables such as passenger cars, washing machines, refrigerators, and other home appliances are in fact production units that consume energy and resources (and hence generate environmental pollutants) to provide services for consumers.

A possible reason for this gap is that services provided by consumer durables go unmeasured in economic censuses, and thus the (environmental) productivity of consumer durables has gained little attention in the literature of efficiency and productivity analysis. However, we cannot ignore the importance of consumer durables in providing services for consumers and in casting pressure on the natural environment. For instance, the use of passenger cars—the main category of consumer durables—is a very convenient and flexible means of transportation in daily life but also an important contributor to emissions of greenhouse gases, air pollutants, and noise. In the European Union, passenger cars on roads amounted to 251 million in 2015 and were responsible for 770 million tonnes of CO_2 emissions, nearly a quarter (22.2%) of total EU emissions during the year; in China, there were 95.1 million registered passenger cars in 2015 and they were estimated to emit approximately 291.7–446.9 million tonnes of CO_2, 2.7–4.2% of China's total emissions in the same year (see Table 2 in Sect. 2).

Therefore, environmental productivity growth in consumer durables is important for environmental protection and sustainable development, and deserves in-depth studies. Since consumer durables can be seen as production units (though very tiny), we can, in principle, estimate environmental productivity change in consumer durables within the existing productivity analysis framework (Chung et al. 1997; Kuosmanen 2013; Lovell 2003), yet such estimation should be consistent with particular features of consumer durables as compared to conventional production units. Those particular features would influence the way of modeling the production activity (polluting technology[3]) for consumer durables and the way of computing and interpreting environmental productivity change. The primary purpose of this chapter is thus to develop an environmental productivity index specially designed for consumer durables.

Since virtually all empirical data are subject to more or less stochastic noise, this chapter presents the first study of environmental productivity growth in consumer durables that takes stochastic noise explicitly into account. We resort to the convex nonparametric least squares (CNLS) approach (Kuosmanen 2008), which deals with stochastic noise in a nonparametric way, to estimate the polluting technology of consumer durables. As noted earlier, only one previous study considers environmental performance of consumer durables, and there is only one previous study

---

[3]Also known as *environmental production technology*.

that applies CNLS to environmental productivity analysis at the sectoral level (Kuosmanen 2013).[4]

The rest of this chapter proceeds as follows: In Sect. 2 we present and analyze the particular features of consumer durables and introduce a typical example. Section 3 elaborates how to specify the polluting technology of consumer durables. Section 4 provides a brief overview of conventional environmental productivity measures and constructs a Malmquist-type index of environmental productivity change for consumer durables. In Sect. 5 we use a unique Finnish data set of passenger cars to demonstrate how to interpret environmental productivity change in consumer durables. Section 6 concludes this chapter.

2 Particular Features of Consumer Durables

The use of consumer durables (passenger cars, refrigerators, washing machines, and other home appliances, etc.) greatly facilitates people's life while at the same time causes much environmental pressure on the society; in this context, environmental productivity growth in consumer durables would be important for environmental protection and sustainable development. Therefore, it is meaningful to assess environmental productivity change in consumer durables as well as the driving forces behind such change. In light of the lack of literature on this subject, we present here the first such study which might help pave the way for future research.

During their use phase, consumer durables are in fact production units that consume energy and resources (and hence generate environmentally bad outputs) to provide services for consumers (see Fig. 1 for an illustration). As a result, we can, in principle, estimate environmental productivity change in consumer durables within the existing productivity analysis framework, which consists of three main stages: (1) modeling the polluting technology of the production units being investigated; (2) estimating the polluting technology for each interval of the study period by using techniques such as CNLS, data envelopment analysis (DEA), parametric programming, and stochastic frontier analysis (SFA); (3) measuring and decomposing environmental productivity change in the production units over the study period based on a selected productivity index, e.g., the Malmquist index (Kuosmanen 2013). Note however that this framework was originally developed for conventional production units. A mechanical application of it to consumer durables may encounter problems or lead to biased or inaccurate estimates, because consumer durables differ from conventional production units in a number of important respects as presented below:

---

[4]Kuosmanen (2013) uses the term StoNED (stochastic nonparametric envelopment of data), but in fact, he only applies CNLS (which is the first stage of StoNED) and does not proceed to further steps.

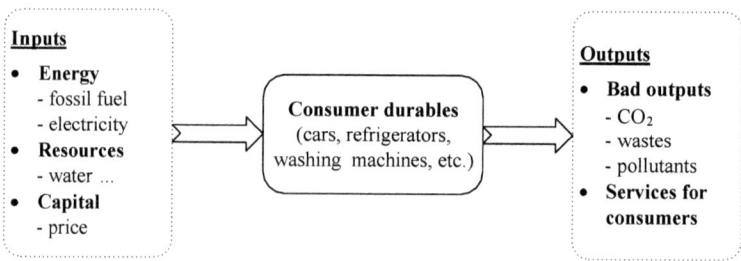

Fig. 1 Illustration of the use phase of consumer durables

1. In a region under consideration, the total fleet of a category of consumer durables can reach a huge size and face the dynamics involving entry of new consumer durables and exit of older ones at each moment.
2. Consumer durables are not decision-making units—their environmental productivity are not influenced by themselves but regulators, producers, consumers, and ambient conditions.[5]
3. Real-world data on environmental costs (fuel consumption and emissions) at the consumer durable level tend to be unavailable or difficult to obtain.[6]
4. A consumer durable usually uses a single type of fuel (gasoline, diesel, or electricity, etc.). The amount of fuel consumption directly determines the level of its CO_2 emissions (see Table 1 for reference).

Taken together, the first and second particular features of consumer durables state that environmental productivity growth in the total fleet of a particular category of consumer durables is driven by three major sources: (1) environmental productivity growth in new consumer durables, mainly influenced by regulators, producers, and consumers; (2) exit of older consumer durables with lower environmental productivity, mainly influenced by regulators and consumers; (3) environmental productivity growth in consumer durables already in use, mainly influenced by regulators, consumers, and ambient conditions. However, it may not be feasible to investigate all these sources of environmental productivity growth

---

[5]For example, fuel consumption of passenger cars on roads are affected by driving behavior, vehicle maintenance, and ambient conditions (e.g., temperature, road, traffic flow, altitude, weather, etc.) (VCA 2016). As a result, even given cars of the same make and model, the actual amounts of fuel consumption may vary significantly.

[6]Estimation of real-world fuel consumption and CO_2 emissions of consumer durables, passenger cars in particular, has attracted a lot of attention. See for example (Alvarez and Weilenmann 2012; André et al. 2006; Dings 2013; Zhang et al. 2014).

Table 1   Correlation coefficients between fuel consumption[a] and emissions of passenger cars

	(1) Gasoline consumption			(2) Diesel consumption		
	ρ	p-value	Count	ρ	p-value	Count
CO_2 emissions (g/km)	0.999	0.000	2095	0.997	0.000	2275
Noise level (dB(A))	0.363	0.000	2095	0.114	0.000	2275
CO emissions (mg/km)	0.057	0.009	2095	0.005	0.798	2275
HC emissions (mg/km)	0.000	0.991	2095	0.312	0.099	29
NO_x emissions (mg/km)	0.071	0.001	2095	0.162	0.000	2275
PM emissions (mg/km)	0.817	0.183	4	0.131	0.000	2275

Source Self-calculation based on the type-approval data for new models of cars (August 2016) collected from the Vehicle Certification Agency (VCA) of the United Kingdom Department for Transport
[a]Fuel consumption is measured in liters per 100 km

(especially the third one) due to the lack of real-world data on environmental costs as suggested by the third particular feature.[7]

In this context, a possible way is to assess environmental productivity growth in new consumer durables using type-approval data (which are more likely to be available), yet this is still challenging within the existing productivity analysis framework. The first particular feature implies that there could be a considerable and variable number of new consumer durables taken in use each year and thus we would be faced with an unbalanced, large-sized panel data set. Although the existing framework can deal with unbalanced panel data by matching observations in adjacent periods and computing (environmental) productivity change for matched observations, it is computationally expensive and probably meaningless to do so in the case of new consumer durables. Moreover, the fourth particular feature highlights the proportional link between fuel consumption and CO_2 emissions of consumer durables. For this reason, several key axiomatic assumptions of a polluting technology, such as free disposability of inputs and weak disposability of good and bad outputs, may no longer hold (Rødseth 2017).

To address these issues, we propose an empirical strategy as follows: The total fleet of a particular category of consumer durables can be decomposed into cohorts of consumer durables taken in use each year (or another time interval) of the study period, that is, yearly cohorts of new consumer durables. We can model the polluting technology of consumer durables by revisiting the general axioms underlying the existing productivity analysis framework (Chung et al. 1997; Färe et al. 1989, 2005; Hailu and Veeman 2000). Then the polluting technology can be estimated for each cohort by one or another technique (e.g., CNLS, DEA, SFA) in terms of the models of new consumer durables. Finally, the environmental productivity

---

[7]An exception is that some real-world data at the aggregate level (e.g., total amount of fuel/ electricity consumption) may be available for consumer durables and those data can be used to estimate other related aggregate measures (e.g., total CO_2 emissions). As such, environmental productivity analysis might be able to be performed at the aggregate level (sector, region, or country).

change from one cohort to another can be computed and decomposed based on a preferred productivity measure. Note that each cohort is represented by a hypothetical consumer durable that possesses the average of inputs and outputs in that cohort (other choices of the hypothetical consumer durable are possible).

The advantages of this empirical strategy lie in the incorporation of the particular features of consumer durables into the existing productivity analysis framework, the higher availability of type-approval data for consumer durables, and the relevance to environmental and climate policy (new consumer durables are subject to increasingly stringent environmental regulations).[8]

2.1 Typical Example

Without loss of generality, this chapter considers passenger cars—the main category of consumer durables—as a typical example to implement our empirical strategy. A passenger car in road traffic serves as a private transportation tool that consumes gasoline, diesel, or alternative fuel to provide transportation services for its user(s) and simultaneously emits CO_2 (the key greenhouse gas), noise, and a variety of air pollutants such as carbon monoxide (CO), nitrogen oxides (NO_x), hydrocarbons (HC), particulate matter (PM), etc. The effects of these emissions are summarized in e.g., (Kortelainen and Kuosmanen 2007; VCA 2016).

Note however that there are a number of important differences between CO_2 emissions and air pollutant emissions from the use of passenger cars. Firstly, the CO_2 emissions and the fuel consumption of a passenger car are directly proportional, which can be shown by calculating their correlation coefficients (0.999 for gasoline and 0.997 for diesel) based on the type-approval data for new models of cars (see Table 1), while the air pollutant emissions (as well as the noise level) of a passenger car are much less correlated with the fuel consumption.[9] Secondly, the type-approval data on fuel consumption and CO_2 emissions are comparable across different models of passenger cars but this is not the case for air pollutant emissions (VCA 2016). Thirdly, compared to local air pollutants, CO_2, a global pollutant that can remain in the atmosphere for centuries, is much more difficult to be reduced. For the last two differences, in what follows we shall consider CO_2 emissions as the single bad output.

---

[8]See (Yang and Bandivadekar 2017; Yang et al. 2017), for example, for overviews of CO_2 emission/fuel consumption standards for new passenger cars in different countries.

[9]In fact, the air pollutant emissions of a passenger car are also associated with a broad range of factors such as the vehicle technology (e.g., end-of-pipe abatement) and maintenance, fuel quality, driving behavior, and ambient conditions. See (VCA 2016) for a more detailed discussion.

Table 2 CO_2 emissions from passenger cars registered in Europe and China in 2015

	European Union	China
Number of registered cars (million)	251.0	95.1
Cars per 1000 people	499	69
Annual CO_2 emissions of all cars (million tonnes)	770.0	$\sim 291.7\text{–}446.9^a$
Annual CO_2 emissions per car (tonnes)	3.1	$\sim 3.1\text{–}4.7^a$
Proportion of total CO_2 emissions (%)	22.2	$\sim 2.7\text{–}4.2^a$

Sources The figures were collected from and self-calculated based on (1) Emission Database for Global Atmospheric Research (EDGAR), release version 4.3.2, European Commission, Joint Research Centre (JRC)/PBL Netherlands Environmental Assessment Agency; (2) European Vehicle Market Statistics Pocketbook 2015/16, International Council on Clean Transportation Europe; (3) Statistical Communique of the People's Republic of China on the 2015 National Economic and Social Development (in Chinese), National Bureau of Statistics of China; (4) Green Vehicle Guide, U.S. Environmental Protection Agency
[a]As there are no reliable CO_2 emissions data available for passenger cars registered in China, we estimated the annual CO_2 emissions of all cars in China in 2015 by multiplying the number of registered cars by the annual CO_2 emissions per car in the EU (3.1 tonnes) and in the United States (4.7 tonnes), respectively

In 2015, passenger cars on EU roads amounted to 251 million and were responsible for 770 million tonnes of CO_2 emissions, nearly a quarter (22.2%) of total EU emissions during the year; meanwhile, there were 95.1 million passenger cars on China's roads and they were estimated to emit approximately 291.7–446.9 million tonnes of CO_2, 2.7–4.2% of China's total emissions during the year (see Table 2). Compared to the EU, China's passenger car fleet has a quite smaller size and accounts for a much lower proportion of total CO_2 emissions. However, as shown in Fig. 2, the fleet has experienced a dramatic expansion over the past few

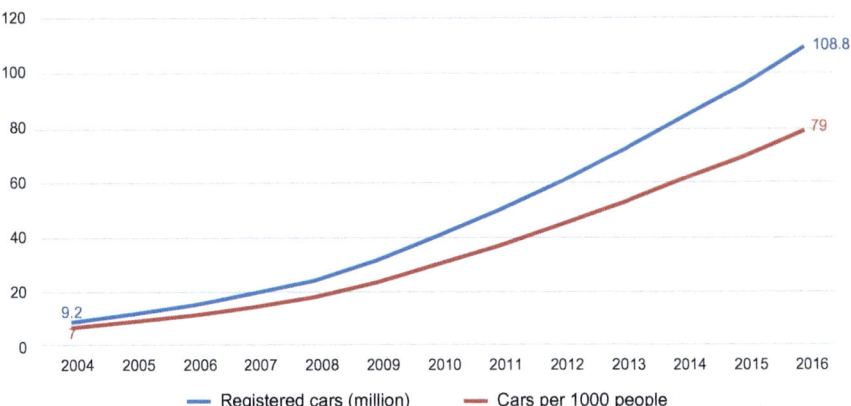

Fig. 2 Growth in the number of registered passenger cars in China, 2004–2016. *Source* Statistical Communiques of the People's Republic of China on the National Economic and Social Development, 2004–2016 (in Chinese), National Bureau of Statistics of China

decades, and cars per 1000 people in China increased rapidly from 7 in 2004 to 79 in 2016, though still quite lower than developed countries (499 for the EU in 2015). In view of China's fast-growing economy, the fleet seems very likely to reach a considerable size and contribute to a fairly huge amount of CO_2 emissions in future years.

Given the importance of passenger cars in sustainable development, both the EU and China have set mandatory CO_2 emission/fuel consumption targets for new passenger cars. For new cars sold in Europe, the average CO_2 emissions shall not exceed 95 g/km by 2021 (European Parliament, the Council 2009); and for new cars sold in China, the average fuel consumption should reach 5 liters per 100 km (~ 120 g/km of CO_2) by 2020 (Ministry of Industry and Information Technology of the People's Republic of China 2015).

3 Conceptual Modeling of Consumer Durables

The purpose of this section is to specify the polluting technology of passenger cars during their use phase, which is a key step of the empirical strategy outlined in Sect. 2. This section has two parts. The first part reviews the general axioms of the production theory and gives a conventional specification of the polluting technology for passenger cars; the second part examines whether the conventional specification is consistent with the particular features of consumer durables and presents a final specification of the polluting technology that is appropriate and specific to passenger cars.

3.1 Conventional Specification of Polluting Technology

Consider a production unit that employs an input vector $\mathbf{x} \in \Re_+^P$ to produce an output vector $\mathbf{y} \in \Re_+^Q$ For each period t, the production technology is represented by the production possibility set

$$T^t = \{(\mathbf{x}, \mathbf{y}) | \mathbf{x} \text{ can produce } \mathbf{y} \text{ in period } t\} \qquad (1)$$

T^t consists of all technologically feasible combinations of $\mathbf{x}$ and $\mathbf{y}$ in period t and requires the following axiomatic assumptions (Färe and Primont 1995):

1. T^t is closed, convex, and bounded;
2. Inactivity is possible: $(\mathbf{x}, \mathbf{0}) \in T^t$;
3. No free lunch: $(\mathbf{0}, \mathbf{y}) \notin T^t$;
4. Free disposability of inputs: if $(\mathbf{x}, \mathbf{y}) \in T^t$ and $\tilde{\mathbf{x}} \geq \mathbf{x}$ then $(\tilde{\mathbf{x}}, \mathbf{y}) \in T^t$;
5. Free disposability of outputs: if $(\mathbf{x}, \mathbf{y}) \in T^t$ and $\tilde{\mathbf{y}} \leq \mathbf{y}$ then $(\mathbf{x}, \tilde{\mathbf{y}}) \in T^t$.

For joint production of good outputs $\mathbf{u} \in \Re_+^R$ and bad outputs $\mathbf{b} \in \Re_+^{Q-R}$, the axiom of free disposability of outputs are replaced by the following three axioms (Färe et al. 2005):

6. Free disposability of good outputs: if $(\mathbf{x}, \mathbf{u}, \mathbf{b}) \in T^t$ and $\tilde{\mathbf{u}} \le \mathbf{u}$ then $(\mathbf{x}, \tilde{\mathbf{u}}, \mathbf{b}) \in T^t$;
7. Weak disposability of good and bad outputs: if $(\mathbf{x}, \mathbf{u}, \mathbf{b}) \in T^t$ and $0 \le \theta \le 1$ then $(\mathbf{x}, \theta\mathbf{u}, \theta\mathbf{b}) \in T^t$;
8. Null-jointness: if $(\mathbf{x}, \mathbf{u}, \mathbf{b}) \in T^t$ and $\mathbf{b} = \mathbf{0}$ then $\mathbf{u} = \mathbf{0}$.

Given Axioms 1–4 and 6–8, we can completely characterize T^t (which is now a polluting technology) by the traditional Shephard input and output distance functions (Färe and Primont 1995; Shepard 1953, 1970), which are respectively expressed as

$$DI^t(\mathbf{x}, \mathbf{u}, \mathbf{b}) = \sup\{\phi > 0 | (\mathbf{x}/\phi, \mathbf{u}, \mathbf{b}) \in T^t\}$$
$$DO^t(\mathbf{x}, \mathbf{u}, \mathbf{b}) = \inf\{\sigma > 0 | (\mathbf{x}, \mathbf{u}/\sigma, \mathbf{b}/\sigma) \in T^t\}$$
(2)

The Shephard input distance function $DI^t(\cdot)$ measures the largest proportion by which we can deflate the input vector $\mathbf{x}$ onto the frontier of T^t while keeping the output vectors $\mathbf{u}$ and $\mathbf{b}$ constant; the Shephard output distance function $DO^t(\cdot)$ measures the largest proportion by which we can expand $\mathbf{u}$ and $\mathbf{b}$ onto the frontier given the input vector $\mathbf{x}$. The evaluated production unit is said to be environmentally efficient if $DI^t(\cdot) = 1$ or $DO^t(\cdot) = 1$, and environmentally inefficient if $DI^t(\cdot) > 1$ or $DO^t(\cdot) < 1$. Since $DO^t(\cdot)$ simply expands good and bad outputs simultaneously onto the frontier, the more general directional distance function, which allows simultaneous contraction of bad outputs and expansion of good outputs (Chung et al. 1997), is more often used in the literature. Mathematically, the directional output distance function is defined in terms of T^t as

$$\overrightarrow{D}^t(\mathbf{x}, \mathbf{u}, \mathbf{b}; \mathbf{g_u}, -\mathbf{g_b}) = \sup\{\delta \ge 0 | (\mathbf{x}, \mathbf{u} + \delta\mathbf{g_u}, \mathbf{b} - \delta\mathbf{g_b}) \in T^t\}$$
(3)

where $(\mathbf{g_u}, -\mathbf{g_b})$ is the directional vector corresponding to $\mathbf{u}$ and $\mathbf{b}$. One need to specify *ex ante* an appropriate directional vector in spite of the generality of the directional distance function. $(\mathbf{u}, -\mathbf{b})$ is a commonly-used directional vector, and given that, $\vec{D}^t(\mathbf{x}, \mathbf{u}, \mathbf{b}; \mathbf{u}, -\mathbf{b})$ measures the largest proportion by which we can simultaneously expand good outputs $\mathbf{u}$ and contract bad outputs $\mathbf{b}$ onto the frontier of T^t given inputs $\mathbf{x}$. To put it another way, the directional distance function seeks the maximum ratio of good outputs to bad outputs for given inputs (Färe et al. 2004). The evaluated production unit is said to be environmentally efficient if $\vec{D}^t(\mathbf{x}, \mathbf{u}, \mathbf{b}; \mathbf{u}, -\mathbf{b}) = 0$, and environmentally inefficient if $\vec{D}^t(\mathbf{x}, \mathbf{u}, \mathbf{b}; \mathbf{u}, -\mathbf{b}) > 0$.

It should be noted that in addition to the axioms inherited from the polluting technology T^t, these multiple-output distance functions also need to satisfy axiomatic properties such as the linear homogeneity of the Shephard distance functions or the translation property of the directional distance function [see e.g., (Färe and

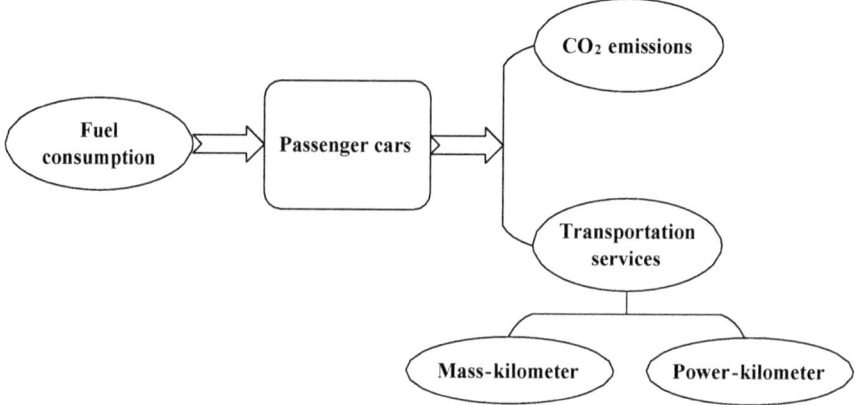

Fig. 3 Conventional specification of the polluting technology for passenger cars

Grosskopf 2000, 2006; Färe and Primont 1995; Färe et al. 2005) for detailed discussions].

Since passenger cars jointly produce transportation services and CO_2 emissions during their use phase, a conventional specification can be readily set for the polluting technology of passenger cars as shown in Fig. 3. Fuel consumption (gasoline, diesel, natural gas, or electricity) is the single input, CO_2 emissions are the bad output, and transportation services (measured by mass-kilometer and power-kilometer)[10] are the good outputs. One might argue that it is necessary to consider also car price as an input, analogous to the capital input in conventional efficiency and productivity analysis. In fact, whether or not car price should be included as an additional input is an open question that depends on whose perspective one takes. There are, generally speaking, three perspectives: consumers', producers', and regulators'. Let us assume that consumers, producers, and regulators are all rational, and concerned with environmental productivity growth in passenger cars.

- For consumers, price is an important (if not the most important) factor to consider in the purchase decision of a passenger car. They are facing an optimization problem: maximization of the amount of transportation services subject to price (budget) and CO_2 emission constraints, or minimization of price and CO_2 emissions given a certain amount of transportation services.
- For producers, the objective is to produce passenger cars that not only meet CO_2 emission standards set by regulators, but also are compatible with demand and purchasing power of consumers.

---

[10]The measures are analogous to units of transportation measurement, such as passenger-kilometer and freight-kilometer.

- Including car price as an additional input implicitly allows substitution between car price and CO_2 emissions—the price of a car may be lower in exchange for more CO_2 emissions while maintaining the same level of transportation services. This leads to a question: is low price a valid excuse to emit more CO_2 emissions? The answer is probably "no" from regulators' perspective.

Therefore, in summary, car price should be included as an additional input if one takes the perspective of consumers or producers; and it should not be included if one takes the perspective of regulators. The current study follows the latter.

3.2 Direct Proportionality and Materials Balance

The fourth particular feature of consumer durables indicates the direct proportionality between the amount of fuel consumption and the level of CO_2 emissions during the use of passenger cars. This connects to the materials balance principle, which argues some general axioms of the production theory may be inconsistent with the laws of thermodynamics [see e.g., Chap. 3 and (Coelli et al. 2007; Førsund 2008; Rødseth 2016, 2017) for detailed discussions]. The materials balance principle is defined in terms of Fig. 3 as follows:

$$\lambda b = \rho x - \pi' \mathbf{u} - a \qquad (4)$$

where x is the input (fuel consumption); $\mathbf{u}$ is the vector of good outputs (mass-kilometer and power-kilometer); b is the bad output (CO_2 emissions); $\rho > 0$, π, and $\lambda > 0$ stand for the content of carbon in x, $\mathbf{u}$, and b, respectively; a denotes the amount of emissions reduction through end-of-pipe abatement. Since mass-kilometer and power-kilometer do not contain carbon (i.e., $\pi = \mathbf{0}$) and there is currently no end-of-pipe abatement for CO_2 emissions from passenger cars (i.e., $a = 0$), Eq. 4 collapses to

$$b = \frac{\rho}{\lambda} x \qquad (5)$$

where $\frac{\rho}{\lambda} > 0$ is the CO_2 emissions factor of the fuel consumed. For example, burning a liter of gasoline produces about 2.3 kg of CO_2, while burning a liter of diesel produces about 2.7 kg of CO_2.[11] Thus we can state that, for a fleet of passenger cars using the same type of fuel, a constant CO_2 emissions factor can be reasonably assumed across the fleet, which we would refer to as the *direct proportionality assumption*. More importantly, Eq. 5 reveals that the materials balance principle and the fourth particular feature of consumer durables are equivalent in the current context, both leading to the direct proportionality assumption.

---

[11]See the websites for more information: https://www.eia.gov/tools/faqs/faq.php?id=307&t=11, https://ec.europa.eu/clima/policies/transport/vehicles/cars.

As a result, Axioms 2 (inactivity is possible), 4 (free disposability of inputs), 7 (weak disposability of good and bad outputs), and 8 (null-jointness) underlying the conventional model specification in Fig. 3 are no longer valid.[12]

- Inactivity is not possible as CO_2 will be inevitably produced from burning a finite amount of fuel. Suppose, when a passenger car is stopped but with its engine running, it produces zero mass-kilometer and power-kilometer but non-zero CO_2 emissions.
- It is not feasible to increase the fuel consumption of a passenger car with its CO_2 emissions held constant, or to decrease its CO_2 emissions with its fuel consumption held constant, in the sense that given one of them the other is uniquely determined. As such, Axioms 4 and 7 cannot be true.[13]
- Axiom 8 implies that it holds for any amount of fuel consumption (Rødseth 2017). But in fact, when there are no CO_2 emissions from a passenger car there is no fuel consumption, i.e., if $b = 0$ then $x = \frac{\lambda}{\rho} b = 0$.

Moreover, the distance functions defined in Eqs. 2 and 3 are problematic due to the direct proportionality assumption. It is infeasible for any evaluated passenger car to use a smaller amount of fuel to produce the same transportation services and CO_2 emissions (corresponding to DI^t), or to use the same fuel consumption to produce either larger amounts of transportation services and CO_2 emissions (corresponding to DO^t) or more transportation services but less CO_2 emissions (corresponding to $\vec{D}^t$). Thus, every passenger car evaluated would be environmentally efficient irrespective of the distance function used, and this is apparently unrealistic.

In summary, the conventional specification of the polluting technology for passenger cars is not consistent with the particular features of consumer durables. To address this problem, we can simply exclude either fuel consumption or CO_2 emissions from the specification without loss of information (Kuosmanen 2013), because from the modeling viewpoint, the two contain equivalent information. For the current study, fuel consumption can be excluded since the focus is placed on CO_2 emissions.

Figure 4 presents the final specification of the polluting technology for passenger cars, where CO_2 emissions are treated as the single input and transportation services (mass-kilometer and power-kilometer) are the outputs. The treatment of CO_2 emissions can be interpreted in two ways: one is that CO_2 emissions act as a perfect proxy for fuel consumption, breaking the direct proportionality between them; the other is that the use of passenger cars consumes "*services from natural*

---

[12]See Rødseth (2017) for a more general discussion on the consistency between the general axioms of the production theory and the materials balance principle.

[13]The direct proportionality assumption implicitly assumes that all fuel in the tank is burned into CO_2. It is possible that only part of the measured amount of fuel is burned while the other is wasted, and in this circumstance, Axioms 4 and 7 hold. Nevertheless, this possibility can be ruled out under type-approval test conditions or in the case that CO_2 emissions data are estimated by multiplying the measured amount of fuel by a constant emissions factor.

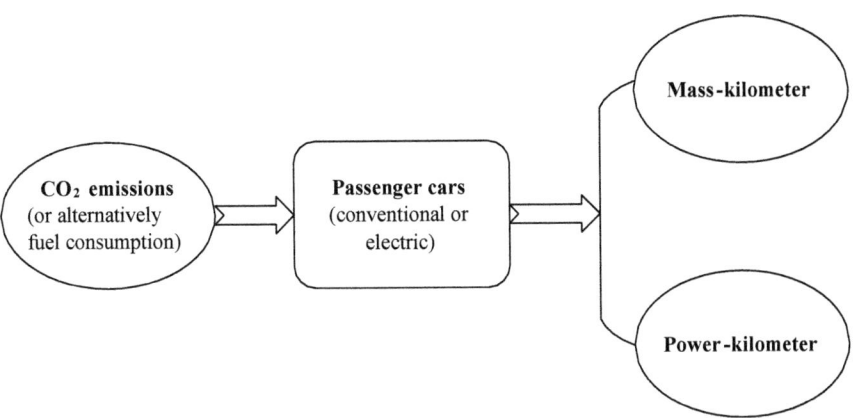

Fig. 4 Final specification of the polluting technology for passenger cars

assets" to dispose of CO_2 emissions (OECD 2011), that is, from the perspective of society (or regulators), CO_2 emissions are regarded as an environmental cost that needs to be reduced. The final specification satisfies the original Axioms 1–5 (which can be easily verified) and we can simply resort to the traditional Shephard distance functions to characterize the polluting technology of passenger cars.

As shown in Fig. 4, the final specification applies to not only conventional passenger cars powered by gasoline, diesel or alternative fuel, but also electric cars. There is also a direct proportional link between the CO_2 emissions of an electric car (for which it should be responsible) and the amount of electricity consumed. We can find out on average how much CO_2 emissions are produced per kilowatt-hour of electricity in the region considered. Furthermore, such way of modeling can be readily extended to other consumer durables, e.g., refrigerators, washing machines, air conditioners, etc.

4 Measurement of Environmental Productivity

4.1 Brief Overview of Conventional Measures

In the case of single good output (u) and single environmental factor (e), the level of environmental productivity in period t and the change in environmental productivity from period t to $t + 1$ are simply defined as

$$EP^t = u^t/e^t$$
$$EP(t, t+1) = \frac{u^{t+1}/e^{t+1}}{u^t/e^t} \tag{6}$$

where e can be either a bad output or an energy or resource input. Note that u and e could be aggregate measures, e.g., gross domestic product (GDP) and total pollutants or emissions.

Equation 6 is seen as the partial measure of environmental productivity in the context of multiple-input and/or multiple-output polluting technologies. Examples of the partial measure include energy productivity (economic output per unit of energy input) (Berndt 1990; Chang and Hu 2010) and carbon productivity (economic output per unit of CO_2 emissions) (Kaya and Yokobori 1998; Meng and Niu 2012). In addition, the reciprocal of the partial measure is widely used in practice, such as energy intensity, carbon intensity, fuel economy of vehicles (fuel consumption divided by mileage traveled), etc. These partial indicators are very intuitive but likely to be problematic due to the absence of other factors in the underlying polluting technology (Kuosmanen 2013).

Total-factor productivity (TFP) indices are therefore generally used in the literature to assess environmental productivity change in multiple-input and/or multiple-output settings. The estimation of environmental TFP is quite challenging because one must somehow manage to aggregate the inputs and the outputs, especially without readily available price data for environmental bads [see e.g., (Kuosmanen 2013) for a more detailed discussion]. In this context, the Malmquist TFP index proposed by Caves et al. (1982) [or one of its many variants such as the Malmquist-Luenberger index proposed by Chung et al. (1997)] has been the most common environmental TFP indicator, because it does not require price data for environmental bads, but rather employ shadow prices of technology distance functions.

Assume for the moment that the Shephard input and output distance functions defined in Eq. 2 are known, we can derive the input- and output-oriented Malmquist indices of environmental productivity change, respectively, as follows:

$$
\begin{aligned}
MI(t, t+1) &= \left(\frac{DI^t(\mathbf{x}^t, \mathbf{y}^t)}{DI^t(\mathbf{x}^{t+1}, \mathbf{y}^{t+1})} \times \frac{DI^{t+1}(\mathbf{x}^t, \mathbf{y}^t)}{DI^{t+1}(\mathbf{x}^{t+1}, \mathbf{y}^{t+1})} \right)^{1/2} \\
MO(t, t+1) &= \left(\frac{DO^t(\mathbf{x}^{t+1}, \mathbf{y}^{t+1})}{DO^t(\mathbf{x}^t, \mathbf{y}^t)} \times \frac{DO^{t+1}(\mathbf{x}^{t+1}, \mathbf{y}^{t+1})}{DO^{t+1}(\mathbf{x}^t, \mathbf{y}^t)} \right)^{1/2}
\end{aligned} \tag{7}
$$

It is said that there is environmental productivity growth from period t to $t+1$ if the value of $MI(t, t+1)$ or $MO(t, t+1)$ is greater than unity, and environmental productivity decline if the value is less than unity.

Alternatively, we can derive the Malmquist index based on the directional output distance function defined in Eq. 3 [which is generally referred to as the Malmquist-Luenberger index (Chung et al. 1997)] as follows:

$$ML(t, t+1) = \left(\frac{1 + \vec{D}^t\left(\mathbf{x}^t, \mathbf{u}^t, \mathbf{b}^t; \mathbf{g}_u^t, -\mathbf{g}_b^t\right)}{1 + \vec{D}^t\left(\mathbf{x}^{t+1}, \mathbf{u}^{t+1}, \mathbf{b}^{t+1}; \mathbf{g}_u^{t+1}, -\mathbf{g}_b^{t+1}\right)} \right.$$

$$\left. \times \frac{1 + \vec{D}^{t+1}\left(\mathbf{x}^t, \mathbf{u}^t, \mathbf{b}^t; \mathbf{g}_u^t, -\mathbf{g}_b^t\right)}{1 + \vec{D}^{t+1}\left(\mathbf{x}^{t+1}, \mathbf{u}^{t+1}, \mathbf{b}^{t+1}; \mathbf{g}_u^{t+1}, -\mathbf{g}_b^{t+1}\right)} \right)^{1/2} \quad (8)$$

Likewise, $ML(t, t+1)$ indicates environmental productivity growth from period t to $t + 1$ if its value is greater than unity, and environmental productivity decline if the value is less than unity.

The Malmquist indices can be decomposed into two components, namely technical change (TC) and efficiency change (EC) (Chung et al. 1997; Nishimizu and Page 1982). Taking the input-oriented Malmquist index as an example, the decomposition proceeds as follows:

$$MI(t, t+1) = MITC(t, t+1) \times MIEC(t, t+1)$$

$$MITC(t, t+1) = \left(\frac{DI^{t+1}(\mathbf{x}^t, \mathbf{y}^t)}{DI^t(\mathbf{x}^t, \mathbf{y}^t)} \times \frac{DI^{t+1}(\mathbf{x}^{t+1}, \mathbf{y}^{t+1})}{DI^t(\mathbf{x}^{t+1}, \mathbf{y}^{t+1})} \right)^{1/2} \quad (9)$$

$$MIEC(t, t+1) = \frac{DI^t(\mathbf{x}^t, \mathbf{y}^t)}{DI^{t+1}(\mathbf{x}^{t+1}, \mathbf{y}^{t+1})}$$

The technical change component accounts for the shift of frontier over time: there is technical progress from period t to $t + 1$ if $MITC(t, t + 1) > 1$, and technical regress if $MITC(t, t + 1) < 1$. As for the efficiency change component $MIEC(t, t + 1)$, a value greater (or less) than unity indicates that the evaluated production unit is catching up to (or moving farther from) the frontier.[14]

The standard techniques for estimating distance functions include parametric programming (Aigner and Chu 1968), DEA (Charnes et al. 1978), and SFA (Aigner et al. 1977; Meeusen and Van den Broeck 1977). Since the multiple-output distance functions must satisfy axiomatic properties such as the linear homogeneity of the Shephard distance functions or the translation property of the directional distance function, and in SFA one cannot impose such properties globally, in this context, parametric estimation of distance functions is usually based on parametric programming (Färe et al. 2005). DEA has an advantage over parametric programming in that it does not require any parametric specification of the functional form but is based on some general axioms of the production theory. However, both DEA and parametric programming are deterministic methods that assume away random noise. This is a major shortcoming because virtually all empirical data are subject to more or less noise. In order to simultaneously impose the axiomatic properties

---

[14]Färe et al. (1994) proposes a third component: *scale efficiency change* under variable returns to scale (VRS). Yet, no consensus has been reached on the derivation and interpretation of this component. See (Färe et al. 1997; Ray and Desli 1997) for a critical exchange on this topic and (Lovell 2003) for a more detailed discussion.

required by the distance functions and deal with stochastic noise in a nonparametric way, one can resort to CNLS (Kuosmanen 2008) or stochastic nonparametric envelopment of data (StoNED) (Kuosmanen and Kortelainen 2012).

Having briefly described the conventional measures of environmental productivity, we will turn our attention in the next subsection to consumer durables—how the Malmquist-type index can be applied to the current context of consumer durables.

4.2 Malmquist-type Index for Consumer Durables

Depending on the polluting technology of passenger cars specified in Fig. 4 and the perspective that we take (i.e., that of regulators, which seeks to reduce CO_2 emissions from passenger cars), an input-oriented Malmquist-type index of environmental productivity change would best suit the current study.

Suppose now that we have data on a total fleet of passenger cars using the same type of fuel, this fleet can be decomposed into cohorts of cars taken in use each year (e.g., cohorts of 2016, 2015, 2014,…), i.e., yearly cohorts of new cars. Following Kuosmanen (2008, 2012), consider the model

$$x_i^t = g^t(\mathbf{y}_i^t) + \varepsilon_i^t \tag{10}$$

where x_i^t denotes the CO_2 emissions of passenger car i in cohort t, $\mathbf{y}_i^t$ is the vector of transportation services (mass-kilometer and power-kilometer), g^t is an increasing and convex emissions generating function, characterizing the best-practice frontier of the polluting technology, and ε_i^t is a composite error term that combines both an inefficiency term μ_i^t and a stochastic noise term v_i^t (i.e., $\varepsilon_i^t = \mu_i^t + v_i^t$). We can equivalently write Eq. 10 in terms of car models as

$$x_m^t = g^t(\mathbf{y}_m^t) + \varepsilon_m^t \tag{11}$$

where each $m = 1,\dots, M^t$ characterizes a subset of identical new cars (i.e., a car model) within cohort t, M^t is the number of car models, and $\varepsilon_m^t = \mu_m^t + v_m^t$. Note that we assume that μ_m^t, v_m^t, and $\mathbf{y}_m^t$ are uncorrelated with each other, and $E(\mu_m^t) = Z^t > 0, E(v_m^t) = 0$. To empirically estimate the polluting technology, we can estimate Eq. 11 separately for each cohort by employing the CNLS approach (the first stage of StoNED).

The CNLS approach produces a consistent estimator of the expected level of CO_2 emissions, and for each cohort t the estimator is obtained by solving the following quadratic programming problem (Kuosmanen 2008, 2012)

$$\min_{\gamma,\alpha,\beta,\varepsilon} \sum_{m=1}^{M^t} \left(\varepsilon_m^t\right)^2$$

$$s.t.$$

$$x_m^t = \gamma_m^t + \varepsilon_m^t \quad \forall m \tag{12}$$

$$\gamma_m^t = \alpha_m^t + \left(\beta_m^t\right)' \mathbf{y}_m^t \quad \forall m$$

$$\gamma_m^t \geq \alpha_k^t + \left(\beta_k^t\right)' \mathbf{y}_m^t \quad \forall m, k$$

$$\beta_m^t \geq 0 \quad \forall m$$

where γ_m^t is the CNLS estimator of the expected CO_2 emissions of car model m in cohort t given the transportation services $\mathbf{y}_m^t$; α_m^t and β_m^t—specific to each car model —are the intercept and the slope coefficients that define tangent hyperplanes to the convex piece-wise linear CNLS frontier, and notably β_m^t measures the CO_2 emissions increased by producing one additional unit of transportation services (i.e., shadow prices).

The CNLS frontier is an average-practice frontier of the polluting technology, rather than the best-practice frontier $g^t\left(\mathbf{y}_m^t\right)$. Mathematically,

$$E\left[x_m^t \middle| \mathbf{y}_m^t\right] = E\left[g^t\left(\mathbf{y}_m^t\right) + \varepsilon_m^t \middle| \mathbf{y}_m^t\right]$$
$$= E\left[g^t\left(\mathbf{y}_m^t\right) + \mu_m^t + v_m^t \middle| \mathbf{y}_m^t\right] \tag{13}$$
$$= g^t\left(\mathbf{y}_m^t\right) + Z^t$$

To estimate Z^t and $g^t\left(\mathbf{y}_m^t\right)$, one should proceed to further stages of StoNED [see (Kuosmanen and Kortelainen 2012; Kuosmanen et al. 2015) for more details]. But for this study, we do not need to do that because CNLS can produce consistent shadow price estimates that are required by a Malmquist-type index (Kuosmanen et al. 2015).

When it comes to computing the CNLS estimator, there are several points worth mentioning. First, prior to the computation we divide both sides of Eq. 11 by kilometer to obtain x_m^t measured in grams of CO_2 per kilometer (g/km)[15] and $\mathbf{y}_m^t$ measured in vehicle characteristics: curb weight in kilograms (kg) and engine power in kilowatts (kW). Second, the number of inequalities in Eq. 12 rises as a quadratic function of the number of observations: let the number of observations be ω, the number of inequalities will be $\omega(\omega - 1)$ (Kuosmanen et al. 2015). Although the models of new cars act as observations in the computation, the data size of each cohort could still be very large (see Table 3 for reference), resulting in heavy computational burden. Fortunately, a penalized algorithm proposed by Keshvari (2017) can help to partly ease the computational burden.

The next step is to derive an input-oriented Malmquist-type index based on the estimated CNLS frontier of each cohort. First, we need to construct a hypothetical

---

[15]Type-approval data on the CO_2 emissions of new passenger cars are normally measured in g/km.

Table 3 Descriptive statistics of the input and output variables; 2002–2014

Cohort	CO$_2$ (g/km)						Curb weight (kg)					Engine power (kW)				
	Obs[a]	Mean	WAVG[b]	SD[b]	Min	Max	Mean	WAVG	SD	Min	Max	Mean	WAVG	SDMin	Min	Max
2002	2648	217.42	184.05	47.71	113	499	1461.55	1311.32	258.17	736	2560	116.74	86.50	49.13	33	380
2003	2840	215.95	182.40	48.78	104	530	1477.19	1320.05	274.38	805	2855	118.78	87.05	51.68	37	405
2004	2725	214.00	183.33	49.70	104	475	1477.61	1332.90	280.36	735	3465	119.93	89.14	53.31	37	450
2005	2890	211.30	182.15	50.15	104	520	1479.32	1345.14	273.17	805	2725	122.65	90.19	57.26	37	450
2006	2688	209.64	181.14	50.83	103	630	1491.84	1352.86	279.93	805	2725	127.28	92.05	62.18	37	450
2007	2588	204.84	179.80	50.86	102	630	1493.64	1370.75	274.12	805	2684	129.34	95.13	62.93	38	456
2008	2313	196.18	167.57	47.21	103	495	1472.35	1337.96	264.09	825	2684	125.95	91.30	63.02	40	471
2009	1485	188.98	158.10	46.31	89	470	1478.15	1344.32	266.42	825	2780	127.82	92.47	63.75	40	456
2010	1322	182.09	150.00	47.90	91	415	1481.38	1323.24	285.29	826	3010	131.10	89.39	70.58	40	456
2011	1156	175.02	144.20	46.43	89	355	1500.92	1333.29	293.27	770	2650	134.18	89.37	70.28	44	420
2012	1060	163.39	139.00	41.64	79	398	1486.81	1337.90	288.69	753	3835	130.52	89.32	68.85	44	515
2013	985	154.66	131.49	37.72	81	353	1466.33	1337.78	266.59	750	2580	126.14	89.66	66.63	44	430
2014	915	149.78	127.23	36.26	78	361	1459.04	1317.06	276.87	750	3835	127.19	89.72	67.27	46	460

Source Self-processing based on Open Data for Vehicles 4.3, Finnish Transport Safety Agency

[a]Car models act as observations. It should be pointed out that there was a clear decrease in the number of observations from 2005 to 2014. This is related to the processing of the original data (further details are available upon request)

[b]*WAVG* weighted average; *SD* standard deviation

car to represent each cohort, according to our empirical strategy outlined in Sect. 2. It appears straightforward to define the representative car (RC) of cohort t with the average CO_2 emissions, curb weight, and engine power. Specifically, the average CO_2 emissions of cohort t are calculated as

$$\bar{x}^t = \sum_{i=1}^{N^t} x_i^t / N^t \qquad (14)$$

where N^t is the number of passenger cars within cohort t. Equivalently, we can calculate the average CO_2 emissions as the weighted average of model specific emissions, that is,

$$\bar{x}^t = \sum_{m=1}^{M^t} w_m^t x_m^t / N^t \qquad (15)$$

where w_m^t is the number of new cars that belong to car model m in cohort t. Note that the average curb weight and engine power of cohort t can be calculated likewise.

The use of a RC implies identical shadow prices across car models in a cohort, which is consistent with the perspective of regulators. Given the RC of each cohort t, we can define an input-oriented Malmquist-type index for passenger cars, as shown below:

$$MC(t, t+1) = \left(\frac{D^t(\bar{x}^{t+1}, \bar{\mathbf{y}}^{t+1})}{D^t(\bar{x}^t, \bar{\mathbf{y}}^t)} \times \frac{D^{t+1}(\bar{x}^{t+1}, \bar{\mathbf{y}}^{t+1})}{D^{t+1}(\bar{x}^t, \bar{\mathbf{y}}^t)} \right)^{1/2} \qquad (16)$$

where $D^t(\bar{x}^t, \bar{\mathbf{y}}^t)$ measures the distance of the RC of cohort t relative to the CNLS frontier of cohort t, $D^t(\bar{x}^{t+1}, \bar{\mathbf{y}}^{t+1})$ measures the distance of the RC of cohort $t + 1$ relative to the CNLS frontier of cohort t, and so forth. It is said that there is environmental productivity growth in new passenger cars from cohort t to $t + 1$ if the value of $MC(t, t + 1)$ is greater than unity, and environmental productivity decline if the value is less than unity.

The four distance measures in Eq. 16 are calculated as

$$
\begin{aligned}
D^t(\bar{x}^t, \bar{\mathbf{y}}^t) &= \frac{\max\left\langle \alpha_m^t + \left(\boldsymbol{\beta}_m^t\right)' \bar{\mathbf{y}}^t \right\rangle}{\bar{x}^t} \\[2ex]
D^t\left(\bar{x}^{t+1}, \bar{\mathbf{y}}^{t+1}\right) &= \frac{\max\left\langle \alpha_m^t + \left(\boldsymbol{\beta}_m^t\right)' \bar{\mathbf{y}}^{t+1} \right\rangle}{\bar{x}^{t+1}} \\[2ex]
D^{t+1}(\bar{x}^t, \bar{\mathbf{y}}^t) &= \frac{\max\left\langle \alpha_m^{t+1} + \left(\boldsymbol{\beta}_m^{t+1}\right)' \bar{\mathbf{y}}^t \right\rangle}{\bar{x}^t} \\[2ex]
D^{t+1}\left(\bar{x}^{t+1}, \bar{\mathbf{y}}^{t+1}\right) &= \frac{\max\left\langle \alpha_m^{t+1} + \left(\boldsymbol{\beta}_m^{t+1}\right)' \bar{\mathbf{y}}^{t+1} \right\rangle}{\bar{x}^{t+1}}
\end{aligned}
\qquad (17)
$$

where $\max\langle\cdot\rangle$ is designed to obtain the reference point on the CNLS frontier of cohort t or $t + 1$ for a given RC, in accordance with the third constraint in Eq. 12.

In a conventional way, we can decompose $MC(t, t + 1)$ into two components representing the effects of technical change and efficiency change:

$$MC(t, t+1) = MCTC(t, t+1) \times MCEC(t, t+1)$$

$$MCTC(t, t+1) = \left(\frac{D^t(\bar{x}^t, \bar{y}^t)}{D^{t+1}(\bar{x}^t, \bar{y}^t)} \times \frac{D^t(\bar{x}^{t+1}, \bar{y}^{t+1})}{D^{t+1}(\bar{x}^{t+1}, \bar{y}^{t+1})} \right)^{1/2} \quad (18)$$

$$MCEC(t, t+1) = \frac{D^{t+1}(\bar{x}^{t+1}, \bar{y}^{t+1})}{D^t(\bar{x}^t, \bar{y}^t)}$$

Unlike in conventional Malmquist indices, the two components in the current context can be interpreted as follows:

- The technical change component $MCTC(t, t + 1)$ accounts for the shift in the CNLS frontier made up by models of new cars. Technical progress, i.e., $MCTC$ $(t, t + 1) > 1$, indicates that models of new cars in cohort $t + 1$ become overall more environmentally efficient than those in cohort t, and technical regress, i.e., $MCTC(t, t + 1) < 1$ indicates that models of new cars become overall less environmentally efficient. Note that this component depends on the car industry, which is regulated by the government through supply-side measures (recall the second particular feature of consumer durables discussed in Sect. 2).
- If the value of $MCEC(t, t + 1)$ is greater (or less) than unity, it shows that the environmental efficiency of cohort $t + 1$ improves (or deteriorates) compared to cohort t. The environmental efficiency of a cohort depends on the composition of its RC, that is, the popularity of environmentally efficient car models (or the proportion of environmentally efficient new cars). Therefore, efficiency improvement from cohort t to $t + 1$ can be interpreted that the popularity of environmentally efficient car models rises from year t to $t + 1$. Note that this component captures changes in consumer behavior, whether due to changes in consumer preferences or incentives set by the government (e.g., changes in tax policy).

Finally, it is worth noting that the Malmquist-type index constructed in terms of passenger cars can be readily extended to other consumer durables.

5 Empirical Case: New Passenger Cars in Finland

In this section, we apply the proposed Malmquist-type index for passenger cars to a unique Finnish data set that covers all vehicles in road traffic in Finland in 2015. The purpose is to demonstrate the interpretation of the proposed index through investigating the environmental productivity change in new, gasoline-fueled passenger cars registered in Finland from 2002 to 2014 and the driving forces behind the change.

Table 3 presents the descriptive statistics of the input and output variables for the cohorts of new gasoline cars. Each observation in a cohort is a subset of identical cars (in terms of CO_2 emissions, curb weight, and engine power), i.e., a car model. Note that the descriptive statistics are model-specific, and the model-specific weighted average CO_2 emissions, curb weight, and engine power constitute the RC of each cohort (see Eq. 15 for reference). As shown in the table, there was a clear decline in both the average and the weighted average CO_2 emissions over the years 2002–2014, whereas neither the curb weight nor the engine power saw such a decline. Further, the weighted average input and output variables were always lower than the arithmetic averages during the years.

Table 4 reports the empirical results for the cohorts of new gasoline cars, including the estimates of the Malmquist-type index (*MC*) and the two components, namely technical change (*MCTC*) and efficiency change (*MCEC*). In order to gain intuition, we have subtracted unity from the estimates, thereby expressing them in the form of percentage change (Färe et al. 1994). As can be seen in the table, all the estimates of *MC* and *MCTC* were positive, while *MCEC* had both positive and negative estimates. Overall, the environmental productivity of new gasoline cars registered in Finland grew at an average of 3.22% per year from 2002 to 2014. The main driver of this growth was the technical progress that occurred in models of new gasoline cars, which had an average annual growth rate of 3.08% over the years. In the meantime, however, the annual rate of efficiency change averaged 0.14%, quite close to zero, that is, the popularity of environmentally efficient car models overall remained unchanged.

Table 4 Empirical results for the cohorts of new gasoline cars in Finland; 2002–2014

Period	Environmental productivity change (%)	Technical change (%)	Efficiency change (%)
2002–2003	1.42	1.32	0.10
2003–2004	0.57	1.61	−1.02
2004–2005	1.54	1.50	0.03
2005–2006	1.31	1.48	−0.17
2006–2007	2.26	3.15	−0.86
2007–2008	4.71	2.67	1.99
2008–2009	6.53	3.63	2.80
2009–2010	3.87	4.51	−0.61
2010–2011	4.49	5.64	−1.09
2011–2012	3.91	4.47	−0.53
2012–2013	5.77	4.90	0.84
2013–2014	2.27	2.05	0.22
Mean	3.22	3.08	0.14

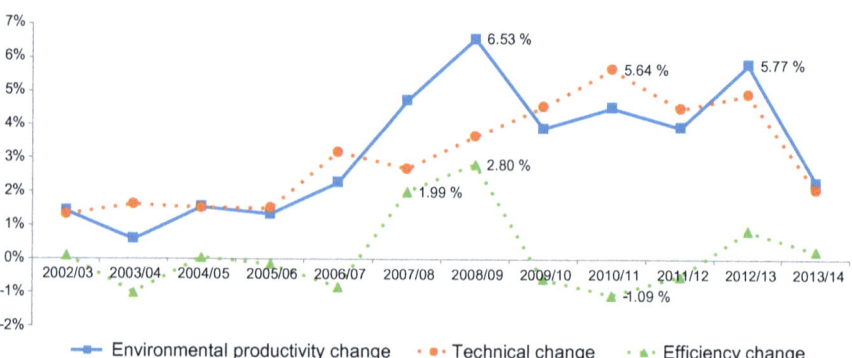

Fig. 5 Environmental productivity change, technical change, and efficiency change in the cohorts of new gasoline cars in Finland; 2002–2014

Figure 5 depicts the trends in *MC*, *MCTC*, and *MCEC* from 2002 to 2014. Technical progress developed at relatively low rates during the first four periods (2002–2003, 2003–2004, 2004–2005, and 2005–2006), and after this it entered a stage of rapid growth. At that stage, technical progress accelerated steadily until it reached a peak growth rate of 5.64% in the period 2010–2011; but after the peak, technical progress declined to reach a low point in the last period (2013–2014). In a different manner, *MCEC* basically fluctuated at zero with small ranges, except the periods 2007–2008 and 2008–2009 when there were remarkable efficiency improvements of 1.99% and 2.80%, respectively. Finally, environmental productivity growth, not surprisingly, evolved in almost the same way as its major driver, technical progress, but was clearly boosted or hindered by the efficiency change component during certain periods.

In summary, 95.7% (3.08/3.22) of the environmental productivity growth in new gasoline cars from 2002 to 2014 should be attributed to the technical progress that occurred in models of new cars—car models provided by the car industry became more environmentally efficient over the years. On the other hand, Finnish car consumers contributed, on average, almost zero to the environmental productivity growth. But this does not mean that consumer behavior can only play a minor role, in fact, it has great potential of pushing the environmental productivity growth up to a higher level. For instance, Finland introduced a CO_2 emissions based vehicle tax in 2008,[16] and around that year, the popularity of environmentally efficient car models increased dramatically. From the perspective of regulators, in order to continue improving the environmental productivity of new passenger cars, they should not only encourage car manufacturers to intensify their efforts in green technological innovations but also stimulate consumers to purchase environmentally efficient passenger cars.

---

[16]See https://www.trafi.fi/en/road/taxation/vehicle_tax/structure_and_amount_of_tax   for   more information.

6 Concluding Remarks

In this chapter, we have constructed an input-oriented Malmquist-type index specially for consumer durables (passenger cars in particular). This index is capable of measuring and decomposing environmental productivity change in new consumer durables. The empirical strategy proposed and the methodology used in this chapter have the following key advantages:

1. The particular features of consumer durables are explicitly taken into account and incorporated into the existing productivity analysis framework. Specifically, our specification of the polluting technology for passenger cars considers CO_2 emissions as the input and transportation services as the outputs, thereby breaking the direct proportionality between fuel consumption and CO_2 emissions. The aggregation of passenger cars into their respective models and the use of a representative car make it possible to compute the Malmquist-type index based on large-sized and unbalanced panel data.

2. The CNLS approach proposed by Kuosmanen (2008) is used to estimate the polluting technology. This approach is capable of dealing with stochastic noise without pre-specifying any functional form and of handling data sets with thousands of observations by running the penalized algorithm developed by Keshvari (2017).

3. This study is of interest to regulators as new consumer durables are subject to increasingly stringent environmental regulations. The exclusion of car price from the polluting technology specification and the idea of using a representative car (which implies a unified set of shadow prices) are consistent with the perspective of regulators.

In order to illustrate the interpretation of the proposed index, we have applied it to investigate the environmental productivity change in new gasoline cars in Finland from 2002 to 2014. The empirical study has found that the environmental productivity of new gasoline cars in Finland grew at an average rate of 3.22% per year between 2002 and 2014. Over 95% of the growth was due to the technical progress that occurred in models of new gasoline cars over the years. Although the contribution of Finnish car consumers to the growth was, on average, negligible, they played an important role around 2008 when Finland introduced a CO_2 emissions based vehicle tax.

As regards future research, it would be interesting to investigate environmental productivity growth in other kinds of new cars and other new consumer durables given data availability. It might also be possible to use more hypothetical consumer durables in a cohort (representing, e.g., brands, regions, etc.). In addition, estimation techniques other than the CNLS approach and more productivity indices can be applied to this emerging study of consumer durables.

The reader should bear in mind that this study is based on type-approval data, which might be subject to test manipulation [e.g., the Volkswagen scandal (Blackwelder et al. 2016)]. Another limitation is that we did not discuss the returns to scale property of the polluting technology. We defer this to future work.

Acknowledgements The author is indebted to Timo Kuosmanen for his valuable guidance, advice, and comments, which greatly improved the presentation of this chapter. I am also grateful to Knox Lovell for his constructive comments and suggestions; to Ruizhi Pang, Xuejie Bai, and Knox Lovell for the nice invitation to contribute to this edited volume; to Abolfazl Keshvari for his kind assistance in computation; and to the participants at the 2016 Asia-Pacific Productivity Conference and the 7th Helsinki Workshop on Efficiency and Productivity Analysis for helpful suggestions. This research was financially supported by the Sustainable Transitions of European Energy Markets (STEEM) project and the Foundation for Economic Education (LSR) (no. 160358). The trip to the 2016 Asia-Pacific Productivity Conference was financially supported by the HSE Foundation (no. 4-759). These financial supports are greatly acknowledged. Of course, the usual disclaimers apply.

References

Aigner D, Lovell CK, Schmidt P (1977) Formulation and estimation of stochastic frontier production function models. Journal of Econometrics 6(1):21–37.

Aigner DJ, Chu SF (1968) On estimating the industry production function. The American Economic Review 58(4):826–839.

Alvarez R, Weilenmann M (2012) Effect of low ambient temperature on fuel consumption and pollutant and CO_2 emissions of hybrid electric vehicles in real-world conditions. Fuel 97:119–124.

André M, Joumard R, Vidon R, Tassel P, Perret P (2006) Real-world European driving cycles, for measuring pollutant emissions from high- and low-powered cars. Atmospheric Environment 40(31):5944–5953.

Aparicio J, Barbero J, Kapelko M, Pastor JT, Zofío JL (2017) Testing the consistency and feasibility of the standard Malmquist-Luenberger index: Environmental productivity in world air emissions. Journal of Environmental Management 196:148–160.

Arabi B, Munisamy S, Emrouznejad A, Shadman F (2014) Power industry restructuring and eco-efficiency changes: A new slacks-based model in Malmquist–Luenberger index measurement. Energy Policy 68:132–145.

Arabi B, Doraisamy SM, Emrouznejad A, Khoshroo A (2017) Eco-efficiency measurement and material balance principle: An application in power plants Malmquist Luenberger index. Annals of Operations Research 255(1–2):221–239.

Berndt ER (1990) Energy use, technical progress and productivity growth: A survey of economic issues. Journal of Productivity Analysis 2(1):67–83.

Blackwelder B, Coleman K, Colunga-Santoyo S, Harrison JS, Wozniak D (2016) The Volkswagen Scandal. URL http://scholarship.richmond.edu/robins-case-network/17/.

Caves DW, Christensen LR, Diewert WE (1982) The economic theory of index numbers and the measurement of input, output, and productivity. Econometrica: Journal of the Econometric Society pp 1393–1414.

Chang TP, Hu JL (2010) Total-factor energy productivity growth, technical progress, and efficiency change: An empirical study of China. Applied Energy 87(10):3262–3270.

Charnes A, Cooper WW, Rhodes E (1978) Measuring the efficiency of decision making units. European Journal of Operational Research 2(6):429–444.

Chung YH, Färe R, Grosskopf S (1997) Productivity and undesirable outputs: A directional distance function approach. Journal of Environmental Management 51(3):229–240.

Coelli T, Lauwers L, Van Huylenbroeck G (2007) Environmental efficiency measurement and the materials balance condition. Journal of Productivity Analysis 28(1–2):3–12.

Dings J (2013) Mind the Gap! Why official car fuel economy figures don't match up to reality. Tech. rep., URL https://www.transportenvironment.org/publications/mind-gap-why-official-car-fuel-economy-figures-donE28099t-match-reality.

Du J, Chen Y, Huang Y (2017) A Modified Malmquist-Luenberger Productivity Index: Assessing Environmental Productivity Performance in China. European Journal of Operational Research.

Emrouznejad A, Yang Gl (2016) CO_2 emissions reduction of Chinese light manufacturing industries: A novel RAM-based global Malmquist–Luenberger productivity index. Energy Policy 96:397–410.

European Parliament, the Council (2009) Regulation (EC) No 443/2009 of the European Parliament and the Council of 23 April 2009 setting emission performance standards for new passenger cars as part of the Community's integrated approach to reduce CO_2 emissions from light-duty vehicles. Url http://eur-lex.europa.eu/LexUriServ/LexUriServ.do?uri=OJ:L:2009: 140:0001:0015:EN:PDF.

Färe R, Grosskopf S (2000) Theory and application of directional distance functions. Journal of Productivity Analysis 13(2):93–103.

Färe R, Grosskopf S (2006) New directions: Efficiency and productivity, vol 3. Springer Science & Business Media.

Färe R, Primont D (1995) Multi-output production and duality: Theory and applications. Kluwer Academic Publishers, Boston.

Färe R, Grosskopf S, Lovell CK, Pasurka C (1989) Multilateral productivity comparisons when some outputs are undesirable: A nonparametric approach. The Review of Economics and Statistics pp 90–98.

Färe R, Grosskopf S, Norris M, Zhang Z (1994) Productivity growth, technical progress, and efficiency change in industrialized countries. The American Economic Review pp 66–83.

Färe R, Grosskopf S, Norris M (1997) Productivity growth, technical progress, and efficiency change in industrialized countries: Reply. The American Economic Review pp 1040–1044.

Färe R, Grosskopf S, Hernandez-Sancho F (2004) Environmental performance: An index number approach. Resource and Energy economics 26(4):343–352.

Färe R, Grosskopf S, Noh DW, Weber W (2005) Characteristics of a polluting technology: Theory and practice. Journal of Econometrics 126(2):469–492.

Førsund FR (2008) Good modelling of bad outputs: Pollution and multiple- output production. Tech. rep., Memorandum//Department of Economics, University of Oslo.

Hailu A, Veeman TS (2000) Environmentally sensitive productivity analysis of the Canadian pulp and paper industry, 1959–1994: An input distance function approach. Journal of Environmental Economics and Management 40(3):251–274.

He F, Zhang Q, Lei J, Fu W, Xu X (2013) Energy efficiency and productivity change of China's iron and steel industry: Accounting for undesirable outputs. Energy Policy 54:204–213.

Kaya Y, Yokobori K (1998) Environment, energy and economy: Strategies for sustainability. Tech. rep., Aspen Inst., Washington, DC (United States); Brookings Institution, Washington, DC (United States).

Keshvari A (2017) A penalized method for multivariate concave least squares with application to productivity analysis. European Journal of Operational Research 257(3):1016–1029.

Kortelainen M, Kuosmanen T (2007) Eco-efficiency analysis of consumer durables using absolute shadow prices. Journal of Productivity Analysis 28(1–2):57–69.

Kuosmanen T (2008) Representation theorem for convex nonparametric least squares. The Econometrics Journal 11(2):308–325.

Kuosmanen T (2012) Stochastic semi-nonparametric frontier estimation of electricity distribution networks: Application of the StoNED method in the Finnish regulatory model. Energy Economics 34(6):2189–2199.

Kuosmanen T (2013) Green productivity in agriculture: A critical synthesis. Tech. rep., Report prepared for the OECD Joint Working Party on Agriculture and the Environment.

Kuosmanen T, Kortelainen M (2012) Stochastic non-smooth envelopment of data: Semi-parametric frontier estimation subject to shape constraints. Journal of Productivity Analysis 38(1):11–28.

Kuosmanen T, Johnson A, Saastamoinen A (2015) Stochastic nonparametric approach to efficiency analysis: A unified framework. In: Data Envelopment Analysis, Springer, pp 191–244.

Lin B, Fei R (2015) Regional differences of CO_2 emissions performance in Chinas agricultural sector: A Malmquist index approach. European Journal of Agronomy 70:33–40.

Liu X, Zhou D, Zhou P, Wang Q (2017) Dynamic carbon emission performance of Chinese airlines: A global Malmquist index analysis. Journal of Air Transport Management 65:99–109.

Lovell CK (2003) The decomposition of Malmquist productivity indexes. Journal of Productivity Analysis 20(3):437–458.

Meeusen W, Van den Broeck J (1977) Efficiency estimation from Cobb- Douglas production functions with composed error. International Economic Review pp 435–444.

Meng M, Niu D (2012) Three-dimensional decomposition models for carbon productivity. Energy 46(1):179–187.

Ministry of Industry and Information Technology of the People's Republic of China (2015) Explanatory notes regarding fuel consumption limits for passenger cars (in Chinese). Url http://chinaafc.miit.gov.cn/n2257/n2260/c97720/content.html.

Nishimizu M, Page JM (1982) Total factor productivity growth, technological progress and technical efficiency change: Dimensions of productivity change in Yugoslavia, 1965–78. The Economic Journal 92(368):920–936.

OECD (2011) Towards green growth: Monitoring progress. OECD, Paris.

Ray SC, Desli E (1997) Productivity growth, technical progress, and efficiency change in industrialized countries: Comment. The American Economic Review 87(5):1033–1039.

Rødseth KL (2016) Environmental efficiency measurement and the materials balance condition reconsidered. European Journal of Operational Research 250(1):342–346.

Rødseth KL (2017) Axioms of a polluting technology: A materials balance approach. Environmental and Resource Economics 67(1):1–22.

Shao Y, Wang S (2016) Productivity growth and environmental efficiency of the nonferrous metals industry: An empirical study of China. Journal of Cleaner Production 137:1663–1671.

Shen Z, Boussemart JP, Leleu H (2017) Aggregate green productivity growth in OECDs countries. International Journal of Production Economics 189:30–39.

Shepard RW (1953) Cost and production functions. Princeton University Press, Princeton.

Shepherd RW (1970) Theory of cost and production functions. Princeton University Press, Princeton.

Song M, Zheng W, Wang S (2017) Measuring green technology progress in large-scale thermoelectric enterprises based on Malmquist–Luenberger life cycle assessment. Resources, Conservation and Recycling 122:261–269.

Sueyoshi T, Goto M, Wang D (2017) Malmquist index measurement for sustainability enhancement in Chinese municipalities and provinces. Energy Economics 67:554–571.

Vehicle Certification Agency of the United Kingdom Department for Transport (2016) Explanatory notes regarding CO_2, fuel consumption testing and more. Url http://www.dft.gov.uk/vca/fcb/new-car-fuel-consump.asp.

Yang Z, Bandivadekar A (2017) 2017 Global update: Light-duty vehicle green- house gas and fuel economy standards. Tech. rep., International Council on Clean Transportation.

Yang Z, Mock P, German J, Bandivadekar A, Lah O (2017) On a pathway to de-carbonization—A comparison of new passenger car CO_2 emission standards and taxation measures in the G20 countries. Transportation Research Part D: Transport and Environment.

Yao X, Guo C, Shao S, Jiang Z (2016) Total-factor CO_2 emission performance of China's provincial industrial sector: A meta-frontier non-radial Malmquist index approach. Applied Energy 184:1142–1153.

Yu C, Shi L, Wang Y, Chang Y, Cheng B (2016) The eco-efficiency of pulp and paper industry in China: An assessment based on slacks-based measure and Malmquist–Luenberger index. Journal of Cleaner Production 127:511–521.

Yu Y, Choi Y, Wei X, Chen Z (2017a) Did China's regional transport industry enjoy better carbon productivity under regulations? Journal of Cleaner Production 165:777–787.

Yu Y, Qian T, Du L (2017b) Carbon productivity growth, technological innovation, and technology gap change of coal-fired power plants in China. Energy Policy 109:479–487.

Zhang C, Liu H, Bressers HTA, Buchanan KS (2011) Productivity growth and environmental regulations-accounting for undesirable outputs: Analysis of china's thirty provincial regions using the Malmquist–Luenberger index. Ecological Economics 70(12):2369–2379.

Zhang N, Choi Y (2013) Total-factor carbon emission performance of fossil fuel power plants in China: A metafrontier non-radial Malmquist index analysis. Energy Economics 40:549–559.

Zhang N, Zhou P, Kung CC (2015) Total-factor carbon emission performance of the Chinese transportation industry: A bootstrapped non-radial Malmquist index analysis. Renewable and Sustainable Energy Reviews 41:584–593.

Zhang S, Wu Y, Liu H, Huang R, Un P, Zhou Y, Fu L, Hao J (2014) Real-world fuel consumption and CO_2 (carbon dioxide) emissions by driving conditions for light-duty passenger vehicles in China. Energy 69:247–257.

Zhou P, Ang B, Han J (2010) Total factor carbon emission performance: A Malmquist index analysis. Energy Economics 32(1):194–201.

Part II
Studies in Energy and Environment

Chapter 5
Revisiting Reasons for Ten Years of Power Shortages in China

Hui-Xian Wang, Hong-Zhou Li, Tao Zou and Yuki Tamai

1 Introduction

During the first decade of the 21st century, China experienced serious nationwide power shortage. According to Yu et al. (2008) and the 2003 to 2011 versions of *China Power Yearbook*, there were 12 provincial administrative regions that were forced to limit residential as well as non-residential electricity consumption due to shortages in power supply in 2002. The number further increased to 21 and 27 provinces in 2003 and 2004 respectively (Bai 2006). For example, in March 2003 Shanxi province artificially cut off the power supply for 10,051 times, equalling to a power shortage of 52.52 million kWh. In Changsha, a city in Hunan province, all consumers except 49 important entities (Yu et al. 2008) were without power supply for several hours every fourth day from November 2003 onwards (Wu et al. 2004). According to Bai (2006), the nationwide power shortage in 2004 amounted to 60 billion kWh. Although the central government has not released more accurate information regarding the power shortage since 2005, it has been said that at least 23 provinces suffered from this (Bai 2006) during that year. After 2005, during a two-year period, some mitigation of the power shortage was achieved, but in 2008 the power supply shortage rose again. Recently, as the aftermath of four-trillion

H.-X. Wang
School of Japanese Studies, Dalian University of Foreign Languages, Dalian, China
e-mail: huixiamw@126.com

H.-Z. Li (✉)
Center for Industrial and Business Organization, Dongbei University of Finance and Economics, Dalian, China
e-mail: lee_hongzhou@163.com

T. Zou
School of Public Management, Shandong University of Finance and Economics, Jinan, China

Y. Tamai
Faculty of Urban Management, Fukuyama City University, Fukuyama, Japan

© Springer Nature Singapore Pte Ltd. 2018
R. Pang et al. (eds.), *Energy, Environment and Transitional Green Growth in China*, https://doi.org/10.1007/978-981-10-7919-1_5

economic stimulus plan, the situation has become worse, since in 2011 shortages even happened during months when there were relatively low periods of power consumption. Because of the fundamental role of the electric power industry in economic growth, and the increasing importance of China's economy in the world market as well as global production chains, it is necessary for researchers to provide more objective and independent explanations for power shortage so that policy-makers can take measures based on academic results in order to prevent the recurrence of these in the future. The findings obtained from this study will help inform Chinese policy-makers with respect to the relationship between productivity, the coal-electricity conflict and power shortage. Further, our findings will contribute to the existing literature by bringing new knowledge about the problems faced by transitional economies when they undergo the switch from a highly centralised administrative mechanism to a market-oriented one.[1]

The discussion flow behind our study to identify the causes of or reasons for the power shortage is as follows: firstly, we examine whether there was underinvestment in installed capacity. If there was not, we estimate the efficiency levels as well as productivity change and the sources of the latter of the power generation sector. Again, if the performance levels are not low enough to confirm that low performance are the main contributor to the power shortage, we resort to existing literature and ask business leaders in the power sector for their opinion on the reasons for power supply shortages and then link their insights with our empirical results on efficiency and productivity.

Nationwide power supply shortages could result from two reasons. First, the installed capacity of power generation is too low in order to satisfy demand in certain periods of time. Second, the performance of the electric power industry is inefficient, which manifests as an inability to fully utilise the installed capacity. However, it seems that the first reason is not supported by literature with regards to China. According to Li (2010), the increase in power consumption during 2003–2009 was 68.3%, much lower than the growth of 98.3% in the installed capacity of power generation. Furthermore, the top five power generation group corporations in China have expanded their installed capacity by as much as 173% during the same period.[2] Yu et al. (2008) also report a similar relationship between the capacity and demand for electric power in China. Given that there was no power shortage before 2002 and the increase of the power capacity was bigger than that of power consumption after 2002, we exclude the first cause of the nationwide power shortage in this study. In other words, China's electric power shortage of the past ten years may be largely attributed to the low performance of power plants. In order to obtain as

---

[1]While in recent years, due to both domestic and overseas economic downturn, the demand for mass products was weakness and many enterprises suffered from overcapacity, which leaded to the decrease of operating rate in enterprises. As a result, the power supply was greater than the relatively weak demand in the recent years.

[2]The top five power generation group corporations include China Huaneng Group, China Guodian Corporation, China Datang Corporation, China Huadian Corporation and China Power Investment Corporation. They are all large state-owned electricity generation companies.

objective and accurate measures of power plant productivity as possible, taking into account the somewhat limited data accessibility and availability, this study employs two distinct production frontier-based methodologies, one a non-parametric and the other a parametric method. Given the relative advantages and disadvantages of these two methods, e.g. no need for arbitrary model specification in the case of the non-parametric method and a capability of accommodating statistical error in the case of the parametric method, empirical results from a single methodology are sometimes less convincing and reliable. As a consequence, conclusions and insights based on these kinds of results are often handled with reservation. However, if we use the same sample but with different methods, and if they lead to robustly similar results, the policy implications of the results would make more sense. From the methodological viewpoint, compared to the parametric method the non-parametric one has advantages in that it avoids arbitrary function specification and distributional assumptions imposed on error terms, though the non-parametric method is unable to deal with any statistical errors (Coelli et al. 2005). For example, any possible impacts of the 2008 snow disaster on the power generation sector in China will be treated as changes in productivity itself, in the estimation of the non-parametric method, whereas in the case of the parametric method it will be treated properly as a random disturbance. On the other hand, the arbitrary assumptions on function specification and the distribution form of error terms imposed by the parametric method make it more subjective and demanding in calculation. Finally, we inter-test the estimated efficiency levels results from these two methods. Taking all the aforementioned arguments into consideration, we decided to employ both methods in this study in order to obtain as full a picture of the efficiency and productivity levels of the power plants in China as possible.

We decided to employ Data Envelopment Analysis (hereinafter DEA) as a presentative of the non-parametric method and Stochastic Frontier Analysis (hereinafter SFA) as a presentative of the parametric method in what follows. Both are suitable in frontier-based estimation of efficiency and productivity, and further can be used to decompose productivity change. When it comes to other possible methodologies of estimating productivity change that are not used in this study, such as non-parametric Tornqvist or the Fisher index, in addition to the need for price information (which is not available for this study), neither of these are frontier-based and consequently are less comparable with the SFA method. Further, from the viewpoint of completeness of Total Factor Productivity (TFP) decomposition, the frontier-based Hicks-Moorsteen method which was first suggested by O'Donnell (2008) and can be performed by free software DPIN (O'Donnell 2010; See et al. 2015), is superior to the Malmquist productivity index.[3] However, the Hicks-Moorsteen method decomposes TFP change into technical change, pure efficiency change, scale efficiency

---

[3]When compared with Tornqvist or the Fisher index, the Hicks-Moorsteen method has no need for price information. When compared with the Malmquist productivity index, it imposes no assumption on returns to scale and firm behavior while it is capable of decomposing TFP changes into different sources. For more details on these methods, see O'Donnell (2012a) and O'Donnell (2012b).

change and mixed efficiency change. These are not, however, comparable to the results from the SFA model because it only decomposes TFP change into technical change, pure efficiency change and scale efficiency change.

The rest of the paper is structured as follows. Section 2 presents a literature review on relevant empirical studies. Section 3 depicts methodologies used in this study. Section 4 reports descriptive statistics of data and the concrete model specification. Section 5 reports the results of the efficiency and productivity estimates; the comparison between results from two methods and analysis are also conducted in this part. Finally, some concluding comments and policy insights are presented in Sect. 6.

2 Literature Review

Literature concerning performance estimation in the electric power industry can be classified into four groups: (i) technical or cost efficiency estimation; (ii) estimation on determinants of efficiency; (iii) estimation on economies of scope and/or scale and; (iv) estimation on productivity change (by means of the Malmquist productivity index or other indices) within a given period (Li et al. 2015). Considering that both Chen et al. (2015) and Li et al. (2015) provide detailed literature reviews on this topic, our study here limits the literature review to the most related and/or representative researches on the performance evaluation for the Chinese power generation sector in chronological order.

Both theoretical methodologies on efficiency estimation and their empirical applications in the power generation sector, which mainly motivated to identify the impacts of ownership (public vs. private) on the performance of power generation plants, have been carried out prosperously since the late 1950s in developed countries (See and Coelli 2012). Until recent years, China has seldom been the target of this kind of research due to the non-existence or non-disclosure of qualified data as well as ideological issues. Our research shows that Yang and Yu (1996) is the first and the most important academic research to focus on the qualitative examination on the Chinese electric power industry (Zhang and Chen 2011; Wang et al. 2012; Zhao et al. 2012). Being the first quantitative study, Lam and Shiu (2001) published their empirical research on the efficiency estimation for China's power generation sector using the Malmquist productivity index. More specifically, they regard provincial administrative regions as decision making units (hereinafter DMUs) and applied the DEA approach to measure the technical efficiency of thermal power generation plants in 30 sample regions using data from 1995 to 1996. Their results show that the average efficiency score increased from 88.8% in 1995 to 90.3% in 1996, with the lowest score of 66.1% in the sample. The paper also identifies the determinants of the efficiency using the DEA-Tobit model and finds that only the capacity factor and fuel efficiency are significant factors affecting technical efficiency. Three years later, Lam and Shiu (2004) published the second DEA-based paper on Chinese power generation which extends the estimation target from efficiency to as well efficiency as productivity using data for 1995, 1996, 1998 and 2000. Their results show that the average efficiency score decreased from 93.7% in 1995 to 91.3% in 1998, but then increased to 93.5% in 2000. The TFP growth between 1995 and 2000 was 2.1% per year on average, with the main contribution coming from the technological change in the means of technical innovation. Yang and Pollitt (2009) is another example of DEA-based empirical research on the same topic. However, this study is different from studies of Lam and Shiu (2001, 2004) in three aspects: first, DMUs in Yang and Pollitt (2009) are 221 Chinese coal-fired power plants instead of provincial administrative regions; second, data is cross-sectional rather than panel; and the last but most important aspect is that the DEA model specification utilised in the paper could incorporate undesirable outputs (pollutants jointly produced with the generation of power) as well as uncontrollable environmental variables.

SFA-based efficiency estimation studies on the Chinese electric power generation sector have not been published in mainstream academic literature until Du et al. (2013) mainly due to the data-demanding characteristic of the parametric method. Du et al. (2013) used a sample including 2093 plants, almost all the fossil-fired generation plants in China, to test the effects of electricity reforms on the productivity and efficiency of China's fossil-fired power plants. Unfortunately, although the model proposed by Battese and Coelli (1995) is used to estimate efficiency levels, the paper does not report any information on efficiency levels of the power plants, but only the determinants of them. Li et al. (2015) employ six different stochastic cost frontier models to estimate the efficiency levels using a panel data of 20 power plants listed in the Chinese securities market during 2002–2011. Their results show that the means of cost efficiency from different models range from 32% of the pooled model to 86% of the true random effects model. Based on these empirical results, they conclude that the coal-electricity pricing linkage scheme in China is a double-edged sword: it provides incentives for less-efficient power plants to increase their efficiency, but imposes a penalty to highly-efficient power plants. From the perspective of methodology, another noteworthy study is Chen et al. (2015). Besides having a relatively big sample size, this research is distinct from existing literature on Chinese electric power generation efficiency estimation in two aspects. The first aspect is that all models used in earlier studies, excluding the true random effects model in Li et al. (2015), assume that all the DMUs (either individual power plants or provincial administrative regions) share the same production frontier, which runs the risk of *confounding between technological differences and technology-specific inefficiency* (Tsionas 2002, p. 128). The random parameter model employed by Chen et al. (2015) gives up the restrictive assumption that all DMUs must share exactly the same frontier, namely the same technological possibilities. In contracts, it separates technical inefficiency from technological differences across DMUs.[4] The second aspect is

---

[4]As shown in model specifications, the true random effects model ($y_{it} = \alpha_0 + X'_{it}\beta + \alpha_i + v_{it} + u_{it}$) assumes that the shape of the frontier for all DMUs is same (shaped by $X'_{it}\beta$) but shifted upward or downward according to the value of a DUM-specific random term (α_i). By contrast, the

that all models mentioned so far are estimated either by linear programming or by the maximum likelihood method, whereas the model employed by Chen et al. (2015) is estimated by the Bayesian method. Compared with estimation techniques, such as maximum likelihood, which are based on sampling theory, the Bayesian method has several desirable virtues.[5] Results from Chen et al. (2015) show that the average efficiency score of power plants is about 0.93, with a minimum value of 0.88. Finally, with increasing attention paid to environmental protection and low-carbon development, researches which take undesirable (or bad) outputs into consideration attract more and more emphasis. Studies in this respect include Xie et al. (2012), Wu et al. (2012), Zhou et al. (2012, 2014), Wang et al. (2013) and Bi et al. (2014).

In addition to those studies published in English journals, an increasing number of studies on performance estimation for the power generation sector are also published in well-known Chinese journals. Yang and Yu (2008) estimate efficiency and productivity of a panel sample covering 28 provincial administrative regions over the 1996–2003 period using the DEA and Malmquist index techniques. Their studies indicate a high technical efficiency level, with even the minimum value being 91%. As for productivity, their findings show that productivity has increased by an average of 2.1% annually and solely due to technological progress (2.2% per year). This result is in line with the findings of Lam and Shiu (2004). Using the three-stage DEA method, Bai and Song (2009) analyse the impact of environmental regulation (restriction on the quantity of SO_2 emissions) on the efficiency of the thermal power sector in 30 provinces in 2004. Their research shows that under non-regulation, weak regulation and strong regulation scenarios, the corresponding average technical efficiency scores change from 70 to 75 and 89%, respectively. This indicates that environmental regulation may help improve the efficiency levels of the thermal power sector as a whole. Li (2009), based on panel data on listed thermal companies over the period of 2001–2007, estimates the efficiency levels of this sector and further identifies determinants of efficiency. The research shows that technical efficiency levels range from 80 to 98%, with a mean value of 87%.

In terms of research scope and variable selection, this study is much analogous to the Zhang and Xia (2011) study, which was designed to gauge technical efficiency levels of the Chinese power generation sector (including not only the thermal or fossil power generation sectors, but also nuclear power, hydroelectric power and renewable resource power, as well as solar power generation) and identify determinants of efficiency. Using the translog production stochastic frontier model proposed by Battese and Coelli (1995), with a data set covering 30 provincial administrative regions over the period of 2003–2009, their research selects capital (installed capacity) and labour as two inputs. Results from this study show that the

---

random parameter model ($y_{it} = \alpha_0 + X'_{it}\beta_i + \alpha_i + v_{it} + u_{it}$) assumes that the shape of the frontier of individual DMUs may be different (shaped by $X'_{it}\beta_i$) if $\beta_i \neq \beta$.

[5]Including: (i) exact inference on efficiencies even in the case of a small sample (Griffin et al. 2007, p. 163; Jondrow et al. 1982, p. 235); (ii) easy incorporation of prior ideas and restrictions such as regularity conditions; and (iii) formal and easy treatment with model uncertainty.

technical efficiency levels of the whole power generation sector are relatively low, ranging from 37 to 53%, with an average value of 47%. Li and Zou (2012), which use data on 27 provincial administrative regions covering the 2000–2009 period, select the same model and variables as Zhang and Xia (2011). Their results show that sample selection does affect empirical findings since technical efficiency levels estimated from Li and Zou (2012) are between 65 and 79%, with a mean of 72%, much higher than those from Zhang and Xia (2011).

3 Methodology on Decomposition of Productivity Change

Since efficiency scores of individual DMUs can be obtained simultaneously in the process of estimation and decomposition of productivity change, we here focus our methodology description on problems concerning productivity instead of efficiency.

3.1 Non-parametric Approach of Decomposing Productivity Change

In this study, non-parametric approach refers to the Malmquist productivity change index, which was first proposed and applied in empirical context by Färe et al. (1994), who incorporated ideas of efficiency measurement from Farrell (1957) and productivity measurement from Caves et al. (1982). In his pioneering article, "The Measurement of Productive Efficiency," Farrell introduced a framework for the measurement of efficiency which can be decomposed into two subcomponents: allocative and technical efficiency. Caves et al. (1982) build their Malmquist productivity index on the base of distance function, which was put forward by Shephard (1953) and Malmquist (1953). To avoid an arbitrary choice of benchmarking technology, Färe et al. (1989) specified the output-based Malmquist productivity change index as the geometric mean of two Caves et al. (1982)-type or CCD-type Malmquist productivity indices. Further, motivated by Nishimizu and Page (1982), who firstly used a parametric approach to decompose the productivity change into technical change and efficiency change, Färe et al. (1992) decomposed, using a non-parametric method, productivity change as follows:

$$M_{FGLR}^O(x_{t+1}, y_{t+1}, x_t, y_t) = \frac{D_0^{t+1}(x_{t+1}, y_{t+1})}{D_0^t(x_t, y_t)}$$
$$\times \left[\left(\frac{D_0^t(x_{t+1}, y_{t+1})}{D_0^{t+1}(x_{t+1}, y_{t+1})}\right)\left(\frac{D_0^t(x_t, y_t)}{D_0^{t+1}(x_t, y_t)}\right)\right]^{1/2} \quad (1)$$

The first term on the right-hand side of Eq. (1) is used to measure the change in technical efficiency, i.e. the change in how far the observed outputs are from the frontier between periods t and $t + 1$, while the geometric mean of the two ratios inside the brackets captures the shift in technology (i.e. the change of the maximum potential outputs given the inputs) between the two periods. By decomposing the Malmquist productivity change index into two subcomponents, Färe et al. (1992) demonstrate that the productivity change could originate from two sources, i.e., from catching up the frontier (technical efficiency change) and from the innovation (technology progress). This is a vital extension to Caves et al. (1982) who deemed the innovation as the sole source of productivity changes and ignored the existence of technical inefficiency. However, Färe et al. (1992) decompose productivity changes on the condition of returns to scale assumption. To release from this assumption, in Färe et al. (1994) the technical efficiency change component in Eq. (1) is further decomposed into pure efficiency change and scale efficiency change. Consequently the Malmquist productivity change index can eventually be written as:

$$M_{FGLR}^{O}(x_{t+1}, y_{t+1}, x_t, y_t) = \frac{D_{0,v}^{t+1}(x_{t+1}, y_{t+1})}{D_{0,v}^{t}(x_t, y_t)} \times \left[\frac{D_{0,v}^{t}(x_t, y_t)}{D_{0,c}^{t}(x_t, y_t)} \middle/ \frac{D_{0,v}^{t+1}(x_{t+1}, y_{t+1})}{D_{0,c}^{t+1}(x_{t+1}, y_{t+1})}\right]$$
$$\times \left[\left(\frac{D_{0,c}^{t}(x_{t+1}, y_{t+1})}{D_{0,c}^{t+1}(x_{t+1}, y_{t+1})}\right)\left(\frac{D_{0,c}^{t}(x_t, y_t)}{D_{0,c}^{t+1}(x_t, y_t)}\right)\right]^{1/2}$$

(2)

where the first term on the right-hand side stands for pure efficiency change (hereinafter PEC), the second term represents scale efficiency change (hereinafter SEC) and the last term captures technical change (hereinafter TC).

To sum up, total productivity factor (hereinafter TFP) change can be defined as a product of pure efficiency change, scale efficiency change and technical change, representing the evidence of catching up, scale fitness and innovation, respectively.

3.2 Non-parametric Approach of Calculating Productivity Change

The output-oriented distance function is the reciprocal of the value of the output-oriented technical efficiency defined by Farrell (1957), namely:

$$D_0^t(x_{kt}, y_{kt}) = [F_o^t(x_{kt}, y_{kt})]^{-1}$$

(3)

where $F_o^t(x_{kt}, y_{kt})$ denotes the output-oriented Farrell efficiency measure that captures the maximum possible expansion of output y for firm k at time t. Suppose there are $k = 1, \ldots, K$ number of firms which produce $m = 1, \ldots, M$ kinds of products, employing $n = 1, \ldots, N$ types of inputs, at each period t, where $t = 1, \ldots, T$. Under such assumptions, $F_o^t(x_{kt}, y_{kt})$ can be calculated by linear programming as follows:

$$F_o^t(x_{kt}, y_{kt}) = max\delta$$

Subject to

$$\delta y_{m,kt} \leq \sum_{k=1}^{k} z_{kt} y_{m,kt}$$

$$x_{n,kt} \geq \sum_{k=1}^{k} z_{kt} x_{n,kt} \tag{4}$$

$$z_{kt} \geq 0$$

Making use of Eq. (3) and (4), the six distance functions in Eq. (2) can be calculated and the value of productivity change can be obtained. In addition, to measure changes in scale efficiency, we can calculate Eq. (4) under variable returns to scale by adding the constraint $\sum_{k=1}^{k} zkt = 1$. The scale efficiency in period t is then calculated as the ratio of the distance function under various returns to scale (hereinafter VRS) to the distance function under constant returns to scale (hereinafter CRS). Consequently the scale efficiency changes are obtained as the ratio of scale efficiencies at periods t and $t + 1$.

3.3 Parametric Approach of Decomposing Productivity Change in the Case of Production Function

Needless to say, Solow (1957) lays the foundation for calculating productivity change using the econometric method. However, from the viewpoint of components of productivity change, Solow's measurement of productivity change is just technical change under assumptions of constant returns to scale and full technical efficiency (i.e. assuming technical efficiency equals one). By mitigating assumptions regarding constant returns to scales imposed on technology, Denny et al. (1981) decompose productivity change into technical change and scale efficiency change. Furthermore, under constant returns to scale assumption and production frontier framework, Nishimizu and Page (1982) decompose productivity change into technical efficiency change and technical change. Finally, Kumbhakar et al. (2000) succeed in decomposing productivity change into technical efficiency change, technical change and scale effects and illustrate, with panel data sets, the developed theoretical framework in the case of production function, cost function and profit function, respectively.

Suppose that a stochastic frontier production function can be expressed as:

$$y_{it} = f(x_{it}', t; \beta) \exp(v_{it}) \exp(-u_{it}) \tag{5}$$

where y_{it} denotes the output of the ith firm ($i = 1, ..., N$) in period t ($t = 1, ..., T$), $f(\cdot)$represents the production technology, x_{it} stands for the vector of input variables, t is the time trend and v_{it} is the error term. u_{it} captures non-negative time-varying inefficiency, i.e. measuring the proportion by which actual y_{it} falls short of maximum possible output ($f(x_{it}', t; \beta) \exp(v_{it})$, known as stochastic frontier output). Technical efficiency is then calculated by $y_{it}/f(x_{it}', t; \beta) \exp(v_{it}) = \exp(-u_{it}) \leq 1$. Incorporating time trend into the production function enables the existence of exogenous technical change, which could shift the production frontier. By taking log and then derivative of production frontier with respect to time t, the rate of exogenous technical change (hereinafter, TC) could be measured.

Since inefficiency term u_{it} is assumed to be time varying, the overall productivity change is also affected by the change in technical efficiency among different periods with given input quantities (Kumbhakar and Lovell 1999). In order to measure this change, we take log derivative of Eq. (5) with respect to time, and then obtain the following formulation.

$$\frac{\ln(y_{it})}{\partial t} = TC_{it} + (-\frac{\partial u_{it}}{\partial t}) \tag{6}$$

where $(-\frac{\partial u_{it}}{\partial t})$ represents technical efficiency change, either negative or positive. Productivity change defined in Eq. (6) assumes input quantities unchanged. If, however, input quantities are also changeable, TFP change (hereinafter, TFPC) can be defined as[6]:

$$T\dot{F}P = \dot{y} - \sum_j \frac{w_j x_j}{\sum_j w_j x_j} \dot{x}_j = \dot{y} - \sum_j S_j^a \dot{x}_j \tag{7.1}$$

where w_j denotes the price of input x_j.

Differentiating Eq. (5) provides:

$$\dot{y} = \frac{\partial \ln y}{\partial t} = \frac{\partial \ln f(x', t; \beta)}{\partial t} + \sum_j \frac{\partial \ln f(x', t; \beta)}{\partial \ln x_j}$$

$$\times \frac{\partial \ln x_j}{\partial x_j} \times \frac{dx_j}{dt} - \frac{\partial u}{\partial t} \tag{7.2}$$

$$= \frac{\partial \ln f(x', t; \beta)}{\partial t} + \sum_j \varepsilon_j \dot{x}_j - \frac{\partial u}{\partial t}$$

where $\sum_j \varepsilon_j = \sum_j \frac{\partial \ln y}{\partial \ln x_j}$ is the measure of returns to scale and ε_j is the jth input elasticity defined at the production frontier, $f(x_{it}', t; \beta) \exp(v_{it})$. Making use of

---

[6]Subscripts i and t are omitted to avoid notational clutter.

formulation (7.1) and (7.2), we finally get the equation proposed by Kumbhakar et al. (2000).

$$
\begin{aligned}
T\dot{F}P &= \frac{\partial \ln f(x', t; \beta)}{\partial t} - \frac{\partial u}{\partial t} + \left(\sum_j \varepsilon_j - 1\right) \sum_j \lambda_j \dot{x} + \sum_j (\lambda_j - S_j^a) \dot{x} \\
&= TC + TEC + \left(\sum_j \varepsilon_j - 1\right) \sum_j \lambda_j \dot{x} + \sum_j (\lambda_j - S_j^a) \dot{x}
\end{aligned}
\tag{8}
$$

where $\lambda_j = \varepsilon_j / \sum_j \varepsilon_j$. In Eq. (8), TFP change is decomposed into four parts: the rate of technical change, the rate of technical efficiency change, the rate of scale economy change and the rate of allocative efficiency change.

3.4 Parametric Approach of Calculating Productivity Change

For estimating and decomposing productivity change, a combination between production function or cost function, or profit function and Cobb-Douglass, or translog functional form is necessary. In the case of translog form production function, which will be used in this paper, productivity can be estimated using the following specification:

$$
\begin{aligned}
\ln Y_{it} &= \beta_0 + \sum_{n=1}^{K} \beta_n \ln \mathrm{x}_{n,it} + \frac{1}{2} \sum_{n=1}^{K} \sum_{m=1}^{K} \beta_{mn} \ln \mathrm{x}_{n,it} \ln \mathrm{x}_{m,it} \\
&\quad + \sum_{i=1}^{K} \beta_{nt} \ln \mathrm{x}_{n,it} t + \frac{1}{2} \beta_{tt} t^2 + \beta_t t + V_{it} - U_{it}
\end{aligned}
\tag{9}
$$

Using Eq. (6)–(8), we get the formula to calculate subcomponents of TFP change for ith DMU between t and $t - 1$ period, this is:

$$
TC_{it} = \frac{\partial \ln y_{it}}{\partial t} = \sum_{i=1}^{K} \beta_{it} \ln \mathrm{x}_{n,it} + \frac{1}{2} \beta_{tt} t + \beta_t \text{ with } t = 2, \ldots T
\tag{10.1}
$$

However, given that the technology change in non-parametric methodology is calculated as geometric mean of technology change between t and $t - 1$ periods (see Eq. (2)), to maintain comparability between two methods, we follow the definition used in Coelli et al. (2003, p. 33), namely:

$$
TC_{it} = \frac{1}{2}(TC_{it} + TC_{it-1}) \text{ with } t = 2, \ldots T
\tag{10.2}
$$

Technical efficiency change in two periods can be calculated as:

$$TEC_{it} = -\frac{(u_{it} - u_{it-1})}{t - (t - 1)} = u_{it-1} - u_{it} = \ln TE_{it} - \ln TE_{it-1} \qquad (10.3)$$

In order to calculate the scale efficiency change, we need the elasticity of inputs, which can be obtained by:

$$\varepsilon_{n,it} = \frac{\partial \ln y_{it}}{\partial \ln x_{n,it}} = \beta_{n,t} + \sum_{m=1}^{K} \beta_{nm} \ln x_{m,it} + \beta_{nt} t \qquad (10.4)$$

Then the scale efficiency change between t and $t - 1$ periods can be calculated by:

$$SEC_{it} = \left(\sum_{n} \varepsilon_{n,t} - 1\right) \sum_{n} \left[(\varepsilon_{n,t} / \sum_{n} \varepsilon_{n,t})(\ln x_{n,it} - \ln x_{n,it-1})\right] \qquad (10.5)$$

Using Eqs. (10.1)–(10.5), productivity change between t and $t - 1$ periods can be calculated and decomposed into three components in the case of the translog form stochastic production frontier model.

4 Data Selection and Model Specification

4.1 Model Specification

In the model specification for the power generation sector, our literature review shows that in most of the recent studies generated power is used as an output variable, while labour, capital stock and consumed fuel are used as input variables. However, as far as China's power generation sector is concerned, researchers have been confronted with a data compatibility problem which will be detailed as follows. First of all, since there are no panel data for labour input in individual provincial administrative regional power generation sectors it is, in most of the studies concerning China, replaced by labour input in the generation and transmission (including both low voltage distribution and high voltage transmission) of heating and electric power sectors (data published by *China Statistics Yearbook* periodically). Given that labour input in the generation and transmission sectors are highly positively related with labour input in the power generation sector, which includes not only the thermal or fossil power generation sub-sectors but also nuclear power, hydroelectric power and renewable resource power, including solar power generation sub-sectors, it follows that this proxy variable is incompatible with labour input in thermal power generation sub-sectors (although some researchers, e.g. Bai et al. (2009) used this in a mismatched way). Second, the amount of coal consumed by the thermal power generation sub-sector is published at individual provincial administrative regional levels. However, by definition, it is not compatible with the amount of power generated by the whole sector. One may attempt to use this variable as the proxy of the amount of fuels consumed by the whole power generation sector on the assumption that electric power generated by different sub-sectors accounted for a similar share across sample regions. The fact is that the share of the thermal power sub-sector in the whole power that is generated varies significantly across regions. For example, the share in Shanghai is about 100% during the sample period, while it is about 30% in Qinghai province and 50% in the Guangxi autonomous region. As a result, even serving as a proxy, the amount of coal consumed by the thermal power generation sub-sector is still not compatible with the amount of power generated by total sub-sectors. Given that the objectives we intend to achieve in this study make the amount of power generated by all types of sub-sectors absolutely necessary and that we have access to corresponding labour input and capital inputs, we decided to exclude fuels consumed from input variables because neither direct data on fuels consumed nor a suitable proxy variable for them are attainable.

Excluding fuels consumption from input means that we assume that there was no difference in the impact of fuel consumption on productivity across DMUs over the sample period.[7] it is a slightly strong and pragmatic assumption. However, based on the reasons listed below, this was the best option available. First, both total factor productivity and partial productivity are used to estimate the DMUs' performance. The latter method is, however, often criticised due to its bias in ranking individual performance (Toby and Boaz 2008). Exclusion of fuels input may change estimates for individual DMUs since the true impact of fuels consumption on productivity across DMUs over the sample period is different. However, as our objective is not to compare and rank individual performance, the result of this assumption in our case is consequently not so problematic. Second, what we are most concerned about, however, is whether our treatment will lead to a systematic bias in the average value of the performance, which is the key in our attempt to explain power shortage. The preliminary performing of the model shows that results related to levels of productivity and efficiency from *both methods* under such treatment (namely, excluding fuels consumption from input) are lower than the maximum average value and higher than the minimum value of the relevant existing empirical studies, rather than an unacceptably high or low value (see Table 3 in Sect. 5). This means that our treatment of excluding fuels consumption from input does not change the average values of productivity and efficiency essentially and does not lead to a systematic bias. Third, the objective of this study is to reveal reasons for the power shortage, instead of an accurate estimation of the performance of the

---

[7]The same treatment is employed by other empirical studies concerning performance estimation for the Chinese power generation sector, e.g., Yang and Yu (2008), Zhang and Xia (2011) and Li and Zou (2012).

Chinese power generation sector. Consequently, as long as the estimated performance is neither too high, e.g. more than 90%, which means power shortage is hardly caused by low performance, nor too low, e.g. less than 50%, which means that low performance is the only, or at least the primary, cause of the power shortage, our final conclusion on the reasons for the power shortage will not be affected by modest changes in the levels of performance estimation.

For performance estimation, we need to specify the stochastic production frontier function model, originally developed by Aigner et al. (1977) and Meeusen et al. (1977), and further extended by many researches such as Pitt and Lee (1981), Schmidt and Sickles (1984), Battese and Coelli (1992, 1995), and Greene (2005). Since we intend not only to calculate the TFP change, but also to identify factors influencing the technical efficiency of power plants in China, we decide to choose the model developed by Battese and Coelli (1995) by which one can achieve the aforementioned research objectives simultaneously. Accordingly, the translog form specification of Battese and Coelli (1995) used in this study can be written as:

$$
\begin{aligned}
\ln Y_{it} = {} & \beta_0 + \beta_1 \ln L_{it} + \beta_2 \ln K_{it} + \beta_3 t + \frac{1}{2}\beta_4 (\ln L_{it})^2 \\
& + \frac{1}{2}\beta_5 (\ln K_{it})^2 + \beta_6 \ln L_{it} \ln K_{it} \\
& + \frac{1}{2}\beta_7 t^2 + \beta_8 t \ln L_{it} + \beta_9 t \ln K_{it} + V_{it} - U_{it}
\end{aligned}
\tag{11}
$$

$$
U_{it} = \delta_0 + \delta_1 GDP_{it} + \delta_2 auxi_{it} + \delta_3 coaleffi_{it} + \delta_4 util_{it} + \delta_5 stru_{it} + \delta_6 reg_{it} \tag{12}
$$

with $u_{it} \sim idd(z_{it}\delta, \sigma_u^2)$ and $v_{it} \sim idd(0, \sigma_v^2)$.

where Y_{it}, L_{it} and K_{it} represent generated power, labour input and installed capacity of power generation of i province at t period, respectively. Equation (12) is used to identify factors that affect technical inefficiency of power plants[8]; GDP_{it} is used to reflect the regional economic development level which may affect efficiency from the demand side, $auxi_{it}$ stands for the ratio of auxiliary power to power generated[9]; $coaleffici_{it}$ represents fuel consumption, being also used to capture the efficiency of installed generator sets; $util_{it}$ represents the utilisation rate of thermal power installed capacity and $stru_{it}$ represents the share of power generated by fuelling coal to total power generated in observations (both these variables may impact efficiency from the supply side). reg_{it} is a DMUmy intended to capture the impacts of the "coal-power price linkage scheme" which has been implemented since 2005.

---

[8]We will not offer any analysis on factors that impact technical inefficiency of power plants in this paper.

[9]Auxiliary power is consumed by the power plants during their production process, capturing the technical efficiency of installed generator sets.

Table 1 Data description and source

Variable	Description	Unit	Data sources
Y_{it}	Power generated	10^8 kW	China Power Yearbook
L_{it}	Labour input	10^5 Person	China Labour Statistics Yearbook
K_{it}	Installed capacity	10^5 kW	China Power Yearbook
GDP_{it}	Provincial GDP	10^9 RMB	China Statistics Yearbook
$auxi_{it}$	Power consumed	%	China Power Yearbook
$coaleffi_{it}$	Fuel consumption	g/kWh	China Power Yearbook
$util_{it}$	Utilisation rate of thermal power installed capacity	%	China Power Yearbook
$stru_{it}$	Power generation structure	%	China Power Yearbook
reg_{it}	Policy DMUmy	0 or 1	

4.2 Data Description

Our empirical study uses a panel data covering 27 provinces, autonomous regions and municipalities during 2000–2010. In line with Lam and Shiu (2004), each provincial region is taken as a decision making unit in the output-oriented non-parametric method. Electric power generated by power plants is considered the output variable,[10] and labour and capital are two inputs used in the power generation process. As noted above, labour input is the number of employees working in generation and transportation (including both distribution and transmission) in the heating power and electric power sectors, and capital is measured with installed generating capacity. The detailed information on data collection and processing is shown in Table 1, while Table 2 provides a summary of statistics of the variables used in the study. GDP is adjusted for inflation using the GDP index and measured in 2000 Chinese RMB.

As can be seen in Table 2, being consistent with Chinese GDP growth during the sample period, the average annual power generated per province increased from 48.5 billion kWh in 2000 to 150.1 billion kWh in 2010. The increase in power demand pulled up investments in power generating equipment, as reflected in the variable of installed capacity (K_{it}), which rose from 113.1 million kW in 2000 to 342.3 million kW in 2010. However, as far as the labour input is concerned, it increased slightly from 99.6 thousand per province on average to 107.6 thousand.

---

[10]The environmental issue, especially the relationship between efficiency (and/or productivity) and emission reduction is a hot issue in researches on the Chinese power generation industry (Yang and Pollitt 2009; Bi et al. 2014). However, since the production function model can only deal with multi-inputs and single output, consequently adding undesirable output to the DEA model will raise the problem of incomparability in estimated results obtained from the SFA and DEA models; furthermore, the designated objective of this study is to find out reasons for power shortages during the last decade in China, so exclusion of undesirable output may not impact our analysis materially.

Table 2 The means of variables during the sample period

	2000	2001	2002	2003	2004	2005	2006	2007	2008	2009	2010
Y_{it}	485	526	587	677	785	892	1020	1163	1228	1309	1501
L_{it}	9.96	10.00	10.19	10.27	10.34	10.31	10.39	10.43	10.37	10.38	10.76
K_{it}	1131	1202	1266	1389	1582	1849	2227	2565	2824	3111	3423
GDP_{it}	3523	3539	3543	3641	3855	4039	4144	4346	4620	4536	4795
$auxi_{it}$	6.08	6.11	5.99	6.05	5.82	5.82	5.85	5.84	5.75	5.61	5.41
$coaleffi_{it}$	369	360	358	362	353	345	341	331	323	317	311
$util_{it}$	0.50	0.50	0.53	0.58	0.61	0.60	0.57	0.56	0.52	0.50	0.52
$stru_{it}$	0.76	0.77	0.78	0.81	0.80	0.78	0.80	0.81	0.79	0.80	0.79
reg_{it}	0	0	0	0	0	1	1	1	1	1	1

Taking all those variables into consideration, it is safe to argue that investments in installed capacity were highly capital and/or technologically intensive, which brought about technical progress in the power industry of China, as will be shown in Sect. 5. Another variable that is worth noting is the utilisation rate of installed capacity, ranging from 0.50 to 0.61, and being clearly lower than expected. Given that China was in a state of power shortage during this period, the low utilisation rate is especially conspicuous and worth thinking about. We will come back to this problem in Sect. 5.

5 Estimation Results and Analysis

5.1 Technical Efficiency

Table 3 shows the comparison of the estimated results on the performance of the Chinese power generation sector from different empirical studies. The current present study shows that the efficiency scores from DEA the minimum and the maximum value among the 297 observations are 51% and 1, and the annual average value ranges from 83 to 88%, with a sample period mean of 85%. For efficiency scores from SFA, the corresponding values are 37, 99, 67–79 and 73%. When compared with existing studies, our DEA-based means of efficiency scores are slightly lower than those found in Lam and Shiu (2001, 2004), and Yang and Pollitt (2009), and higher than those of Bai and Song (2009). As to SFA-based means, our results are lower than Li (2009), higher than Zhang and Xia (2011), and similar to Li and Zou (2012).

More detailed distribution patterns of efficiency scores from the present study can be found in Figs. 1 and 2. As shown in Figs. 1 and 2, estimates from the non-parametric method with an average value of 85% are higher than those from the parametric method with an average value of 73%. The difference in estimates may largely result from different benchmarks against which the efficiency levels of the other DMUs are evaluated. More specifically, take the efficiency score for Province A in the year 2000 as an example. Under the DEA method, the 27 provinces in 2000 constitute a sub-sample within which the efficiency score of Province A is estimated against the best performance in these 27 observations.[11] Similarly, the efficiency scores of other individual provinces in other years are also

---

[11]The other way to estimated efficiency levels of individual provinces under the DEA method is to regard the whole sample as a whole and estimate each individual against the best performance in this sample, just like under the SFA method. However, doing it in such a way means that the panel structure of the data is neglected and assumes that there is no technological progress over eleven years of the sample period (see Fried et al. 2007 for more detailed explanations). Given that the power generation sector is a capital- and technical-intensive industry and with the vast investments of China's power generation in the sample period, we think our treatment is more appropriate in taking the background of this research into account than the alternative.

Table 3 Comparison of relevant empirical studies on the Chinese power generation sector

	Sample period	Research method	Research target (DMU)	Maximum value	Minimum value	Range of mean	TFP (TC)
Present study	*2000–2010*	*DEA-TE*	*The whole sector (province)*	*1*	*0.51*	*0.83–0.88*	*2.23 (1.95)*
		SFA-TE		*0.99*	*0.37*	*0.67–0.79*	*0.97 (0.80)*
Lam and Shiu (2001)	1995–1996	DEA-TE	Thermal power (province)	1	0.69	0.89–0.90	
Lam and Shiu (2004)	1995–1996; 1998-2000	DEA-TE	Thermal power (province)	1	0.73	0.91–0.94	2.1 (2.2)
Yang and Pollitt (2009)	2002	DEA-TE	Coal-fired (plant)	1	0.60	0.88–0.95	
Li et al. (2015)	2002–2011	SFA-CE	Thermal power (plant)	1	0.21	0.32–0.86	
Chen et al. (2015)	1999–2011	SFA-CE (Bayesian)	Fossil-fuel (plant)			0.84–0.96	
Yang and Yu (2008)	1996–2003	DEA-TE	The whole sector (province)			0.92–0.94	2.1 (2.2)
Bai and Song (2009)	2004	DEA-TE	Thermal power (province)	1	0.16	0.70	
Li (2009)	2001–2007	SFA-TE	Thermal power (plant)			0.80–0.98	
Zhang and Xia (2011)	2003–2009	SFA-TE	The whole power sector			0.37–0.53	
Li and Zou (2012)	2000–2009	SFA-TE	Thermal power (province)	0.98	0.36	0.65–0.79	

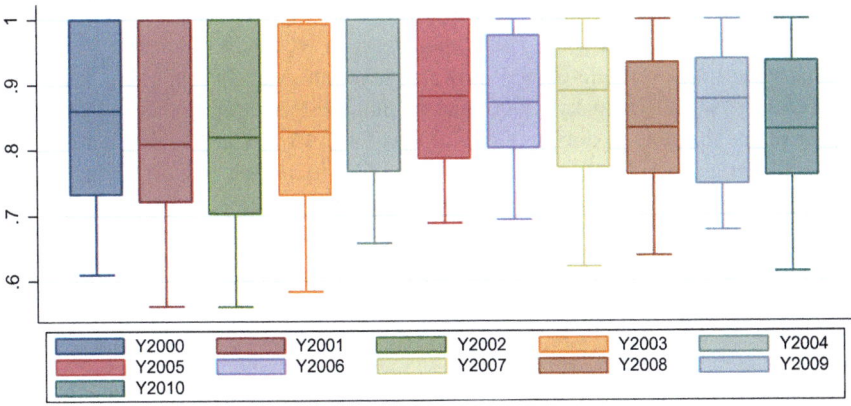

Fig. 1 Technical efficiency of China's power generation sector estimated from DEA

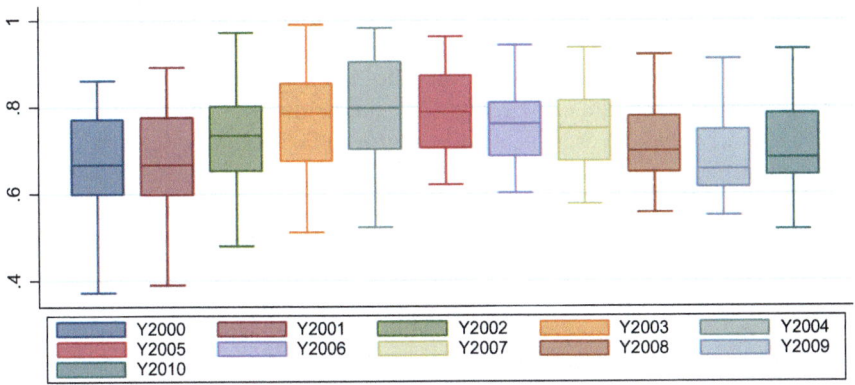

Fig. 2 Technical efficiency of China's power generation sector estimated from SFA

estimated through the same way. By contrast, under the SFA method, the efficiency score for Province A in the year 2000 is estimated against the best performance in the whole sample which consists of 297 (the product of 27 provinces and 11 years) observations. Since the best performance in sub-groups must be inferior or at best equal to the best performance in the whole group, it follows that the estimated efficiency score of the same observation under the DEA method must be no smaller than those estimated under the SFA method.

Although results show that efficiency levels of the Chinese power generation sector have room for improvement and may be one reason for the power shortage during the sample period of 2000–2010, we cannot conclude that it is the main or only cause of the power shortage. This is because compared with the pre-2000 efficiency levels when there was no power shortage (see Lam and Shiu 2001, 2004), the efficiency levels for 2000–2010 were not significantly lower, and therefore cannot solely explain the increase in power shortages. When compared internationally, See and Coelli (2012) find that average technical efficiency scores for public-owned and private-owned power plants in Malaysia are 68 and 88% respectively, while Vaninsky (2006) shows that the technical efficiency of electric power plants in the U.S. during 2000–2004 is 94%. Consequently, it is hard to say that an average efficiency value of 73 or 85% in power plants in developing countries like China is too low to bring out power shortages.

5.2 TFP Change and Its Sources

Table 4 shows the statistical summary of productivity change index and its decomposition calculated by non-parametric DEA and parametric SFA methods. As expected, there are considerable differences in both the TFP change index and their components between two methods. For example, the average annual TFP growth estimated from DEA is 2.23%, which is quite a bit higher than the 0.97% received by the SFA. Further, the DEA method estimates a positive average scale efficiency change over the sample period while the SFA shows a negative change. Notwithstanding, there are some remarkable similarities between results from two methods. First, they both estimate a positive growth in productivity change; second, they both estimate that technical progress is the major contributor to productivity growth; third, the Spearman's rho between annual TFP change from two methods is 0.97, showing high consistency in tendency of annual TFP change. The results can be explained by the fact of Chinese electric power industry regulatory reform. As is known, technical progress means a shift in the production frontier, resulting mostly from innovation, which could be embedded in new equipment investment. In 2002, the State Power Corporation, which had been the vertical monopolist in the electric power industry, was separated into five independent power generation group corporations (see footnote 1). In order to acquire market share as soon as possible, the top five corporations sharply increased their installed capacity simultaneously, leading to a second investment rush in electricity generation (Zhao et al. 2012).[12] Li (2010) shows that there was a 98.3% growth in generation capacity in the whole nation and 173% growth in the top five during the period from 2005 to 2009. Innovations embedded in new generating units shifted the frontier and served as the main sources of TFP change in the Chinese electric power industry, as is reflected in Table 4.

The results from both methods related to pure efficiency change (PEC), while another source of TFP change roughly reflected a trend of increase in technical efficiency measurements during the first half of the last decade, and a trend of

---

[12]The first time an investment rush happened was in 1985, when the Chinese government began allowing private investment in electricity generation in response to a serious supply shortage of electric power.

Table 4 Annual Productivity change index and its decomposition (%)

	N-TC[a]	P-TC[b]	N-PEC	P-PEC	N-SEC	P-SEC	N-TFP	P-TFP
2000–01	2.90	−0.20	−1.60	2.06	0.40	−0.13	1.70	1.73
2001–02	8.50	−0.04	−0.30	6.82	−0.10	−0.13	7.10	6.65
2002–03	6.90	0.13	1.10	6.39	−0.12	−0.23	6.80	6.29
2003–04	−2.50	0.35	4.70	3.05	2.60	−0.36	4.70	3.04
2004–05	1.30	0.61	0.70	−0.50	0.10	−0.48	2.20	−0.37
2005–06	−2.00	0.90	−0.40	−4.00	1.50	−0.67	−1.00	−3.77
2006–07	3.80	1.19	−0.21	−1.53	−1.40	−0.54	0.20	−0.88
2007–08	−3.90	1.45	−0.22	−5.02	4.10	−0.41	−2.20	−3.98
2008–09	0.50	1.71	0.10	−5.79	−4.00	−0.44	−3.40	−4.52
2009–10	4.00	1.94	−0.10	4.00	2.30	−0.45	6.20	5.49
Average[c]	1.95	0.80	0.38	0.55	0.54	−0.38	2.23	0.97

[a]The N—refers to indices calculated by non-parametric method
[b]The P—refers to indices calculated by parametric method
[c]Arithmetic means of individual indices

decrease for the second half. We argue that this tendency may be in line with the situation of the Chinese electric power industry in the last decade. As mentioned earlier, the vertical monopolist "The State Power Corporation of China" was dismantled in 2002 and in its place five independent power generation group corporations were established, which compete in the power generation sector against each other as well as against other existing little independent power plants. Market pressure as well as relatively low efficiency during the monopoly period enabled the improvement of the efficiency of the newly founded five corporations. Furthermore, other existing power plants had to improve efficiency when faced with competition from big rivals. All these facts contributed to technical efficiency gains from 2000 to 2005. However, it could be predicted that with an increasing number of idle staff personnel and loss of motivation for managers to struggle with a bad business environment due to the sharply increasing price of coal and low utilisation rates, technical efficiency began changing from an upward tendency to a downward tendency around the year 2004, as shown in Table 3.[13]

When compared with Lam and Shiu (2004) who report an average annual increase of 2.1% in TFP over the period of 1995–1996 and 1998–2000, our findings

---

[13]Losses incurred by state-owned enterprises due to policy intervention are usually termed "policy-induced losses". Because of the information asymmetry problem between government and enterprises, it is very hard for the state to distinguish between the policy-induced losses and the enterprises' operational losses. The managers of state-owned enterprises have an incentive to ascribe all their losses like managerial slacks, on-job consumption and other agency problems—no matter whether the losses are due to the policy burdens, their own incompetence or opportunistic behavior—to state policy. We are unsure whether or not this phenomenon existed in state-owned power plants in the last decade. If it did happen, this agency problem will be another reason for negative technical efficiency changes.

show that there is no TFP decrease during the sample period, and accordingly TFP is hardly the reason for power shortages. In fact, TFP increased by 2.23% (DEA) or 0.97% (SFA) annually during this period. Taking estimated results of efficiency levels as well as TFP change into consideration, it is hard to reach a conclusion that low performance is the major cause of the power shortage that happened in the first decade of the 21st century in China. There must be other reasons for the power shortages.

5.3   Reasons for Low Utilisation Rates of Installed Capacity

Figure 3 offers information on utilisation rates of the installed thermal power capacity during the sample period. Utilisation rates range from 0.27 to 0.76 with an average rate of 0.55. Needless to say, this is a low rate level by any standard. The co-existence of sufficient installed capacity, not-so-bad technical efficiency levels and productivity growth rate of the power generation sector motivate us to investigate further the cause of the low utilisation rate which may directly lead to the power supply shortage. The reason for running down the power plant may be due to technical problem (maintenance), managerial decision (cost-benefit analysis) or other reasons. After interviewing business leaders in the power sector and carefully reviewing the literature, the second reason became especially attractive as the potential candidate for the reason for the power shortage.

The literature review shows that Zhang and Chen (2011), Zhao et al. (2012) and Wang et al. (2013) have all identified the coal-power conflicts between coal production and power generation corporations. Conflicts are mainly due to the uneven marketisation reform progress implemented in the coal and power generation industries in China. More specifically, according to Li et al. (2015, p. 297), to stabilise the electricity price and provide more incentive to coal mines to increase

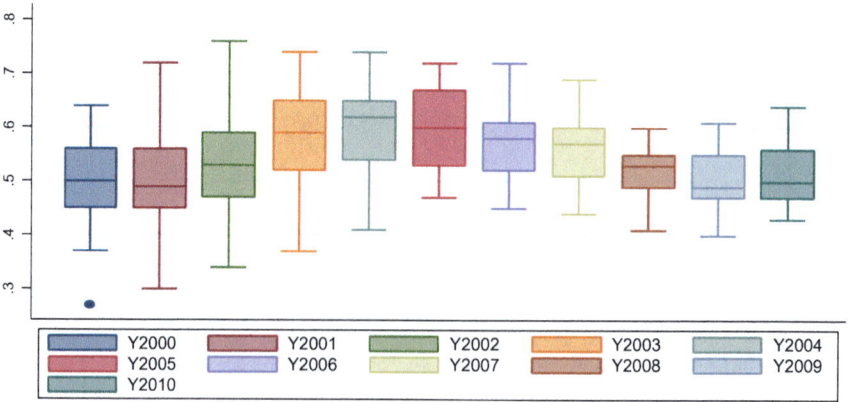

Fig. 3 Box plot of utilisation rate of thermal power installed capacity during the sample period

output, China's central government introduced the dual-track pricing scheme in the coal industry in 1985, which requires qualified coal mines to sell a certain amount of thermal coal to qualified thermal power plants (usually large state-owned power plants) at a government-guided price. Output beyond the quota can be priced 50 or 100% higher and sold freely on the market. At the same time, the price for electric power has been under the strict control of the National Development and Reform Commission and cannot be changed accordingly with the market-oriented coal price. As a result, when the gap between the government-guided price and market price is big, coal production corporations are reluctant to increase the quantity of coal sold at a government-guided price. The higher the coal market price, the more serious the reluctance is. On the other hand, to satisfy the increasing need in coal consumption resulting from the increasing need for electric power, thermal power plants had to buy more and more coal at a market price. This creates profitability problems for the thermal power producers, since the government-decided electric power price[14] is determined by using the government-guided coal price in the electricity price formula.

Figure 4 presents the coal price index, soaring from 100 in 2002 to 179.78 in 2011, largely beyond the change of the Producer Price Index or PPI. Since coal-purchasing costs account for about 70% of the total cost in coal-fired power plants, continuously increasing the coal price brought serious financial problems to the power generation industry [see e.g. Wang et al. (2013)]. It follows that the mismatch between the market-oriented coal pricing mechanism and government-guided power pricing scheme provided power plants with a serious incentive to make themselves incompatible with the state's demands: if they ran the power plants in such a way that supply met the demand for electricity, they would have incurred greater financial losses. In order to deal with this distorted institutional arrangement and reduce their financial losses, the rational reaction is to purposely reduce the quantity of thermal power generation, which is also shown as a low utilisation rate of these plants, which can lead to less need for coal to be bought at the market price (the dual-track pricing scheme in the coal industry ensures that power plants can buy a certain amount of coal below the market price).

We also checked the possible impacts of variable renewable energy (VRE) such as solar and wind on the utilisation rate of conventional capacity. According to *The National Economic and Social Development Statistical Bulletin of 2014*, which is issued by the National Bureau of Statistics of China, the total installed capacity in 2014 was 1.36 billion kW, of which thermal, wind and solar generation capacity was about 0.92 billion, 95.81 million and 26.52 million kW, equalling to a share of 67.3, 7.0 and 1.9% respectively. Further, according to *The 21st Century Economic Report (5 February 2015)*, the total amount of power generated in 2014 was 5463.8 billion kWh, of which the amount of power generated by the thermal power, wind

---

[14]In order to link the benchmarking on-grid electric price with the coal price in the market, the Chinese government introduced a coal-electricity price linkage scheme characterised by cost-sharing between power plants and electricity users in 2004, while according to Li et al. (2015), it served as a double-edged sword and hardly functioned as expected.

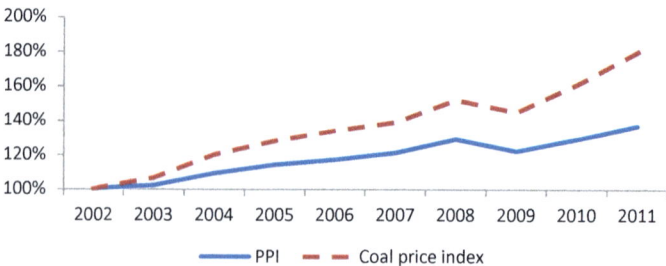

Fig. 4 The comparison of change between the coal price index and PPI

power and solar power sectors was 4170, 156.3 and 23.1 billion kWh, equalling to a share of 76.3, 2.9 and 0.4% respectively. That is to say, even after years of promotion by the central government of the use of variable renewable energy, the share of them in both installed capacity and generated power is still too low to significantly influence the utilisation rate of thermal power installed capacity.

To summarise, one can conclude that low utilisation rates like the ones in China's power generation plants in the last decade are more likely to result from the strategic decision of managers, rather than being the results of low demand for electricity or equipment maintenance.

6   Concluding Remarks

In searching for causes for the ten years of power shortage that happened last decade, we first analysed whether there was underinvestment in installed capacity. Studies of Li (2010) and others show that it is safe to conclude that insufficient level of generation capacity is not a cause of nationwide power shortages. Next we examined the role of performance as a reason for power shortages by estimating efficiency levels as well as productivity change and its sources in the power generation sector. Results show that the average efficiency score from DEA and SFA is 85 and 73%, respectively. Further, TFP increased by 2.23% (DEA) or 0.97% (SFA) annually. Taking estimated results of efficiency levels as well as TFP change into consideration, it is hard to reach a conclusion that low performance was the major cause of the power shortage in the first decade of the 21st century in China. Finally, we examined the role of managerial decisions as a cause of power shortages. We did this by interviewing business leaders and examining the existing literature. According to these, there were incentive-related problems which originated originating from the relationship between the market-oriented coal pricing mechanism, the government-determined electric power pricing regime and invalid coal-electricity pricing linkage. That is to say, as the coal price rose, thermal power plants began to slip into the red. To reduce operational losses, managers decided to reduce coal use by artificially lowering the utilisation rate which eventually leads to the phenomenon of power supply shortage.

From the perspective of policy implications, our study reflects difficulties faced by transition economies in their shift from centralised-governance to market-oriented mechanism. The problem is not that policy-makers in those economies do not know what to do, but rather that achieving one policy intention is often at the cost of sacrificing or harming the other objective, which is also pursued by other policy designs, namely so-called transitional costs. For example, to stabilise and even lower the price of electricity for macroeconomic reasons, the Chinese government's intervention in pricing could be justified. However, doing so creates incentive problems in power plants when the coal price is in a state of continuous increase. In 2012, the dual-track pricing policy was eventually abolished and calculation formulas of the electricity price as well as the coal-power price linkage scheme were also correspondingly adjusted.[15] Given that both theory and practices in developed economies show that the power supply sector is contestable and should be subject to market mechanisms, a gradual removal of price controls on electricity should be carried out. However, more attention should be paid to network operations which are characterized by a natural monopoly. Finally, predicting sources of productivity change in China's electricity generation sector in the next few years, we argue that productivity growth through technological progress resulting from equipment investments may be hard to be achieved given the fact of excessive installed capacity and the decreasing growth rate of the Chinese economy from now on. If that is true, technical efficiency improvements will be and should be the main source of productivity growth in the Chinese power generation sector.

Acknowledgements We are grateful for the financial support from the Planning Foundation of the Ministry of Education of China for Research in Humanities and Social Sciences "Theory and Application Research on the Incorporation of Efficiency-improving Design into Cost-plus Regime" (17YJA790042) and Project of Key Discipline in Industrial Economics of DUFE.

References

Aigner D. J., Lovell C. A. K. and Schmidt P. Formulation and estimation of stochastic frontier production function models. Journal of Econometrics, vol. 6, 1977, pp. 21–37.
Bai X.J. and Song Y. Environment regulation, technology innovation and efficiency improvement of Chinese Thermal power industry, China Industrial Economics, No.8, 2009, pp. 68–77.
Bai X.J. Reasons for and responses to current power shortage in our country. The dissertation submitted to Shaanxi Normal University for master's degree 2006.

---

[15]*Instruction on Further Reform Concerning Thermal Coal Market* issued in December 2012 amended the coal-power price linkage scheme; namely, when the price of thermal coal rises or falls by 5% or more over the last continuous 12 months, thermal power plants will be allowed to add 90% of the price changes into the electricity pricing formula, pre-determined by the central regulatory agency, and absorb 10% of the price changes by cost saving, instead of passing all the changes on to the electricity end users. Before 2012, the proportion that power plants had to internally absorb was 30% of upward changes in the coal price.

Battese G. E. and Coelli T. J. A model for technical inefficiency effects in a stochastic frontier production function for panel data. Empirical Economics, vol. 20(2), 1995, pp. 325–332.

Battese G. E. and Coelli T. J. Frontier production functions, technical efficiency and panel data: with application to paddy farmers in India. Journal of Productivity Analysis, vol. 1, 1992, pp. 153–169.

Bi G. B., Song W., Zhou P. and Liang L. Does environmental regulation affect energy efficiency in China's thermal power generation? Empirical evidence from a slacks-based DEA model. Energy Policy, vol. 66, 2014, pp. 537–546.

Caves D. W., Christensen L. R. and Diewert W. E.The economic theory of index numbers and the measurement of input, output, and productivity. Econometrica, vol. 50(6), 1982, pp. 1393–1414.

Chen Z.F., Barros C. P. and Borges M. R. A Bayesian stochastic frontier analysis of Chinese fossil-fuel electricity generation companies, Energy Economics 48 (2015) , pp. 136–144.

Coelli T.J., Estache A., Perelman S. and Trujillo L. A Primer on Efficiency Measurement for Utilities and Transport Regulators, The International Bank for Reconstruction and Development. 2003, THE WORLD BANK.

Coelli T. J., Rao D. S. P., O'Donnel C. J. l and Battese G. E. An Introduction to Efficiency and Productivity Analysis. 2005, New York, Springer.

Denny M., Fuss M., and Waverman L. The substitution possibilities for energy. In modelling and measuring natural resource substitution. Edited by Berndt E. R. and Field, B. C., 1981, MIT Press, Cambridge, MA.

Du L.M., He Y.N. and Yan J.Y. The effects of electricity reforms on productivity and efficiency of China's fossil-fired power plants: An empirical analysis, Energy Economics 40 (2013), pp. 804–812.

Färe R., Grosskopf S., Lindgren B. and Roos P. Productivity developments in Swedish hospitals: a Malmquist output index approach. Carbondale: Department of Economics, Southern Illinois University, 1989.

Färe R., Grosskopf S., Lindgren B. and Roos P. Productivity changes in Swedish pharmacies 1980-1989: a nonparametric Malmquist approach. Journal of Productivity Analysis, vol. 3,1992, pp. 85–101.

Färe R., Grosskopf S., Norris M. and Zhang Z. Productivity growth, technical progress and efficiency change in industrialized countries. American Economic Review, vol. 84, 1994, pp. 66–84.

Farrell M. J. The measurement of productive efficiency. Journal of the Royal Statistical Society, Series A (General), vol. 120, 1957, pp. 253–281.

Fried H., Lovell K. and Schmidt S. The measurement of productive efficiency and productivity. Oxford University Press.

Greene W. Fixed and random effects in stochastic frontier models. Journal of Productivity Analysis, vol. 23, 2005, pp. 7–32.

Jondrow J., Materov I., Lovell K. and Schmidt P. On the estimation of technical inefficiency in the stochastic frontier production function model. Journal of Econometrics 19(2/3), 1982, pp. 233–238.

Kumbhakar S. C. Estimation and decomposition of productivity change when production is not efficient: a panel data approach. Econometric Review, vol. 19, 2000, pp. 426–460.

Kumbhakar S.C. and Lovell C.A.K. Stochastic Frontier Analysis, 2000, Cambridge University Press.

Lam P. L. and Shiu A. A data envelopment analysis of the efficiency of China's thermal power generation. Utilities Policy, vol. 10, 2001, pp. 75–83.

Lam P. L. and Shiu A. Efficiency and productivity of China's thermal power generation. Review of Industrial Organization, vol. 24, 2004, pp. 73–93.

Li S. The research on the endogenous barriers to entry into China's generation market. The dissertation submitted to Dongbei University of Finance and Economics for Ph.D. degree 2010.

Li H.Z. and Zou T. An empirical analysis of efficiency and determinants on power generation industry of China, Reform 10 (2012), pp. 44–50.

Li H.Z., Tian X.L., and Zou T. Impact analysis of coal-electricity pricing linkage scheme in China based on stochastic frontier cost function, Applied Energy 151 (2015), pp. 296–305.

Li T. Productive factors, power price regulation reform and the efficiency of thermal power plants: stochastic frontier evidence from A-share listed companies, Journal of Finance and Economics, Vol.35 No.4, 2009, pp. 107–118.

Malmquist S. Index numbers and indifference surfaces. Trabajos de Estadistica, vol. 4, 1953, pp. 209–242.

Meeusen W. and Broeck J. Efficiency estimation from Cobb-Douglas production functions with composed error. International Economic Review, vol. 18, 1977, pp. 435–444.

Nishimizu M., Page J. M. Total factor productivity growth, technological progress and technical efficiency change: dimensions of productivity change in Yugoslavia, 1965-78. The Economic Journal, vol. 92(368) , 1982, pp. 920–936.

O'Donnell C.J. Nonparametric estimates of the components of productivity and profitability change in U.S. agriculture Am. J. Agric. Econ., 94 (4) (2012a), pp. 873–890.

O'Donnell C.J. An aggregate quantity framework for measuring and decomposing productivity change. J. Prod. Anal., 38 (2012b), pp. 255–272.

O'Donnell C.J. An Aggregate Quantity-Price Framework for Measuring and Decomposing Productivity and Profitability Change. Centre for Efficiency and Productivity Analysis Working Papers. University of Queensland.

O'Donnell C.J. DPIN Version 1.0: A Program for Decomposing Productivity Index Numbers, Centre for Efficiency and Productivity Analysis Working Papers. 2010, University of Queensland.

Pitt M. and Lee L. The measurement and sources of technical inefficiency in Indonesian weaving industry. Journal of Development Economics, vol. 9, 1981, pp. 43–64.

Schmidt P. and, Sickles R. C. Production frontiers and panel data. Journal of Business and Economic Statistics, vol. 4, 1984, pp. 367–374.

See K. F. and Coelli T. An analysis of factors that influence the technical efficiency of Malaysian thermal power plants. Energy Economics, vol. 34, 2012, pp. 677–685.

See K.F. and Li F. Total factor productivity analysis of the UK airport industry: A Hicks-Moorsteen index method, Journal of Air Transport Management, vol. 43, issue C, 2015, pp. 1–10.

Shephard R. W. Cost and Production Functions, 1953, Princeton: Princeton University Press.

Solow R. M. Technical change and the aggregate production function. The Review of Economics and Statistics, vol. 39(3), 1957, pp. 312–320.

Toby B. and Boaz M. Use of total factor productivity analyses in network regulation case studies of regulatory practice. 2008, working paper of The Brattle Group.

Tsionas E.G. Stochastic frontier models with random coefficients. J. Appl. Econ. 17 (2), 2002, pp. 127–147.

Griffin, J.E., Steel, M.F.J. Bayesian stochastic frontier analysis using WinBUGS. J Prod Anal 27, 2007, pp. 163–176.

Vaninsky A. Efficiency of electric power generation in the United States: analysis and forecast based on data envelopment analysis. Energy Economics, vol. 28, 2006, pp. 326–338.

Wang Y.S., Xie B.C., Shang, L.F. and Li, W.H. Measures to improve the performance of China's thermal power industry: in view of cost efficiency. Applied Energy, vol. 112, 2013, pp. 1078–1086.

Wang Q. and Chen X. China's electricity market-oriented reform: from an absolute to a relative monopoly. Energy Policy 51, 2012, pp. 143–148.

Wu F., Fan L.W., Zhou P. and Zhou D.Q. Industrial energy efficiency with CO2 emissions in China: a nonparametric analysis. Energy Policy vol. 49, 2012, pp. 164–172.

Wu Y.S.H. and Jiang Y.Q. and Zhong W. Causes of and solution to current power shortage in our country. Journal of Electric Power Technologic Economics, No. 5, 2004, pp. 4–7.

Xie B.C., Fan Y. and Ou Q.Q. Does generation form influence environmental efficiency performance? An analysis of China's power system. Applied Energy, 96(1), 2012, pp. 261–271.

Yang M. and Yu X. China's Power Management. Energy Policy 24 (8), 1996, pp. 735–757.

Yang S.Y. and Yu L.C. The efficiency and productivity in China's electricity supply system, Collected Essays on Finance and Economics, No.3, 2008, pp. 15–20.

Yang H. and Pollitt M. Incorporating undesirable outputs into Malmquist TFP Index: environmental performance growth of Chinese coal-fired power plants. European Journal of Operational Research, 197 (2009), pp. 1095–1105.

Yu L. and Wang J. Vertical dual-track pricing system: an economic analysis on and solution to power supply shortages in China, China Industrial Economics. vol. 10, 2008, pp. 43–52.

Zhang V. Y. and Chen Y. Vertical relationships in China's electricity industry: the quest for competition?. Utilities Policy, vol. 19, 2011, pp. 142–153.

Zhao X. L., Lyon T. P. and Song C. Lurching towards markets for power: China's electricity policy 1985–2007. Applied Energy, vol. 94, 2012, pp. 148–155.

Zhang G.X. and Xia D.W. Ownership structure, environment regulation and efficiency of Chinese power generation Industry- stochastic frontier production function analysis based on provincial panel data during 2003-2009, China Industrial Economics, No.6, 2011, pp. 130–140.

Zhou P., Ang B.W. and Wang H. Energy and CO2 emission performance in electricity generation: a non-radial directional distance function approach. Eur. J. Oper. Res. 221(3), 2012, pp. 625–635.

Zhou P., Sun Z.R. and Zhou D.Q. Optimal path for controlling CO2 emissions in China: a perspective of efficiency analysis. Energy Econ. vol.45, 2014, pp. 99–110.

Chapter 6
Allocation Schemes and Efficiencies of China's Carbon and Sulfur Emissions

Zhongqi Deng, Ruizhi Pang and Yu Fan

1 Introduction

With the rapid development of global economies and societies, human survival is encountering enormous challenges from environmental pollution and greenhouse gas emissions (Currie et al. 2015). Reducing emissions and safeguarding the sustainability of economic and social development have become critical concerns around the word (Martin et al. 2014; Fowlie 2010), so understanding the most efficient ways to reduce local pollution sources can significantly improve well-being in both developed and developing countries (Greenstone and Hanna 2014). In accepting pollution emissions as undesirable outputs, it is thus necessary to explore production efficiency and allocation schemes.

Discussions during the 2009 Copenhagen Climate Change Conference (so-called the "one last chance to save the mankind") covered both the promises of the first phase of the Kyoto Protocol (2008–2012) and the global emissions reduction agreement in the following phase (2012–2020). Thereafter, climate change summits in Cancun, Durban, Doha, Warsaw, Lima, and Paris all focused global attention on environmental and resource issues. Since the Chinese economic reforms of 1978, the total energy consumption in China has witnessed a sharp increase, with China surpassing the United States becoming the largest energy-consuming nation in 2010 (Statistical Review of World Energy). In 2013, China consumed 3.75 billion tons of coal equivalent energy, representing 22.4% of the total global amount. This enormous

Z. Deng (✉)
School of Economics, Sichuan University, Chengdu 610065, China
e-mail: zhongqideng@sina.com

R. Pang
College of Economics and Social Development, Nankai University, Tianjin 300071, China

Y. Fan
Nanjing Chemical Industry Park Administration Committee, Nanjing 210047, China

© Springer Nature Singapore Pte Ltd. 2018
R. Pang et al. (eds.), *Energy, Environment and Transitional Green Growth in China*, https://doi.org/10.1007/978-981-10-7919-1_6

consumption of energy contributed respectively to 90 and 80% of Chinese SO_2 and CO_2 emissions, thus encroached the threshold of ecological bearing capacity (Pang et al. 2015a; UKCIP 2002).[1] Consequently, energy conservation and emissions reduction have become unavoidable tasks in China.

As one of the major economic powers in the world, China has taken enormous efforts to conserve energy and reduce emissions. As part of the Twelfth Five-Year Plan Work Program on the Emissions Reduction of Greenhouse Gases, the Chinese government stated that "by the end of 2015, the national carbon intensity level should decline by 17% from the end of 2010." Every province (or city) was assigned a specific carbon dioxide emission reduction target. In addition, in the Twelfth Five-Year Plan Work Program on Integrated Energy Conservation and Emissions Reduction, the Chinese government also stipulated sulfur dioxide emission reduction target of 2015 for various provinces and cities.

These policy documents presented a rigid restraint to regional economic and social development. However, based on the mid-term evaluation of China's Twelfth Five-Year Plan, it is apparent that "the economic indicators have been fulfilled while the environmental indicators lag behind." For example, energy consumption intensity fell only 5.5% from 2011 to 2012, 11.5% away from the target value of 16%. The survey results for carbon intensity were also barely satisfied, with a total decline of only 6.6% from 2011 to 2012. In addition, nitrogen oxide emissions increased by 5.74% in 2011.[2] In short, China has not achieved the projected periodical targets for energy conservation and emissions reduction. What could be the main reason for the failure to achieve the periodical targets? Is this phenomenon reasonable or inevitable? Is the administrative allocation scheme that sets one target to fit all provinces and cities economically reasonable? How does one distribute provincial emissions quotas with the total national emissions remaining unchanged? How does one balance fairness and efficiency when allocating emissions rights?

Reflecting on these questions, this paper aims to determine an optimal approach for emissions control and allocation that does not rely on technological production progress. An optimal allocation scheme is required to meet not only the emissions reduction targets but also the potential requirements of provincial economic development. These purposes can be realized through a zero-sum gain data envelopment analysis (ZSG-DEA) approach. This approach is specifically oriented to maximize the technical efficiency of reducing carbon and sulfur emissions in

---

[1]"Beijing's skyscrapers receded into a dense gray smog Thursday as the capital saw the season's first wave of extremely dangerous pollution, with the concentration of toxic small particles registering more than two dozen times the level considered safe", reported by Associated Press on January 16, 2014.

[2]In the Twelfth Five-Year Plan Work Program on the Integrated Energy Conservation and Emissions Reduction, the Chinese government stated that by 2015 the country's total nitrogen oxide emission should be controlled within 20.462 million ton, downward at least 10% from the end of 2010.

various provinces with fully utilizing potential emissions reduction ability. Under the constraint of unchanged total emissions, the final target is to achieve the reallocation of provincial emissions.

2 Research Method and Data Processing

2.1 Existing Research on Allocation Mechanism

Resource allocation has been a recently trending topic in economics (Hsieh and Klenow 2009; Asker et al. 2014). Barzel and Sass (1990) researched the allocation of resources through voting and Ergin (2002) introduced a model of resource allocation based on priorities to address the question how to allocate Pareto efficiently. Additionally, Gollin et al. (2014) researched the misallocation of labor in the agricultural sector, which is also based on the efficiency principle.

In terms of emission-right allocation, Bastianoni et al. (2004) discussed the geographical approach, consumer responsibility approach, and carbon emission added approach to assign the responsibility for greenhouse gas. Edwards and Hutton (2001) used a computable general equilibrium (CGE) model to evaluate the methods of allocating carbon permits within the UK. Ferng (2003) studied the carbon emission allocation from the perspectives of benefit principle and ecological deficit within Taiwan. Bohm and Larsen (1994) studied the allocation of CO_2 emissions in EU member countries on the basis that the marginal revenue of emission reduction equals to its marginal costs. Besides, Burtraw et al. (2005) and Palmer (2009) studied the allocation of gas emissions in electronical industries under a trading mode, which is also available for the ZSG scheme of this paper.

In general, the goal of allocation schemes is to optimize cost, profit, or efficiency (Demailly and Quirion 2008). As a non-parametric method, DEA (data envelopment analysis) has been widely applied to energy allocation (e.g., Korhonen and Syrjänen 2003; Pang et al. 2015b). However, the application of DEA in an allocation scheme can be subject to the limitation of a fixed sum in a particular input (or output), which means that the gains from a DMU (Decision Making Unit) are equal to losses elsewhere, that is, the so-called Zero-Sum Game. Under this condition, traditional parametric and non-parametric methods usually cannot solve this allocation problem. Lins et al. (2003) initially proposed the ZSG-DEA model and applied it to evaluate the national award-winning efficiency in the Sydney Olympic Games. Many scholars subsequently applied this model, including Gomes and Lins (2007), Chiu et al. (2013), Wang et al. (2013), and Pang et al. (2015a). By using the model, this paper intends to reallocate Chinese provincial carbon and sulfur emissions in 2010 and 2015 to maximize overall efficiency, thus guiding the setting of China's emissions-reduction targets in the future.

2.2 Zero-Sum Gain Model

This paper determines the input and output variables by considering technical rationality in the production process. Population, capital stock and energy consumption are designated as inputs, represented by X_1, X_2 and X_3, respectively; gross regional product (GRP), carbon-dioxide emission and sulfur-dioxide emission are designated as outputs, represented by Y_1, Y_2, and Y_3, respectively. To evaluate the technical efficiency of undesirable outputs objectively, this paper adheres to the basic viewpoints of Environmental Production Technology (EPT):

1. In actual manufacturing process, undesired outputs are inevitable (null-joint), so good outputs cannot be produced without producing bad outputs.
2. All other things being equal, effort is required to "get rid of" an unwanted by product, as required by regulation, so reductions in inputs and undesired outputs will lead to a simultaneous reduction in desired outputs (weak disposability).

In addition to EPT, the following three lemmas should be noted before putting the ZSG-DEA model forward:

Lemma 1 In a ZSG-DEA model, the incentive that moves a decision-making unit (DMU) to an efficient frontier is equivalent to the incentive in a traditional DEA model.

Lemma 2 All DMUs can achieve 100% efficiency after a proportional reallocation of emissions, which is a sufficient but not necessary condition.

Lemma 3 No matter whether there exists internal competition or cooperation among DMUs within an inefficient (efficient) set, the relationship between ZSG-DEA efficiency and DEA efficiency is always valid.

These lemmas are derived by the authors, but the proofs of Lemma 1–3 refer to Lins et al. (2003), Gomes and Lins (2007), and Pang et al. (2015a), respectively, so they are not demonstrated forthwith. Lemma 1 indicates that the incentive distortion of DMUs is not in existence under the ZSG-DEA model. Lemma 3 indicates that the internal game among DMUs has no significance, internal behaviors can thus be described as a "black box" to simplify the model analysis. The definitions of inefficient and efficient sets will be given later. Lemma 2 indicates that even when total emissions and technical levels remain the same, efficiency maximization and Pareto improvement can be realized only by reallocating the (input or output) factors; this is the theoretical foundation of this paper.

The basic model of DEA in Eq. (1) is different from the traditional models of CCR and BCC. In Eq. (1), θ_{1k} and θ_{2k} are handled separately, which shows that to become effective in technology a DMU can reduce Y_2 and Y_3 by different proportions. Here, θ_{1k} and θ_{2k} are referred to as the emission efficiency of carbon dioxide and sulfur dioxide, respectively, under the conditions of current population, capital stock, and energy consumption. The objective function is the weighted sum of θ_{1k} and θ_{2k}, which are endowed with equal weight in this paper (that is, 0.5), Wang et al. (2013) also adopted a similar weight scheme. Different weights can also be set in various situations. λ_j represents DMU_j's contribution to the efficient frontier and the restraint $\sum \lambda = 1$ shows that the return to scale is variable.

$$Min\ 0.5\theta_{1k} + 0.5\theta_{2k}$$

$$s.t.\ \sum_{j=1}^{n} \lambda_j X_{ij} \leq X_{ik},\ i = 1,2,3;\ \sum_{j=1}^{n} \lambda_j Y_{1j} \geq Y_{1k};\ \sum_{j=1}^{n} \lambda_j Y_{2j} = \theta_{1k} Y_{2k} \tag{1}$$

$$\sum_{j=1}^{n} \lambda_j Y_{3j} = \theta_{2k} Y_{3k};\ \sum_{j=1}^{n} \lambda_j = 1;\ \lambda_j \geq 0,\ j = 1,2,\ldots,n$$

Based on Eq. (1) and Lemma 1, this paper carries out a non-radial allocation for the carbon dioxide emission (Y_2) and sulfur dioxide emission (Y_3), resulting in a ZSG-DEA model oriented by undesired outputs, as indicated in Eq. (2). In practice, all DMUs strive to reduce the emissions of carbon and sulfur. In Eq. (2), the expressions $Y_{2k}(1 - h_{1k})$ and $Y_{3k}(1 - h_{2k})$ respectively represent the carbon dioxide emission and sulfur dioxide emission that must be reduced by the kth DMU. These reductions will be distributed to the other $n - 1$ DMUs through a Proportional Reduction Strategy while maintaining the same total emissions of carbon and sulfur. After the reallocation, all DMUs are mapped to a new efficient frontier (see Lemma 2). At this point, the efficiencies of all the DMUs reach 100%, thus realizing Pareto Optimality. To maintain the same total emissions, a portion of the undesired outputs must be distributed to efficient DMUs to compensate for the lost undesired outputs of inefficient DMUs, thus the ZSG-DEA efficient frontier will remain at a lower level than before. As for Eq. (2), problems occur with existing literature such as Gomes and Lins (2007), and Chiu et al. (2013), so this paper makes some corrections in the following paragraphs.

$$Min\ 0.5h_{1k} + 0.5h_{2k}$$

$$s.t.\ \sum_{j=1}^{n} \lambda_j X_{ij} \leq X_{ik},\ i = 1,2,3;\ \sum_{j=1}^{n} \lambda_j Y_{1j} \geq Y_{1k}$$

$$\lambda_k h_{1k} Y_{2k} + \sum_{j \neq k}^{n} \lambda_j Y_{2j} \left[1 + \frac{Y_{2k}(1 - h_{1k})}{\sum_{j \neq k} Y_{2j}} \right] = h_{1k} Y_{2k}$$

$$\lambda_k h_{2k} Y_{3k} + \sum_{j \neq k}^{n} \lambda_j Y_{3j} \left[1 + \frac{Y_{3k}(1 - h_{2k})}{\sum_{j \neq k} Y_{3j}} \right] = h_{2k} Y_{3k} \tag{2}$$

$$\sum_{j=1}^{n} \lambda_j = 1;\ \lambda_j \geq 0,\ j = 1,2,\ldots,n$$

If a regulatory authority is sufficiently effective and competent to influence the decision-making process of the DMUs, then the abovementioned allocation method is the most efficient. This allocation method not only ensures the realization of the overall targets of emission reduction, but also stimulates all DMUs to reach an efficient frontier. However, the calculation process of Eq. (2) is rather complex and involves nonlinear programming. Therefore, this paper engages in a step-by-step calculation: First, this paper calculates the θ_{1k} and θ_{2k} values corresponding to each province and city with Eq. (1). Then, following Gomes and Lins (2008) as well as Pang et al. (2015a), this paper solves h_{1k} and h_{2k} with Eq. (3).

$$h_{1p} = \theta_{1p} \left[1 + \frac{\sum\limits_{p \in w} Y_{2p}(1 - q_{kp}h_{1p})}{\sum\limits_{p \notin w} Y_{2p}} \right], \; h_{2p} = \theta_{2p} \left[1 + \frac{\sum\limits_{p \in w'} Y_{3p}(1 - q'_{kp}h_{2p})}{\sum\limits_{p \notin w'} Y_{3p}} \right] \quad (3)$$

In this equation $q_{kp} = \theta_{1k}/\theta_{1p}$ and $q'_{kp} = \theta_{2k}/\theta_{2p}$ (see Pang et al. 2015a). Inefficient set w is the set composed of all DUMs in which θ_{1k} values are not equal to 100%. The other inefficient set w' refers to the set of DMUs in which θ_{2k} values are not equal to 100%. According to Lemma 3, the relationship displayed by Eq. (3) has nothing to do with the games inside the inefficient set (w or w'). In this paper, h_{1k} and h_{2k} represent the ZSG addition coefficients of carbon and sulfur emissions, respectively. Furthermore, by using Eq. (3), it is easy to calculate these addition coefficients when all the provinces and cities reach the new ZSG frontier. The provinces and cities whose ZSG addition coefficient of carbon emission surpasses 100% (implying advanced carbon-emission technology) could increase their local carbon emissions; similarly, provinces and cities whose ZSG addition coefficient of sulfur emission surpasses 100% could increase their local sulfur emissions.

This paper then expands the ZSG-DEA model of Eq. (2) into a multi-dimensional situation and substitutes Eq. (3) into Eq. (2). Because $0.5h_{1k} + 0.5h_{2k}$ is independent for each DMU, minimizing each $0.5h_{1k} + 0.5h_{2k}$ is equivalent to minimizing the sum, $\sum_{k=1}^{n}(0.5h_{1k} + 0.5h_{2k})$. Therefore, this paper obtains Eq. (4). Because the allocation of carbon-dioxide and sulfur-dioxide emissions could be viewed as a special trade between efficient DMUs and inefficient DMUs, this paper places all originally inefficient DMUs into the inefficient set. DMUs in the inefficient set have redundant undesired outputs (carbon or sulfur emissions), so it is possible to allocate these redundancies to the originally efficient DMUs. In this manner, the final allocation results can be obtained with a single calculation, which is a major innovation offered by this paper.

$$Min \sum_{k=1}^{n} (0.5h_{1k} + 0.5h_{2k})$$

$$s.t. \sum_{j=1}^{n} \lambda_j X_{ij} \leq X_{ik}, \ i = 1,2,3; \ \sum_{j=1}^{n} \lambda_j Y_{1j} \geq Y_{1k}$$

$$\sum_{p \in w} \lambda_p q_{pk} h_{1k} Y_{2k} + \sum_{p \notin w} \lambda_p Y_{2j} \left[1 + \frac{\sum_{p \in w} Y_{2p}(1 - q_{pk}h_{1k})}{\sum_{p \notin w} Y_{2p}} \right] = h_{1k} Y_{2k} \quad (4)$$

$$\sum_{p \in w'} \lambda_p q'_{pk} h_{2k} Y_{3k} + \sum_{p \notin w'} \lambda_p Y_{3j} \left[1 + \frac{\sum_{p \in w'} Y_{3p}(1 - q'_{pk}h_{2k})}{\sum_{p \notin w'} Y_{3p}} \right] = h_{2k} Y_{3k}$$

$$\sum_{j=1}^{n} \lambda_j = 1; \ \lambda_j \geq 0, \ j = 1, \ldots, n$$

In conclusion, the calculation steps can be summarized as follows:

1. Calculate Eq. (1) by using the original input and output data to identify the efficient and inefficient DMUs.
2. Calculate Eq. (4) to solve the ZSG-DEA addition coefficients, h_{1k} and h_{2k}, for various DMUs.
3. Multiply h_{1k} and h_{2k} with the corresponding original CO_2 and SO_2 emissions, respectively, to obtain the emissions data after reallocation.

Finally, Eq. (1) can be recalculated with the reallocated emissions data, in which case it is noted that all the DMUs will have 100% technological efficiency, thus realizing the maximum of efficiency (see Lemma 2, and it will also be tested in the empirical analysis section later).

2.3 Variable Selection and Data Sources

This paper selects 30 Chinese provinces and cities in 2010 and 2015 as samples.[3] Relevant economic and energy data primarily come from China Statistic Yearbook (2011–2014) and China Energy Statistic Yearbook (2011–2014). Using 2008 as the base year, this paper adjusts all the nominal variables to a real price level. The estimated values of 2015 primarily come from the Twelfth Five-Year Plan Work Program on the Emissions Reduction of Greenhouse Gases [China's National Development and Reform Commission (2011), no. 41] and the Twelfth Five-Year

---

[3]These two years are selected because that 2010 and 2015 are the final year of China's Eleventh and Twelfth Five-Year Plan, respectively, so this paper can obtain relevant documents and reports. Some data of 2015 are simulated values.

Plan Work Program on Integrated Energy Conservation and Emissions Reduction [CNDRC (2011), no. 26]. With considering technology rationality in the production process based on ZSG Environmental Production Technology, this paper regards population,[4] capital stock[5] and energy consumption in each province and city as input variables, and regards provincial gross regional product and the emissions of carbon dioxide and sulfur dioxide[6] as output variables. Table 1 lists the summary statistics of these variables and indicates that while the sulfur emission has declined the other inputs and outputs have increased, particularly the capital stock, which has more than doubled.

To estimate carbon dioxide emission in 2010, this paper uses various energy consumption values as basic data, including 16 major energy sources: coal, fine washed coal, other washed coal, coke, crude oil, gasoline, kerosene, diesel, fuel oil, liquefied LPG, coke oven gas, other gases, refinery gas, natural gas, thermal, and electricity. All the energy consumption data come from the Regional Energy Balance Sheet of the China Energy Statistic Yearbook. The conversion formula of carbon dioxide emission refers to IPCC (2006):

$$CO_2 = \frac{44}{12} \sum_{i=1}^{16} (E_i \times NCV_i \times CEF_i \times COF_i) \qquad (5)$$

where E_i denotes the consumption of different fuels; NCV_i denotes net heat value; COF_i denotes the carbon emission factor of unit heat value; COF_i denotes the carbon oxidation rate; and 44/12 is the gasification coefficient of carbon dioxide. The average net heat values of different forms of energy sources come from Appendix 4 of the China Energy Statistical Yearbook; the carbon-emission factors come from the 2006 IPCC Guidelines for National Greenhouse Gas Inventories (Vol. 2, Chapter 1, Table 1.3). China's Twelfth Five-Year Plan Work Program on the Emissions Reduction of Greenhouse Gases clarifies the range of decline in carbon dioxide emission per GRP (gross regional product) from 2010 to 2015, from which the carbon density can be calculated. This value is then multiplied by the estimated GRP in 2015 to estimate the CO_2 emissions in each province and city in 2015. The rationality of the administrative allocation scheme and other schemes will be discussed later.

---

[4]The population in 2015 are estimated based on the population of 2013 with using 0.72% as the annual growth rate, because the Twelfth Five-Year Plan Work Program on National Population Growth stipulated that "control the annual growth rate of population within 0.72%".

[5]This paper uses Perpetual Inventory Method (PIM) to estimate the real capital stocks of various provinces in 2010 and 2015. When estimating the capital stocks in 2015, this paper uses the provincial capital stocks in 2013 as base, and assumes that the growth rate of Chinese material capital stock is 14%.

[6]The regional sulfur-emission control plan in the Annex 4 of China's Twelfth-Five Plan Work Program on the Integrated Energy Conservation and Emissions Reduction provides the provincial target of sulfur-dioxide emission, this paper uses it directly as the estimated value of administrative allocation of 2015.

Table 1 Summary statistics of input-output variables in 2010 and 2015

Variable	Year	Mean	Std. dev.	Min	Max
Population (X_1) (10,000)	2010	4436.12	2708.88	563.00	10440.96
	2015	4571.96	2767.18	586.14	10797.83
Capital stock (X_2) (100 million yuan)	2010	39963.33	26216.18	5192.27	108096.30
	2015	80445.15	50216.62	12092.57	208646.20
Energy consumption (X_3) (10,000 ton of standard coal)	2010	15583.79	9521.93	1672.25	40345.02
	2015	17777.40	10682.77	1934.11	45734.30
Gross Regional Product (Y_1) (100 million yuan)	2010	11517.94	9102.42	1063.79	37317.13
	2015	20071.28	15070.42	1952.21	61215.20
Carbon dioxide emission (Y_2) (10,000 ton)	2010	41162.20	27669.44	5468.14	121160.50
	2015	57290.57	36385.07	8160.16	162243.10
Sulfur dioxide emission (Y_3) (10,000 ton)	2010	72.83	41.15	2.88	153.78
	2015	59.72	33.74	2.36	126.10

Note Both the capital stock and the gross regional product are measured by real price. There 30 samples in each year. Yuan is the unit of RMB
Source See the section of Variable Selection and Data Sources

3 Empirical Analysis

3.1 Comparison Between ZSG Allocation, National Administrative Allocation, and Actual Emissions in 2010

In the Eleventh Five-Year Plan, China encouraged the building of desulfurization facilities in thermal power plants to ensure that sulfur-dioxide emission would be reduced by 10% by the end of 2010 as a curb to acid rain. The government also promulgated the Eleventh Five-Year Plan Work Program on the Emission Control of Major Pollutants, in which the control plan of sulfur emission for each province and city was specifically set. Because carbon-intensity control was not included in the comprehensive evaluation system of economic and social development during China's Eleventh Five-Year Plan, this section primarily discusses the differences in sulfur-dioxide emission between provincial administrative allocation, actual emission, and ZSG allocation in 2010 (refer to Table 2). The ZSG allocation of provincial sulfur dioxide denotes the quota after reallocating the actual emission of each province by using the optimized approach of this paper.

3.1.1 Twenty Provinces or Cities Were Assigned an Excessively High Administrative Sulfur-Emission Quota

Based on the prescribed provincial reduction target, the government stressed emission reduction in all provinces and cities (except for Hainan, Gansu, Qinghai,

Table 2 Provincial administrative allocation actual emission and ZSG allocation of sulfur dioxide in 2010 (10,000 ton)

	SEE	Admin. allocation		Actual emission		ZSG allocation	
		2010	Change	2010	Change	2010	Change
Beijing	1.00	15.20	−20.4	11.51	−39.7	36.66	91.9
Tianjin	1.00	24.00	−9.4	23.52	−11.2	74.94	182.8
Hebei	0.24	127.10	−15.0	123.38	−17.5	93.64	−37.4
Shanxi	0.07	130.40	−14.0	124.92	−17.6	25.84	−83.0
Inner Mongolia	0.06	140.00	−3.8	139.41	−4.3	28.63	−80.3
Liaoning	0.21	105.30	−12.0	102.22	−14.6	67.73	−43.4
Jilin	0.20	36.40	−4.7	35.63	−6.7	23.2	−39.3
Heilongjiang	0.18	49.80	−2.0	49.02	−3.5	27.47	−45.9
Shanghai	1.00	38.00	−25.9	35.81	−30.2	114.12	122.5
Jiangsu	1.00	112.60	−18.0	105.05	−23.5	334.77	143.8
Zhejiang	0.81	73.10	−15.0	67.83	−21.1	175.49	104.1
Anhui	0.18	54.80	−4.0	53.21	−6.8	31.02	−45.7
Fujian	0.28	42.40	−8.0	40.91	−11.3	36.42	−21.0
Jiangxi	0.14	57.00	−7.0	55.71	−9.1	24.92	−59.3
Shandong	0.54	160.20	−20.0	153.78	−23.2	262.53	31.1
Henan	0.27	139.70	−14.0	133.87	−17.6	116.66	−28.2
Hubei	0.22	66.10	−7.8	63.26	−11.8	44.13	−38.5
Hunan	0.18	83.60	−9.0	80.13	−12.8	44.75	−51.3
Guangdong	1.00	110.00	−15.0	105.05	−18.8	334.78	158.7
Guangxi	0.09	92.20	−9.9	90.38	−11.7	24.99	−75.6
Hainan	1.00	2.20	0.0	2.88	30.9	9.18	317.3
Chongqing	0.09	73.70	−11.9	71.94	−14.1	20.97	−74.9
Sichuan	0.15	114.40	−11.9	113.1	−12.9	53.23	−59.0
Guizhou	0.04	115.40	−15.0	114.88	−15.4	14.86	−89.1
Yunnan	0.13	50.10	−4.0	50.07	−4.1	20.55	−60.6
Shaanxi	0.11	81.10	−12.0	7.86	15.6	26.14	−71.6
Gansu	0.08	56.30	0.0	55.18	−2.0	13.98	−75.2
Qinghai	1.00	12.40	0.0	14.34	15.6	45.71	268.6
Ningxia	0.41	31.10	−9.3	31.08	−9.4	40.18	17.1
Xinjiang	0.09	53.56	0.0	58.85	9.9	17.29	−67.7

Note SEE denotes the sulfur-emission efficiency. The column of "change" is to measure the change between the allocations of 2010 and the real emission of 2005 (unit is %)

Source The data of "ZSG allocation" are calculated by the authors. The data of "administrative allocation" come from the Eleventh Five-Year Plan Work Program on the Emissions Control of Major Pollutants [China's National Development and Reform Commission (2006), no. 70] and Xinjiang, which retained the same sulfur emission in 2010 as in 2005). As for the ZSG allocation, the quotas in various provinces and cities were not identical and were in fact inconsistent with the administrative quotas. For example, the ZSG quotas in 10 provinces and cities, including Guangdong, Jiangsu, Zhejiang, Shandong, Shanghai, Tianjin, Qinghai, Beijing, Ningxia, and Hainan, surpassed the administrative quotas, and the total increase of ZSG allocation surpassed 200%.

In terms of sulfur-emission efficiency, the top ten provinces and cities were Beijing, Tianjin, Shanghai, Jiangsu, Guangdong, Hainan, Qinghai, Zhejiang, Shandong, and Ningxia. However, the Chinese government set a relatively more difficult emission-reduction target for these locales; for example, Beijing was assigned a 20.4% reduction from 2005 to the end of 2010 (Shanghai 25.9%, Jiangsu 18%, and Shandong 20%). Conversely, those with lower sulfur-emission efficiency (lower than 0.2) had a relatively lower emission-reduction target; for example, Anhui and Yunnan were required to reduce emission by only 4% (Inner Mongolia 3.8%, Heilongjiang 2%). It seems that an unfair phenomenon of "whipping the fast and hardworking" existed under the national administrative allocation, similarly to the A-J effect in the price regulation field.

Achieving nationwide sulfur-emission-reduction target requires elevating sulfur emission efficiency, which is a rigid restraint for the provinces and cities with lower sulfur-emission efficiency. The ZSG allocation scheme of this paper is beneficial for the provinces and cities with higher sulfur-emission efficiency but "punishes" those with lower efficiency, thus conforming to the efficiency principle and incentive requirement.

3.1.2 Significant Provincial Difference in the Completion Degree of Sulfur-Dioxide-Emission Reduction

Although most provinces and cities met the administrative target (except for Hainan, Qinghai, and Xinjiang), the degree of completion varied from province to province (see Table 2). Areas, such as Beijing, Zhejiang, Jiangsu, Shanghai, and Hubei, achieved an additional reduction of more than 4%, whereas the additional reduction was less than 1% in Inner Mongolia, Guizhou, Ningxia, and Yunnan. Based on the two indicators of sulfur-emission efficiency and completion degree of the administrative target, this paper could roughly divide these 30 provinces and cities into four categories (see Fig. 1).

The first category includes the provinces and cities with high efficiency and good performance in sulfur reduction, represented by Beijing, Shanghai, Jiangsu, and Zhejiang. Due to advanced reduction technology, these provinces and cities already reached their best level under the current macroeconomic production framework and could even surpass the administrative target.

The second category includes the provinces and cities with high efficiency but poor performance in sulfur reduction, represented by Tianjin, Qinghai, and Hainan. The sulfur-emission efficiency in these provinces and cities achieved 100%, but

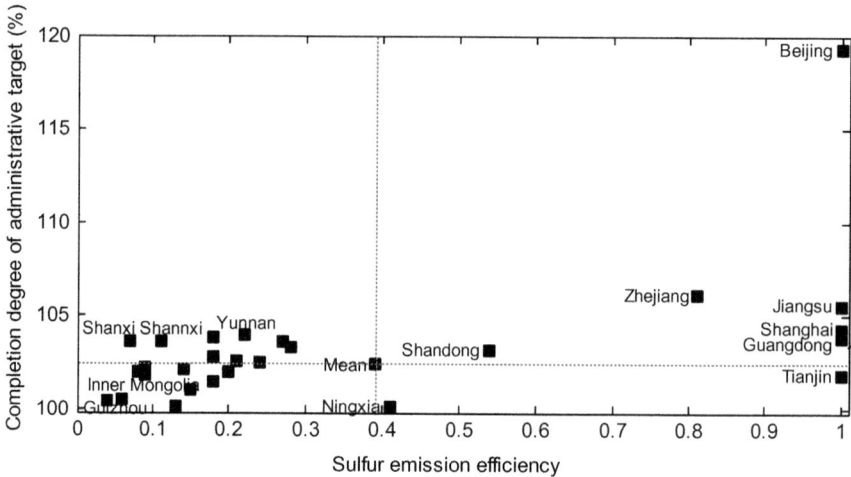

Fig. 1 Sulfur-emission efficiency and completion degree of administrative target (2010)

because of their economic development structure[7] and/or the restraint of reduction technology (such as Qinghai and Hainan), they could barely (or merely) reach the administrative target.

The third category includes the provinces and cities with lower efficiencies but good performance in sulfur reduction, represented by Shanxi, Hunan, and Shaanxi. The sulfur-emission efficiency in these provinces and cities was lower than 0.2, with Shanxi at only 0.06. Under the current population, energy consumption, and capital input circumstances, although the actual sulfur emission was excessive, it was not difficult to achieve the administrative target because the national administrative target was too low and there was significant room for reducing emission.

The fourth category includes the provinces and cities that performed poorly in both efficiency and completion degree, represented by Guizhou, Inner Mongolia, and Xinjiang. They encountered enormous challenge in energy conservation and emission reduction. They should urgently address these issues and take measures such as optimizing energy structure, raising sulfur-emission efficiency, and introducing advanced reduction technology, to reach the administrative target.

3.1.3 The Middle and Western Regions Should Shoulder More Responsibilities in Terms of Reducing Sulfur Emission

The administrative scheme to allocate sulfur-emission right will lead to hardship in the provinces and cities that have higher sulfur-emission efficiency (such as Tianjin,

---

[7]In Tianjin, the industrial section accounts for an excessive proportion in economic structure (being 48% in 2010), and the heavy industry accounts for 84% in the industrial section in 2010.

Qinghai, and Hainan) in accomplishing their administrative reduction target, but relief in the provinces and cities that have greater emission but lower efficiency (such as Shanxi, Shaanxi, and Hunan). Moreover, the administrative allocation could lead to backwardness in terms of energy conservation and emissions reduction in the provinces such as Guizhou and Xinjiang.

Figure 2 shows the results in three major economic regions of China. The government administratively prescribed that "by the end of 2010, sulfur emissions in the eastern, middle, and western regions should be reduced by at least 16.3, 9.8, and 8.7%, respectively." These three major economic regions met this goal by the end of 2010, realizing reduction of 20.2, 13.0, and 9.0%, respectively. As for the completion degree, in the eastern region it was the best, followed by the middle and western regions.

According to Fig. 2, actual emission of sulfur dioxide was greatest in the western region, reaching 8.2 million ton and 37.4% of total emission nationwide; after the ZSG allocation, this region received the lowest allocation of sulfur emission right that is only 3.1 million ton. Most the provinces and cities in the western region had lower sulfur-emission efficiency (including Guizhou, Inner Mongolia, Shaanxi, and Xinjiang), but the protective administrative allocation in this region might have aggravated this result. Similarly, the administrative allocation in the middle region was also greater than the ZSG allocation. To narrow the gap between the eastern, middle, and western regions, it is necessary to utilize incentives and punitive measures, enhance inter-regional negotiation and cooperation on emissions-reduction technology and management mechanism, as well as accelerate the spread of advanced technology and management concepts.

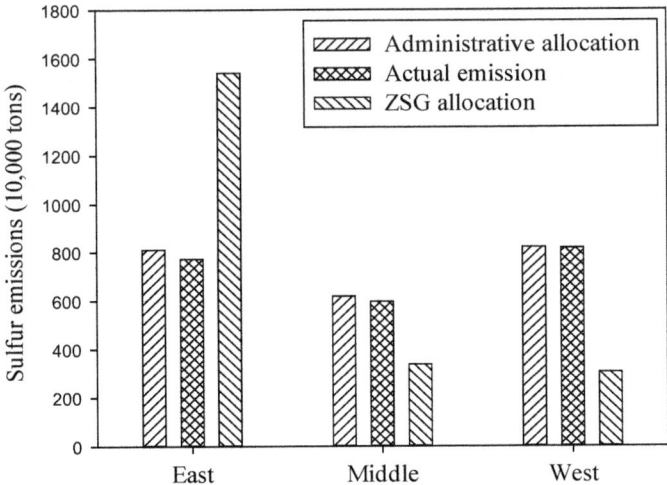

Fig. 2 Administrative allocation, actual emission, and ZSG allocation of SO_2 in the eastern, middle, and western of China (2010). *Source* Calculated by the authors through the data in Table 2

3.2 Comparison Between the ZSG Allocation and Administrative Allocation in 2015

3.2.1 Under the ZSG Allocation Scheme, There Were 16 Provinces and Cities in China that Must Lower Their Administrative Quota of Carbon Emission

As shown in Table 3, among these 16 provinces or cities, Shanxi, Inner Mongolia, Hebei, and Liaoning, where carbon emission efficiency was lower than 0.4, would receive lower carbon emission quota under the ZSG allocation scheme. For example, the ZSG allocation of Shanxi was reduced to 320.128 million ton from the 967.760 million ton original emission (a decreasing of 66.92%). The carbon emission quota in Inner Mongolia also needed to decline by 559.750 million ton. Under current economic structure, these resource-oriented provinces and cities would have difficulty realizing the ZSG allocation target. Therefore, they could purchase emission right from the areas with excess carbon emission quotas, which is a tradeoff between environmental sustainability and economic development.

On the other hand, under the ZSG scheme, there were 14 provinces and cities that obtained more carbon emission quotas, including economically developed provinces and cities, such as Beijing, Shanghai, Jiangsu, and Guangdong. These provinces and cities already had optimized scale of carbon emission (with carbon emission efficiency of 100%; see Table 3 for details). For example, Guangdong was administratively required to realize a carbon intensity of 1.22 ton/10,000 yuan; under the ZSG scheme, it was permitted to increase emission by 872.250 million ton—an increase of 99.46% in carbon intensity that reached 2.43 ton/10,000 yuan. Because the energy consumption structure in Guangdong was dominated by hydropower and nuclear power, the increased carbon emission would not necessarily lead to a simultaneous growth in GRP. Therefore, Guangdong might choose to "sell" its carbon-emission right of 872.250 million ton to other provinces. Besides, other regions, such as Zhejiang, Fujian, Jiangxi, and Chongqing, could also acquire more carbon-emission quotas under the ZSG scheme, thus lessening the pressure to reduce their emission.

3.2.2 When Allocating Emission with an Administrative Scheme, the Chinese Government Adopted a Unified Standard to Fit All Regions

In the attachment to China's Twelfth Five-Year Plan Work Program on the Emissions Reduction of Greenhouse Gases, there are clear statements on the necessary level of carbon intensity decline in 2015 for various provinces and cities. This paper measures the decrease in carbon intensity from 2011 to 2015 under the ZSG allocation scheme and compares it to the administrative scheme, thus demonstrating that there is an enormous gap between the ZSG allocation target and

Table 3 China's provincial carbon-emission ZSG-allocation and carbon-intensity in 2015

	CEE	Estimated emission	ZSG allocation	Difference	Rank	Carbon intensity	
						Admin.	ZSG
Beijing	1.00	214.32	427.48	213.16	6	0.95	1.90
Tianjin	1.00	302.99	604.34	301.35	5	1.82	3.64
Hebei	0.29	1203.84	685.21	−518.63	28	3.68	2.10
Shanxi	0.17	967.76	320.13	−647.63	30	6.65	2.20
Inner Mongolia	0.20	936.92	377.17	−559.75	29	4.82	1.94
Liaoning	0.31	1030.11	644.27	−385.84	27	3.29	2.06
Jilin	0.41	395.77	323.51	−72.26	18	2.64	2.16
Heilongjiang	0.35	504.09	347.33	−156.76	23	3.03	2.09
Shanghai	1.00	366.86	731.73	364.88	4	1.47	2.93
Jiangsu	1.00	1065.05	2124.35	1059.30	1	1.56	3.11
Zhejiang	0.81	655.28	1057.86	402.58	3	1.51	2.44
Anhui	0.39	523.74	403.23	−120.51	19	2.38	1.83
Fujian	0.60	378.39	456.06	77.68	9	1.50	1.81
Jiangxi	0.59	287.74	341.10	53.36	10	1.74	2.06
Shandong	0.46	1602.88	1474.62	−128.27	20	2.54	2.33
Henan	0.43	929.71	792.06	−137.66	22	2.50	2.13
Hubei	0.45	609.91	549.28	−60.63	16	2.14	1.93
Hunan	0.55	497.68	544.24	46.55	11	1.76	1.92
Guangdong	1.00	876.99	1749.24	872.25	2	1.22	2.43
Guangxi	0.57	297.83	340.91	43.08	12	1.79	2.05
Hainan	1.00	93.16	185.81	92.65	7	2.56	5.11
Chongqing	0.57	274.90	310.22	35.32	13	1.88	2.12
Sichuan	0.51	580.27	588.44	8.17	14	1.91	1.94
Guizhou	0.28	444.63	247.88	−196.74	24	4.81	2.68
Yunnan	0.35	431.32	298.82	−132.51	21	3.18	2.21
Shaanxi	0.31	573.10	359.34	−213.76	25	3.09	1.94
Gansu	0.39	293.62	226.74	−66.88	17	4.05	3.13
Qinghai	1.00	88.48	176.49	88.01	8	3.64	7.27
Ningxia	0.42	220.11	182.25	−37.86	15	7.43	6.15
Xinjiang	0.27	478.39	255.73	−222.66	26	4.95	2.65
Total	–	17125.81	17125.81	0.00	–	–	–

Note The unit of emission (allocation) is million ton. The column of "difference" is obtained by using the ZSG allocation to minus the estimated emission. The column of "Rank" is arranged in descending order according to the "difference" quantity. The carbon intensity is referred to as the carbon dioxide emission of unit GRP, and unit is ton/million yuan

Source The ZSG allocation is calculated by the authors. The carbon intensity data of administrative allocation come from the Twelfth Five-Year Plan Work Program on the Emissions Reduction of Greenhouse Gases [China's National Development and Reform Commission (2011), no. 41]

the administrative allocation target. Although the carbon-intensity reduction target under the national administrative allocation scheme varies from province to province, it remains at approximately 17% overall; see Fig. 3. However, under the ZSG allocation scheme, the target has extreme ranges from −80% to 73%.

Comparing the two schemes, there are 14 provinces and cities in which the administrative allocation target surpasses that of the ZSG quota. The most severe gap between the two schemes lies in Qinghai province at 89.51%. Under the ZSG allocation scheme, the carbon intensity in Beijing, Tianjin, Shanghai, Jiangsu, Zhejiang, Guangdong, Hainan, and Qinghai in 2005 are permitted to go beyond their 2010 level. Although the carbon intensity in Qinghai and Hainan provinces in 2010 was 4.049 and 2.879 ton/10 thousand yuan, respectively, their respective total carbon emission was only 88.484 and 93.155 million ton; therefore, under the ZSG allocation scheme, they were permitted to increase carbon emission. As for the provinces and cities with high GRP, including Beijing, Shanghai, and Guangdong, they could raise their carbon dioxide emission in 2015 under the ZSG allocation scheme. There are 16 provinces or cities in which administrative control target is less strict than ZSG control, including the major energy output provinces (Shanxi and Inner Mongolia) and industrial provinces (Hebei and Liaoning), these areas would face greater pressure of emission reduction under the ZSG scheme.

A statement in the Twelfth Five-Year Plan Work Program on Integrated Energy Conservation and Emissions Reduction specifies emission target of sulfur dioxide for various provinces and cities by the end of 2015. See Table 4 for their comparison with the sulfur-emission allocation under the ZSG scheme. Although administrative control no longer enforces a unified degree of decline for sulfur dioxide in all provinces and cities, there is an almost antipodal situation between the administrative allocation and the ZSG allocation.[8] In addition, the problem of "whipping the fast and hardworking" but "rewarding the slow and freeloading" still exists under the administrative allocation scheme. For provinces and cities with higher sulfur emission efficiency such as Beijing, Jiangsu, Shanghai, Zhejiang, and Guangdong, the government has greater expectation on sulfur-emission reduction, whereas the less efficient areas such as Hebei, Shanxi, Liaoning, Shaanxi, and Xinjiang are permitted to increase sulfur-dioxide emission.

3.2.3 Nationwide, 19 Provinces and Cities Were Being Granted an Excessively High Administrative Sulfur-Emission Quota

Among these 19 provinces and cities, Inner Mongolia, Shanxi, Guizhou, and Shaanxi must continue their emission reduction program. As for Hebei, Liaoning

---

[8]Shanghai, Guangdong, Beijing, Jiangsu, Tianjin, and Zhejiang need to lower emissions under the administrative allocation scheme but increase emissions under the ZSG scheme. On the contrary, Yunnan, Xinjiang, Gansu, Shaanxi, Jilin, Shanxi, Heilongjiang, Liaoning, Hebei, and Hubei need to increase emissions under the administrative allocation scheme but reduce emissions under the ZSG allocation scheme.

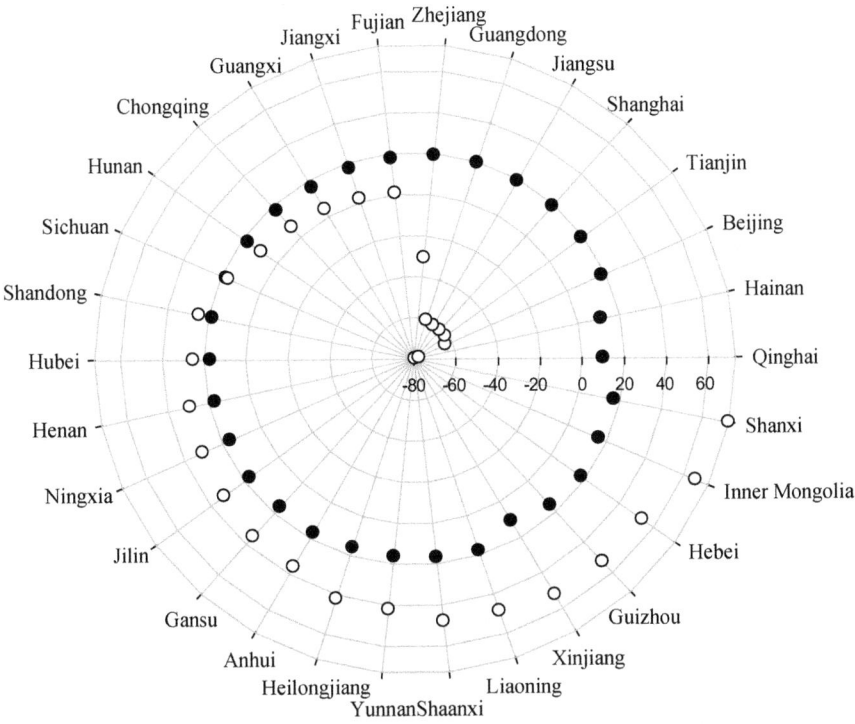

Fig. 3 Reduction degree of carbon intensity under the two allocation schemes (%). *Source* Negative reduction degree means increasing. The reduction degrees of carbon intensity under the administrative allocation scheme come from the Twelfth Five-Year Plan Work Program on the Emissions Reduction of Greenhouse Gases [China's National Development and Reform Commission (2011), No. 41], and the data of ZSG allocation scheme are calculated by Table 3

and Henan, their secondary industry constitutes a major proportion in their industrial structure, which needs to transform and upgrade. Provinces and cities such as Shanxi, Inner Mongolia, and Guizhou are traditionally energy exporter. Based on local resource reserve and economic structure, it is unrealistic to change their energy consumption structure over a short period of time. Therefore, it is more feasible for them to improve energy efficiency and take advantage of their local strengths by exploiting emerging alternative energies such as solar and wind energy.

On the other hand, there are 11 provinces and cities in the country that receive higher quotas under the ZSG scheme than under the administrative control. There are seven provinces and cities in which ZSG quotas increase by 266% relative to the administrative quotas, namely Beijing, Shanghai, Jiangsu, Guangdong, Tianjin, Hainan, and Qinghai. Because sulfur emission in these provinces and cities have already met the optimal scale (the sulfur emissions efficiency being 100%), they

Table 4 China's provincial allocations of sulfur-dioxide emission in 2015

	SEE	Admin. allocation		ZSG allocation		Difference	Rank
		2015	Change	2015	Change		
Beijing	1.00	9.00	−21.81	32.94	186.17	23.94	8
Tianjin	1.00	21.60	−8.16	79.05	236.10	57.45	5
Hebei	0.17	125.50	1.72	77.54	−37.15	−47.96	25
Shanxi	0.05	127.60	2.15	25.13	−79.88	−102.47	29
Inner Mongolia	0.06	134.40	−3.59	29.28	−79.00	−105.12	30
Liaoning	0.18	104.70	2.43	70.46	−31.07	−34.24	22
Jilin	0.17	40.60	13.95	25.38	−28.77	−15.22	14
Heilongjiang	0.15	50.30	2.61	27.11	−44.69	−23.19	16
Shanghai	1.00	22.00	−38.56	80.52	124.84	58.52	4
Jiangsu	1.00	92.50	−11.95	338.53	222.26	246.03	1
Zhejiang	0.66	59.30	−12.58	143.62	111.74	84.32	3
Anhui	0.17	50.50	−5.09	31.18	−41.41	−19.32	15
Fujian	0.28	36.50	−10.78	37.89	−7.39	1.39	11
Jiangxi	0.13	54.90	−1.45	26.66	−52.15	−28.24	19
Shandong	0.37	160.10	4.11	214.15	39.26	54.05	6
Henan	0.21	126.90	−5.21	96.03	−28.27	−30.87	20
Hubei	0.23	63.70	0.70	54.02	−14.61	−9.68	12
Hunan	0.22	65.10	−18.76	53.14	−33.68	−11.96	13
Guangdong	1.00	71.50	−31.94	261.67	149.10	190.17	2
Guangxi	0.14	52.70	−41.69	26.65	−70.52	−26.05	18
Hainan	1.00	4.20	45.83	15.37	433.72	11.17	10
Chongqing	0.12	56.60	−21.32	24.41	−66.06	−32.19	21
Sichuan	0.20	84.40	−25.38	60.79	−46.25	−23.61	17
Guizhou	0.05	106.20	−7.56	19.88	−82.69	−86.32	28
Yunnan	0.10	67.60	35.01	23.59	−52.89	−44.01	23
Shaanxi	0.09	87.30	12.12	27.99	−64.06	−59.31	27
Gansu	0.08	63.40	14.90	18.35	−66.75	−45.05	24
Qinghai	1.00	18.30	27.62	66.97	367.04	48.67	7
Ningxia	0.43	36.90	18.73	58.24	87.40	21.34	9
Xinjiang	0.08	72.70	23.53	20.45	−65.24	−52.25	26

Note SEE denotes the sulfur-emission efficiency. The column of "difference" is calculate by using the ZSG allocation to minus the administrative allocation. Ranking is arranged in descending order according to the "difference" quantity

Source Both the sulfur-emission efficiency and the data of ZSG allocation are calculated by the authors with the original data introduced in the section of Variable Selection and Data Sources. The data of administrative allocation come from the Twelfth Five-Year Plan Work Program on the Integrated Energy Conservation and Emissions Reduction [China's National Development and Reform Commission (2011), no. 26]

could choose to lease their extra emission right. Similarly, Zhejiang, Ningxia, Shandong, and Fujian could possibly emit more sulfur dioxide in the ZSG allocation scheme, but there is still room for them to reduce emission because their sulfur emission efficiency is lower than 100%; see Table 4 for details. Therefore, these four provinces still have an incentive to reduce sulfur emission by optimizing their energy-usage structure and promoting desulfurization technology.

4 Conclusions

Under the framework of a macro total factor production function, this paper selects relevant theories on environmental production technology as a starting point to explore the allocations of carbon and sulfur emissions. An output-oriented model is initially used to describe the total factor production process. We place carbon and sulfur emissions into the production process in the form of undesirable outputs, a ZSG efficiency distribution model is then established by combining the ZSG-DEA approach and environmental production technology. Using mathematical software to solve the programming problem, the distribution schemes of China's carbon and sulfur emissions are analyzed. This paper focuses on the calculation of ZSG efficiency based on 2010 historical data, as well as evaluates and compares the differences between administrative allocation, ZSG allocation, and actual emissions. We also offer an optimal proposal for China's carbon and sulfur emissions allocation in 2015. The following conclusions are drawn.

First, China's Central Government adopts an allocation scheme of "one size fits all" to set emissions-reduction target, leading to a malpractice of "whipping the fast and hardworking" but "rewarding the slow and freeloading." Therefore, some provinces (Tianjin, Qinghai, Hainan, and others with higher sulfur emissions efficiencies) must struggle to fulfill their administrative targets, whereas other provinces (Shanxi, Shaanxi, Hunan, and others with greater emissions but lower efficiencies) can easily meet their targets. This leads to provinces with significant emissions (including Guizhou, Inner Mongolia, and Xinjiang) lagging further behind. In contrast, the ZSG allocation scheme, based on the emissions efficiency of all provinces and cities, emphasizes the overall Pareto optimal and simultaneously considers economic, environmental, and energy factors, thereby leading to widely ranging administrative allocation results. After the ZSG reallocation in 2015, 11 provinces obtain higher sulfur quotas than that in the administrative allocation, whereas 19 other provinces continue their emissions reduction apart from their administrative quotas. The latter are primarily resource-oriented provinces, so it is more difficult for them to realize the ZSG reduction target under their present economic structure; however, they can purchase emissions right from other provinces.

Second, comparisons between the administrative allocation of China's Central Government and the ZSG allocation show that provinces and cities with high emissions efficiency were generally assigned higher reduction targets by the government than that under the ZSG allocation, whereas provinces with lower emissions efficiency were assigned lower administrative emissions reduction targets. As for regional distribution, the western region was the most inefficient in terms of sulfur emission, but the government implemented an administrative protection that is not conducive to narrowing the gap between the east and west. Therefore, the government should adjust the current administrative scheme and offer necessary incentives. Based on the Pareto optimality of efficiency, this paper introduces the allocation of carbon and sulfur emissions into a total factor production framework to demonstrate that, although carbon and sulfur emissions are inevitable with economic outcomes, they can be controlled more effectively and reasonably than in the traditional administrative allocation scheme.

Because the allocation of emissions right involves many crucial issues in various dimensions, such as resource reserve, energy consumption structure, emissions reduction potential and industrial structure, a slight difference in the allocation of the emissions right could lead to profound influence in various provinces and cities in terms of the optimization of industrial structure, energy production and consumption policies. This paper's conclusions can offer some useful policy implications for future emissions reduction in China. To reduce carbon and sulfur emissions more efficiently, China must focus on the middle and western provinces that hold the greater capacity for emissions reduction. The government should also strive to build inter-regional cooperative industrial platforms and encourage enterprises with greater efficiency to offer technological support to those who are lacking to narrow the gap between the western and eastern regions. When prescribing the emissions control for different provinces and regions, the government should simultaneously consider fairness and efficiency. Finally, it is essential to improve the performance of pilot projects in which carbon and sulfur emissions are sold and/or traded, perfect the design of national carbon and sulfur trading mechanisms, and add environmental evaluation to the assessment of local government performance.

Acknowledgments Zhongqi Deng acknowledges financial support from the Social Science Foundation of China on "the study of the optimal city size in China under the triple effects of growth, environment and congestion". Ruizhi Pang acknowledges the Humanities and Social Sciences Project of the Ministry of Education of China (no. 15YJA790049) and Collaborative Innovation Center for China Economy.

References

Asker, J., A. Collard-Wexler, and J. De Loecker (2014), "Dynamic Inputs and Resource (Mis) Allocation", *Journal of Political Economy,* 122: 1013–1063.

Barzel, Y. and T.R. Sass (1990), "The Allocation of Resources by Voting", *Quarterly Journal of Economics,* 105(3): 745–771.

Bastianoni, S., F.M. Pulselli, and E. Tiezzi (2004), "The Problem of Assigning Responsibility for Greenhouse Gas Emissions", *Ecological Economics,* 49(3): 253–257.

Bohm, P., and B. Larsen (1994), "Fairness in a Tradeable-permit Treaty for Carbon Emissions Reductions in Europe and the Former Soviet Union", *Environment and Resource Economics*, 4 (3): 219–239.

Burtraw, D., K. Palmer, and D. Kahn (2005), "Allocation of CO_2 Emissions Allowances in the Regional Greenhouse Gas Cap-and-Trade Program", discussion paper in *Resources for the Future*, 5–25.

China's National Development and Reform Commission (2006), The Eleventh Five-Year Plan Work Program on the Emission Control of the Major Pollutants, document of China's State Council, no. 70.

China's National Development and Reform Commission (2011), The Twelfth Five-Year Plan Work Program on the Emission Reduction of the Green-House Gas, document of China's State Council, no. 41.

China's National Development and Reform Commission (2011), The Twelfth Five-Year Plan Work Program on the Integrated Energy Conservation and Emission Reduction, document of China's State Council, no. 26.

Chiu, Y., J. Lin, C. Hsu, and J. Lee (2013), "Carbon Emission Allowances of Efficiency Analysis: Application of Super SBM ZSG-DEA Model", *Polish Journal of Environmental Studies*, 22 (3): 653–666.

Currie, J., L. Davis, M. Greenstone, and R. Walker (2015), "Environmental Health Risks and Housing Values: Evidence from 1,600 Toxic Plant Openings and Closings", *American Economic Review*, 105(2): 678–709.

Demailly, D. and P. Quirion (2008), "European Emission Trading Scheme and Competitiveness: A Case Study on the Iron and Steel Industry", *Energy Economics*, 30(4): 2009–2027.

Edwards, T.H., and J.P. Hutton (2001), "Allocation of Carbon Permits within a Country: A General Equilibrium Analysis of the United Kingdom", *Energy Economics*, 23(4): 371–386.

Ergin, H. (2002), "Efficient Resource Allocation on the Basis of Priorities", *Econometrica*, 70(6): 2489–2497.

Ferng, J. (2003), "Allocating the Responsibility of CO_2 Over-emissions from the Perspectives of Benefit Principle and Ecological Deficit", *Ecological Economics*, 46(1): 121–141.

Fowlie, M. (2010), "Emissions Trading, Electricity Restructuring, and Investment in Pollution Abatement", *American Economic Review*, 100(3): 837–869.

Gollin, D., D. Lagakos, and M.E. Waugh (2014), "The Agricultural Productivity Gap", *Quarterly Journal of Economics*, 129(2): 939–93.

Gomes, E.G. and M.P.E. Lins (2007), "Modeling Undesirable Outputs with Zero Sum Gains Data Envelopment Analysis Models", *Journal of the Operational Research Society*, 59: 616–623.

Greenstone, M., and R. Hanna (2014), "Environmental Regulations, Air and Water Pollution, and Infant Mortality in India", *American Economic Review*, 104(10): 3038–3072.

Hsieh, C.T., and P.J. Klenow (2009), "Misallocation and Manufacturing TFP in China and India", *Quarterly Journal of Economics*, 124(4): 1403–1448.

IPCC, 2006, *IPCC Guidelines for National Greenhouse Gas Inventories*, Tokyo IGES.

Korhonen, P.J., and M.J. Syrjänen (2003), "Evaluation of Cost Efficiency in Finnish Electricity Distribution", *Annals of Operations Research*, 121(1–4): 105-122.

Lins, M.P.E., E.G. Gomes, J.C.C.B. Soares de Mello, and A.J.R. Soares de Mello (2003), "Olympic Ranking Based on a Zero Gains Sum Gains DEA Model", *European Journal of Operational Research*, 148(2): 312–322.

Martin, R., M. Muûls, L.B. De Preux, and U.J. Wagner (2014), "Industry Compensation under Relocation Risk: A Firm-level Analysis of the EU Emissions Trading Scheme", *American Economic Review*, 104(8): 2482–2508.

Palmer, K., D. Burtraw, and A. Paul (2009), "Allocation Allowances in a CO_2 Emissions Cap-and-Trade Program for the Electricity Sector in California", discussion paper in *Resource for the Future*, 9–41.

Pang, R., Z. Deng, and Y. Chiu (2015a), "Pareto Improvement through A Reallocation of Carbon Emission Quotas", *Renewable and Sustainable Energy Reviews*, 50: 419–430.

Pang, R., Z. Deng, and J. Hu (2015b), "Clean energy use and total-factor efficiencies: An international comparison", *Renewable and Sustainable Energy Reviews*, 52: 1158–1171.

UKCIP (2002), *Climate Change Scenarios for the United Kingdom: The UKCIP Scientific Report*, Oxford: UK Climate Impacts Programme.

Wang, K., X. Zhang, Y. Wei, and S. Yu (2013), "Regional Allocation of CO_2 Emissions Allowance over Provinces in China by 2020", *Energy Policy*, 54(3): 214–229.

Chapter 7
Carbon Productivity and Carbon Shadow Price in China's Power Industry: An Endogenous Directional Distance Function Approach

Yujiao Xian and Ke Wang

1 Introduction

China's economy has experienced a rapid growth along with fast-paced urbanization and industrialization. However, the great achievement of economic development has led to some increasing environmental pressure, such as energy resource overshoot, air pollution, and greenhouse gas (GHG) emissions. How to control the energy-related GHG emissions, which is mainly CO_2 emissions, has become one of the most urgent challenges that need to be addressed in China. In 2013, the statistics of International Energy Agency shows that the power industry sector produces nearly 50% of China's carbon emission (IEA 2015). Therefore, controlling CO_2 emissions of China's power industry sector should be regarded as priority for national carbon emission reduction. The evaluation of carbon performance (e.g., carbon efficiency, productivity and shadow price) makes the effort of environmental protection accountable and helps to prioritize actions and formulate policies for economic growth, energy saving, and CO_2 emissions control. In this regard, it is essential for China to improve the carbon performance in power industry sector.

When measuring the carbon efficiency with the consideration of both intended and unintended outputs (e.g., pollutants), the directional distance function (DDF) based nonparametric DEA technique is considered an effective approach that

Y. Xian · K. Wang (✉)
Center for Energy and Environmental Policy Research & School of Management
and Economics, Beijing Institute of Technology, Beijing, China
e-mail: wangkebit@bit.edu.cn

K. Wang
Sustainable Development Research Institute for Economy and Society of Beijing,
Beijing, China

K. Wang
Beijing Key Lab of Energy Economics and Environmental Management, Beijing, China

© Springer Nature Singapore Pte Ltd. 2018   161
R. Pang et al. (eds.), *Energy, Environment and Transitional Green
Growth in China*, https://doi.org/10.1007/978-981-10-7919-1_7

can expand intended outputs and control unintended outputs or inputs simultaneously (Chambers et al. 1996; Managi and Jena 2008; Chang and Hu 2010; Wang et al. 2013). The techniques for estimating efficiency scores and shadow prices of pollutants through DDF can be divided into the parametric technique (e.g., Stochastic Frontier Analysis, SFA) and the non-parametric technique (e.g., DEA). The former usually requires a specific assumption on production function such as the quadratic directional distance function (Kumbhakar and Lovell 2000). Examples of its applications can be found in Chambers (2002), Färe et al. (2006), Wei et al. (2013) and Molinos-Senante et al. (2015). While the latter does not need any assumption on production function and is based on the data construction of all observed inputs and outputs. It has been widely utilized to the issues of energy and environmental such as Watanabe and Tanaka (2007), Zhou et al. (2008), Wang et al. (2012), Lin et al. (2013), Shortall and Barnes (2013), Li and Lin (2015). In this paper, we will use the non-parametric DEA technique for the carbon efficiency and productivity evaluation.

In the empirical applications of DDF based on the DEA model, the directional vector is usually selected directly by the researchers in advance. This selection is arbitrary and could not guarantee to capture the largest distance to the efficient frontier. Thus, some researchers introduced an endogenous DDF method based on the DEA model to identify the largest efficiency improvement potentials (Färe et al. 2013; Zofio et al. 2013; Hampf and Krüger 2015; Wang et al. 2016a; Lee 2014, 2016). In our paper, we will use the endogenous DDF technique to estimate carbon efficiency without market prices. In addition, previous studies of endogenous DDF method based on the DEA model mainly focus on the theory development and efficiency evaluation. In this study, we develop the dual form of the endogenous DDF technique which is further utilized to estimate the shadow price of CO_2 emissions in China's power industry sector.

Regarding the carbon efficiency and productivity change, Malmquist productivity index, Malmquist-Luenberger productivity index and Luenberger productivity indicator are the most common indexes, and they are equivalent in principle. When calculating these indexes, there are usually three disadvantages: (i) non-circular; (ii) possible infeasible situation; and (iii) different measures for cross-period units (Färe and Grosskopf 1996). In order to solve these problems, Pastor and Lovell (2005) developed a Malmquist index under a global frontier that is composed with the data in all periods under investigation. It satisfies circularity and is immune to infeasible solution, as well as can generate a single measure for cross-period units. Many studies had employed the global frontier in empirical analysis (e.g., Kumar 2006; Asmild and Tam 2007; Herrala and Goel 2012; Fan et al. 2015). Thus, in this study, we also employ the global Luenberger indicator to analyze the efficiency change of power industry sector of China's 30 provinces and four areas (i.e., north-eastern area, eastern area, central area and western area).

It is also important to explore the contribution of the sources to carbon productivity change. In our study, the global carbon Luenberger productivity indicator is decomposed into three compositions: best practice gap change (*BPC*), pure efficiency change (*PEC*) and scale efficiency change (*SEC*). Therefore, it can help to identify the effects of technical progress, catch-up and scale management in carbon productivity growth.

The remaining part of this chapter is organized as follows: Sect. 2 describes the endogenous directional distance function model, presents the estimation method of shadow price of unintended outputs, and introduces the global Luenberger productivity indicator and its decomposition. Section 3 shows our data source. Section 4 first analyzes the carbon productivity change among the power industry sector of China's 30 provinces and their corresponding four areas; then it provides an empirical estimation and the convergence analysis of the relative shadow price of CO_2 emissions among areas and provinces. Section 5 shows the conclusions and provides several policy implications.

2 Methodologies

2.1 Endogenous Directional Distance Function

Assuming we observe n (j = 1, 2, ..., n) DMUs with m (i = 1, 2, ..., m) inputs x, s (r = 1, 2, ..., s) intended (or good) outputs y and h (f = 1, 2,..., h) unintended (or bad) outputs u. The corresponding production possibility set then can be denoted by:

$$T = \left\{ (x, y, u) \in R_+^{m+s+h} : x \text{ can produce}(y, u) \right\} \tag{1}$$

It is often assumed to satisfy several technically and economically reasonable characteristics including: (i) Convexity (Shephard 1970); (ii) Free disposability of inputs and intended (or good) outputs (Färe and Primont 1995); (iii) Weak disposability of unintended (or bad) outputs associated with intended (or good) outputs which implies any proportional reduction of intended and unintended outputs together is feasible in the production possibility set (Färe and Grosskopf 2004); and (iv) Null-jointness of intended (or good) and unintended (or bad) outputs which indicates intended outputs and unintended outputs are simultaneously generated.

To identify the production possibility set based on the empirical data, we use non-parametric directional distance function approach in this study. In contrast to parametric approach, the non-parametric approach does not need a specific form of the production function or any assumption on the inefficiency distribution.

The output-oriented DDF can be defined as:

$$\vec{D}(x, y, u; \vec{g}) = max\left\{ \beta : \left(x, y + \beta\vec{g}_y, u - \beta\vec{g}_u\right) \in T \right\} \tag{2}$$

in which β (> 0 or = 0) is the inefficiency score and $\vec{g} = \left(\vec{g}_y, -\vec{g}_u\right)$ is the directional vector.

In most applications for evaluating efficiency and productivity, the directional vector is arbitrarily pre-selected by the researchers. However, there may be some disadvantages in this arbitrary selection process. First, intended and unintended outputs are usually assigned the same weight associate with the pre-selected direction, and thus, they do not have any trade-offs in production process. Second, the inefficiency scores may be underestimated when some non-zero slacks exist on outputs (Fukuyama and Weber 2009). Third, there may be a downward-sloping segment on the efficient production frontier when utilizing the weak disposability characteristic mentioned above, i.e., the frontier may have a segment with negative slope (Picazo-Tadeo and Prior 2009; Chen and Delmas 2012). Therefore, some inefficient units located on this part may be misclassification as efficient units along with these arbitrary directions. In order to solve these problems, Färe et al. (2013) proposed a technique to obtain an endogenous directional vector by maximizing the inefficiency score of the unit under evaluation. Hereafter, Hampf and Krüger (2015) developed a more general model to obtain the direction along which each unit can identify the furthest distance to the efficient production frontier. The associated output-oriented model for the under evaluation decision making unit, DMU_{j_0}, can be shown as follows:

$$\max_{\beta, \lambda_j, \alpha_{r j_0}, \delta_{f j_0}} \beta$$

$$s.t. \quad x_{i j_0} \geq \sum_{j=1}^{n} x_{ij} \lambda_j, \quad i = 1, 2, \ldots, m$$

$$y_{r j_0} + \beta \alpha_{r j_0} y_{r j_0} \leq \sum_{j=1}^{n} y_{rj} \lambda_j, \quad r = 1, 2, \ldots, s$$

$$u_{f j_0} - \beta \delta_{f j_0} u_{f j_0} = \sum_{j=1}^{n} u_{fj} \lambda_j, \quad f = 1, 2, \ldots, h \qquad (3)$$

$$\sum_{r=1}^{s} \alpha_{r j_0} + \sum_{f=1}^{f} \delta_{f j_0} = 1$$

$$\beta, \lambda_j, \alpha_{r j_0}, \delta_{f j_0} \geq 0, j = 1, 2, \ldots, n, \ r = 1, 2, \ldots, s, \ f = 1, 2, \ldots, h.$$

In Model (3), λ_j represents the intensity variable, whereas $\alpha_{r j_0}$ and $\delta_{f j_0}$ are the weight variables for intended output r and unintended output f, respectively. Moreover, the non-negative restriction on α and δ means that only the directions $\vec{g} = (\vec{g}_y, -\vec{g}_u) = (\alpha \otimes y, -\delta \otimes u)$ that do not reduce intended outputs or increase unintended outputs can be obtained. Note $\otimes$ denotes the Hadamard product of two vectors.

2.2 Shadow Price Estimation of Unintended Output

Obviously, Model (3) is a nonlinear programming problem which can be transformed into a linear programming problem by introducing two new variables, $\beta_1 = \beta \times \alpha$ and $\beta_2 = \beta \times \delta$. The linear model then can be read as:

$$\max_{\beta_{1r},\beta_{2f},\lambda_j} \sum_{r=1}^{s} \beta_{1r} + \sum_{f=1}^{h} \beta_{2f}$$

$$s.t. \quad x_{ij_0} \geq \sum_{j=1}^{n} x_{ij}\lambda_j, \ i = 1, 2, \ldots, m$$

$$y_{rj_0} + \beta_{1r} y_{rj_0} \leq \sum_{j=1}^{n} y_{rj}\lambda_j, \ r = 1, 2, \ldots, s \tag{4}$$

$$u_{fj_0} - \beta_{2f} u_{fj_0} = \sum_{j=1}^{n} u_{fj}\lambda_j, \ f = 1, 2, \ldots, h$$

$$\beta_{1r}, \beta_{2f}, \lambda_j \geq 0, \ j = 1, 2, \ldots, n.$$

In Model (4), β_{1r} and β_{2f} are the inefficiency scores for the intended output r and the unintended output f, respectively.

Let v, μ and ω be the decision variables indicating the dual multipliers of the constraints of inputs, intended outputs and unintended outputs in Model (4). We can transfer Model (4) to Model (5), which is the dual form of Model (4).

$$\min_{v_i,\mu_r,\omega_f} \sum_{i=1}^{m} x_{ij_0} v_i - \sum_{r=1}^{s} y_{rj_0}\mu_r + \sum_{f=1}^{h} u_{fj_0}\omega_f$$

$$s.t. \quad \sum_{i=1}^{m} x_{ij} v_i - \sum_{r=1}^{s} y_{rj}\mu_r + \sum_{f=1}^{h} u_{fj}\omega_f \geq 0, \ \forall j$$

$$\sum_{r=1}^{s} y_{rj_0}\mu_r \geq 1, \tag{5}$$

$$\sum_{f=1}^{h} u_{fj_0}\omega_f \geq 1,$$

$$v_i, \mu_r \geq 0, \ i = 1, 2, \ldots, m; \ r = 1, 2, \ldots, s.$$

Considering v_i, μ_r and ω_f as the shadow price for inputs i, intended output r and unintended output f, respectively. We treat $\sum_{r=1}^{s} y_{rj}\mu_r$ as total revenue for DMU$_j$, and $\sum_{i=1}^{m} x_{ij} v_i + \sum_{f=1}^{h} u_{fj}\omega_f$ as total cost for DMU$_j$. Then we define the negative profit for each DMU$_j$ as $\sum_{i=1}^{m} x_{ij_0} v_i - \sum_{r=1}^{s} y_{rj_0}\mu_r + \sum_{f=1}^{h} u_{fj_0}\omega_f$, and thus, Model (5) seeks to minimize the negative profit of each DMU$_j$. This optimization is based on dual shadow prices. As it stands, in Model (5), the first constraint means that the efficient profit from inputs and outputs must be positive. It is crucial to note here that the value of dual variables of unintended outputs can be considered as a cost with the constraint that they are positive. Following Hailu (2003), or Førsund (2009) in considering positive dual price for the unintended output, it indicates that the revenue from the intended outputs has to at lest compensate the cost of inputs and the unintended outputs (i.e., the negative revenue). The economic implication of this result is relevant and intuitive: if the dual prices of the unintended outputs are negative, obviously, the producers' revenue then will be from both intended and unintended outputs are no longer 'bad' in the economic sense.

Consequently, the relative shadow price of unintended output f, p_{u_f}, associated with the intended output r can be obtained as follows:

$$p_{u_f} = \frac{p_{y_r} \times \omega_f}{\mu_r} \tag{6}$$

where p_{y_r} is the market price of intended output r. Thus, on the one hand, p_{u_f} can be considered as the relative market price of unintended output f. On the other hand, the relative shadow price can be considered as the opportunity abatement cost regarding the corresponding economic benefits, and it therefore represents the marginal abatement cost of unintended outputs which means the trade-off between generating intended outputs and unintended outputs.

2.3 Global Luenberger Productivity Indicator

As mentioned above, the global production technology can overcome the weaknesses of traditional productivity indexes in computing carbon productivity change.

Assume we observe T ($t = 1, 2, \ldots, T$) time periods, a global benchmark technology T^G hence can be defined as $T_V^G = T_V^1 \cup T_V^2 \cup \ldots \cup T_V^T$ and $T_C^G = T_C^1 \cup T_C^2 \cup \ldots \cup T_C^T$ (Pastor and Lovell 2005). The subscribe V and C represent the technology exhibiting variable returns to scale (VRS) and constant returns to scale (CRS).

Consequently, the global Luenberger productivity indicator (*GLPI*) can be defined on CRS as follows:

$$\begin{aligned} GLPI_C^G\left(x^t, y^t, u^t; x^{t+1}, y^{t+1}, u^{t+1}\right) &= \vec{D}_C^G(x^t, y^t, u^t) - \vec{D}_C^G\left(x^{t+1}, y^{t+1}, u^{t+1}\right) \\ &= \beta_C^G(x^t, y^t, u^t) - \beta_C^G\left(x^{t+1}, y^{t+1}, u^{t+1}\right) \end{aligned} \tag{7}$$

where $\vec{D}_C^G(x, y, u) = \max\{\beta : (x, y + \beta\alpha \otimes y, u - \beta\delta \otimes u) \in T_C^G\}$ is the directional distance function, and similarly, $\otimes$ denotes the Hadamard product of two vectors. Specifically, $GLPI_C^G > 0$ indicates the productivity growth; $GLPI_C^G = 0$ indicates the productivity remains at the same level; and $GLPI_C^G < 0$ indicates the productivity decline. Following Färe et al. (1994b), we can decompose *GLPI* into pure efficiency change (*PEC*), scale efficiency change (*SEC*) and best practice gap change (*BPC*) as follows:

$$PEC = \beta_V^t(x^t, y^t, u^t) - \beta_V^{t+1}\left(x^{t+1}, y^{t+1}, u^{t+1}\right) \tag{8}$$

$$SEC = \left[\beta_C^t(x^t, y^t, u^t) - \beta_V^t(x^t, y^t, u^t)\right] \\ - \left[\beta_C^{t+1}\left(x^{t+1}, y^{t+1}, u^{t+1}\right) - \beta_V^{t+1}\left(x^{t+1}, y^{t+1}, u^{t+1}\right)\right] \tag{9}$$

$$BPC = \left[\beta_C^G(x^t, y^t, u^t) - \beta_C^t(x^t, y^t, u^t)\right] \\ - \left[\beta_C^G\left(x^{t+1}, y^{t+1}, u^{t+1}\right) - \beta_C^{t+1}\left(x^{t+1}, y^{t+1}, u^{t+1}\right)\right] \tag{10}$$

Here, technical efficiency captures the movement towards to (or away from) the efficient production frontier, and thus, *PEC* measures technical efficiency change under *VRS*; Scale efficiency denotes the deviation from the optimal production scale that generates the largest marginal benefit and the observed production scale, and thus, *SEC* measures the change of this deviation between two adjacent periods; Best practice gap is the distance between the global production frontier and each period production frontier, and thus, *BPC* measures the change of technological gap between two adjacent periods.

Obviously that the sum of *PEC*, *SEC* and *BPC* equals to *GLPL*:

$$GLPI_C^G\left(x^t, y^t, u^t; x^{t+1}, y^{t+1}, u^{t+1}\right) = PEC + SEC + BPC \tag{11}$$

Note that the positive values of these three components respectively indicates pure efficiency improvement, scale efficiency increase, and technical progress, while the negative values of these three components respectively indicates pure efficiency deterioration, scale efficiency decrease, and technical regress; zero values on these three components indicate no change.

3 Data

We apply the endogenously non-parametric DDF model and the global carbon Luenberger productivity indicator to the power industry sector in China's 30 provinces during the 12th Five-Year Plan period (2011–2015). Hong Kong, Macau, Taiwan and Tibet are not included in this sample because some of their data are missing and these regions are not involved in China's polices for energy saving and carbon emissions reduction.

Three inputs, one intended output and one unintended output are used in our calculation. The intended output and unintended output are defined as the gross electricity generation and total CO_2 emissions, respectively. Each province is considered as generating these outputs by using employee, fuel consumption and electricity generation installed capacity. The data on the employee is obtained from the China Industry Economy Statistical Yearbook, while the data on the fuel consumption, the installed capacity and the gross electricity generation are obtained from the Wind database. CO_2 emissions are calculated from the fuel consumption.

Table 1 Descriptive statistics

Inputs and outputs (units)	No. of observations	Mean	Std. Dev.	Min.	Max.
Employee (thousand persons)	150	94.29	51.42	9.20	212.35
Fuel consumption (million ton coal equivalent)	150	52.04	32.49	4.90	140.01
Installed capacity (million kW)	150	42.06	24.28	4.25	104.02
Electricity (billion kWh)	150	1715.85	1079.25	169.07	4651.43
CO_2 emissions (million ton CO_2)	150	131.19	100.04	10.48	417.67

Specifically, we use the carbon emission factors for combusting coal, oil and natural gas to calculate the fuel consumption related CO_2 emissions, and these factors are obtained from the National Greenhouse Gas Inventories of IPCC Guidelines. In addition, electricity prices are the feed-in tariffs which are obtained from the Price Division of National Development and Reform Commission of People's Republic in China. The specifically descriptive statistics are presented in Table 1.

4 Empirical Analyses

How to improve carbon productivity and reduce carbon emissions abatement cost is an important issue to control CO_2 emissions. In this section, we first provide an analysis of carbon productivity change and its decomposition, and then we show the relative shadow prices of CO_2 emissions for each area and specific regions.

4.1 Carbon Productivity Change Analysis

In order to identify the sources of *GLPI* change for four areas, the decomposition of average *GLPI* into *BPC*, *PEC* and *SEC* is reported in Table 2. The last column presents the *GLPI*, *BPC*, *PEC* and *SEC* of each area during the entire study period. It can be seen that only western area shows the increase in *GLPI*, while all the other three areas show the decrease in *GLPI*. Furthermore, the technical progress is the primary driving force for the growth of *GLPI* during 2011–2015, while pure efficiency deterioration always provides negative contribution on the growth of *GLPI*. It implies that, on average, all areas are away from the efficient production frontier in our study period. In addition, scale efficiency increases in central area and western area, whereas it decreases in eastern area and north-eastern area during the entire study period. This finding implies that the eastern and north-eastern areas in China have both failed in moving toward more optimal scales of generating electricity and emitting CO_2 during 2011–2015.

Table 2 Decomposition of global carbon productivity indicator for each area

Areas	Indicators	2011–2012	2012–2013	2013–2014	2014–2015	2011–2015
Eastern area	GLPI	−0.065	0.086	−0.041	0.014	−0.005
	BPC	−0.079	0.124	0.015	0.003	0.064
	PEC	−0.024	−0.010	−0.059	0.058	−0.035
	SEC	0.038	−0.028	0.003	−0.047	−0.034
Central area	GLPI	−0.045	0.105	−0.084	−0.103	−0.128
	BPC	0.022	−0.016	0.145	−0.066	0.085
	PEC	−0.095	0.085	−0.222	−0.031	−0.264
	SEC	0.028	0.036	−0.006	−0.006	0.051
Western area	GLPI	0.039	0.042	0.046	−0.061	0.066
	BPC	0.084	−0.068	0.120	−0.026	0.111
	PEC	−0.019	0.045	−0.075	−0.049	−0.098
	SEC	−0.026	0.066	0.001	0.013	0.053
North-eastern area	GLPI	−0.043	0.013	0.009	−0.024	−0.045
	BPC	0.031	−0.025	0.096	0.034	0.136
	PEC	−0.059	0.011	−0.073	−0.032	−0.153
	SEC	−0.014	0.027	−0.014	−0.027	−0.027

In conclusion, policies focused on developing new technologies of electricity generation, energy utilization and carbon control among areas might not be enough, more efforts are required to encourage technical efficiency catching-up and economic scale management in improving carbon productivity in China's power industry.

In order to obtain a better understanding of carbon productivity change and its decomposition, we additionally compare these indicators among China's 30 provinces. Figure 1 illustrates the average GLPI and its decomposition indicators

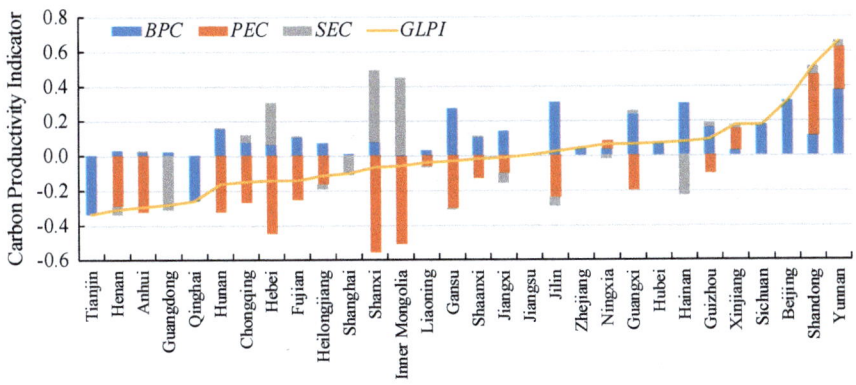

Fig. 1 Carbon productivity indicators and their decomposition for specific regions

(*BPC*, *PEC* and *SEC*). It can be seen that about 40% regions whose *GLPI* range from 2.3 to 65.7% experience carbon productivity growths. Among these regions, Yunnan shows the highest growth rate (65.7%), followed by Shandong (51.4%), Beijing (31.1%), Sichuan (17.9%) and Xinjiang (17.7%). Their carbon productivity growths are almost driven by pure efficiency increase and technical progress (i.e., the reduction on best practice gaps). Hence, promoting the progress on technology of energy utilization and CO_2 emissions control is an efficient way for carbon productivity growth. On the contrary, there are 17 regions present carbon productivity decrease (range from −1.2 to −33.5%) and in which, the primary driving force for productivity decline of about 70% regions is pure efficiency decrease. Accordingly, policies focused on encouraging technical efficiency catching-up among regions are still very important in improving carbon productivity among regions.

4.2   Relative Shadow Price of CO_2 Emissions

In addition to the carbon efficiency and productivity evaluation, we further estimate the relative shadow prices of CO_2 emissions for the power industry sector in China's 30 provinces. The relative shadow price can be considered as the opportunity abatement cost regarding to economic electricity generation, and it therefore represents the marginal abatement cost of CO_2 emissions which means the trade-off between producing electricity and emitting CO_2 emissions. The larger relative shadow price represents it is more expensive to control additional carbon emissions.

Figure 2 depicts the weighted average shadow prices for four areas during 2011–2015. It can be seen that the dynamic trends of the relative shadow prices of CO_2 emissions show great disparity among areas, but all of them are characterized by a rising trend during the 12th Five Year Plan period. In specific, the CO_2 emissions abatement cost of China's power industry sector fluctuates with a range from 494 to 965 yuan/ton during 2011–2015. The lowest 5-year price appears in the eastern area with a range from 390 to 620 yuan/ton, and the highest price appears in the

Fig. 2 Weighted average shadow prices of four areas

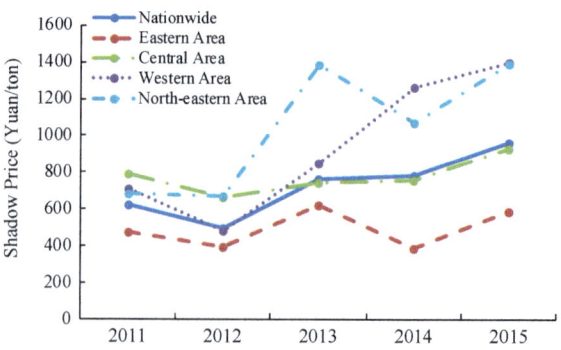

north-eastern area with a range from 668 to 1389 yuan/ton. The CO_2 emissions abatement cost of power industry sector in central area is relatively stable around 780 yuan/ton during 2011–2015, and the cost in western area has been the highest one since 2014. The results indicate that China has made some efforts to build an environmental-friendly and energy-efficient society since the beginning of the 12th Five-Year Plan, and the stricter policies and regulations implemented to reduce carbon emissions had begun to gradually increase the costs of additional emissions reduction.

In order to present a further insight into the relative shadow prices comparison, we apply the ANOVA test to identify the price difference, which assumes the mean value between different groups (areas and years) have no significant difference. The test results for four areas and five years are listed in Table 3. The second row is the test result among four areas, while the third row is the test result among five years. It can be found that there is significant difference (at 0.05 levels) in the relative shadow prices among different years and areas. This finding indicates that there is still obviously unbalanced level of CO_2 emissions abatement costs among China's areas, indicating the utilization of electricity generation and emission control technologies are inequitable.

Figure 3 depicts the annual average shadow prices for each region in terms of the regional electricity generation during the study period. It can be found that, among the power industry sector of China's 30 provinces, Fujian evidences the lowest annual average shadow prices of CO_2 emissions, while Chongqing has the

Table 3 ANOVA analysis of shadow prices

	df	F	P-value
Area	4	2.214	0.003
Year	5	3.301	0.013

H_0: There is no difference among groups

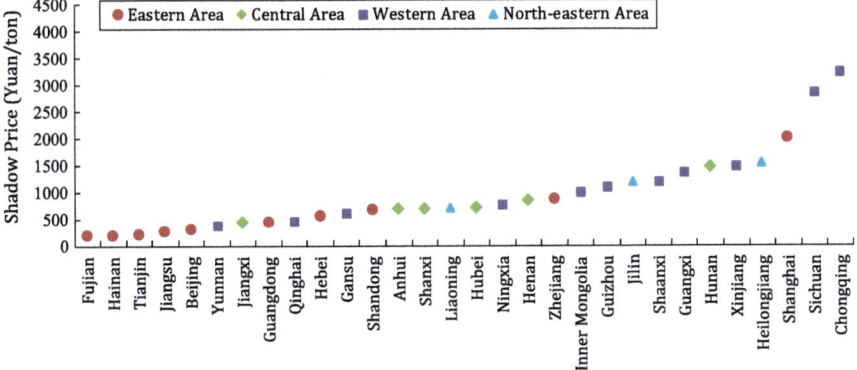

Fig. 3 Annual average shadow prices for specific regions

highest CO_2 emissions abatement cost. In specific, the annual average shadow prices of CO_2 emissions of Chongqing, Sichuan, Shanghai are ranked top three among 30 regions which are all above 2000 yuan/ton; while the annual average shadow prices of CO_2 emissions of Fujian, Hainan, Tianjin and Jiangsu are all below 300 yuan/ton and ranked bottom among 30 regions. The CO_2 emissions abatement cost is significantly different between specific regions, implying that the level of economic production scale and electricity generation technology among China's regions is obviously unbalanced and inequitable. Since the relative shadow price is significantly various across provinces, one suggestion is that the Chinese government should give more impetus to the implementation of regional carbon emissions trading scheme (Wang et al. 2016b). The government has set some targets of CO_2 emissions intensity reduction in the 12th Five Year Plan, and assigned them to different provinces. Through the regional carbon emission trading, the regions whose relative shadow prices are higher can acquire abatement cost savings. In specific, these regions can decide whether to implement an emissions abatement strategy or to purchase allowances from the regions with lower relative shadow prices in carbon emissions trading market. Hence, the difference on relative shadow prices of CO_2 emissions among provinces and areas will provide a necessity and possibility in CO_2 emissions abatement cost savings from the regional carbon emissions trading in China's power industry sector.

In order to provide a further insight into the difference of relative shadow prices between areas and provinces, we apply the analysis of sigma (σ) convergence and beta (β) convergence. σ convergence is sufficient but not necessary for β convergence. The σ convergence is to explore the trend of the static measure of shadow prices dispersions among areas and provinces, and the β convergence is to test the negative relationship between initial shadow price and its growth rate (if $0 < \beta < 1$). Figure 4 presents the σ convergence and Table 4 shows the β convergence across all areas and provinces. On the one hand, there has been a clear increase in the dispersions of shadow prices distributions both among areas and

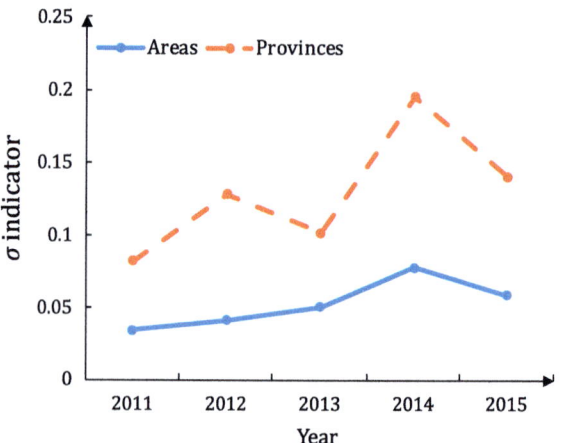

Fig. 4 σ indicator of areas and provinces

Table 4 β indicator of areas and provinces

	β indicator	P-value
Area	0.72	0.01
Year	0.73	0.00

among provinces and thus evidence for sigma non-convergence. It suggests that the gaps of relative shadow prices among areas and among provinces become larger during the 12th Five Year period in China. On the other hand, the β indicator among areas and provinces are 0.72 and 0.73 respectively, which suggest the existence of beta convergence over the study period. Hence, most areas or provinces, which have the low initial shadow price, have relatively high growth rate of shadow price on average. One possible reason is that the reduction potentials of shadow price is less in the areas and provinces with low shadow prices, and thus, the growth rate would be higher.

5 Conclusions and Policy Implications

GHG emissions abatement is considered one of the most urgent problems, as China and the rest of world all are facing serious challenges from global warming and environmental degradation. Although China's pilot CO_2 emissions trading market has been in place for a few years, its market operation has not yet reached expectation. If the environmental policies and carbon trading market were efficient, a price on carbon emission permit or a carbon tax would equal the marginal abatement cost. As the largest sector of China's carbon emissions, the power industry sector is critical in saving energy and controlling CO_2 emissions. Evaluating carbon efficiency and productivity, and estimating the CO_2 emissions abatement cost for the power industry sector in China are necessary for understand the current CO_2 emissions performance and CO_2 abatement cost, which could provide valuable policy making supports for further mitigation efforts.

In this study, we apply an endogenously developed DDF method to evaluate the carbon efficiency and productivity of the power industry sector of China's 30 provinces and their corresponding four areas during 2011–2015. In addition, the relative shadow prices (i.e., the marginal abatement costs) of CO_2 emissions of the power industry sector for these 30 provinces and the corresponding four areas during this period are estimated.

On the one hand, the results of carbon productivity evaluation indicate that:

(i) Only the average *GLPI* of the western area shows an increase during our study period, indicating the carbon productivity growth of the power industry sector only appears in China's western area during the 12th FYP period.

(ii) On the average of four areas, the primary driving force for carbon productivity increase can be attributed to technical progress (i.e., the decrease of best practice gaps), while the primary driving force for carbon productivity decrease can be attributed to the lack of catch-up effect (i.e., pure efficiency deterioration). Moreover, scale efficiency increase promotes the carbon productivity growth in central area and western area, whereas scale efficiency decrease drags the carbon productivity growth in eastern area and north-eastern area.

(iii) There are 12 regions performed growth whereas 17 regions performed decline in carbon productivity. In general, the pure efficiency decrease provides the greatest contribution in carbon productivity decline for most regions.

(iv) At the current stage, developing new technologies of electricity generation, energy utilization and carbon control might not be enough, while encouraging technical efficiency catching-up and economic production scale management will play a more important role in improving the carbon productivity of China's power industry sector. In addition, promoting some clean and renewable energy projects may help to reduce the over dependence on traditional fossil fuel consumption so as to realize the carbon efficiency improvement and abatement cost reduction in this industry.

On the other hand, the results of relative shadow prices estimation indicate that:

(v) On the weighted average of all 30 regions, the CO_2 emissions abatement cost of China's power industry sector increases during the 12th Five Year Plan period from 494 to 965 yuan/ton.

(vi) There is statistically significant shadow prices difference between China's areas and provinces. The highest weighted average CO_2 emissions abatement cost appears in the north-eastern area with a range from 668 to 1389 yuan/ton, while the lowest weighted average CO_2 emissions abatement appears in the eastern area with a range from 390 to 620 yuan/ton.

(vii) The average CO_2 emissions abatement cost of Chongqing is highest, and that of Fujian is lowest. There is still obviously unbalanced and inequitable levels of economic production scale, electricity generation and carbon abatement technologies among China's regions. The large gap on CO_2 emissions abatement cost in power industry sector among different regions provide a necessity and possibility to reduce the national total carbon abatement cost through regional and national carbon emissions trading schemes.

(viii) The shadow prices are sigma non-convergence and beta convergence among areas and provinces. It suggests that although the initial shadow price and its growth rate are negatively correlated on average, both the gaps of relative shadow prices among areas and among provinces become larger during the 12th Five Year period.

Acknowledgements We gratefully acknowledge the financial supports from the National Natural Science Foundation of China (grant Nos. 71471018, 71521002 and 71761137001), the Social Science Foundation of Beijing (grant No. 16JDGLB013), the National Key R&D Program (grant No. 2016YFA0602603), the Joint Development Program of Beijing Municipal Commission of Education, Fok Ying Tung Education Foundation (161076) and International Clean Energy Talent Program (2017) from Chinese Scholarship Council (No. 201702660030).

References

Asmild, M., Tam, F., 2007. Estimating global frontier shifts and global Malmquist indices. Journal of Productivity Analysis. 27(2): 137–148.

Chambers, R., 2002. Exact nonradial input, output, and productivity measurement. Economic Theory. 20: 751–765.

Chambers, R., Färe, R., Grosskopf, S., 1996. Productivity growth in APEC countries. Pacific Economic Review. 1:181–190.

Chang, T. P., Hu, J. L., 2010. Total-factor energy productivity growth, technical progress, and efficiency change: An empirical study of China. Applied Energy. 87(10): 3262–3270.

Chen, C. -M., Delmas, M.A., 2012. Measuring Eco-Inefficiency: A New Frontier Approach. Operations Research. 60(5): 1064–1079.

Fan, M.T., Shao, S., Yang, L.L., 2015. Combining global Malmquist-Luenberger index and generalized method of moments to investigate industrial total factor CO2 emission performance: A case of Shanghai (China). Energy Policy. 79:189–201.

Färe, R., Primont, D., 1995. Multi-Output Production and Duality: Theory and Applications. Boston/ Kluwer Academic Publishers.

Färe, R., Grosskopf, S., 1996. Intertemporal Production Frontiers: With Dynamic DEA. Kluwer Academic Publishers, Boston.

Färe, R., Grosskopf, S., 2004. New Directions: Efficiency and Productivity. Boston: Kluwer Academic Publishers.

Färe, R, Grosskopf, S., Norris, M., Zhang, Z., 1994b. Productivity growth, technical progress and efficiency change in industrialized countries. The American Economic Review. 84(1):66–83.

Färe, R., Grosskopf, S., Weber, W. L., 2006. Shadow prices and pollution costs in U.S. agriculture. Ecological Economics. 56: 89– 103.

Färe, R., Grosskopf, S., Wittaker, G., 2013. Directional Output Distance Functions: Endogenous Constraints Based on Exogenous Normalization Constraints. Journal of Productivity Analysis. 40: 267–269.

Fukuyama, H., Weber, W. L., 2009. A directional slacks-based measure of technical inefficiency. Socio-Economic Planning Sciences. 43: 274–287.

Førsund, F., 2009. Good modeling of bad outputs: pollution and multiple-output production. International Review of Environmental and Resource Economics. 3:1–38.

Hampf, B., Krüger, J. J., 2015. Optimal Directions for Directional Distance Functions: An Exploration of Potential Reductions of Greenhouse Gases. American Journal of Agricultural Economics. 97: 920–938.

Hailu, A., 2003. Non-parametric productivity analysis with undesirable outputs: reply. American Journal of Agricultural Economics. 85 (4): 1075–1077.

Herrala, R., Goel, R. K., 2012. Global CO2 efficiency: Country-wise estimates using a stochastic cost frontier. Energy Policy. 762–770.

IEA. CO2 Emissions from fuel combustion highlights. International Energy Agency. ⟨http://www.iea.org/media/statistics/co2highlights.pdf⟩; 2015 [accessed 04.25.17].

Kumar, S., 2006. Environmentally sensitive productivity growth: a global analysis using Malmquist–Luenberger index. Ecological Economics. 56 (2): 280–293.

Kumbhakar, S.C., Lovell, C.A.K., 2000. Stochastic Frontier Analysis. Cambridge, UK: Cambridge University Press.

Lee, C.-Y., 2014. Meta-data envelopment analysis: Finding a direction towards marginal profit maximization. European Journal of Operational Research. 237: 207–216.

Lee, C.-Y., 2016. Nash-profit efficiency: A measure of changes in market structures. European Journal of Operational Research. 255: 659–663.

Li, K., Lin, B., 2015. Metafroniter energy efficiency with CO2 emissions and its convergence analysis for China. Energy Economics. 230–241.

Lin, E. Y., Chen, P., Chen, C., 2013. Measuring the environmental efficiency of countries: a directional distance function metafrontier approach. Journal of Environmental Management. 134–142.

Managi, S., Jena, P.R., 2008. Environmental productivity and Kuznets curve in India. Ecological Economics. 65:432–440.

Molinos-Senante, M., Hanley, N., Salagarrido, R., 2015. Measuring the CO2 shadow price for wastewater treatment: A directional distance function approach. Applied Energy. 144: 241–249.

Pastor, J.T., Lovell, C.A.K., 2005. A global Malmquist productivity index. Economics Letters. 88:266–271.

Picazo-Tadeo, A. J., Prior, D., 2009. Environmental Externalities and Efficiency Measurement. Journal of Environmental Management. 90: 3332–3339.

Shephard, R.W., 1970. Theory of Cost and Production Functions. Princeton, NJ: Princeton University Press.

Shortall, O. K., Barnes, A. P., 2013. Greenhouse gas emissions and the technical efficiency of dairy farmers. Ecological Indicators. 29:478–488.

Wang, K., Wei, Y. M., Zhang, X., 2012. A comparative analysis of China's regional energy and emission performance: Which is the better way to deal with undesirable outputs? Energy Policy. 46:574–584.

Wang, K., Wei, Y. M., Zhang, X., 2013. Energy and emissions efficiency patterns of Chinese regions: a multi-directional efficiency analysis. Applied Energy. 104:105–116.

Wang, K., Xian, Y., Wei, Y. M., Huang, Z. M., 2016a. Sources of carbon productivity change: A decomposition and disaggregation analysis based on global Luenberger productivity indicator and endogenous directional distance function. Ecological Indicators. 66: 545–555.

Wang, K, Xian, Y., Zhang, J., Li, Y., Che, L, 2016b. Potential carbon emission abatement cost recovery from carbon emission trading in China: An estimation of industry sector. Journal of Modelling in Management, 11(3), 842–854.

Watanabe, M., Tanaka, K., 2007. Efficiency analysis of Chinese industry: A directional distance function approach. Energy Policy. 35 (12): 6323–6331.

Wei, C., Loschel, A., Liu, B., 2013. An Empirical Analysis of the CO2 Shadow Price in Chinese Thermal Power Enterprises. Energy Economics. 40: 22–31.

Zhou, P., Ang, B. W., Poh, K. L., 2008. A survey of data envelopment analysis in energy and environmental studies. European Journal of Operational Research. 189:1–8.

Zofio, J. L., Paster, J. T., & Aparicio, J., 2013. The directional profit efficiency measure: On why profit efficiency is either technical or allocative. Journal of Productivity Analysis, 40(3): 257–266.

Chapter 8
The Context-Dependent Total-Factor Energy Efficiency of China's Regions

Jin-Li Hu and Tzu-Pu Chang

1 Introduction

This chapter applies the context-dependent total-factor energy efficiency (CD-TFEE) to find the levels of frontiers of China's regions. CD-TFEE is an approach that combines context-dependent data envelopment analysis (CD-DEA) by Seiford and Zhu (2003) and total-factor energy efficiency (TFEE) by Hu and Wang (2006). The levels of frontiers from CD-TFEE are determined by a decision-making unit's (DMU's) efficiency in using energy, while those from CD-DEA are determined by the overall technical efficiency (OTE). Since a DMU may have different efficiency levels in different inputs, the levels of frontiers decided by CD-TFEE may not be the same as those resulting from CD-DEA.

Ever since the economic reforms starting in 1978, China has been experiencing rapid economic growth with a rising need for imported energy. Although China's total coal consumption is structurally declining, its imported oil is basically increasing. SO_2 emissions are a serious problem for air pollution, especially as industrial clusters are the main source for SO_2 emission (Myllyvirta 2016). Consequently, efficient energy use at the regional level is now an urgent task for China as it targets to save energy and reduce emissions at the same time.

J.-L. Hu (✉)
Institute of Business and Management, National Chiao Tung University,
Taipei City, Taiwan
e-mail: jinlihu@mail.nctu.edu.tw

T.-P. Chang
Department of Finance, National Yunlin University of Science and Technology,
Yunlin County, Taiwan

© Springer Nature Singapore Pte Ltd. 2018
R. Pang et al. (eds.), *Energy, Environment and Transitional Green
Growth in China*, https://doi.org/10.1007/978-981-10-7919-1_8

2 Methodology

Professor Joe Zhu personally describes CD-DEA as an 'onion-peeling' approach. DMUs can be categorized by different levels of efficiency frontiers. Hu and Wang (2006) define total-factor energy efficiency (TFEE) as a ratio of target energy input to actual energy input:

$$TFEE = Target\ Energy\ Input/Actual\ Energy\ Input \qquad (1)$$

The target energy is the projected amount found by a DEA model. Since the target energy input is never greater than the actual energy input, a TFEE score is between zero and one—that is, since $0 \le$ target energy input $\le$ actual energy input, then $0 \le$ TFEE ≤ 1 must hold. A TFEE score of one implies full energy efficiency, while a TFEE score of zero implies extremely inefficient use of energy.

The relation between overall technical efficiency (OTE) and TFEE can be described as follows:

$$
\begin{aligned}
TFEE &= 1 - Total\ Input\ Slack/Actual\ Input \\
&= 1 - (Non\text{-}radial + Radial\ Slacks)/Actual\ Input \\
&\le 1 - Radial\ Slack/Actual\ Input \\
&= Overall\ Technical\ Efficiency\ (OTE)
\end{aligned} \qquad (2)
$$

It is noteworthy that the above inequality is based on Farrell efficiency, which incorporates proportional adjustments of all inputs. However, Färe and Lovell (1978) consider that Russell efficiency is better behaved with less assumptions and higher discriminating power than Farrell efficiency. Therefore, this chapter calculates both CD-DEA and CD-TFEE by using Russell efficiency measures that relax all inputs to be proportional contracted with the same ratio.

The CD-DEA was proposed in 2003 and since then many studies have applied or extended it in many research fields. In terms of energy and environment field, Wu et al. (2016) use the CD-DEA technique to calculate the reduction targets of CO_2 emission and energy consumption for industrial sectors in China. Bi et al. (2014) treat CD-DEA as a clustering approach and further evaluate the environmental performance of regions in China. To our best knowledge, there is no literature combine CD-DEA technique with TFEE framework. Although the idea of Wu et al. (2016) who used CD-DEA rank frontier levels of regional CO_2 emission and energy intensity in China may be somewhat close to this chapter, the chapter is the first one to formally compare CD-DEA and CD-TFEE.

3 Context-Dependent DEA and TFEE

According to Seiford and Zhu (2003), the CD-DEA procedure is as follows:

(1) Run the DEA model on all observations in the same year.
(2) Eliminate the DMUs whose overall technical efficiency (OTE) equals 1, making the remaining (OTE-inefficient) DMUs form a new second-level OTE-efficient frontier.
(3) Repeat the procedure to remove the new second-level OTE-efficient frontier, and then a third-level OTE-efficient frontier is formed.
(4) If required, repeat above procedure until all DMUs are OTE-efficient.

The CD-DEA procedure determines the levels of frontiers by their OTE scores found by a DEA model.

By replacing the efficiency concept of OTE with TFEE, the CD-TFEE procedure is as follows:

(1) Run the DEA model on all observations in the same year.
(2) Eliminate the DMUs whose TFEE equals 1, making the remaining (TFEE-inefficient) DMUs form a new second-level TFEE-efficient frontier.
(3) Repeat the procedure to remove the new second-level TFEE-efficient frontier, and then a third-level TFEE-efficient frontier is formed.
(4) If required, repeat above procedure until all DMUs are TFEE-efficient.

In other words, in the CD-TFEE procedure the levels of frontiers are determined by their TFEE scores instead of OTE scores. Moreover, as mentioned above, CD-DEA and CD-TFEE may produce different levels of efficiency frontiers. From policymakers' perspectives, CD-TFEE should be more relevant to find out benchmarks of energy efficiency.

4 Russell-Based Directional Distance Function (RDDF) with Undesirable Outputs

According to the procedures of CD-OTE and CD-TFEE introduced above, we use a Russell-based directional distance function (RDDF) model to calculate the efficient frontiers. First, suppose that there are K DMUs using M inputs, $X = (x_{1k}, x_{2k}, \ldots, x_{mk}) \in R_+^M$, to jointly produce N desirable outputs, $Y^g = (y_{1k}^g, y_{2k}^g, \ldots, y_{nk}^g) \in R_+^N$, and J undesirable outputs, $Y^b = (y_{1k}^b, y_{2k}^b, \ldots, y_{jk}^b) \in R_+^J$. In line with the assumptions of Färe et al. (1996), the DEA technology can be expressed as follows:

$$
\begin{aligned}
T = \{(X, Y^g, Y^b) : &\sum_{k=1}^{K} \lambda_k x_{mk} \leq x_m, \ m = 1, 2, \ldots, M \\
&\sum_{k=1}^{K} \lambda_k y_{nk}^g \geq y_n^g, \ n = 1, 2, \ldots, N \\
&\sum_{k=1}^{K} \lambda_k y_{jk}^b = y_j^b, \ j = 1, 2, \ldots, J \\
&\lambda_k \geq 0, \ k = 1, 2, \ldots, K\}.
\end{aligned}
\tag{3}
$$

Here, λ_k state the intensity variables representing the weight of each DMU. With respect to computing the efficient frontier with undesirable outputs, the literature commonly uses the distance function (DF) and directional distance function (DDF) (Hu and Chang 2016a). Aside from those two approaches, this article applies a more flexible method, the Russell-based directional distance function, which allows us to expand desirable outputs and contract both inputs as well as undesirable outputs at different proportions simultaneously.

As for the linear programming problem of RDDF, we define DDF as (Chung et al. 1997):

$$\overrightarrow{D}(X, Y^g, Y^b; g_X, g_{Y^g}, g_{Y^b}) = \max\{\beta : (X - \beta g_X, Y^g + \beta g_{Y^g}, Y^b - \beta g_{Y^b}) \in T\}, \quad (4)$$

where the non-zero vector (g_X, g_{Y^g}, g_{Y^b}) denotes the directions in which inputs and desirable and undesirable outputs are adjusted by an equal scale. Note that $\overrightarrow{D}(X, Y^g, Y^b; g_X, g_{Y^g}, g_{Y^b}) \geq 0$ and $\overrightarrow{D}(X, Y^g, Y^b; g_X, g_{Y^g}, g_{Y^b}) = 0$ if and only if (X, Y^g, Y^b) is on the production frontier. However, some inputs, such as labor and capital, may not be freely adjusted in the short run. Therefore, Hu and Chang (2016a) consider that the quasi-fixed inputs assumption proposed by Ouellette and Vierstraete (2004) is closer to reality.

In this RDDF with the quasi-fixed inputs model, we assume that the energy input (e) can be adjusted, while all other M-1 inputs are quasi-fixed. That is, the energy is only adjustable input in this DEA model to shift an inefficient DMU to the efficiency frontier, hence providing a higher discriminative power on TFEE scores (Chang 2013). Both desirable and undesirable outputs can be adjusted by different scales, meaning that there is no unique direction. Letting $(g_X, g_{Y^g}, g_{Y^b}) = (X, Y^g, Y^b)$, the RDDF with quasi-fixed inputs for the oth DMU can be expressed by the following linear programming problem:

$$\overrightarrow{D}(X, Y^g, Y^b) = \max \frac{1}{1 + N + J} \left(\beta^e + \sum_{n=1}^{N} \beta_n^g + \sum_{j=1}^{J} \beta_j^b\right)$$

$$\text{s.t.} \sum_{k=1}^{K} \lambda_k e_k \leq (1 - \beta^e) e_o,$$

$$\sum_{k=1}^{K} \lambda_k x_{mk} \leq x_{mo}, m = 1, 2, \ldots, M - 1 \qquad (5)$$

$$\sum_{k=1}^{K} \lambda_k y_{nk}^g \geq (1 + \beta_n^g) y_{no}^g, n = 1, 2, \ldots, N$$

$$\sum_{k=1}^{K} \lambda_k y_{jk}^b = (1 - \beta_j^b) y_{jo}^b, j = 1, 2, \ldots, J$$

$$\lambda_k \geq 0, \beta^e \geq 0, \beta_m^x \geq 0, \beta_n^g \geq 0, \beta_j^b \geq 0, k = 1, 2, \ldots, K.$$

According to Eq. (4), $\overrightarrow{D}(X, Y^g, Y^b)$ denotes the inefficiency level for the oth DMU, implying that the oth DMU is efficient if and only if all βs are equal to zero. Moreover, β^e, β_n^g, and β_j^b are the inefficiency level of energy input, desirable output, and undesirable output, respectively.[1]

We note that β^e and β_j^b range from zero to unity, while β_n^g ranges from zero to infinite. In order to ensure the upper bound of efficiency score is one, we define that the OTE score found by the above DEA model is $1/[1 + \overrightarrow{D}(X, Y^g, Y^b)]$, while the TFEE score is $1/(1 + \beta^e)$ for DMU$_o$.

5 Data Sources and Variables

Table 1 depicts the variables. Following Hu and Wang (2006) and Hu and Chang (2016b), there are four input variables: capital, labor, energy, and farmland (as a proxy for biomass energy). Two output variables are included: GDP (as a desirable output) and SO$_2$ (as an undesirable output). Regional data in 2014, including GDP, SO$_2$, labor, and farmland, are obtained from *China Statistical Yearbook* (National Bureau of Statistics of China 2015). Regional energy consumption comes from *China Energy Statistical Yearbook*.

Regional capital stocks are estimated by the following steps. First, Shan (2008), one of the classic studies in the literature for estimating China's regional capital stocks, applies the perpetual inventory method from 1952 to 2006 for this data. Second, based on Shan's data, we extend regional capital stocks data from 2006 into 2014 by the same approach, i.e.:

$$K_t = K_{t-1}(1 - \delta) + I_t, \qquad (6)$$

where K_t is capital stock; I_t is gross fixed capital formation in year t, and δ is the depreciation rate and assumed to be 10.96%. Note that GDP and capital stock are converted into real variables at the 1978 price level.

6 Frontier Levels by CD-DEA and CD-TFEE

China's regions can be categorized into three areas: east (E), central (C), west (W). The average per capita income rankings for these three areas in China, from the highest to the lowest, are east, central, and west (Lei 1996).

---

[1]Apparently, RDDF with the quasi-fixed inputs model is a non-radial DEA model. It is a more generalized model than other non-radial DEA models (such as slack-based model). For details, please refer to Färe and Grosskopf (2010).

Table 1 China's regional output and input data in 2014

Id	Name	Area	GDP (100 Million RMB in 1978)	SO₂ (10 k ton)	Capital (100 Million RMB in 1978)	Labor (10 k Per-sons)	Energy (10 k ton of standard coal equivalence)	Farm area (1000 acres)
1	Beijing	E	3573.28	7.89	3651.48	1156.70	6831.20	196.10
2	Tianjin	E	3981.76	20.92	1791.82	877.21	7955.00	479.03
3	Hebei	E	6731.88	118.99	4584.55	4202.66	29320.21	8713.08
4	Shanxi	C	2655.35	120.82	1322.15	1895.70	19863.00	3783.43
5	Inner Mongolia	W	3606.72	131.24	6914.27	1485.40	18309.06	7355.96
6	Liaoning	E	6610.11	99.46	1026.12	2626.00	20585.67	4164.09
7	Jilin	C	2871.09	37.23	1941.08	1447.17	8483.40	5615.29
8	Heilongjiang	C	3480.52	47.22	1082.02	2182.50	11954.90	12225.92
9	Shanghai	E	8187.52	18.81	8435.33	1365.60	11084.63	356.98
10	Jiangsu	E	16423.93	90.47	12212.33	4760.83	29863.03	7678.62
11	Zhejiang	E	8351.22	57.41	3194.02	3902.94	18826.00	2274.00
12	Anhui	C	4567.60	49.30	644.64	4311.00	12011.02	8945.53
13	Fujian	E	4698.30	35.59	1110.00	2700.93	12109.72	2305.24
14	Jiangxi	C	3048.86	53.44	4778.34	2603.30	8055.40	5570.55
15	Shandong	E	12526.32	159.02	7328.63	6606.50	35362.60	11037.93
16	Henan	C	7172.78	119.82	6407.71	6520.00	22890.00	14378.30
17	Hubei	C	5918.74	58.38	2488.92	3687.50	16320.00	8112.26
18	Hunan	C	4422.95	62.38	992.73	4044.13	15316.84	8764.47
19	Guangdong	E	14929.59	73.01	9665.64	6183.23	28669.57	4744.95
20	Guangxi	W	2517.32	46.66	1583.65	2795.00	9515.34	5929.94
21	Hainan	E	736.32	52.69	160.88	543.10	1819.93	859.61

(continued)

Table 1 (continued)

Id	Name	Area	GDP (100 Million RMB in 1978)	SO₂ (10 k ton)	Capital (100 Million RMB in 1978)	Labor (10 k Per-sons)	Energy (10 k ton of standard coal equivalence)	Farm area (1000 acres)
22	Chongqing	W	2886.20	3.26	915.89	1771.33	7693.96	3540.35
23	Sichuan	W	6572.12	79.64	3837.41	4833.00	19878.10	9668.61
24	Guizhou	W	1467.46	92.58	684.32	1909.69	9708.78	5516.46
25	Yunnan	W	2204.90	63.67	213.03	2950.00	10454.83	7194.43
26	Shaanxi	W	3390.87	78.10	2329.08	2149.00	11728.08	4262.14
27	Gansu	W	1847.08	57.56	2820.68	1519.86	7521.45	4197.51
28	Qinghai	W	360.43	15.43	383.24	317.30	3991.70	553.70
29	Ningxia	W	393.86	37.71	316.97	358.70	4946.10	1253.16
30	Xinjiang	W	1401.62	85.30	1367.72	1142.00	14926.08	5517.63

Note E East, C Central, W West

Tables 2 and 3 show the frontier levels found by CD-DEA and CD-TFEE for China's regions in 2014, respectively. Guanxi (W) and Gansu (W) are on level 5 by CD-DEA, while they both are on level 1 by CD-TFEE. This is because Guanxi and Gansu use energy efficiently, but use other inputs inefficiently, hence making the frontier levels found by CD-DEA and CD-TFEE different.

Table 2 indicates that there are five levels of efficiency frontiers for the overall use of resources in China. Only nine out of China's thirty regions are on level 1 as found by CD-DEA, showing that more than two-thirds of China's regions still have much room to improve their overall technical efficiency. Nine out of eleven western

Table 2 Levels of quasi-fixed DDF OTE frontiers of China's regions in 2014

Id	Name	Area	Level 1	Level 2	Level 3	Level 4	Level 5
1	Beijing	E	1.000				
2	Tianjin	E	1.000				
3	Hebei	E	0.497	0.568	0.739	1.000	
4	Shanxi	C	0.376	0.429	0.518	1.000	
5	Inner Mongolia	W	0.212	0.434	1.000		
6	Liaoning	E	1.000				
7	Jilin	C	0.604	0.676	1.000		
8	Heilongjiang	C	0.628	1.000			
9	Shanghai	E	1.000				
10	Jiangsu	E	0.818	1.000			
11	Zhejiang	E	0.937	1.000			
12	Anhui	C	1.000				
13	Fujian	E	1.000				
14	Jiangxi	C	0.486	0.667	1.000		
15	Shandong	E	0.631	0.710	1.000		
16	Henan	C	0.542	0.618	0.818	0.891	1.000
17	Hubei	C	0.677	0.823	1.000		
18	Hunan	C	0.735	1.000			
19	Guangdong	E	0.883	1.000			
20	Guangxi	W	0.529	0.595	0.754	0.818	1.000
21	Hainan	E	1.000				
22	Chongqing	W	1.000				
23	Sichuan	W	0.616	0.701	0.909	1.000	
24	Guizhou	W	0.331	0.443	0.509	1.000	
25	Yunnan	W	1.000				
26	Shaanxi	W	0.546	0.584	0.753	1.000	
27	Gansu	W	0.333	0.394	0.664	0.711	1.000
28	Qinghai	W	0.055	0.197	0.417	0.512	1.000
29	Ningxia	W	0.025	0.167	0.317	0.406	1.000
30	Xinjiang	W	0.068	0.209	0.394	0.476	1.000

Note E East, *C* Central, *W* West

regions are on the fourth or fifth OTE frontiers, showing low overall efficiency levels in resource use. This reflects the 'double deterioration' phenomenon in China with both low economic development and low resource efficiency for some regions (Hu et al. 2005).

Table 3 indicates that there are five levels of efficiency frontier for energy use in China in 2014. Eleven regions in China are on level 1 of TFEE frontiers—that is, almost two-thirds of China's regions can find domestic benchmarks to improve their energy efficiency. However, six out of the eleven western regions are on efficiency levels 4 and 5 in energy use, while four out of them are on efficiency level

Table 3 Levels of quasi-fixed DDF TFEE frontiers of China's regions in 2014

Id	Name	Area	Level 1	Level 2	Level 3	Level 4	Level 5
1	Beijing	E	1.000				
2	Tianjin	E	1.000				
3	Hebei	E	0.677	0.464	0.635	1.000	
4	Shanxi	C	0.468	0.392	0.410	1.000	
5	Inner Mongolia	W	0.687	0.509	1.000		
6	Liaoning	E	1.000				
7	Jilin	C	0.679	0.650	1.000		
8	Heilongjiang	C	0.776	1.000			
9	Shanghai	E	1.000				
10	Jiangsu	E	0.992	1.000			
11	Zhejiang	E	0.973	1.000			
12	Anhui	C	1.000				
13	Fujian	E	1.000				
14	Jiangxi	C	0.779	0.688	1.000		
15	Shandong	E	0.770	0.708	1.000		
16	Henan	C	0.503	0.830	0.864	0.948	1.000
17	Hubei	C	0.898	0.800	1.000		
18	Hunan	C	0.764	1.000			
19	Guangdong	E	0.982	1.000			
20	Guangxi	W	1.000				
21	Hainan	E	1.000				
22	Chongqing	W	1.000				
23	Sichuan	W	0.719	0.661	0.912	1.000	
24	Guizhou	W	0.815	0.415	0.462	1.000	
25	Yunnan	W	1.000				
26	Shaanxi	W	0.865	0.589	0.802	1.000	
27	Gansu	W	1.000				
28	Qinghai	W	0.515	0.409	0.427	0.427	1.000
29	Ningxia	W	0.595	0.354	0.353	0.353	1.000
30	Xinjiang	W	0.646	0.393	0.424	0.424	1.000

Note E East, *C* Central, *W* West

1 in energy use. This implies that the western regions may have relatively better performance in energy use than their use of other inputs.

Among the eleven eastern regions, six are on the level 1 (Beijing, Tianjin, Liaoning, Shanghai, Fujian and Hainan), three are on level 2 (Jiansu, Zhejiang, and Guandong), one is on level 3 (Shandong), and one is on level 4 (Hebei) of TFEE frontiers in 2014. Among the eight central regions, one is on level 1 (Anhui), two are on level 2 (Heilongjiang and Hunan), three are on level 3 (Jilin, Jiangxi, and Hubei), one is on level 3 (Jiangxi), one is on level 4 (Shanxi), and one is on level 5 (Henan) of TFEE frontiers in 2014. Among the eleven western regions, two are on level 1 (Yunnan and Gansu), one is on level 3 (Inner Mongolia), three are on level 4 (Sichuan, Guizhou, and Shaanxi), and three are on level 5 (Qinhai, Ningxia, and Xinjiang) of TFEE frontiers in 2014. The CD-TFEE results hence show that east area is the benchmark for the central and west area to improve their energy efficiency.

The reasons why the eastern regions in China have higher energy efficiency are multiple, usually referring to higher levels of income, value-added, technology, education, urbanization, equipment, transportation, residential environment, etc. (Liu et al. 2012; Wei and Liao 2016) In summary, the key driving force for improving energy efficiency is still economic development which includes economic, social, and environmental aspects.

7 Concluding Remarks

This chapter demonstrates how to apply the CD-TFEE procedure to categorize China's regions into levels of frontiers. The results found by CD-DEA and CD-TFEE are typically different since CD-TFEE highlights the energy efficiency benchmarking instead of overall efficiency benchmarking. It is found that more than half of the eastern regions are on the level 1 of TFEE frontiers, being energy efficiency benchmarks for other regions in China. The CD-TFEE procedure can be applied to regions or sectors in other economies, in order to find benchmarks for a DMU to improve its energy efficiency.

References

Bi, G.B., W. Song and J. Wu (2014), "A Clustering Method for Evaluating the Environmental Performance based on Slacks-based Measure," Computers & Industrial Engineering, 72, 169–177.

Chang, M.C. (2013), "A Comment on the Calculation of the Total-factor Energy Efficiency (TFEE) Index," Energy Policy, 53, 500–504.

Chung, Y.H., R. Färe and S. Grosskopf (1997), "Productivity and Undesirable Outputs: A Directional Distance Function Approach," Journal of Environmental Management, 51, 229–240.

Färe, R. and S. Grosskopf (2010), "Directional Distance Functions and Slacks-Based Measures of Efficiency," European Journal of Operational Research, 200, 320–322.

Färe, R., S. Grosskopf and D. Tyteca (1996), "An Activity Analysis Model of the Environmental Performance of Firms—Application to Fossil-Fuel-Fired Electric Utilities," Ecological Economics, 18, 161–175.

Färe, R. and C.A.K. Lovell (1978), "Measuring the Technical Efficiency of Production," Journal of Economic Theory, 19, 150–162.

Hu, J.L. and T.P. Chang (2016a), "Total-factor Energy Efficiency and Its Extensions: Introduction, Computation and Application," in Data Envelopment Analysis: A Handbook of Empirical Studies and Applications, edited by Joe Zhu, pp. 45–69, Springer.

Hu, J.L. and T.P. Chang (2016b), "Energy and Pollution Efficiencies in China's Regions," in China's Energy Efficiency and Conservation: Household Behaviour, Legislation, Regional Analysis and Impacts, edited by Elspeth Thomson and Bin Su, pp. 61–74, Springer.

Hu, J.L., H.J. Sheu and S.F. Lo (2005), "Under the Shadow of Asian Brown Clouds: The Unbalanced Regional Productivities in China and Environmental Concerns," International Journal of Sustainable Development and World Ecology, 12(4), 429–442.

Hu, J.L. and S.C. Wang (2006), "Total-Factor Energy Efficiency of Regions in China," Energy Policy, 34(17), 3206–3217.

Lei, X. (1996), "Analysis of the Income Situation of the Chinese Peasantry since Reform and Openness," Chinese Economic Studies, 29(6), 62–67.

Liu, J. S. Dong, Y. Li, Q. Mao, J. Li and J. Wang (2012), "Spatial Analysis on the Contribution of Industrial Structural Adjustment to Regional Energy Efficiency: A Case Study of 31 Provinces across China," Journal of Resources and Ecology, 3(2), 129–137.

Myllyvirta, L. (2016), "New Trends in China Energy Consumption," Greenpeace. Downloaded from https://www.brookings.edu/wp-content/uploads/2016/07/PPT_Lauri-Myllyvirta.pdf. Accessed on June 15, 2017.

National Bureau of Statistics of China (2015), China Statistical Yearbook 2015, Beijing. Website: http://www.stats.gov.cn/tjsj/ndsj/2015/indexeh.htm.

Ouellette, P. and V. Vierstraete (2004), "Technological Change and Efficiency in the Presence of Quasi-fixed Inputs: a DEA Application to the Hospital Sector," European Journal of Operation Research, 154, 755–763.

Seiford, L.M. and J. Zhu (2003), "Context-dependent Data Envelopment Analysis Measuring Attractiveness and Progress," Omega, 31(5), 397–408.

Shan, H. (2008), "Reestimating the Capital Stock of China: 1952–2006," Journal of Quantitative &Technical Economics, 10, 17–31. (in Chinese).

Wei, Y. and H. Liao (2016), Energy Economics: Energy Efficiency in China, Springer.

Wu, J., Q. Zhu and L. Liang (2016), "CO2 Emissions and Energy Intensity Reduction Allocation over Provincial Industrial Sectors in China," Applied Energy, 166, 282–291.

Chapter 9
Was Economic Growth in China Environmentally Friendly? A Case Study of the Chinese Manufacturing Sector

Sung Ko Li and Xinju He

1 Introduction

The Chinese economy has experienced fast economic growth since the inception of economic reforms started in late 1970s. The real GDP per capita of China increased 2240% from 1978 to 2016, compared with a 183% increase in the US during the same period.[1] However, after three decades of successful reform, many problems still exist. Aware of the importance of efficient production and environmental protection, the Chinese central government decided to address these two issues. In regard to production, the Thirteenth Five-year plan emphasized using reform to "improve the market environment and mechanisms to encourage fair competition and survival of the fittest" and policies must aim at "improving the quality and efficiency of the supply system" (National Development and Reform Commission 2016, Chap. 5). Regarding the environment, the plan listed "green development" as one of the five focus areas for the period 2016–2020 (National Development and Reform Commission 2016, Part 1). This paper separates these two issues in the efficiency analysis of the Chinese manufacturing sector.

A large literature has emerged to evaluate China's productivity and efficiency performance using data of different levels, including firm (Jefferson et al. 1996, 2003), industry (Lam and Shiu 2001), city (Wu 2000) and province (Zheng et al. 1998, 2003). These early studies ignored the environmental costs of China's industrial growth. Despite increased government efforts to protect against air and water pollution, concentrations of pollutants continued to be among the highest in the world (Li and Zhang 2014). The environmental costs in terms of premature

---

[1]Computed from the series of GDP per capita (2010 constant US$) downloaded from the "Indicators" webpage, World Bank. (https://data.worldbank.org/indicator/NY.GDP.PCAP.KD).

S. K. Li (✉) · X. He
Hong Kong Baptist University, Kowloon Tong, China
e-mail: skli@hkbu.edu.hk

© Springer Nature Singapore Pte Ltd. 2018
R. Pang et al. (eds.), *Energy, Environment and Transitional Green Growth in China*, https://doi.org/10.1007/978-981-10-7919-1_9

death due to pollution-related illness were also large. A study projected that the cumulative losses of human life could be large through 2020 if the trend is not contained (Zhao et al. 2013).

Environmental efficiency has been widely studied in recent literature. However, the concept of environmental efficiency has not been clearly distinguished. Many studies adopt a measure that simultaneously expands desirable outputs and contracts undesirable outputs. Some treat the measurement as technical efficiency (Färe et al. 1989). Others treat it as environmental efficiency (Hua et al. 2007; Park et al. 2016). Two recent research efforts are: (i) separating the production of undesirable outputs from the production of desirable outputs (Malikov et al. 2015); (ii) separating the treatment of undesirable outputs from the production process of desirable and undesirable outputs (Wu et al. 2015).

In this paper, we believe that desirable and undesirable outputs should be included in the same production process because they are produced simultaneously. Further, the treatment of undesirable outputs after production is not considered because it is a different issue from evaluating performance during the production process. We adopt Kuosmanen's (2005) empirical production technology that production set is convex with weak disposability in undesirable outputs. We think that economic performance and environmental performance in production are two different concepts and should be treated differently. So two types of efficiency are then defined according to different objectives. Our study provides answers to the following questions: First, in the presence of undesirable outputs, has the economic performance of the manufacturing sector improved over the studied period? Second, has the manufacturing sector become environmentally friendly over the studied period? Third, has the manufacturing sector given up the environment to achieve more profits?

In Sect. 2, we discuss two types of technical efficiency. Section 3 explains the method of measurement. Then we apply the method in Sect. 3 to measure efficiency in the Chinese manufacturing sector in Sect. 4, where Chinese city-level data are utilized to estimate the two types of technical efficiency. Their dynamic changes are discussed, too. Section 5 explores the policy choices faced by different provinces. By investigating the changes over time, we also evaluate the effects of the Great Western Development strategy. Section 6 concludes the paper.

2 Protecting the Environment Versus the Production of Goods

Although China has been growing fast in the last several decades, the pollution problem has become serious. For example, the smog in Beijing was so serious that local authorities declared a five-day pollution "red alert" on December 16, 2016. As most pollutants are undesirable outputs during the production of desirable outputs, studying the efficiency of production must consider the undesirable outputs. This paper studies the industrial production of Chinese cities from two angles.

We consider three parties in our discussions: the firm owner, the manager of the firm, and the policy maker. The objective of the firm owner is to maximize profits. The manager is responsible for the production process and he may or may not aim at profit-maximizing. The policy maker's objective is to maximize social welfare.

Factories in the manufacturing sector utilize inputs to produce desirable outputs, which are economic goods that can generate revenue for the producer. The objective of the firm owner is to maximize profits. When desirable outputs are inefficiently produced, inputs are underutilized in the sense that more desirable outputs can be produced with the existing factor inputs. We say that the firm is *desirable output-oriented technically inefficient*. The firm owner has an incentive to eliminate such inefficiency to increase profits. Efficient production of desirable outputs is consistent with the policy maker's objective because society's resources can be better utilized. The existence of such inefficiency can be explained by X-efficiency theory or principal-agent problem in the literature, see for example, Frantz (1988). Efficiency can be achieved by replacing the current manager if the manager does not improve or by forcing a long-lasting inefficient firm out of the market if the firm does not improve. Such actions require a competitive market environment in both the labor market and product market. Providing a competitive market environment is the job of the policy maker. Such policy is market-oriented in which the policy maker affects the market environment and allows the firm to choose its optimal production plan.

Pollutants such as sulfuric acid, sooty particles, etc. are economic bads that come with the production of desirable outputs. They are undesirable outputs of the production process and their existence lowers society's welfare. When excessive undesirable outputs are produced during the production process, it is possible to reduce them without decreasing the quantities of desirable outputs and increasing the quantities of inputs. We say that the firm is *environment-oriented technically inefficient*. To protect the environment, effective measures include disposing of undesirable outputs once they appear or adopting production processes that generate less undesirable outputs. Both are costly to implement and will be detrimental to the profit level. Private firms have little or no incentive to get rid of undesirable outputs but the policy maker wants to eliminate them. Hence a competitive market environment cannot force a private firm to minimize undesirable outputs through profit motive. In contrast, the policy maker can persuade private firms to generate less undesirable outputs either by providing positive incentives (i.e., subsidy) or negative incentives (i.e., punishment). This requires direct government intervention in the production process. This type of policy is government-oriented in which the optimal choice of the firm's production plan is directly influenced by the policy maker through affecting the revenue and costs of the firm.

We argue that the above two inefficiencies should be treated differently. If both inefficiencies appear, the objective of a party determines its response. Firm owners care about desirable outputs only. They will push managers to eliminate desirable output-oriented technical efficiency to generate higher revenue without increasing costs. The existence of undesirable outputs is not on the agenda of firm owners.

In contrast, more desirable outputs and less undesirable outputs are both objectives of the policy maker. The exact target depends on the relative importance of desirable and undesirable outputs.

3 Technical Efficiency Measures with Undesirable Outputs

Denote inputs, desirable outputs, and undesirable outputs by $x \in \mathbb{R}_+^N$, $g \in \mathbb{R}_+^M$, and $b \in \mathbb{R}_+^L$, respectively. The production set is $\Im := \{(x; g, b) : x \text{ can produce } (g, b)\}$. This set consists of all feasible production activities $(x; g, b)$. When production does not take place on the production frontier, technical inefficiency appears. In the literature of gauging the performance of production units in the presence of undesirable outputs, efficiency measures are based on different orientations. Some typical examples are:

1. $E_1 = \min_\lambda \{\lambda : (\lambda x^j, b^j, g^j) \in \Im\}$. See Färe et al. (1996), Yaisawarng and Klein (1994), and Hailu and Veeman (2001).
2. $E_2 = \min_\lambda \{\lambda : (x^j, \lambda b^j, g^j) \in \Im\}$. See Tyteca (1997).
3. $E_3 = \max_\beta \{\beta : (x^j, b^j - \beta b^j, g^j + \beta g^j) \in \Im\}$. See Färe et al. (1989) and Ball et al. (2001).

In previous studies, the authors chose the orientations arbitrarily without justifying why we should choose a particular orientation. In the above examples, E_1 is not related to environmental efficiency because the reduction of undesirable outputs is not considered in the measure. E_2 deals with environmental efficiency but technical efficiency is not involved. E_3 expands desirable outputs and contracts undesirable outputs simultaneously. Environmental efficiency cannot be isolated.

We separate the two types of efficiency and name the measures we use as follows:

1. Desirable output-oriented measure of technical efficiency:

$$E_g = 1/\max_\theta \{\theta : (x; \theta g, b) \in \Im\}.$$

2. Environment-oriented measure of technical efficiency:

$$E_b = \min_\lambda \{\lambda : (x; g, \lambda b) \in \Im\}.$$

The value of each measure ranges from 0 to 1. A larger value means higher efficiency and the value of 1 identifies operation on the frontier. Thus, the desirable output-oriented measure of technical efficiency expands desirable outputs only and captures the inefficient behavior of managers to produce desirable outputs. On the other hand, the environment-oriented measure of technical efficiency contracts undesirable outputs only and reflects the inability of avoiding undesirable outputs. These two types of efficiencies are treated separately. Which one to use depends on whether the objective is environmental protection or economic performance. In later discussions, we say E_g and E_b measure the economic performance and environmental performance of the firm respectively.

These two measures are computed using an empirical piecewise linear production frontier constructed from the data. To model undesirable outputs in the production process, early applications treated pollutants as undesirable outputs and estimated their shadow prices (Pittman 1983). Some later researchers treated the undesirable outputs as inputs (Liu and Sharp 1999; Hailu and Veeman 2001; Dyckhoff and Allen 2001). A popular method was initiated by Färe et al. (1989) who used weak disposability to model undesirable outputs. Kuosmanen (2005) modified the model of Färe et al. (1989) to introduce an empirical production technology that is convex with strongly disposable inputs and desirable outputs but undesirable outputs are weakly disposable.

Suppose there are K firms. The observed production data for firm k is $(x^k; g^k, b^k), k = 1, \ldots, K$. To evaluate the efficiency of a firm $(x^0; g^0, b^0)$, we adopt Kuosmanen's (2005) empirical production technology because it is consistent with the convexity assumption in other DEA models. Under variable returns to scale, the two measures are:

$$
(E_g)^{-1} = \max_{\theta, \mu, z} \left\{ \begin{array}{l} \theta : \sum_{k=1}^{K} z_k g^k \geq \theta g^0, \sum_{k=1}^{K} z_k b^k = b^0, \sum_{k=1}^{K} (z_k + \mu_k) x^k \leq x^0, \\ \sum_{k=1}^{K} (z_k + \mu_k) = 1, z_k \geq 0 \, for \, k = 1, \ldots K \end{array} \right\}.
$$

$$
E_b = \max_{\lambda, \mu, z} \left\{ \begin{array}{l} \lambda : \sum_{k=1}^{K} z_k g^k \geq g^0, \sum_{k=1}^{K} z_k b^k = \lambda b^0, \sum_{k=1}^{K} (z_k + \mu_k) x^k \leq x^0, \\ \sum_{k=1}^{K} (z_k + \mu_k) = 1, z_k \geq 0 \, for \, k = 1, \ldots K \end{array} \right\}.
$$

4 Data and Results

We use the analytical framework proposed above to analyze the efficiency and pollution problems of China. The data of industrial production for 312 Chinese cities from 2003 to 2014 are published in the China Environmental Statistical Yearbook. After discarding observations with missing values during the investigated period, 294 prefecture level cities are available for further analysis. The desirable output is gross industrial output value. The three undesirable outputs used in the analysis are: waste dust emission, waste gas and waste water. The inputs used in the analysis are: fixed assets, labor, water used and energy consumption.

The fixed assets here refer to the total value of durable equipment, machines, building and land for production. All published data are the aggregate of all firms in the city. Since the firm number is available, we use the firm average data of each city in the computation. Thus, each observation is an average firm of the city. The estimated frontier is closer to the production technology of a typical firm and the efficiency scores reflect firms' behaviors. The descriptive statistics of our data set of 2003, 2009 and 2014 are reported in Table 1.

The efficiency scores of various measures were computed. The geometric means of desirable output-oriented and environment-oriented efficiency for each year are reported in Table 2. The two measures E_g and E_b are those discussed in the previous section and their empirical technologies consist of undesirable outputs. TE_o is the inverse of Farrell output-oriented measure of technical efficiency in which the data consist of desirable outputs and inputs only.

Both measures E_g and TE_o are the technical efficiency in the direction of desirable outputs. The difference is that undesirable outputs are included in the estimation of E_g but not in TE_o. Thus the empirical production frontier of E_g better reflects the "true" production process. The values of TE_o were about 20% smaller than E_g during the studied period.

Result 1 *When the production process includes both desirable and undesirable outputs, ignoring undesirable outputs in the empirical production frontier underestimates the economic performance of the firm.*

The above result shows that, excluding undesirable outputs, firms are perceived to be less efficient in the use of TE_o than their actual behavior. Hence undesirable outputs should be included in the modeling of the empirical production frontier.

Levels of Efficiency

The Chinese government has implemented many policies to encourage market competition and environmental protection. One major issue is to investigate the seriousness of technical inefficiency in the manufacturing sector during the studied period in the production of desirable and undesirable outputs. If the answer is "Yes", then nothing should be done with respect to technical inefficiency. In contrast, if the answer is "No", there is high potential to increase desirable outputs and decrease undesirable outputs, so something must be done.

For each measure reported in Table 2, a larger value means improvement in efficiency and a value of 1 means that the firm is technically efficient in the corresponding orientation. We can see that on average both E_g and E_b are far from 1 with scores less than 0.81 and 0.33 respectively. This indicates that the production of manufacturing goods and the jointly produced pollutants were far from the production frontier during 2003–2014. It is possible that, without adding resources, firms in the manufacturing sector could produce more desirable outputs and less undesirable outputs. Compared with best practice firms, the potential of reducing undesirable outputs was much larger. Furthermore, the value of E_g was much closer to 1 than the value of E_b. This means that the firm was closer to the frontier in the direction of desirable outputs and far from the frontier in the direction of

Table 1 Descriptive statistics of inputs and outputs of 2003, 2009, 2014

	2003				2009				2014			
	Mean	Std	Min	Max	Mean	Std	Min	Max	Mean	Std	Min	Max
Desirable output												
g1	70.5	58.0	3.5	619.6	147.0	111.0	38.5	907.6	337.1	327.6	89.1	4493.5
Undesirable outputs												
b1	15.8	16.1	0.7	137.6	9.2	18.7	0.8	294.0	7.9	7.7	0.8	83.3
b2	292.4	807.3	1.2	8453.7	345.9	1535.2	0.5	24711.0	422.8	1378.3	0.1	20583.0
b3	1706.4	2260.6	0.4	18023.1	1674.5	3239.8	2.9	38073.3	4191.5	5733.5	6.2	38442.3
Inputs												
x1	389.0	272.6	48.2	2022.4	252.6	156.3	64.6	1169.1	308.0	226.0	38.4	1497.1
x2	48.7	60.9	2.6	705.0	79.5	122.4	9.7	1431.4	162.9	262.1	21.0	2360.0
x3	22.6	36.5	0.8	397.3	10.9	19.7	0.3	186.3	11.9	24.3	0.5	297.5
x4	1277.1	7236.9	17.6	123238.6	925.8	1998.5	6.7	18438.9	1228.3	3075.5	28.8	46482.2

Number of observations = 294

g (Firm average industrial output value (million rmb)), b1 (Firm average waste water (10 k ton)), b2 (Firm average waste gas (ton)), b3 (Firm average dust emission (ton)), x1 (Firm average number of employees), x2 (Firm average fixed assets (million RMB)), x3 (Firm average water used (10 K ton)), x4 (Firm average energy consumption (ton ce))

Table 2 Geometric mean of different oriented efficiency from 2003 to 2014

Year	E_g	E_b	TE_o
2003	0.59	0.12	0.44
2004	0.61	0.14	0.50
2005	0.69	0.15	0.55
2006	0.67	0.17	0.55
2007	0.71	0.23	0.56
2008	0.75	0.26	0.58
2009	0.76	0.27	0.62
2010	0.76	0.33	0.61
2011	0.75	0.29	0.59
2012	0.79	0.26	0.63
2013	0.81	0.32	0.65
2014	0.78	0.27	0.63

undesirable outputs. This is expected because undesirable outputs are byproducts of the production process and are costly to dispose of. Once appearing, the firm has no motive to dispose of them.

Result 2 *The production of desirable and undesirable outputs in the Chinese manufacturing sector was highly inefficient during 2003–2014. The production activity was farther from the production frontier in the direction of undesirable outputs.*

Result 2 shows that both desirable output-oriented technical efficiency and environment-oriented technical efficiency are low so that there is much room for improvement of both economic and environmental performance in the manufacturing sector.

Dynamic Changes of Efficiency

Another concern is the dynamic changes of the two types of technical efficiency. If one type of technical efficiency has been improving during the studied period, then the policy during the period was on the right track and need not be changed. Otherwise, low efficiency prevailed over time. New policies must be implemented to address the issue of inefficiency.

We can see that the values of both E_g and E_b in 2014 were much higher than those in 2003 (from 0.59 to 0.78 for E_g and 0.12 to 0.27 for E_b). However, E_g shows an increasing trend which, allowing for fluctuation, was not destructed throughout 2003–2014. However, the value of E_b increased continuously from 0.12 to 0.33 from 2003 to 2010 and dropped to 0.27 in 2014. To investigate the existence of time trend and the possibility of a break in 2010, define variables $D_t = 1$ for t = 2010, 2011, 2012, 2013, 2014 and $D_t = 0$ otherwise, and $TIME_t = t - 2002$ for t = 2003, …, 2014. We confirm this pattern by running the following two regression equations:

Table 3 The regression of time trend for E_g and E_b

VARIABLES	(1) $\ln(E_g)$	(2) $\ln(E_b)$
D	0.192***	1.238***
	(0.0617)	(0.209)
TIME	0.0427***	0.140***
	(0.00353)	(0.0119)
TIME*D	−0.0314***	−0.162***
	(0.00688)	(0.0233)
Constant	−0.560***	−2.242***
	(0.0158)	(0.0534)
Observations	3540	3540
R-squared	0.078	0.077

Standard errors are in parentheses. "***", "**" and "*" indicate significance at 1%, 5% and 10% levels respectively

$$\ln\left(E_{gt}\right) = \alpha_0 + \alpha_1 D_t + \alpha_3 TIME_t + \alpha_4 D_t \times TIME_t + \varepsilon_t \tag{1}$$

$$\ln(E_{bt}) = \beta_0 + \beta_1 D_t + \beta_3 TIME_t + \beta_4 D_t \times TIME_t + \mu_t \tag{2}$$

Let Period 1 be the time from 2003 to 2009 and Period 2 from 2010 to 2014. In the above two regression models, α_3 is the growth rate of E_g during Period 1 and $(\alpha_3 + \alpha_4)$ the growth rate of E_g during Period 2. Similarly, the growth rates of E_b are β_3 during Period 1 and $(\beta_3 + \beta_4)$ during Period 2. The regression results are listed in Table 3.

All individual coefficients are significant at the 1% level in both Models (1) and (2). Using the Chow test, the coefficients of D and ($TIME \times D$) are jointly and significantly different from zero for each regression equation. This confirms the existence of a break in 2010. The estimated coefficients of the slope dummy ($TIME \times D$) in both models are highly significant. Hence the growth rates of E_g and E_b are different before and after 2010. Model (1) indicates that the average growth rate of the technical efficiency of desirable outputs (E_g) was 4.27% in Period 1 and 1.13% (= 4.27% − 3.14%) in Period 2. Both are significantly different from zero.[2] We can conclude that E_g has been improving over time throughout the whole studied period of 2003–2014 although the growth rate fell after 2010. In Model (2) the growth rate of the environment-oriented technical efficiency (E_b) was 14% in Period 1. This growth rate became −2.2% (= 14.0% − 16.2%) after 2010. This result is summarized as follows:

Result 3 *The technical efficiency of the manufacturing sector improved over time in the directions of producing more desirable outputs and less undesirable outputs*

---

[2]The terms α_3 and $(\alpha_3 + \alpha_4)$ in Model (1) are significantly different from zero at 5% level of significance by the t-test and Wald test respectively.

up to 2010 during the studied period. After 2010, the trend of improvement continued for the desirable output-oriented technical efficiency but the environment-oriented technical efficiency became stagnant.

Results 2 and 3 show that the problem of inefficient production of undesirable outputs is more serious than that of desirable outputs.

Convergence Between Environmentally Friendly and Unfriendly Cities

We explore Results 2 and 3 further in detail by different groupings. We believe that some groups of cities are more environmentally friendly than others. The issue is whether such difference converges over time. Three groupings were considered:

Grouping 1: Green cities versus non-green cities

In China, 47 cities are named "environmentally friendly city". These environmentally friendly cities have more restrictions on pollution and put more effort into environmental protection. We expect that green cities do a better job of environmental protection compared with non-green cities.

Grouping 2: Industrial cities versus non-industrial cities

In China, 124 cities are named "industrial city". These industrial cities set up industrial zones and many polluted industries centralize into them. We expect that industrial cities perform worse than non-industrial cities in environmental protection.

Grouping 3: Eastern versus non-eastern cities

From the empirical data, it is observed that eastern cities are more efficient in the production of both desirable and undesirable goods. The behaviors of other regions are similar. Hence non-eastern cities are grouped together.

The geometric averages of the two types of efficiency scores of each group are listed in Table 4.

Table 4 Geometric mean of efficiency for different groups from 2003 to 2014

Year	Grouping 1		Grouping 2		Grouping 3	
	E_g	E_b	E_g	E_b	E_g	E_b
2003	0.75(0.56)	0.28(0.11)	0.55(0.62)	0.10(0.15)	0.67(0.54)	0.19(0.10)
2004	0.81(0.58)	0.36(0.12)	0.58(0.63)	0.11(0.17)	0.74(0.54)	0.23(0.11)
2005	0.81(0.67)	0.37(0.13)	0.68(0.70)	0.12(0.19)	0.78(0.64)	0.25(0.12)
2006	0.81(0.64)	0.39(0.15)	0.63(0.69)	0.12(0.22)	0.76(0.62)	0.28(0.13)
2007	0.84(0.69)	0.46(0.20)	0.68(0.74)	0.18(0.28)	0.79(0.67)	0.31(0.20)
2008	0.84(0.72)	0.47(0.23)	0.74(0.75)	0.23(0.28)	0.81(0.71)	0.33(0.22)
2009	0.83(0.74)	0.47(0.24)	0.73(0.78)	0.22(0.31)	0.79(0.74)	0.36(0.23)
2010	0.85(0.75)	0.54(0.30)	0.73(0.79)	0.28(0.37)	0.81(0.73)	0.42(0.28)
2011	0.84(0.73)	0.41(0.27)	0.72(0.77)	0.25(0.31)	0.81(0.71)	0.33(0.27)
2012	0.85(0.77)	0.39(0.25)	0.76(0.80)	0.23(0.29)	0.82(0.76)	0.31(0.24)
2013	0.85(0.80)	0.45(0.30)	0.77(0.83)	0.27(0.36)	0.84(0.79)	0.40(0.29)
2014	0.82(0.77)	0.37(0.26)	0.74(0.81)	0.22(0.33)	0.83(0.74)	0.35(0.24)

Note that in Table 4, Grouping 1 means the green cities versus non-green cities, Grouping 2 means the industrial cities versus non-industrial cities, and Grouping 3 means the eastern cities versus non-eastern cities. The numbers without brackets are the geometric means of green cities, industrial cities and eastern cities, whereas the numbers in brackets are the geometric means for non-green cities, non-industrial cities and non-eastern cities. From the table, it is observed that the groups with the expectation of being environmentally friendly were more efficient in reducing undesirable outputs compared with other cities which are expected to be less environmentally friendly during 2003–2014. This justifies the three groupings. Further, they were more efficient in the production of desirable outputs, too.

Since the patterns of these three groupings are similar, we discuss Grouping 1 (green and non-green cities) only. The geometric means of output-oriented technical efficiency and environment-oriented technical efficiency are shown in Fig. 1.

In Fig. 1, the trends of all series show the pattern identified in the previous discussion. Both the desirable output-oriented efficiency and environment-oriented efficiency are improving over time for green and non-green cities. However, it gives us additional information. We observed that the gap between output-oriented technical efficiency was narrower over time from 2003 to 2014. On the other hand, the gap between environment-oriented technical efficiency first widened. Although it finally narrowed, this gap remained wide in 2014. To investigate the convergence issue, we ran the following two regression equations.

Let $diff_t^i = E_t^{i,green} - E_t^{i,non-green}$ be the difference between the geometric means of the technical efficiency of green and non-green cities related to i at time t, i = g (output-oriented), b (environment-oriented), and t = 2003, ..., 2014. We refer to $diff^i$ as a i efficiency gap. If this difference has a time trend for each group, then

$$diff_t^g = \alpha_0 + \alpha_1 TIME_t + \varepsilon_t \tag{3}$$

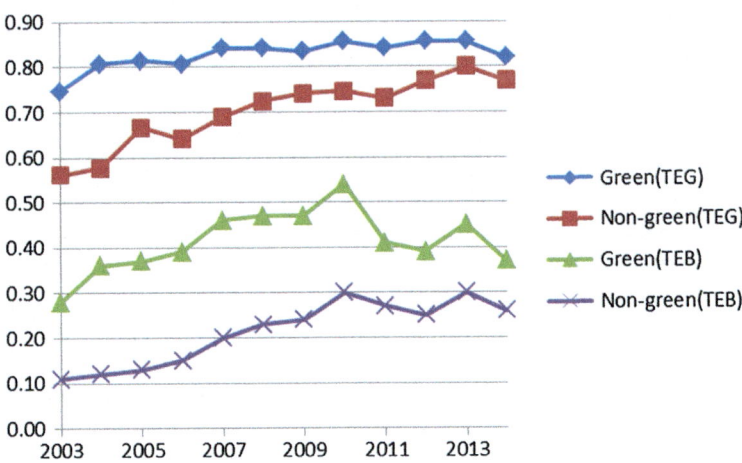

Fig. 1 Efficiencies of different orientations of green and non-green cities

Table 5 Regressions of convergence between green and non-green cities

VARIABLES	(3) diff^g (output-oriented)	(4) diff^b (environment-oriented)
TIME	−0.0137***	−0.00958**
	(0.00180)	(0.00356)
Constant	0.214***	0.262***
	(0.0133)	(0.0262)
Observations	12	12
R-squared	0.853	0.421

Standard errors are in parentheses. "***", "**" and "*" indicate significance at 1%, 5% and 10% levels respectively

$$diff_t^b = \beta_0 + \beta_1 TIME_t + \mu_t \qquad (4)$$

where $TIME_t$ is defined as before. In our sample, $diff > 0$ for both orientations. When the coefficient of $TIME$ is negative, the value of $diff$ falls and the gap narrows over time. Similarly, if the coefficient of $TIME$ is positive, the gap widens over time. The regression results are presented in Table 5.

From Table 5, the coefficient of $TIME$ is significantly negative for each model. This means that the desirable output-oriented efficiency gap and the environment-oriented efficiency gap between green and non-green cities were narrower over time during the studied period. However, β_1 is less than α_1 in absolute value. So the convergence between green and non-green cities was slow in environment-oriented technical efficiency. The same conclusion holds for the other two groupings.

Result 4 *The gap between environmentally friendly cities and unfriendly cities has been narrowing over time. But the convergence speed was much faster in output-oriented technical efficiency than the environment-oriented technical efficiency.*

Recall the discussion in Sect. 2 that market-oriented policies are more suitable for dealing with desirable output-oriented technical efficiency and government-oriented policies are better for environment-oriented technical efficiency. Combining Results 2, 3 and 4, we arrive at the followings:

a. The market mechanism works well for the manufacturing sector of China. Although Result 2 shows that the production of undesirable outputs was far from the production frontier, such type of inefficiency has been improving over time (Result 3), and the efficiency gap between green and non-green cities became very small at the end of the studied period (Result 4).

b. Government policies through positive and negative incentives are necessary to protect the environment. It is because the environment-oriented technical efficiency was very low (Result 2), and it did not improve over time (Results 3 and 4).

5   The Environmentally Unfriendly Provinces

From Result 2, we know that there is much room for improvement for the manufacturing sector in the production of desirable and undesirable outputs. Although firms are improving over time, they are still far from the production frontier, especially for the lower rank cities. For example, out of the 294 cities in 2014, 112 and 80 cities were on the frontier in the direction of desirable outputs and in the direction of undesirable output respectively. However, the geometric means of E_g and E_b are 0.78 and 0.27 respectively. Thus, cities at the bottom badly performed for both orientations. Pushing them to the production frontier is crucial in creating a clean environment. In this section, we investigate the characteristics of the most inefficient provinces.

We first computed the average output-oriented technical efficiency and average environment-oriented technical efficiency for each province and for each year. Then they were classified according to these two types of efficiency. For each year and each type of efficiency, the top 10 most efficient provinces fell within the "above average" group; the bottom 10 most inefficient provinces fell within the "below average group"; other provinces fell within the "average" group. The following table shows the pattern of provinces according to the classification for the period 2012–2014.[3] In this table, moving from left to right across a row signals deterioration in environment-oriented technical efficiency, and moving down a column means deterioration in output-oriented technical efficiency. Thus, cities in the upper left cell of the table are the best performing in terms of both type of efficiency, whereas cities in the lower right cell are the worst performing. And we group the 30 provinces (excluding Tibet, Hong Kong, Macau, and Taiwan) into four regions: Eastern region (E), North-Eastern (NE), Middle region (M) and Western region (W).

By grouping the 30 provinces (excluding Tibet, Hong Kong, Macau, and Taiwan) into four regions: Eastern region (E), North-Eastern (NE), Middle region (M), and Western region (W), we summarize the patterns in Table 6 as follows:

Group A: Efficiency in both desirable outputs and undesirable outputs

This group contains the cities in the most upper left cell of the table. There are eight provinces in this group. All of them, except Jilin, are in the eastern region. These provinces did well in both producing desirable outputs and avoiding undesirable outputs. Cities in these provinces were relatively close to the production frontier. Further improvements are likely through technological changes: increasing the productivity of producing desirable outputs and the ability of disposing of undesirable outputs.

---

[3]When a province is in the same group in two years during 2012–2014, it is classified as that group. Five provinces are in three different groups during 2012–2014. We consider their grouping in 2011 to determine their categories.

Table 6 Categories of provinces for 2012–2014

		Environment-oriented technical efficiency (E_b)		
		Above average	Average	Below average
Output-oriented technical efficiency (E_g)	Above average	E-Beijing E-Guangdong E-Jiangsu E-Hainan E-Shanghai E-Shangdong E-Tianjin NE-Jilin		(M-Jiangxi) (W-Guanxi)
	Average	(NE-Liaoning)	(E-Hebei) E-Zhejiang (M-Henan) (M-Hubei) (M-Hunan) (W-Chongqing) W-Xinjiang W-Inner Mongolia	E-Fujian
	Below average		(M-Anhui) (W-Sichuan) W-Shaanxi	NE-Heilongjiang M-Shanxi W-Gansu W-Guizhou W-Ningxia W-Qinghai W-Yunan

Group B: Efficiency in desirable outputs but inefficiency in undesirable outputs

This group includes cities, Guangxi and Jiangxi, in the second and third cells in the first row. They did relatively well in the production of desirable outputs but produced excessive unnecessary undesirable outputs. Thus, decreasing undesirable outputs but leaving desirable outputs more or less unchanged is a suitable direction for improvement. Since firms usually have no incentive to dispose of undesirable outputs, government-oriented policies are needed to push firms to reduce undesirable outputs produced during the production process for further improvement.

Group C: Efficiency in undesirable outputs but inefficiency in desirable outputs

The first column on the left excluding the first cell in the table belongs to this group. Only one province, Liaoning, is in this group. Liaoning did environmentally well in keeping undesirable outputs at a low level. Emphasis should be put on increasing desirable outputs. As discussed in Sect. 2, this indicates problems in market force and the incentive system of managers. Market-oriented policy to encourage more competition is one way to force firms to make further improvements.

Group D: Inefficiency in both desirable outputs and undesirable outputs

The cell in the center and the three lower right cells belong to this group which consists of cities with low scores in both desirable output-oriented technical efficiency and environment-oriented technical efficiency. In Table 6, a low average score means inefficient performance. Thus, provinces in this group have high potential to produce more desirable outputs and less undesirable outputs. These are highly inefficient provinces. For improvement, increasing desirable outputs only, reducing undesirable outputs only, or simultaneously doing both are feasible. As simultaneously increasing desirable outputs and reducing undesirable outputs may be difficult, these provinces face a tradeoff between economic growth (output-oriented improvement) and environmental protection (environment-oriented improvement). Most of the provinces in this group are in the middle or western regions. In particular, the lower right cell is the worst. Most provinces in this cell are in the western region. Special attention should be paid to them.

Several observations emerge from the preceding discussions. First, in terms of both types of efficiency, Middle and Western China lag behind other regions. The western region was worse than the middle region during 2003–2014. From the Central Government's point of view, China needs to choose appropriate policies to remedy the regional imbalance. Second, our model derives different improvement directions for provinces, which is not found in other studies. For example, provinces in Group A were close to the frontier, so a strategy of promoting innovation of new technology is appropriate. On the other hand, Guangxi, Jiangsu and Liaoning need to concentrate on one direction only. Finally, provinces in Group D have potential to produce more desirable outputs and less undesirable outputs without adding new resources. Innovation of the latest technology is not urgent.

Result 5 *Eastern provinces were more efficient in the production of desirable outputs and were more environmentally friendly during the studied period. Western provinces lagged far behind eastern provinces and middle provinces in terms of the production of both desirable and undesirable outputs.*

Western provinces were not always the worst in terms of output-oriented and environment-oriented technical efficiency. We follow the same rules of the above table to categorize all provinces for 2003–2005. The results are presented in Table 7. Provinces which improved their relative positions from 2003 to 2005 are expressed in parentheses whereas provinces which deteriorated in their relative positions are underlined. Although eastern provinces dominated the upper left cell in both periods 2003–2005 and 2012–2014, the relative performance between middle provinces and western provinces has changed. From 2003 to 2005, all six middle provinces were in the lower-right three cells. In particular, three out of five provinces in the worst lower-right cell were from the middle region. In contrast, there were only two western provinces. The middle region was the worst performing region. On the other hand, from 2012 to 2014, all middle provinces except one improved in at least one orientation. In contrast, five out of seven provinces in the worst lower-right cell were from the West during the same period. Although some western provinces did improve, in general the manufacturing sector in the

Table 7 Categories of provinces for 2003–2005

		Environment-oriented technical efficiency (E_b)		
		Above average	Average	Below average
Output-oriented techncial efficiency (E_g)	Above average	E-Beijing E-Jiangsu E-Guangdong E-Hainan E-Shangdong E-Shanghai E-Tianjin E-Zhejiang NE-Jilin W-Xinjiang		
	Average		E-Fujian (NE-Liaoning) NE-Heilongjiang W-Inner Mongolia W-Yunan	(W-Guanxi) (E-Hebei) (M-Hubei) (M-Henan) (W-Chongqing)
	Below average		M-Shanxi W-Gansu W-Guizhou W-Qinghai W-Shaanxi	W-Ningxia (W-Sichuan) (M-Anhui) (M-Hunan) (M-Jiangxi)

western region has fallen to the bottom in both production of desirable and undesirable outputs.

Result 6 *During the growth of the manufacturing sector from 2003 to 2014, the following were found:*

1. *Eastern provinces were consistently performing the best.*
2. *Middle provinces improved relative to western provinces.*
3. *The western region became the worst performing region. Provinces are lagging behind other provinces in both output-oriented technical efficiency and environment-oriented technical efficiency.*

In the first two decades after the economic reforms in China since 1978, economic policies were biased toward the coastal region. This has been successful for the industrial sector as seen from Results 5 and 6. However, such policy has further worsened regional income inequality. To achieve balanced regional growth, the central government adopted the "Great Western Development" (GWD) strategy in 1999. In the second 10 years (2009–2018) of GWD, the focuses were infrastructure improvement, environmental protection, and social development, which have been formally incorporated into China's 12th Five-year Program for National Social and Economic Development (2011–2015). The infrastructure development is aimed at stimulating economic growth in the western region through strengthening the link between this region and other regions. A necessary condition for shortening the gap between the western and eastern regions is efficient production of desirable outputs with minimum byproducts that hurt the environment. The above result shows that, for the manufacturing sector, the GWD strategy has yet to achieve its goal.

6 Conclusion

In this paper, we analyzed the productive performance of the Chinese manufacturing sector during 2003–2014. We measured the desirable output-oriented technical efficiency and environment-oriented technical efficiency and argued that they reflect economic and environmental performance. The policies to deal with them are market-oriented for the former and government-oriented for the latter.

Our study shows that the sampled cities were in general very inefficient in regard to the two efficiencies discussed in Sect. 2. Some groups of cities are more efficient than others in both efficiencies. For example, green cities are more efficient than non-green cities. The market force worked well. On the one hand, there was a trend of improving desirable output-oriented technical efficiency during the studied period and there is no evidence that the trend will stop. On the other hand, the gap of desirable output-oriented technical efficiency between green and non-green cities was large at first but converged fast. Such gap was narrowed to a very low level by the end of the studied period. This shows that the desirable output-oriented technical inefficiency can be cured by the current market mechanism. This may be evidence of the success of market reform in China.

Our study also shows that the production of the manufacturing sector was not environmentally friendly. Although there was a trend of improving environment-oriented technical efficiency, such trend stopped significantly in the last several years of the studied period. Further, the gap of environment-oriented technical efficiency between green and non-green cities was large throughout the studied period. Although there was indication of convergence, it was slow. By the end of the studied period, the environment-oriented technical efficiency remained at a very low level and the gap between green and non-green cities was still wide. Therefore, new actions from the government must be taken.

We also found that the performance of the manufacturing sector in the western region was not very bad at the beginning of the studied period. However, several western provinces have improved their relative position but more fell to the bottom by the end of the same period.[4] As the Great Western Development strategy (GWD) has been implemented since 1999 to promote balanced regional growth in China, our results lead to the following conclusion: (i) The improving provinces, Guangxi, Sichuan, and Chongqing, are relatively more developed provinces in the

---

[4]These provinces did improve during 2003–2014. They fell to the bottom because other provinces improved much faster.

western region. If the manufacturing sector was affected by the GWD, then it suggests that more developed provinces gained from the GWD strategy. (ii) The western provinces at the bottom are less developed. The GWD strategy was not strong enough to make the manufacturing sector in the less developed provinces more competitive in terms of both environmental protection and productivity improvement.

If our study of the manufacturing sector reflects more or less the whole economy, then the government must be more active in protecting the environment while the market reform continues.

References

Ball, V.E., R. Fare, S. Grosskopf, and R. Nehring. 2001. Productivity of the U.S. Agricultural Sector: The Case of Undesirable Outputs. In Hulten, Charles; Dean, Edwin R.; Harper, Michael J. Eds., New Developments in Productivity Analysis, Chicago: University of Chicago, 541–586.

Dyckhoff, H., and K. Allen, 2001. Measuring Environmental Efficiency with Data Envelopment Analysis (DEA). European Journal of Operational Research 132: 312–325.

Färe, R., S. Grosskopf, C.A.K. Lovell, and C. Pasurka. 1989. Multilateral Productivity Comparisons When Some Outputs are Undesirable: A Nonparametric Approach. Review of Economics and Statistics 71: 90–98.

Färe, R., S. Grosskopf, and D. Tyteca. 1996. An Activity Analysis Model of the Environmental Performance of Firms - Application to Fossil-Fuel-Fired Electric Utilities. Ecological Economics 18: 161–175.

Frantz, R.S. 1988. X-Efficiency: Theory, Evidence and Applications. Boston: Kluwer Academic Publishers.

Hailu, A., and T.S. Veeman. 2001. Non-Parametric Productivity Analysis with Undesirable Outputs: An Application to the Canadian Pulp and Paper Industry. American Journal of Agricultural Economics 83: 805–816.

Harbaugh, W.T., A. Levinson, and D.M. Wilson. 2002. Reexamining the Empirical Evidence for an Environmental Kutznets Curve. Review of Economics and Statistics 84:541–551.

Hua, Z., Y. Bian, and L. Liang. 2007. Eco-efficiency Analysis of Paper Mills Along the HuaiRiver: an Extended DEA Approach. Omega 35: 578–587.

Jefferson, G.H., T.G. Rawski, and Y. Zheng. 1996. Chinese Industrial Productivity: Trends, Measurement Issues and Recent Developments. Journal of Comparative Economics, 23: 146–180.

Jefferson, G.H., A.G.Z. Hu, X. Guan, and X. Yu. 2003. Ownership, Performance, and Innovation in China's Large- and Medium-size Industrial Enterprise Sector. China Economic Review 14: 89–113.

Kuosmanen, T. 2005. Weak Disposability in Nonparametric Production Analysis with Undesirable Outputs. American Journal of Agricultural Economics 87: 1077–1082.

Lam, P., and A. Shiu. 2001. A Data Envelopment Analysis of the Efficiency of China's Thermal Power Generation. Utilities Policy 10: 75–83.

Li, M., and L. Zhang. 2014. Haze in China: Current and future challenges. Environmental Pollution, 189: 85–86.

Liu, W., and J. Sharp. 1999. DEA Models via Goal Programming. In Westermann, G. (Ed.),Data Envelopment Analysis in the Service Sector. Deutscher Universitätsverlag, Wiesbaden. 79–101.

Malikov, E., S.C. Kumbhakar, and E.G. Tsionas. 2015. "Bayesian Approach to Disentangling Technical and Environmental Productivity." Econometrics 3: 443–465.

National Development and Reform Commission. 2016. The 13th Five-Year Plan for Economic and Social Development of the People's Republic of China. Beijing, China: Central Compilation & Translation Press. (Translated by Compilation and Translation Bureau, Central Committee of the Communist Party of China).

Park, Y.S., S.H. Lim, G. Egilmez, and J. Szmerekovsky. 2016. Environmental Efficiency Assessment of US Transport Sector: A Slack-based Data Envelopment Analysis Approach. Transportation Research Part D: Transport and Environment. https://doi.org/10.1016/j.trd.2016.09.009.

Pittman, R.W. 1983. "Multilateral Productivity Comparisons with Undesirable Outputs." Economic Journal 93: 883–891.

Tyteca, D. 1997. Linear Programming Models for the Measurement of Environment Performance of Firms - Concepts and Empirical Results. Journal of Productivity Analysis 8: 183–197.

Wu, J., L. Lv, J. Sun, and X. Ji. 2015. A Comprehensive Analysis of China's Regional Energy Saving and Emission Reduction Efficiency: From Production and Treatment Perspectives. Energy Policy 84: 66–176.

Wu, Y. 2000. Is China's Economic Growth Sustainable? A Productivity Analysis. China Economic Review 11: 278–296.

Yaisawarng, S., and J.D. Klein. 1994. The Effects of Sulfur Dioxide Controls on Productivity Change in the US Electric Power Industry. Review of Economics and Statistics 76: 447–460.

Zheng, J., S. Liu, and A. Bigsten. 1998. Ownership Structure and Determinants of Technical Efficiency: An Application of Data Envelopment Analysis to Chinese Enterprises (1986–90). Journal of Comparative Economics 26: 465–484.

Zheng, J., X. Liu, and A. Bigsten. 2003. Efficiency, Technical Progress, and Best Practice in Chinese State Enterprises (1980–1994). Journal of Comparative Economics 31: 134–152.

Zhao, B., S. Wang, X. Dong, J. Wang, L. Duan, X. Fu, J. Hao, and J. Fu. 2013. Environmental Effects of the Recent Emission Changes in China: Implications for Particulate Matter Pollution and Soil Acidification. Environmental Research Letters 8: 024031.

Chapter 10
Environmental and Energy Efficiencies Using the Stochastic Frontier Cost Function Type

Sangmok Kang

1 Introduction

Recently, it is recognized that the increase of CO_2 emission as a main factor of greenhouse gas emission is a phenomenon raised from fossil fuel use by most of environmental economists. As fossil fuel is a chief factor of CO_2 emission, it is an important time to reduce use of fossil fuels, preparing for increase of greenhouse gases. Thus, this paper is to measure simultaneous performance considering CO_2 emission and fossil fuel use, and apply empirical test to measure it. As the data of fossil fuels and CO_2 emission as usage data is available for the OECD countries, the environment efficiencies for CO_2 emission and the energy efficiency for fossil fuel are measured at the same time.

As the literature review shows, the measure of environmental efficiencies appears to have a certain limit to premise the assumption of weak disposability and strong disposability, or null-jointness between desirable outputs and undesirable outputs. Namely, the existing studies use the unrealistic assumptions that desirable outputs and undesirable outputs make a change given the constant state of input directly connected with pollutants, or use labor and capital stock with pollutants directly.[1]

There are other types of studies which measure environmental efficiencies based of stochastic frontier analysis (SFA). These studies are Reinhard et al. (1999, 2000, 2002), Gang and Felmingham (2004), Herrala and Goel (2012), and Lansik and

---

[1]Färe et al. (1989), Färe et al. (1996), Chung et al. (1997), Zofio and Prieto (2001), and Färe et al. (2007) assume the weak disposability of pollutants, and null-jointness among good outputs and bad outputs. They connect pollutants with labor forces and capital stocks unrelated directly or assume frontier considering only good outputs and bad outputs without inputs.

S. Kang (✉)
Department of Economics, Pusan National University, Busan, South Korea
e-mail: smkang@pusan.ac.kr

© Springer Nature Singapore Pte Ltd. 2018
R. Pang et al. (eds.), *Energy, Environment and Transitional Green Growth in China*, https://doi.org/10.1007/978-981-10-7919-1_10

Wall (2014). Reinhard et al. (1999) measured environmental efficiency of dairy farms using SFA, and Reinhard et al. (2000) estimated environmental efficiency of the same dairy farms using SFA and DEA (data envelopment analysis), based on output and input approaches. Reinhard et al. (2002) attempted to have a two-stage approaches, which measured environmental efficiency first, and regressed it with some impact factors. Gang and Felmingham (2004) measured environmental efficiencies and its impacting factors in the Australian irrigation industry using input-oriented approach such as Reinhard et al. (2002).[2] Their environmental efficiencies were based on estimates of technical efficiency. They additionally estimated the potential reduction of the environmentally detrimental salt emissions resulting from the improvement of environmental inefficiency in addition.

Herrala and Goel (2012) measured the environmental efficiencies for 170 countries making use of stochastic cost frontier analysis. They used CO_2 emission as dependent variable, and GDP, population, and national land as independent variables. Lansik and Wall (2014) introduced several methods such as ecological efficiency and material flow balance approach as frontier approach explaining environmental efficiencies.

However, these studies on stochastic frontier analysis excepting Herrala and Goel (2012) take desirable output as a dependent variable, and pollutants as independent variables of inputs, when estimating environmental efficiency.[3] Differentiating from previous studies, the current research uses pollutant as a dependent variable, and simultaneously measures environmental efficiency and energy efficiency for fossil fuel. This is distinguished from the previous studies in that this article use stochastic cost frontier analysis, and simultaneously estimate environmental efficiency and energy efficiency for fossil fuel in the one model, which influences pollutants.

The remainder of the paper is organized as follows. Section 2 introduces theoretic model on environmental efficiency and energy efficiency. Section 3 explains the descriptive statistics data in OECD countries, and empirical test results. Section 4 draws final conclusions.

---

[2]In the input approach, the pollutant should be reduced with other inputs such like labor forces, energy inputs, and capital stocks, whereas the pollutant should be decreased by itself in the output approach, Two approach are common in that they intent to minimize a pollutant. The strong point of input approach is that it may minimize one more pollutants simultaneously. But the output approach can do not so, because we can put only one pollutant as dependent variable. For more information on this, please refer to Kang (2015).

[3]Here, these studies mention Reinhard (1999, 2000, 2002), and Gang and Felmingham (2004).

2 Theoretic Model

Environmental efficiency is measured as minimum pollutant over actual pollutant as a harmful pollutant needs to minimize. There are two methods in estimating the environmental efficiency based on the definition of environmental efficiency. First, pollutants are considered to be inputs, and minimized in the production function. Second, pollutants are defined as outputs, and minimized in the cost function. And then, a majority of studies considered pollutants as inputs, especially in the case of using desirable outputs and undesirable outputs at the same time. Alternative approach that treats pollutants as outputs and minimize them in the cost function will be used to measure the environmental efficiency. The stochastic cost frontier model in the theoretic model is introduced. This article particularly divides the types of efficiencies into environmental efficiency and energy efficiency for fossil fuels in the one single model. The model for measuring two efficiencies together will be introduced.

First, environmental efficiency is defined as follow;

$$
\begin{aligned}
EE_Z &= \min\{\theta : \theta \cdot Z \in T(y, Z)\} \\
&= \min\{\theta : \theta \cdot Z \geq Z^*\} \\
&= \min\{\theta : \theta \geq Z^*/Z\} \\
&= Z^*/Z
\end{aligned}
\tag{1}
$$

where, Z: actual pollutant, Z^*: minimum pollutant, θ: environmental efficiency. Environmental efficiency has a value less than 1. A pollutant is considered as a dependent variable, but also it is treated as a byproduct to be minimized.

Meanwhile, as Herrala and Goel (2012) defined, y is desirable outputs vector, and Z is pollutants vector to be minimized in production possibility set (T). However, differentiating from Herrala and Goel (2012), this article do not use environmental efficiency decided by regulation policy, but use environmental efficiency defined on the cost frontier, which is measured as minimum pollutants over actual pollutants. The basic model here premises the production technology such that pollutants are explained by desirable outputs and inputs. That is,

$$
Z \geq T(y, x) \tag{2}
$$

where, pollutant Z is the function of desirable outputs (y) and inputs (x). Namely, a production function uses x and produce y and Z simultaneously. Equation (2) means that Z should be minimized in producing given y. Thus, Min (Z) = T(y, x). Combined Eqs. (1) with (2), environmental efficiency based on stochastic cost frontier is defined as

$$\exp(-u_{it}) = \min(Z_{it})/Z_{it} \tag{3}$$

Now, stochastic frontier cost function including random error and environmental inefficiency error is expressed as

$$Z_{it} = T(y_{it}, x_{it} : \beta) \cdot \exp(v_{it}) \cdot \exp(u_{it}) \tag{4}$$

where, pollutants (Z) as a dependent variable is the function of y, x, random error (v), and environmental inefficiency error (u). Equation (4) can be transformed into the logarithm type of translog stochastic cost frontier function as

$$
\begin{aligned}
\ln(Z_{it}) &= \beta_0 + \beta_1 \ln y_{it} + \beta_2 \ln K_{it} + \beta_3 \ln L_{it} + \beta_4 \ln f\!f_{it} + \beta_5 \ln n\!f_{it} \\
&\quad + 1/2\,\beta_6 \ln^2 y_{it} + 1/2\,\beta_7 \ln^2 K_{it} + 1/2\,\beta_8 \ln^2 L_{it} + 1/2\,\beta_9 \ln^2 f\!f_{it} + 1/2\,\beta_{10} \ln^2 n\!f_{it} \\
&\quad + \beta_{11} \ln y_{it} \cdot \ln K_{it} + \beta_{12} \ln y_{it} \cdot \ln L_{it} + \beta_{13} \ln y_{it} \cdot \ln f\!f_{it} + \beta_{14} \ln y_{it} \cdot \ln n\!f_{it} \\
&\quad + \beta_{15} \ln K_{it} \cdot \ln L_{it} + \beta_{16} \ln K_{it} \cdot \ln f\!f_{it} + \beta_{17} \ln K_{it} \cdot \ln n\!f_{it} \\
&\quad + \beta_{18} \ln L_{it} \cdot \ln f\!f_{it} + \beta_{19} \ln L_{it} \cdot \ln n\!f_{it} + \beta_{20} \ln f\!f_{it} \cdot \ln n\!f_{it} \\
&\quad + v_{it} + u_{it}
\end{aligned}
\tag{5}
$$

where, inputs are classified into capital stock, labor forces, fossil fuels, and non-fossil fuels. As already mentioned, a type of stochastic cost frontier function is used because a pollutant should be minimized. So, the environmental inefficiency error term shows plus (+) sign different from the case of production function. We can estimate environmental efficiency from Eq. (5).

First of all, let's introduce energy efficiency of fossil fuel as one of factors affecting to environmental efficiency. We need to analyze the relation between energy efficiency of fossil fuel and environmental efficiency. The energy efficiency of fossil fuel is defined as

$$EE_{ff} = \min\{\delta : \delta \cdot ff \in T(y, Z)\} \tag{6}$$

following the definition of energy efficiency, the energy efficiency is also defined as follow;

$$EE_{ff} = \min(ff_{it})/ff_{it} \tag{7}$$

where, EE_{ff}: energy efficiency, min(ff): minimum fossil fuel, ff: actual fossil fuel.

Energy efficiency is also defined as minimum fossil fuel over actual fossil fuel. If both of environmental efficiency and energy efficiency are efficient in the Eq. (5), we need to substitute fossil fuel (ff) into $\delta \cdot$ff, and put environmental inefficiency error term (u_{it}) = 0. The stochastic frontier cost function satisfying these conditions is expressed as

$$\ln(Z_{it}) = \beta_0 + \beta_1 \ln y_{it} + \beta_2 \ln K_{it} + \beta_3 \ln L_{it} + \beta_4 \ln ff_{it} + \beta_5 \ln nf_{it}$$
$$+ 1/2\,\beta_6 \ln^2 y_{it} + 1/2\,\beta_7 \ln^2 K_{it} + 1/2\,\beta_8 \ln^2 L_{it} + 1/2\,\beta_9 \ln^2 \delta \cdot ff_{it} + 1/2\,\beta_{10} \ln^2 nf_{it}$$
$$+ \beta_{11} \ln y_{it} \cdot \ln K_{it} + \beta_{12} \ln y_{it} \cdot \ln L_{it} + \beta_{13} \ln y_{it} \cdot \ln \delta \cdot ff_{it} + \beta_{14} \ln y_{it} \cdot \ln nf_{it}$$
$$+ \beta_{15} \ln K_{it} \cdot \ln L_{it} + \beta_{16} \ln K_{it} \cdot \ln \delta \cdot ff_{it} + \beta_{17} \ln K_{it} \cdot \ln nf_{it}$$
$$+ \beta_{18} \ln L_{it} \cdot \ln \delta \cdot ff_{it} + \beta_{19} \ln L_{it} \cdot \ln nf_{it} + \beta_{20} \ln \delta \cdot ff_{it} \cdot \ln nf_{it}$$
$$+ v_{it}$$

$$(8)$$

Thus, Eq. (5) should be equalized with Eq. (8) in order to accomplish overall efficiency including two efficiencies. Namely, to achieve the best practices of two efficiencies, the next condition should be satisfied:

$$\tfrac{1}{2}\beta_9 \ln^2 \delta + (\beta_4 + \beta_{13}\ln y_{it} + \beta_{16}\ln K_{it} + \beta_{18}\ln L_{it}$$
$$+ \beta_{20}\ln nf_{it}) \cdot \ln \delta - u_{it} = 0$$

$$(9)$$

This is a quadratic formula expressed by $\ln\delta$, which can be solved. For simplification, Let's put the coefficient of second item as b. Namely,

$$\beta_4 + \beta_{13}\ln y_{it} + \beta_{16}\ln K_{it} + \beta_{18}\ln L_{it} + \beta_{20}\ln nf_{it} = b \qquad (10)$$

in the Eq. (9), $\ln\delta$ can be solved as

$$\ln \delta = \frac{-b \pm \sqrt{b^2 + 2\beta_9(-u_{it})}}{\beta_9} \qquad (11)$$

thus, inserting the coefficients estimated by Eqs. (5) into (11), we derive the value of δ. The δ is energy efficiency for fossil fuel, and $\exp(-u)$ is environmental efficiency for the pollutant. As a result, we can get environmental efficiency (θ) in the Eq. (5) and energy efficiency (δ) in the Eq. (11), respectively.

The translog cost function is estimated by maximum likelihood estimation (MLE). Based on Stevenson (1980), the following distribution assumption is assumed as:

(1) $v_i \sim$ iid $N(0, \sigma_v^2)$, v_i (random error) is normal distribution.
(2) $u_i \sim$ iid $N + (\mu, \sigma_u^2)$, u (cost inefficient error) is nonnegative half normal.
(3) v_i ↹ u_i are distributed independently of each other and of the regressors.

The truncated normal distribution is assumed for u_i. As mean of this distribution is not 0, but random μ, the truncated normal distribution allows the normal distribution to have a nonzero mode. That is, the truncated normal distribution provides a more flexible pattern of efficiency than half normal distribution. In addition, The panel model of time varying cost efficiency such like Battese and Coelli (1992) is considered in the next empirical test.

3 Empirical Test Results

The proposed theory model is applied to a sample of OECD countries for 1996–2009. The sample data include labor forces, capital stock, fossil fuel, non-fossil fuel, CO_2 emission, and GDP for 27 OECD countries. We use labor forces by OECD statistics, and estimate capital stocks of OECD countries by the perpetual inventory method, which is derived from new investment for OECD countries in the Penn World Table 1. The fossil fuel and non-fossil fuel data, which are marked by ton of oil equivalent, also come from OECD statistics. CO_2 emission comes from United Nations Framework Convention on Climate Change (UNFCCC). The money value data such as capital stock and GDP are transformed into constant value based on 2005 year (2005 = 100). We use per capita variables, which are divided by population.[4] We use a type of stochastic frontier cost function as an estimation method, and estimate two efficiencies with 378 observations for 14 years. Of the 14 years, 4 years results (1996, 2000, 2005, and 2009) representively are presented due to limited space. The summary of statistics for OECD countries is listed in Table 1.

The per capita mean of OECD for 1996–2009 is 10.3 ton (CO_2 emission), 31,002 dollar (GDP), 77,408 dollar (capital stock), 0.49 person (labor forces), 166.5 ton (fossil fuel), and non-fossil fuel (46.8 ton). We can classify Luxembourg, United States, Australia, and Canada as high level countries in terms of per capita fossil fuel use.

As we do not use production function, but use stochastic frontier cost function in the empirical test, this results may be different from those of the production function in the existing studies. The estimation equation of per capita CO_2 emission by the type of stochastic frontier cost function is illustrated in Table 2. As is shown, per capita CO_2 emission is mostly significant for per capital fossil fuel, but not significant for other explainable variables. However, total variance (σ^2), gamma (Υ), and environmental inefficiency error term (μ) are all significant at the one percent level, and over 60% of composite-error terms results from environmental inefficiency error terms. The time-varying environmental inefficiency (eta) is not significant.

While log likelihood value of maximum likelihood estimation (MLE) is 277.9, the value of ordinary least square (OLS) is 212.7, and the LR test shows 130.5. Thus, the null hypothesis, which there are no environmental inefficiency and no change of environmental inefficiency, is rejected in one percent level (threshold value: 9.21) through χ^2 distribution. So, we confirm environmental inefficiency exists. Using the estimated coefficients of the stochastic frontier cost function, we additionally estimate energy efficiency (δ) in Eq. (11).

Meanwhile, Table 3 shows the elasticity of CO_2 emission for GDP and fossil fuel, which is derived from the estimation equation of stochastic frontier cost function. The annual average elasticity of CO_2 emission for GDP is 0.193,

---

[4]If we use total variables, this will be more advantageous to high income countries. Per capita variables are applicable to every countries equitably.

Table 1 Descriptive statistics (1996–2009)

	CO_2/P	GDP/p	K/p	L/p	FE/p	NFE/p
Australia	18.2	35,673	88,409	0.51	278.4	9.4
Austria	8.8	34,651	94,837	0.49	131.8	50.7
Belgium	11.8	32,045	88,635	0.43	224.1	17.3
Canada	17.7	34,489	73,376	0.53	294.7	123.5
Denmark	10.9	33,316	81,875	0.53	172.2	14.2
Finland	11.9	29,924	81,803	0.50	166.9	57.2
France	6.8	30,815	71,353	0.46	107.4	34.1
Germany	10.6	30,879	81,814	0.48	161.3	13.1
Greece	9.5	22,400	59,260	0.43	132.3	4.8
Hungary	5.8	14,568	33,572	0.41	97.4	5.4
Iceland	9.9	38,583	101,780	0.57	146.7	313.2
Ireland	11.0	35,702	81,829	0.47	165.8	4.3
Italy	8.0	28,958	82,407	0.41	132.7	9.0
Japan	9.8	30,607	107,586	0.53	159.7	16.2
Korea, South	10.5	20,573	66,589	0.48	166.2	9.0
Luxembourg	22.1	67,934	150,598	0.65	354.7	4.7
Mexico	3.7	10,774	24,817	0.38	60.8	3.8
Netherlands	10.8	35,580	79,434	0.52	252.8	4.7
New Zealand	8.3	24,910	50,035	0.52	146.8	70.1
Norway	9.4	46,492	118,271	0.52	144.2	268.2
Poland	8.5	12,517	23,081	0.45	110.6	1.0
Portugal	6.0	19,550	56,190	0.51	95.1	13.6
Spain	7.5	26,823	71,483	0.46	122.9	15.8
Sweden	6.1	31,421	62,619	0.51	100.0	107.3
Switzerland	6.1	36,648	115,660	0.60	92.4	62.0
UK	9.2	31,612	56,328	0.49	159.0	7.0
United States	19.1	39,610	86,385	0.50	317.6	22.8
Mean	10.3	31,002	77,408	0.49	166.5	46.8

Unit: ton, dollar, person, ton

inelastistic for 1996–2009. Namely, one percent increase of GDP causes the 0.193% increase of CO_2 emission, implying that the increase of income do not much impact on the increase of CO_2 emission. Whereas, the annual average elasticity of CO_2 emission for fossil fuel is 0.950, close to 1. Namely, the one percent increase of fossil fuel causes 0.95% increase of CO_2 emission, showing that the use of fossil fuel is closely connected with CO_2 emission. The countries that elasticity of CO_2 emission for GDP is high fall on Poland, Luxembourg, Netherlands, and Ireland. On the other hand, of the countries that show very low elasticity of CO_2 emission for GDP, Iceland, Ireland, and Greece specially display minus (−) sign of elasticity, implying that nonetheless of income increase, these countries reduced CO_2 emission effectively.

Table 2 The estimation results of Stochastic Frontier cost function

	Coefficient	Standard deviation	t value
Constant	−1.332	1.173	−1.135
ln(GDP/p)	−0.054	0.547	−0.099
ln(K/p)	0.015	0.504	0.030
ln(L/p)	0.110	0.280	0.391
ln(FE/p)	0.352***	0.225	1.562
ln(NFE/p)	0.146	0.498	0.292
$1/2\ln(GDP/p)^2$	−0.098	0.176	−0.558
$1/2\ln(K/p)^2$	−0.050	0.307	−0.164
$1/2\ln(L/p)^2$	0.199	0.582	0.341
$1/2\ln(FE/p)^2$	0.478*	0.174	2.746
$1/2\ln(NFE/p)^2$	0.009	0.022	0.408
ln(GDP/p)*ln(K/p)	0.118	0.214	0.551
ln(GDP/p)*ln(L/p)	0.082	0.519	0.158
ln(GDP/p)*ln(FE/p)	0.056	0.292	0.192
ln(GDP/p)*ln(NFE/p)	−0.099	0.071	−1.384
ln(K/p)*ln(L/p)	−0.123	0.545	−0.227
ln(K/p)*ln(FE/p)	−0.229	0.240	−0.951
ln(K/p)*ln(NFE/p)	0.075	0.064	1.173
ln(L/p)*ln(FE/p)	−0.055	0.278	−0.198
ln(L/p)*ln(NFE/p)	0.313***	0.192	1.626
ln(FE/p)*ln(NFE/p)	0.048	0.044	1.100
$sigma^2$	0.027*	0.004	6.156
gamma	0.606*	0.065	9.308
mu	0.256*	0.056	4.596
eta	0.009	0.009	1.005
Log likelihood	277.911		
LR test	130.457		
Number of sample	27		
Observation	378		

Note LR of log likelihood test is estimated by $-2(L(H0) - L(H1))$
*Significant at 1% level
***Significant at 10% level

In case of elasticity of CO_2 emission for fossil fuel, Canada, United States, Luxembourg, Australia, and Netherlands show higher elasticity over one, while Mexico, Switzerland, Portugal, France relatively display lower elasticity of CO_2 emission. In these countries, the impact of fossil fuel on CO_2 emission is less sensitive. In conclusion, the impact of fossil fuel on CO_2 emission is more sensitive than that of income.

Table 4 shows the trend of fossil fuel efficiency for 1996–2009, which is derived by estimating Eq. (11). Here, the efficiency of fossil fuel is driven in the stochastic

Table 3 Elasticity of CO_2 emission

	Elasticity for GDP					Elasticity for fossil fuel				
	1996	2000	2005	2009	Mean	1996	2000	2005	2009	Mean
Australia	0.279	0.289	0.300	0.329	0.296	1.158	1.182	1.180	1.119	1.170
Austria	0.099	0.083	0.104	0.095	0.096	0.883	0.865	0.894	0.845	0.876
Belgium	0.226	0.220	0.225	0.215	0.222	1.108	1.111	1.091	1.037	1.096
Canada	0.005	0.016	0.035	0.050	0.029	1.386	1.392	1.373	1.261	1.360
Denmark	0.338	0.240	0.195	0.208	0.238	1.086	0.972	0.909	0.845	0.964
Finland	0.117	0.083	0.089	0.110	0.096	1.037	0.997	0.982	0.940	1.019
France	0.089	0.090	0.102	0.110	0.096	0.842	0.847	0.823	0.755	0.823
Germany	0.257	0.243	0.229	0.212	0.235	0.949	0.933	0.933	0.895	0.935
Greece	0.301	0.320	0.291	0.281	0.309	0.811	0.866	0.873	0.837	0.854
Hungary	0.256	0.256	0.235	0.217	0.250	0.847	0.803	0.848	0.767	0.824
Iceland	−0.045	−0.063	−0.058	−0.096	−0.066	1.007	1.023	0.993	0.912	0.997
Ireland	0.373	0.351	0.331	0.278	0.338	0.860	0.938	0.903	0.834	0.902
Italy	0.248	0.248	0.267	0.239	0.255	0.822	0.842	0.840	0.767	0.828
Japan	0.246	0.251	0.254	0.260	0.253	0.876	0.880	0.877	0.830	0.873
Korea, South	0.301	0.284	0.279	0.293	0.288	0.926	0.947	0.970	0.990	0.957
Luxembourg	0.432	0.375	0.405	0.402	0.400	1.102	1.106	1.216	1.123	1.147
Mexico	0.219	0.226	0.250	0.272	0.246	0.629	0.656	0.637	0.612	0.637
Netherlands	0.393	0.371	0.326	0.307	0.355	1.115	1.097	1.127	1.111	1.110
New Zealand	0.005	0.020	0.042	0.043	0.031	1.070	1.097	1.063	0.987	1.070
Norway	−0.062	−0.085	−0.070	−0.038	−0.061	0.957	0.959	0.973	0.941	0.961
Poland	0.445	0.434	0.395	0.328	0.405	0.937	0.851	0.860	0.884	0.874
Portugal	0.152	0.204	0.272	0.201	0.208	0.704	0.781	0.735	0.698	0.741
Spain	0.166	0.195	0.220	0.195	0.194	0.752	0.850	0.881	0.790	0.839
Sweden	−0.002	−0.042	−0.043	−0.024	−0.030	0.950	0.878	0.846	0.746	0.867
Switzerland	0.104	0.084	0.103	0.090	0.091	0.679	0.678	0.655	0.618	0.663
UK	0.254	0.252	0.246	0.250	0.250	1.040	1.004	0.984	0.897	0.986
United States	0.176	0.197	0.213	0.213	0.201	1.350	1.320	1.271	1.197	1.287
Mean	0.199	0.190	0.194	0.187	0.193	0.959	0.958	0.953	0.898	0.950

frontier cost function. The energy efficiency is defined as minimum energy over actual energy. Annual average efficiency of fossil fuel in the OECD countries for 1996–2009 lied from 0.813 to 0.837, and the level of efficiency had been improved. The improved energy efficiency represents that the gaps of fossil fuel among OECD countries had been reduced gradually. Netherlands, Mexico, Canada, United States, New Zealand, United Kingdom, and Switzerland show higher energy efficiencies. But, the reasons showing high efficiency are different from these countries. High efficiency reflects that actual fossil fuel use comes close to minimum fossil fuel use, whereas low efficiency implies actual use are far away from minimum use in given output condition. So, even though Netherlands, Canada, and United States show high per capita fossil fuel, their fossil fuel uses come close to minimum use of

Table 4 Energy efficiency (1996–2009)

	1996	2000	2005	2009	Mean
Australia	0.766	0.776	0.789	0.800	0.783
Austria	0.756	0.765	0.777	0.785	0.771
Belgium	0.856	0.862	0.869	0.875	0.866
Canada	0.921	0.925	0.930	0.934	0.928
Denmark	0.782	0.787	0.796	0.806	0.793
Finland	0.722	0.730	0.743	0.755	0.737
France	0.788	0.796	0.807	0.815	0.802
Germany	0.751	0.759	0.768	0.776	0.764
Greece	0.725	0.736	0.748	0.758	0.742
Hungary	0.846	0.853	0.861	0.866	0.856
Iceland	0.836	0.843	0.852	0.858	0.847
Ireland	0.770	0.780	0.792	0.799	0.785
Italy	0.804	0.812	0.822	0.827	0.816
Japan	0.754	0.763	0.773	0.781	0.768
Korea, South	0.729	0.740	0.755	0.765	0.747
Luxembourg	0.770	0.778	0.791	0.800	0.785
Mexico	0.925	0.929	0.933	0.937	0.931
Netherlands	0.981	0.982	0.983	0.983	0.982
New Zealand	0.864	0.871	0.879	0.885	0.875
Norway	0.820	0.826	0.835	0.844	0.832
Poland	0.742	0.754	0.764	0.772	0.758
Portugal	0.784	0.797	0.812	0.816	0.802
Spain	0.792	0.802	0.814	0.821	0.808
Sweden	0.825	0.830	0.839	0.847	0.835
Switzerland	0.866	0.870	0.877	0.881	0.873
UK	0.865	0.871	0.878	0.884	0.875
United States	0.905	0.910	0.916	0.920	0.913
Mean	0.813	0.820	0.830	0.837	0.825

frontier curve, and they show high fossil fuel efficiencies. While, Mexico and Switzerland relatively have low per capita fossil fuels but, they also come close to minimum use of frontier curve, and also have high efficiencies.

However, Finland, Greece, Korea, Poland, Germany, and Japan display most low efficiencies of fossil fuels. Finland, Korea, and Greece show similar levels of per capital fossil fuel uses and per capita CO_2 emission. Especially, Germany, which shows higher proportion of manufacturing in the overall industry, reports that the average per capita fossil fuel is 161 ton. Then that of France is 107.2 ton. So, the per capita fossil fuel and CO_2 emission of Germany considerably show high levels. Poland's fossil fuel is relatively large but, the sizes of per capital GDP and per capita capital stock are small. So, Poland show low efficiency of fossil fuel.

Table 5 shows the results of environmental efficiency for CO_2 emission. The annual average environmental efficiency of OECD countries for 1996–2009 is 0.750, less than that of energy efficiency (0.850). The distribution of annual environmental efficiency in the OECD countries for the same period lie from 0.737 to 0.762. This mean that in case of the CO_2 emission, the CO_2 emission of individual country is farther away from the performance of the best practice than that of fossil fuel use. Namely, it implies the CO_2 emission has more possibilities to reduce than fossil fuel. As the energy efficiencies year by year have been improved, the environmental efficiencies show the same trend. It means that the gaps of environmental efficiencies among countries have also gradually reduced. Netherlands, Mexico, Canada, The United States, New Zealand, United Kingdom, and

Table 5 Environmental efficiency (1996–2009)

	1996	2000	2005	2009	Mean
Australia	0.663	0.673	0.685	0.695	0.679
Austria	0.657	0.668	0.680	0.690	0.674
Belgium	0.792	0.799	0.807	0.813	0.803
Canada	0.897	0.900	0.905	0.908	0.902
Denmark	0.682	0.692	0.703	0.713	0.698
Finland	0.615	0.626	0.640	0.650	0.633
France	0.709	0.718	0.729	0.737	0.723
Germany	0.640	0.650	0.663	0.673	0.657
Greece	0.612	0.623	0.637	0.647	0.630
Hungary	0.795	0.801	0.809	0.816	0.805
Iceland	0.778	0.785	0.794	0.801	0.789
Ireland	0.664	0.674	0.686	0.696	0.680
Italy	0.715	0.724	0.735	0.743	0.729
Japan	0.636	0.647	0.660	0.670	0.653
Korea, South	0.619	0.630	0.643	0.654	0.636
Luxembourg	0.643	0.654	0.667	0.676	0.660
Mexico	0.904	0.907	0.911	0.914	0.909
Netherlands	0.971	0.972	0.974	0.975	0.973
New Zealand	0.826	0.832	0.839	0.844	0.835
Norway	0.752	0.760	0.769	0.777	0.764
Poland	0.655	0.665	0.678	0.687	0.671
Portugal	0.707	0.716	0.727	0.735	0.721
Spain	0.710	0.719	0.730	0.738	0.724
Sweden	0.768	0.776	0.785	0.792	0.780
Switzerland	0.802	0.809	0.816	0.822	0.812
UK	0.812	0.818	0.825	0.831	0.822
United States	0.866	0.871	0.876	0.880	0.873
Mean	0.737	0.745	0.755	0.762	0.750

Switzerland show very high efficiencies as such like the energy efficiency. This is an anticipated result because CO_2 emission generally has a significant connection with fossil fuel.

On the contrary to this, Greece, Finland, Korea, Japan, Germany, Luxembourg, and Poland show very low performance of environmental efficiency. Of these countries, the rank of environmental efficiency for Luxembourg somewhat remains behind more than the rank of energy efficiency, even though Luxembourg reports very high per capita fossil fuel and per capita CO_2 emission. Japan, and Germany report similar levels of per capita fossil fuel use with Korea, but a little higher level of per capita CO_2 emission than Korea. And then, Poland use more per capita fossil fuel than these countries, but emit less per capita CO_2 emission (8.5 ton) than Finland (11.9 ton), Korea (10.5 ton), and Greece (9.5 ton).

As a result, there are a bigger chance to reduce CO_2 emission because the environmental efficiency of OECD countries is lower than the energy efficiency of fossil fuel.[5]

4 Conclusions

This paper estimated energy efficiency and environmental efficiency together in one single model using a type of stochastic frontier cost function. As Herrala and Goel (2012) tried, stochastic frontier cost function is available to measure environmental efficiency of pollutants in terms of minimization of pollutants. The statistic data of OECD countries were used for the estimation of two simultaneous efficiencies.

The empirical test results showed the existence of environmental inefficiency, and over 60% of composite-error terms results from environmental inefficiency error terms. The time-varying environmental inefficiency (eta) is not significant. The impact of fossil fuel change on CO_2 emission is more sensitive than that of income.

Annual energy efficiency of fossil fuel in the OECD countries for 1996–2009 lied from 0.813 to 0.837, and the energy efficiency level had been improved. The improved energy efficiency represents that the gaps of fossil fuel among countries had been reduced gradually. The annual average environmental efficiency for 1996–2009 is 0.750, less than that of energy efficiency (0.850). This means that the CO_2 emission for individual country is farther away from the best practice than that of fossil fuel. Eventually, this means that there is a significant possibility to reduce not only fossil fuel use but also CO_2 emission.

As empirical results were shown, fossil fuel use is closely related with CO_2 emission, and the increase of fossil fuel efficiency results in improvement of environmental efficiency. Hence, to get the high performance, the effort to reduce

---

[5]In this paper, environmental efficiency is defined as minimum CO_2 over actual CO_2. So, reducing actual CO_2 emission, we can improve environmental efficiency.

CO_2 emission is needed itself, and more basically, the additional effort to transform fossil fuel use into renewable energy should be accompanied. We should make efforts to introduce low-carbon energy system and go technological innovation side by side.

References

Battese, G.E and T.J. Coelli, "Frontier Production Function, Technical Efficiencies and Panel Data: With Application to Paddy Farmers in India," Journal of Productivity Analysis, 3, 1992, 153–169.

Chung, Y.R., Fare, R., Grosskopf, S., "Productivity and Undesirable Outputs: a Directional Distance Function Approach," Journal of Environmental Management 51, 1997, pp. 229–240.

Färe, R., Grosskopf, S., Lovell, C.A.K., Pasurka, C., "Multilateral Productivity Comparisons When Some Outputs are Undesirable: A Nonparametric Approach," Review of Economics and Statistics 71(1), 1989, pp. 90–98.

Färe, R., S. Grosskopf, and Daniel Tyteca, "An Activity Analysis Model of The Environmental Performance of Firms-Application to Fossil Fuel Fired Electric Utilities", Ecological Economics, 18, 1996, 161–175.

Färe, R., S. Grosskopf, and Carl Pasurka, "Environmental Production Functions and Environmental Directional Distance Function," Energy, 32, 2007, pp. 1055–1066.

Gang, L. and Felmingham, "Environmental Efficiency of the Australian Irrigation Industry in Treating Salt Emissions," Australian Economics Papers, 2004. pp. 475–490.

Herrala, R. and R.K. Goel, "Global CO_2 Efficiency: Country-wise Estimates using a Stochastic Cost Frontier," Energy Policy, 45, 2012, pp. 762–770.

Kang, S-M., Efficiency, Productivity, and Performance, Bobmunsa, 2015.

Lansink, A. O. and A. Wall, "Frontier Models for Evaluating Environmental Efficiency: an Overview," Economics and Business Letters, 3(1), 2014, pp. 43–50.

Reinhard, S., Lovell, C.A.K. and G.J. Thijssen, "Econometric Estimation of Technical and Environmental Efficiency: an Application to Dutch Dairy Farms," American Journal of Agricultural Economics, 81, 1999, pp. 44–60.

Reinhard, S., Lovell, C.A.K. and G.J. Thijssen, "Environmental Efficiency with Multiple Environmentally Detrimental Variables: Estimated with SFA and DEA," European Journal of Operational Research, 121, 2000, pp. 287–303.

Reinhard, S., Lovell, C.A.K. and G.J. Thijssen, "Analysis of Environmental Efficiency Variation," American Journal of Agricultural Economics, 84, 2002, pp. 1054–1065.

Stevenson, R.E., "Likelihood Functions for Generalized Stochastic Frontier Estimation," Journal of Econometrics, 13, 1980, 56–66.

Zofio, J.L., Prieto, A.M., "Environmental Efficiency and Regulatory Standards: The Case of CO_2 Emissions From Countries," Resource and Energy Economics, 23, 2001, pp. 63–83.

Chapter 11
Evaluating Performance of New Energy—Evidence from OECD

Ching-cheng Lu, Jin-chi Hsieh, Yung-ho Chiu and Zhen-sheng Lin

1 Introduction

Human civilization has been accompanied by energy development, and energy is closely linked with the progress of human life, science, technology, economy, etc. ever since the Industrial Revolution in the 19th century. Easy access to energy sources has driven the rapid growth of the global economy, resulting in excessive consumption and low efficiency of energy. It also has led to an acceleration in the depletion of limited fossil energy sources as well as the emergence of global climate change, the greenhouse effect, and other environmental issues. This has impacted the global environment and endangered the existence and sustainable development of future generations. Therefore, it is a pressing issue to reduce the use of fossil energy and improve energy efficiency by actively developing new forms of green energy.

Many leaders of countries around the world gathered in Paris to attend the United Nations Framework Convention on Climate Change's Twenty-first Conference of the Parties in 2015 to discuss how to handle the issue of climate change, energy savings, and carbon reduction. Countries are now actively promoting high efficiency and low carbon economies with low carbon emissions, so as to improve the deteriorating environmental quality and achieve the goal of sustainable development. As traditional fossil energy is concentrated in unstable regions, its prices and supply fluctuate greatly and also threaten investments and

C. Lu
Department of Applied Economics, Fo Guang University, Jiaoxi, Taiwan

J. Hsieh
Department of Business Administration, Taipei City University of Science and Technology, Taipei, Taiwan

Y. Chiu (✉) · Z. Lin
Department of Economics, Soochow University, Taipei, Taiwan
e-mail: echiu@scu.edu.tw

© Springer Nature Singapore Pte Ltd. 2018
R. Pang et al. (eds.), *Energy, Environment and Transitional Green Growth in China*, https://doi.org/10.1007/978-981-10-7919-1_11

223

energy security. All countries must seek alternative energies to replace traditional fossil energy and to present opportunities to create a green economy.

The problem of energy demand and environmental protection is an important issue for industrial development. As energy demand continues to grow, carbon dioxide emissions continue to increase, which have a negative impact on climate change. Therefore, attention should be paid in how to balance environmental protection and economic development, improve energy efficiency, and maintain energy security and energy prices. Many countries have set significant policy objectives to reduce carbon emissions and energy use and to improve energy efficiency. The goal is to create a sustainable environment for economic growth and greenhouse gas emission reduction. The fastest way to reduce energy demand is by improving energy efficiency, as it can cut pollution and carbon dioxide emissions due to economic and demographic growth. However, fossil energy will still be used up, and new energy will quickly be developed in all countries of the world, but the costs are still higher than fossil energy, and so the future price of energy will be affected by the efficiency of new energy sources. The development of new energy technologies must exhibit high performance, high efficiency, low cost, and low pollution as necessary conditions, if they are expected to accelerate into the era of new energy use.

Environmental and energy performance assessments make up a good tool in energy development, as the results can help us to discover inefficient consumption, improve it in order to maintain high performance, and reduce energy costs to improve the energy use ratio. A review of the environmental and energy efficiency literature shows that it mostly focuses on using structural equation models to explore the two efficiencies. However, many studies used decision-making units (DMUs) in the same period with the DEA method and did not consider the input-output process across multiple periods in assessing national energy environmental efficiency, such as Dritsaki and Dritsaki (2014), Goto et al. (2014), Sueyoshi and Goto (2015), and Yang et al. (2015). In recent years, some studies have also included time variables in dynamic DEA or two-stage DEA to achieve a dynamic performance evaluation, but they have ignored the progress of energy technologies and the differences in input variables under periods and regions of new energy.

This paper therefore employs the Meta-frontier Dynamic DEA (MFD-DEA) method to assess the performance of energy environmental efficiency in Organization for Economic Co-operation and Development (OECD) countries, in order to investigate the effect of energy environmental efficiency in different regions and to observe the effects of input and output variables and carryover multiple periods in OECD members' energy consumption. The results can help countries take the energy strategy reference and enhance their energy efficiency, develop renewable energy, and reduce carbon emissions. We assess the energy environmental efficiency performance of OECD members in this study by investigating (1) the energy environmental efficiency value, (2) the effects of renewable energy development, (3) the effects of different regions, (4) and strategies for improving energy efficiency.

This study's DMUs are 34 countries of OECD members in this study. The regions are divided into North Western Europe (NWE) (14 countries): United Kingdom (GB), Netherlands (NL), Belgium (BE), Ireland (IE), Luxembourg (LU), Iceland (IS), France (FR), Switzerland (CH), Norway (NO), Germany (DE), Denmark (DK), Sweden (SE), Finland (FI), and Austria (AT); South Eastern Europe (SEE) (11 countries): Estonia (EE), Italy (IT), Greece (GR), Hungary (HU), Tokelau (TK), Spain (ES), Poland (PL), Slovenia (SI), Portugal (PT), the Czech Republic (CZ), and Slovakia (SK); America (4 countries): United States (US), Canada (CA), Mexico (MX), and Chile (CL); and others (5 countries): South Korea (KR), Japan (JP), Israel (IL), New Zealand (NZ), and Australia (AU). The goal is to assess their performances of energy environmental efficiency for the period 2008–2012.

The remainder of this paper is organized as follows: Section 2 is Literature Review. Section 3 is Research Method. Section 4 is Empirical Results and Discussion. Section 5 is Conclusions.

2 Literature Review

The main research of new energy performance has focused on improving energy efficiency and reducing power generation and operating costs in energy applications (such as Yang et al. 2015; Meng et al. 2014, etc.). However, issues concerning the protection of environment are more important, as the phenomenon of global warming is threatening the living environment of all creatures and human beings. Many studies have begun to explore how to reduce greenhouse gas and carbon emission, in order to create a sustainable environment. This study researches OECD member countries and summarizes the empirical literature as follows.

Output is divided into desirable and undesirable categories to evaluate environmental efficiency through the DEA approach. Goto et al. (2014) proposed a balance between industrial pollution and economic growth to attain a sustainable society in the world. With the DEA method, they separated outputs into desirable and undesirable categories to assess the operational efficiency, unified efficiency under natural disposability (UEN), and unified efficiency under natural and managerial disposability (UENM) of various organizations in 47 prefectures' manufacturing and non-manufacturing industries of Japan. They found that the DEA method has an analytical capability to quantify the importance of investment on capital assets for technology innovation and confirms the validity of the Porter hypothesis in Japan's manufacturing industries. They also presented that the emission of greenhouse gases is a main source of unified inefficiency in the two groups of industries. That study suggested those industries need to make better efforts to reduce greenhouse gas emissions and air pollution substances by investing in capital assets for technology innovation. Sueyoshi and Goto (2013, 2015) also proposed desirable and undesirable outputs and used the non-radial DEA model to measure unified and scale efficiencies in coal-fired power plants of the U.S. northeast region. They compared the operational and environmental performances of fossil fuel power plants in Pennsylvania-New Jersey-Maryland Interconnection and California Independent System Operator (2012) and measured the unified efficiency of Japan's fossil fuel power generation during the period 2004–2008 (2011).

Wang et al. (2014) proposed a very important green image for corporate survivability in a global market, stating that the operators of companies need to consider both economic prosperity and pollution prevention in their operations, as a green image is an important strategy for corporate sustainability. They used the DEA method to assess environmental performance, with the variables focusing upon research and development (R&D) strategies as well as technology innovation and selection for the reduction of undesirable outputs (e.g., CO_2 emissions). They applied the proposed approach to 153 observations on S&P 500 corporations of U. S. industrial sectors in 2012 and 2013. Their empirical results confirm that investors pay more serious attention to a company's green image and the reality for a long run sustainability than profitability in a short run concern.

Egilmez and Park (2014) used a two-step hierarchical methodology for an integrated application of the economic input output life cycle assessment (EIO-LCA) and DEA approaches to quantify the transportation-related carbon, energy, and water footprints (FP) of U.S. manufacturing sectors and to evaluate the environmental and economic performances based on eco-efficiency scores. EIO-LCA was employed to quantify the environmental impacts associated with the activities among 276 manufacturing sectors, and DEA approaches assessed the performance of the overall environmental and economic benefit tradeoff by determining the eco-efficiency value of each sector. They found that the vast majority of U.S. manufacturing sectors are inefficient (eco-efficiency <1), with only tobacco manufacturing being eco-efficient; the U.S. average was 0.5; the results indicated that inefficient U.S. manufacturing sectors need to reach an average reduction of 50% on the carbon, energy, and water FP impacts to reach the 100% eco-efficiency frontier. Yago et al. (2015) assessed the eco-efficiency of a group of 113 wastewater treatment plants (WWTPs) in regions across Spain, also used the method to combine life cycle assessment (LCA) and DEA, and found that the effects of their efficiency are contained in the size of the facility, the climatic influence, the influent load, and the over- or underuse of the plant.

Filippini and Wetzel (2014) employed a stochastic frontier panel data model to analyze the cost efficiency of 28 electricity distribution companies in New Zealand for the period between 1996 and 2011. They estimated a total cost function and a variable cost function in order to evaluate the impact of ownership unbundling on the level of cost efficiency. They found that the ownership separation of electricity generation and retail operations from the distribution network has a positive effect on the cost efficiency of distribution companies in New Zealand, and the estimated effect of ownership separation suggests a positive average one-off shift in the level of cost efficiency by 0.242 in the short run and 0.144 in the long run. Xie et al. (2014) proposed that the environmental efficiencies of electric power industries in different countries may serve as a benchmark to evaluate their emission reduction efforts, used the slack based measure data envelopment analysis (SBM-DEA) model to investigate the environmental total factor productivity (TFP) index of electric power industries in 26 OECD (Organization for Economic Cooperation and Development) and BRIC (Brazil, Russia, India, and China) countries from 1996 to 2010, and employed the Tobit regression model to analyze the influence of related factors on TFP and its decompositions. They found that the dynamic environmental efficiency or TFP provides a good perspective for evaluating emission reduction efforts of electric power industries in different countries, and that taking the energy structure and affordability into consideration, environmental TFP may indicate climate change mitigation efforts to a large extent. Galán and Pollitt (2014) presented an extension of dynamic stochastic frontier models that accounts for unobserved heterogeneity in inefficiency persistence and in the technology. High inefficiency persistence and heterogeneity in the Colombian distribution sector are found to be important criteria in inefficiency persistence, customer density, and consumption density for regulatory purposes.

Yang et al. (2015) used the super-efficiency DEA method to assess environmental efficiency and evaluated DMUs in 30 provinces of China in 2000–2010. The results showed that Beijing and Shanghai have better environmental efficiency, and Qinghai has worse performance. They showed that east areas are more efficient in production, while the west areas rank last, with central areas ranking in between during the period studied. They suggested that policies should be established to further promote production efficiency. Meng et al. (2014) studied inefficiency and congestion in 16 Asia-Pacific Economic Cooperation (APEC) countries by using the two-stage DEA approach for the period 1996–2011. They found that energy is congested due to fossil energy in the 16 APEC countries; moreover, the APEC countries should take some useful measures to control the congestion coming from non-fossil energy. There are many studies on environmental and energy issues such as Sueyoshi and Goto (2012), Shrivastava et al. (2012), Amirteimoori and Kordrostami (2012), Shabani et al. (2014), Kuo et al. (2014), Wang and Feng (2015), Sueyoshi and Wang (2014), etc.

Some research studies in recent years have focused on the issue of renewable energy, such as Hong et al. (2013) who assessed the possible contribution of the 12th Five Year Plan for China's future energy system and identified factors (in the period 2011–2015) that might influence its impacts. The current status of renewable energy development in China was first reviewed. They next used an energy system analysis plan to simulate several energy scenarios on an hourly basis and proposed to improve the efficiency of renewable energy technologies and sectors as an important policy in China's energy system. Woo et al. (2015) also used DEA to evaluate the dynamic environment efficiency of renewable energy in OECD; labor, capital, and renewable energy supply are the input items, while the output items are the desirable output of Gross Domestic Product (GDP) and the undesirable output of carbon emissions. They also used the Malmquist productivity index (MPI) to estimate the average efficiency change in the period 2004–2011 and found results that showed geographical differences in environmental efficiency in OECD. Fagiani et al. (2013) analyzed the effects of investors' risk aversion on the performances of support schemes and compared two policy options of a feed-in tariff mechanism and a certificate market system. Their results showed that while a tariff mechanism could obtain better results than a certificate market, its performance is strictly dependent on regulator choices. Menegaki and Gurluk (2013) compared the renewable energy performance of Turkey and Greece, showing that Turkey spends efforts to tacitly comply with European Union legislation and sets ambitious renewable energy targets. Greece, on the other hand, is afflicted by an economic crisis that threatens to retard its renewable energy developments unless it uses renewable energy sources as a means to escape the crisis.

The DEA methods have also been utilized to evaluate energy and environmental efficiency. More scholars are dealing with multiple inputs and outputs at the same time, trying to find the reasons for efficiency and inefficiency and arriving at efficiency goals of input and output items. Energy performance is a complex issue encompassing power plants, fuel energy, hybrid energy, transportation energy, industrial energy consumption, d technology efficiency, etc. and may also include the effects of unintended output pollutants such as CO_2, etc. and the relationships of carbon dioxide (CO_2) emissions between areas and countries. The inputs and outputs of the above literature are more focused on the same period, but input items of labor, capital, energy consumption, etc. and output items of GDP, carbon dioxide emissions, etc. may arise across multiple periods when one is evaluating energy environmental efficiency. This study considers multi-period production processes and the effect of meta-frontier problems in different regions, uses the meta-frontier dynamic DEA approach to evaluate energy environment efficiency, and observes the impact of environmental and energy efficiency over time.

3 Research Method

3.1 DEA Model

The DEA approach is based on the Pareto optimal solution concept using linear programming techniques to evaluate the relative efficiency of a DMU. DEA is an effective evaluating efficiency method to make decisions as to the priority of strategies in a multi-oriented environment. To use it, one has to establish an efficiency index. The efficiency index is formed by the linear programming method with the input and output variables of each DMU efficiency meta-frontier, depending on the frontier-shift between each DMU to determine the relative efficiency of individual DMUs. This concept began with the DEA model of Farrell (1957) and developed into the CCR model of Charnes et al. (1978), with Banker et al. (1984) extending it to the BCC model. However, the CCR and BCC methods mainly focus on the input and output items of the same periods, whereas energy environmental efficiency usually runs across multiple periods.

3.2 Dynamic DEA

The Dynamic DEA (D-DEA) method was started by Klopp (1985), who proposed a window analysis of the D-DEA approach. Färe et al. (1994) followed and proposed the Malmquist index (MPI), but neither analyzed the interaction effect for two carry-over periods. In order to deal with the issue of efficiency for multiple carry-over periods, Färe and Grosskopf (1996) proposed to put the effect of internal linkages into D-DEA. Studies that ensued include Bogetoft et al. (2008), Chen (2009), Kao (2014), Nemoto and Goto (1999, 2003), Park and Park (2009), Sueyoshhi and Sekitani (2005), Chang et al. (2009), etc.

Tone and Tsutsui (2010) extended the model to the Slack-Based Measures (SBM) D-DEA model. Tone and Tsutsui (2014) next proposed the weighted SBM D-DEA model. They used carry-over as the dynamic period link and classified as desirable (good), undesirable (bad), discretionary (free), non-discretionary (fixed), etc. The D-DEA model is divided into input-oriented, output-oriented, and non-oriented types.

We assess the overall efficiency (OE) and term efficiency (TE) with the non-oriented SBM D-DEA approach in this study. Each period has independent input and output in every DMU, and there is a carry-over link from period t to t + 1 so as to find the change across two periods. Figure shows the structure of DN-DEA in this study.

This model sets up n DMUs (j = 1, 2, ..., n) over T periods (t = 1, 2, ..., T). The DMUs have multiple different and independent inputs and outputs in each term, with the z good as a carry-over from period t to period t + 1 herein. The carry-over is guaranteed by Eq. (1):

$$\sum_{j=1}^{n} z_{ijt}^{\alpha} \lambda_j^t = \sum_{j=1}^{n} z_{ijt}^{\alpha} \lambda_j^{t+1} \left(\forall; t = 1, \ldots, T-1 \right) \tag{1}$$

Here, the symbol α shows good (bad, free, fix, etc.), the non-oriented overall efficiency (δ^*) is calculated by Eq. (2), and ω^t and ω_i are weights to term t and the input.

$$\delta^* = \frac{\frac{1}{T}\sum_{t=1}^{T} \omega^t \left[1 - \frac{1}{m+nbad} \left(\sum_{i=1}^{s} \frac{\omega_i^- s_{ij}^-}{x_{iot}} + \sum_{i=1}^{nbad} \frac{s_{it}^{bad}}{z_{iot}^{bad}} \right) \right]}{\frac{1}{T}\sum_{t=1}^{T} \omega^t \left[1 - \frac{1}{s+ngood} \left(\sum_{i=1}^{s} \frac{\omega_i^+ s_{ij}^+}{y_{iot}} + \sum_{i=1}^{ngood} \frac{s_{it}^{good}}{z_{iot}^{good}} \right) \right]} \tag{2}$$

The non-oriented term efficiency (ρ^*) follows as Eq. (3) (Fig. 1).

$$\rho^* = \frac{1 - \frac{1}{m+nbad} \left(\sum_{i=1}^{m} \frac{\omega_i^- s_{iot}^{-*}}{x_{iot}} + \sum_{i=1}^{nbad} \frac{s_{iot}^{bad*}}{z_{iot}^{bad}} \right)}{1 - \frac{1}{s+ngood} \left(\sum_{i=1}^{s} \frac{\omega_i^+ s_{iot}^+}{y_{iot}} + \sum_{i=1}^{ngood} \frac{s_{iot}^{good*}}{z_{iot}^{good}} \right)} \tag{3}$$

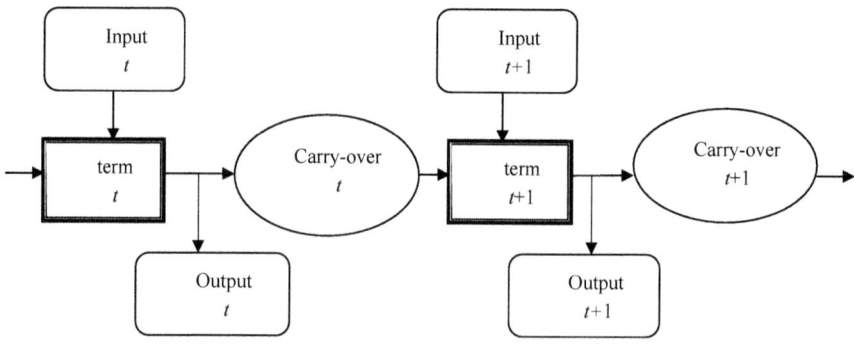

Fig. 1 The structure of dynamic DEA (Tone and Tsutsui 2010)

3.3 Meta-Frontier DN-DEA

Ruttan et al. (1978) defined the meta-frontier as a development curve of all groups, allowing different groups to measure efficiency across a common basis. Battese and Rao (2002) and Battese et al. (2004) proposed that the technical efficiency (TEE) of different groups can be compared with each other through a meta-frontier model. Thanassoulis and Portela (2008) presented the concept of convex meta-frontier and found that groups using advanced technology to produce a product, even under the exchange of technology, will do so due to enhanced technology, leading to more outward expansion and improved business performance during a time period. O'Donnell et al. (2008) set up a meta-frontier model that can accurately calculate the group and meta-frontier technical efficiencies. However, the traditional DEA usually assumes that all producers have the same level of technology, but the assessed DMUs are often in different geographical locations, national policies, socio-economic conditions, etc., which cause different technology levels. Therefore, based on the Tone and Tsutsui (2010) SBM DN-DEA, O'Donnell et al. (2008) meta-frontier model, and the weighted SBM Meta-frontier D-DEA (MFD-DEA) model, we set up the model as follows.

3.3.1 Meta-Frontier (MF)

Under different factors of management type, resources, regulation, environment etc., we assume all units (N) are composed of DMUs in g groups ($N = N_1 + N_2 + \cdots + N_G$); x_{ij} and y_{rj} indicate input item i (i = 1, 2, ..., m) of item j (j = 1, 2, ..., N) and output item r (r = 1, 2, ..., s) of item j (j = 1, 2, ..., N) under the meta-frontier; the k of DMU can choose the most favorable final output weight, so that it get the maximum efficiency value; and the meta-frontier k of DMU efficiency can be solved by the following linear programming (LP):

Min: ρ^*

$$\text{s.t.} \sum_{g=1}^{G}\sum_{\partial=1}^{n} Z_{ijtg}\lambda_{jg}^t = \sum_{g=1}^{G}\sum_{\partial=1}^{n} Z_{ijtg}\lambda_{jg}^{t+1}\ (vi|t=1\ i-1) \tag{4}$$

$$\lambda_{jg}^t \geq 0, S_{it}^- \geq 0, S_{it}^+ \geq 0, S_{it}^{good} \geq 0$$

$$X_{iot} = \sum_{g=1}^{G}\sum_{\partial=1}^{n} X_{ijtg}\lambda_{jg}^t + S_{it}(i=1\cdots m, t=1\cdots i)$$

$$Y_{iot} = \sum_{g=1}^{G}\sum_{\partial=1}^{n} Y_{ijtg}\lambda_{jg}^t - S_{it}^t(i=1\cdots s, t=1\cdots i)$$

$$Z_{iot}^{good} = \sum_{g=1}^{G}\sum_{\partial=1}^{n} Z_{ijtg}^{good}\lambda_{jg}^t - S_{it}^t(i=1\cdots ngood; t=1\cdots i) \tag{5}$$

$$\sum_{g=1}^{G}\sum_{\partial=1}^{n} \lambda_{jg}^t = 1\,(t=1\cdots i)$$

Using Eqs. (3), (4), and (5), we can find the overall technical efficiency (MFOE) value of all DMUs under the meta-frontier.

3.3.2 Group-Frontier (GF)

We divide all DMUs into g groups. Each DMU under the group frontier chooses the most favorable final output weighted, so that the efficiency of the DMUs under the group frontier can be solved by the following equation:

$$\rho_0^* = \frac{\frac{1}{T}\sum_{t=1}^{T} W^t \left[1 - \frac{1}{m+nbad}\left(\sum_{i=1}^{m}\frac{W_i^- S_{it}^-}{X_{iot}} + \sum_{i=1}^{nbad}\frac{S_{it}^{bad}}{Z_{iot}^{bad}}\right)\right]}{\frac{1}{T}\sum_{t=1}^{T} W^t \left[1 + \frac{1}{s+ngood}\left(\sum_{i=1}^{s}\frac{W_i^+ S_{it}^+}{Y_{iot}} + \sum_{i=1}^{ngood}\frac{S_{it}^{good}}{Z_{iot}^{good}}\right)\right]} \tag{6}$$

$$\sum_{j=1}^{n} z_{ijt}^{\alpha}\lambda_j^t = \sum_{j=1}^{n} z_{ijt}^{\alpha}\lambda_j^{t+1}\ (\forall i; t=1,\ldots,T-1) \tag{7}$$

$$x_{iot} = \sum_{j=1}^{n} x_{ijt}\lambda_j^t + s_{it}^-\ (i=1,\ldots,m; t=1,\ldots,T)$$

$$y_{iot} = \sum_{j=1}^{n} y_{ijt}\lambda_j^t - s_{it}^+\ (i=1,\ldots,s; t=1,\ldots,T) \tag{8}$$

$$z_{iot}^{good} = \sum_{j=1}^{n} z_{iot}^{good}\lambda_j^t - s_{it}^{good}\ (i=1,\ldots,ngood; t=1,\ldots,T)$$

$$\sum_{j=1}^{n} \lambda_j^t = 1 (t = 1, \ldots, T)$$

$$\lambda_j^t \geq 0, s_{it}^- \geq 0, s_{it}^+ \geq 0, s_{it}^{good} \geq 0$$

(9)

3.3.3 Technology Gap Ratio (TGR)

Since the meta-frontier contains the group frontier of g groups, the technical efficiency of the meta-frontier (MFE) will be less than the technical efficiency of the group frontier (GFE). The ratio value, called the technical efficiency gap ratio (or technology gap ratio, TGR), is shown as:

$$\text{TGR} = \frac{\rho^*}{\rho_o^{*g}} = \frac{MFE}{GFE}$$

(10)

4 Empirical Result and Discussion

This study focuses on the performance of using new energy in OECD countries. At present, there are 7 major industrial countries and EU members among the 34 OECD member countries. We consider the integrity of using energy data and thus use data for the period 2008–2012 to assess the energy environment performances of OECD members. In this study we use the SBM MFD-DEA model to evaluate the energy environment performances of 34 OECD member countries over 2008–2012. The input variables are gross capital (GC), manpower (MP), renewable energy, other energy usage costs (RE), etc.; the output variable is the non-intended output of carbon dioxide emissions (CO_2). Because CO_2 is a non-intended output, we have to use the translation method with the CO_2 output data to a negative value, add a constant so that the maximum negative value becomes 1, and let the data be adjusted, with the GDP as a carry-over across periods. Because the regional geography and environmental conditions of countries are different, when coupled with GC, MP, RE, etc., the input items, the CO_2 output item, and GDP carry-over variables in the SBM MFD-DEA model can be observed under different energy environment efficiency values. Table 1 lists the variables' definition of inputs, output, and carry-over.

Table 2. shows the descriptive statistics of input and output variable data results and as follows: (A) MP: The average value is 29,058,000 people from 2008 to 2012. The U.S. had the most people employed in 2012 at 159,330,000; on the other hand, IS had the least people employed in 2011 at 186,000. The standard deviation value is 29,058,000 people. (B) GC: The average value is 280.826 billion USD in 2008–2012. The U.S. had the maximum value in 2012 at 3.126 trillion USD, while IS had minimum value in 2010 of 1.837 billion USD. The standard deviation value is 514,216 billion USD. (C) RE: The average value is 50,024 kW in 2006–2013.

Table 1 Variables' definition in this study

Variable		Unit	Definition
Inputs	MP	Thousand people	The number of indirect or direct manpower required for energy production
	GC	Million USD	The funds, equipment, and related costs that must be invested in energy production
	RE	kW	Energy producers use energy from nature, such as solar, wind, hydrogen, etc.
Outputs	CO_2	Million Ton	The amount of carbon dioxide (CO_2) emissions from the production of energy
Carry-over	GDP	Million USD	The total value of all final goods and services produced by the use of factors of production over a period

Source Authors' arrangement

Table 2 Descriptive statistics of input and output variables

Variable		Standard deviation	Average	Maximum	Minimum
Input variables	MP	29,058	17,643	159,330	186
	GC	514,216	280,826	3,126,140	1837
	RE	91,524	50,024	470,793	25
Output variable	CO_2	1024	5918	6333	1

Data source Authors' collection

The U.S. had a maximum value in 2011 of 470,793 kW, while IL had a minimum value in 2008 of 25 kW. The standard deviation value is 91,524. (D) CO_2: The average value of each year increased 5918 million tons; the maximum value was for the U.S. at 6333 million tons in 2008, while the minimum value was 1 million tons. The standard deviation value is 1024 million tons.

We find that the average value of labor (MP) for the 34 OECD member countries changed little within the range 17,513,000–17,811,000 people in 2008–2012, but the GC values significantly increased from 242.672 to 303.243 billion USD in 2009–2012. RE also significantly increased from 47,228 to 54,096 kW in 2008–2011, and GDP significantly grew from 1,224 to 1,378 billion USD in 2009–2011. This shows there was significant performance from using capital investment and using renewable energy to enhance GDP over these years. However, the performance of reducing CO_2 emissions was not significant (5,903 to 5,931). This is an important issue that all OECD members must face together to solve the problem (Table 3).

This study uses the SBM MFD-DEA method to evaluate the energy environmental efficiency of 34 OECD countries for the period 2008–2012. Table 4 shows the results. It showed polarization distribution in meta-frontier overall efficiency (MFOE) of energy environmental efficiency, the effective countries had GB, NL, BE, LU, IE, IS and EE (efficiency value is 1) etc. KR, FI, TK, AU, CA, ES, PL, SI, NZ, PT, CZ, SK, MX, and CL have smaller MFOE values than the average value (0.792), meaning their energy environmental efficiency needs improvement. The

Table 3 The AVE values of input, output, and carry-over variables for 2008–2012

Year	Variables				
	GC	MP	RE	CO_2	GDP
2008	301,281	17,513	47,228	5903	1,307,460
2009	242,672	17,595	48,143	5931	1,223,556
2010	265,053	17,733	50,543	5916	1,283,517
2011	291,879	17,811	54,096	5922	1,378,142
2012	303,243	17,560	50,540	5920	1,352,293

Data source Authors' collection

value of meta-frontier efficiency (MFE) is below the average value of all members of OECD for ES, CA, MX, PL, AU, FI, PL, CZ, NZ, SK, and SI, indicating these countries need specific energy strategies to improve energy environmental efficiency. The MFE values of AT and GR are lower than the average value in 2008–2009, but above the average value in 2010–2012, showing that they attach importance to the issues of energy use and the environment.

We want to understand the impact of geographical location conditions on energy efficiency, and so we divide the full sample into North Western Europe (NWE), South Eastern Europe (SEE), the Americas, and others. NWE contains GB, NL, BE, IE, LU, IS, FR, CH, NO, DE, DK, SE, FI, and AT. SEE contains EE, IT, GR, HU, TK, ES, PL, SI, PT, CZ, and SK. The Americas contains US, CA, MX, and CL. The others contain JP, KR, IL, NZ, and AU. We shall compare the differences in meta-frontier efficiency (MFE), group frontier efficiency (GFE), and technology gap ratio (TGR) variables among the 3 groups of NEW, SEE, and Americas.

Table 5 shows the MFE, GFE, and TGR values of the 14 countries in new, Table 6 shows them for SEE, and Table 7 shows them for the Americas. We see that the average value of MFE is 0.8525 in the NWE group, which is larger than the Americas (0.5968) and SEE (0.4491) groups over 2008–2012. It indicates that NWE countries develop their economies at the same time that their implementation of environmental protection efforts are more efficient.

The average value of GFE is 0.9764 in the SWE group, which is larger than that for the Americas (0.6171) and SEE (0.7578) groups over 2008–2012. The average value of TGR is 0.9753 in the SWE group, which is larger than that for the Americas (0.9739) and SEE (0.9046) groups over 2008–2012. We also find that TGR has the lowest value of 0.6963 by AT in 2009; this value is lower than 0.9 that it was contained SE (2008, 2011 and 2012) and AT (2008 and 2009) etc., and the TGR value of many countries close or equal to 1. This indicates that these countries' energy environmental efficiency is relatively more stable than that of the Americas and SEE. TGR has the lowest value of 0.4108 for TK (2011) in the period 2008–2012 for the SEE group; this value was less than 0.9 that it was contained GR (2008, 2009), TK (2008, 2011, 2012), PL (2008–2012), SI (2008–2012) and CZ (2008, 2009, 2012). It shows that energy environment efficiency performance needs to improve in the SEE group. The TGR value is larger than 0.9 in all countries of the Americas in 2008–2012, meaning that energy environmental efficiency is greatly influenced by geographical location.

Table 4 Energy environmental efficiency of OECD countries over 2008–2012

DMU	Overall efficiency	Rank	Term efficiency				
			2008	2009	2010	2011	2012
US	0.9319	16	0.7344	0.9993	0.9985	0.9992	0.9999
JP	0.9998	12	0.9994	0.9999	0.9999	0.9999	0.9999
DE	0.9499	14	0.9993	0.9994	0.946	0.8278	0.9776
DK	0.9999	8	0.9999	0.9999	0.9999	0.9997	0.9998
GB	1	1	1	1	1	1	1
IT	0.946	15	0.955	0.9979	0.9994	0.8559	0.9223
ES	0.5738	26	0.5541	0.5667	0.5971	0.6032	0.5479
CA	0.6088	25	0.5765	0.5891	0.6216	0.6312	0.6258
MX	0.4235	33	0.4161	0.4283	0.4166	0.4411	0.4161
AT	0.8801	17	0.708	0.6962	1	1	1
KR	0.7642	21	0.6681	0.7045	0.7769	0.6906	0.9999
NL	1	1	0.9999	1	1	1	1
TK	0.6619	23	0.4474	1	1	0.4108	0.47
PL	0.5692	27	0.5775	0.5868	0.5346	0.5694	0.578
FR	0.9999	8	0.9999	0.9999	0.9999	0.9999	0.9999
BE	1	1	1	1	1	0.9999	1
SE	0.8236	19	0.7118	0.9857	0.9749	0.7263	0.7192
CH	0.9999	8	0.9999	0.9999	0.9999	0.9999	0.9999
AU	0.6464	24	0.6413	0.6347	0.6327	0.6532	0.6705
NO	0.9999	8	0.9999	0.9999	0.9999	0.9999	0.9999
GR	0.8523	18	0.6038	0.661	1	1	1
FI	0.6631	22	0.6382	0.6706	0.6799	0.6858	0.641
IE	1	1	0.9999	1	1	0.9999	1
PT	0.488	30	0.4855	0.4839	0.4693	0.5257	0.4747
CZ	0.4391	31	0.4198	0.4367	0.4398	0.4742	0.4207
IL	0.9779	13	0.8898	1	1	1	1
CL	0.4084	34	0.4024	0.4169	0.4082	0.4174	0.3982
HU	0.7941	20	0.5106	0.9841	0.7459	0.807	0.9228
NZ	0.5338	29	0.4981	0.5085	0.5469	0.5695	0.5482
SK	0.437	32	0.4181	0.4497	0.4452	0.4465	0.4255
LU	1	1	1	1	1	1	1
SI	0.5547	28	0.3791	0.395	0.7587	0.6061	0.6281
IS	1	1	1	1	1	1	1
EE	1	1	1	1	1	1	1
Average	0.792	NA	0.7422	0.7998	0.8233	0.7924	0.8055
Maximum	1	NA	1	1	1	1	1
Minimum	0.4084	NA	0.3791	0.395	0.4082	0.4108	0.3982
Standard dev.	0.2181	NA	0.2397	0.2376	0.2252	0.2228	0.2357

Source Authors' collection

Table 5 The MFE, GFE, and TGR value of countries in NWE

Country	2008			2009			2010			2011			2012		
	MFE	GFE	TGR	MFE	GFE	TGR	MFE	GFE	TGR	MFE	GFE	TGR	MFE	GFE	TGR
GB	1	1	1	1	1	1	1	1	1	1	1	1	1	1	1
NL	0.9999	1	0.9999	1	1	1	1	1	1	1	1	1	1	1	1
BE	1	1	1	1	1	1	1	1	1	0.9999	1	0.9999	1	1	1
IE	0.9999	0.9999	1	1	1	1	1	1	1	0.9999	1	0.9999	1	1	1
LU	1	1	1	1	1	1	1	1	1	1	1	1	1	1	1
IS	1	1	1	1	1	1	1	1	1	1	1	1	1	1	1
FR	0.9999	0.9999	1	0.9999	0.9999	1	0.9999	0.9999	1	0.9997	0.9999	1	0.9998	0.9998	1
CH	0.9999	1	0.9999	0.9999	1	0.9999	0.9999	1	0.9999	0.9999	1	0.9999	0.9999	1	0.9999
NO	0.9999	0.9999	1	0.9999	0.9999	1	0.9999	0.9999	1	0.9999	0.9999	1	0.9999	0.9999	1
DE	0.9999	0.9999	1	0.9999	0.9999	1	0.9999	0.9999	1	0.9999	0.9999	1	0.9999	0.9999	1
DK	0.9993	0.9993	1	0.9994	0.9994	1	0.946	0.9555	0.9901	0.821	0.9555	0.9918	0.9746	0.9776	0.9969
SE	0.7118	1	0.7118	0.9857	1	0.9857	0.9749	1	0.9749	0.7263	1	0.7263	0.7192	0.7192	0.7192
FI	0.6382	0.6848	0.9320	0.6706	0.7033	0.9535	0.6799	0.6924	0.9819	0.6858	0.6924	0.9533	0.641	0.6942	0.9234
AT	0.708	0.9998	0.7081	0.6962	0.9998	0.6963	0.9998	1	0.9998	0.9998	1	0.9998	0.9998	1	0.9998
average	0.7643	0.9774	0.9537	0.9537	0.9787	0.9740	0.9002	0.9748	0.9962	0.8100	0.9748	0.9777	0.8345	0.9763	0.9747

Source Authors' collection

Table 6 The MFE, GFE, and TGR values of countries in SEE

Country	2008 MFE	GFE	TGR	2009 MFE	GFE	TGR	2010 MFE	GFE	TGR	2011 MFE	GFE	TGR	2012 MFE	GFE	TGR
EE	1	1	1	1	1	1	1	1	1	1	1	1	1	1	1
IT	0.955	0.973	0.9815	0.9979	0.9999	0.9980	0.9994	1	0.9994	0.8559	0.9309	0.9194	0.9223	0.9278	0.9941
GR	0.6038	0.9996	0.6040	0.661	0.9999	0.6611	1	1	1	1	1	1	1	1	1
HU	0.5035	0.5106	0.9861	0.9841	1	0.9841	0.7459	0.9289	0.8030	0.807	0.8117	0.9942	0.9228	0.9468	0.9747
TK	0.4474	1	0.4474	1	1	1	1	1	1	0.4108	1	0.4108	0.47	1	0.47
ES	0.5364	0.5541	0.9681	0.5667	0.6052	0.9364	0.5971	0.6413	0.9311	0.6032	0.6092	0.9902	0.5465	0.5479	0.9975
PL	0.5775	1	0.5775	0.5868	1	0.5868	0.5346	1	0.5346	0.5694	1	0.5694	0.578	1	0.5780
SI	0.3791	0.5391	0.7032	0.395	0.5134	0.7694	0.4754	0.7587	0.6226	0.5681	0.6061	0.9373	0.5452	0.6281	0.868
PT	0.4855	0.4855	1	0.4839	0.4839	1	0.4693	0.4693	1	0.5257	0.5257	1	0.4747	0.4747	1
CZ	0.4198	0.4882	0.8599	0.4367	0.5131	0.8511	0.4398	0.4592	0.9578	0.4609	0.4742	0.972	0.4207	0.5015	0.8389
SK	0.4178	0.4181	0.9993	0.4497	0.4588	0.9802	0.4452	0.4493	0.9909	0.4465	0.4735	0.9430	0.4178	0.4255	0.9819
average	0.4256	0.7221	0.8383	0.4413	0.7795	0.8879	0.5283	0.7658	0.9830	0.5131	0.7618	0.9021	0.4873	0.7600	0.9117

Source Authors' collection

Table 7 The MFE, GFE, and TGR values of countries in the Americas

Country	2008			2009			2010			2011			2012		
	MFE	GFE	TGR	MFE	GFE	TGR	MFE	GFE	TGR	MFE	GFE	TGR	MFE	GFE	TGR
US	0.7344	0.7453	0.9854	0.9993	1	0.9993	0.9985	1	0.9985	0.9992	1	0.9992	0.9999	1	0.9999
CA	0.5765	0.5868	0.9824	0.5891	0.5976	0.9858	0.6216	0.6404	0.9706	0.6312	0.6372	0.9906	0.6258	0.634	0.9871
MX	0.4161	0.4414	0.9427	0.4283	0.4535	0.9444	0.4166	0.4439	0.9385	0.4411	0.4596	0.9597	0.4161	0.4404	0.9448
CL	0.3898	0.4024	0.9697	0.4169	0.4356	0.9697	0.4082	0.6449	0.9697	0.4174	0.4183	0.9697	0.3982	0.3979	0.9697
average	0.5324	0.5408	0.9701	0.6084	0.6217	0.9748	0.6112	0.6823	0.9693	0.6222	0.6288	0.9798	0.61	0.6181	0.9754

Source Authors' collection

We also study the effects of energy environmental efficiency in order to focus on the issue of using RE and find that the average MFE value of 0.8921 for the top 10 countries is larger than the 0.6334 of the bottom 10 countries over the period 2008–2012. The results are in Tables 8 and 9. The MFOE value is the lowest in CA (0.6088) and the largest in NO, FR, and CH (0.9999). The average value is 0.8906 in the top 10 countries when using RE. The MFOE value is the lowest in CL (0.4084) and the largest in IL (0.9779); the average value is 0.6331 in the bottom 10 countries when using RE. These results indicate that energy and environmental efficiency has a direct impact on using RE; therefore, the governments of all countries in OECD should formulate better policies to encourage using RE.

We use the Wilcoxon test method to understand the effect of energy environmental efficiency with the geography differences among the NWE, SEE, and Americas groups of OECD, with the results shown in Table 10. We find that the

Table 8 The MFE values of the top 10 countries using RE

Country	2008	2009	2010	2011	2012	MFOE
CA	0.5765	0.5891	0.6216	0.6312	0.6258	0.6088
US	0.7344	0.9993	0.9985	0.9992	0.9999	0.9319
NO	0.9999	0.9999	0.9999	0.9999	0.9999	0.9999
JP	0.9994	0.9999	0.9999	0.9999	0.9999	0.9998
FR	0.9999	0.9999	0.9999	0.9997	0.9998	0.9999
DE	0.9993	0.9994	0.946	0.8278	0.9776	0.9499
SE	0.7118	0.9857	0.9749	0.7263	0.7192	0.8236
CH	0.9999	0.9999	0.9999	0.9999	0.9999	0.9999
IT	0.955	0.9979	0.9994	0.8559	0.9223	0.946
AT	0.6413	0.6347	0.6327	0.6532	0.6705	0.6464
average	0.8617	0.9206	0.9173	0.8693	0.8915	0.8906

Source Authors' collection

Table 9 The MFE of the bottom 10 countries using RE

Country	2008	2009	2010	2011	2012	MFOE
SI	0.3791	0.395	0.7587	0.6061	0.6281	0.5547
CL	0.4024	0.4169	0.4082	0.4174	0.3982	0.4084
PL	0.5775	0.5868	0.5346	0.5694	0.578	0.5692
CZ	0.4198	0.4367	0.4398	0.4742	0.4207	0.4391
NZ	0.4981	0.5085	0.5469	0.5695	0.5482	0.5338
GR	0.6038	0.661	1	1	1	0.8523
KR	0.6681	0.7045	0.7769	0.6906	0.9999	0.7642
HU	0.5106	0.9841	0.7459	0.807	0.9228	0.7941
SK	0.4181	0.4497	0.4452	0.4465	0.4255	0.437
IL	0.8898	1	1	1	1	0.9779
Average	0.5367	0.6143	0.6656	0.6581	0.6921	0.6331

Source Authors' collection

Table 10 The Wilcoxon test on AVE of TGR

Test variable	Classification	MFE	AVE of TGR	Wilcoxon Test (p value)
Using RE	Top 10	0.8906		0.0124*
	After 10	0.6331		
Group	NWE		0.9753	0.0084**
	SEE		0.8460	
	NWE		0.9753	0.6793
	Americas		0.9739	
	SEE		0.8460	0.0425*
	Americas		0.9739	

$*p < 0.05$, $**p < 0.01$, $***p < 0.001$
Source Authors' collection

average value of TGR exhibits significant differences in NWE and SEE ($p = 0.0084**$), and there are significant differences in each year from 2008 to 2012, where the p value is respectively $0.0014**$, $0.0014**$, $0.0014**$, $0.0066**$, and $0.0291*$. The average value of TGR is not significantly different within NEW and Americas ($p = 0.6793$), and there are no significant differences in each year from 2008 to 2012. The average value of TGR is significantly different within SEE and Americas ($P = 0.0425*$), and there are significant differences in 2008 and 2010, where the p value is respectively $0.0405*$ and $0.0419*$; the other years do not present any significant correlation. Therefore, energy environmental efficiency is greatly influenced by geographical factors, and each country must develop relevant strategies based on specific environmental conditions to improve energy environmental efficiency. Energy environmental efficiency is significantly correlated within before and last 10 of using RE, where the p value is $0.0124*$.

From the empirical results of this study, we find that equipment investment and output costs are much higher than traditional energy to develop new energy. The costs of the SEE group are due to historical factors in the past under the Soviet Union, and because the growth of economies and technology is slower than those of Western countries; thus, their use of energy efficiency is relatively backward. Although EE and IT are also good in the performance of MFE in this group for the period 2008–2012, the energy performance of other countries in this group is relatively poor, such that MOFE is relatively poor compared with other groups. The MOFE values of NWE and the Americas are significantly better than SEE, because of their strong economic and technological conditions. While the Americas area is a region of large energy consumption, this situation is also shown in its TGR value being higher than the other groups, which is close to 1.

5 Conclusions

We employ the MFD-DEA approach herein to explore the performance of energy environmental efficiency in 34 countries of OECD for the period 2008–2012. Because the demands of energy are sustained and increase with economic development, we hope the results of the study can provide a reference for these countries to develop an energy environmental policy in the future, to use the concepts of minimum inputs and maximum outputs under limited resources, and to understand the important issues of greenhouse gas emissions and climate change. We divide the sample into three groups from 2008 to 2012, made up of NWE, SEE, and Americas. The MFE, GFE and TGR values are calculated to understand the different energy environmental efficiency changes with geographical environmental conditions, and the Wilcoxon test method helps verify the differences among the groups in this study.

We find that the efficiency values of GB, NL, BE, LU, IE, IS, and EE are 1 in 2008–2012. KR, FI, TK, AU, CA, ES, PL, SI, NZ, PT, CZ, SK, MX, and CL have smaller MFOE values than the average value (0.792), showing that their energy environmental efficiency needs improvement. ES, CA, MX, PL, AU, FI, PL, CZ, NZ, SK, and SI need specific energy strategies to improve energy environmental efficiency, because their MFE is below the average value. The average value of MFE of the NWE group is larger than those of the Americas and SEE groups in 2008–2012, indicating that NWE countries developed their economies at the same time as they implemented environmental protection efforts that are more efficient.

The TGR values of many countries in the NWE group are close or equal to 1, meaning that these countries' energy environmental efficiency is relatively more stable than the Americas and SEE. The TGR value is larger than 0.9 for all countries of the Americas in 2008–2012, showing that energy environmental efficiency is greatly influenced by geographical location. Energy environmental efficiency has a direct impact on using RE, and therefore governments of all countries in OECD should formulate better policies to encourage using RE. The average value of TGR shows significant differences in NWE and SEE, and there are significant differences in each year from 2008 to 2012 with the Wilcoxon test method. The average value of TGR has no significant difference within NEW and the Americas. The average value of TGR has a significant difference within SEE and the Americas, and there are significant differences in 2008 and 2010; other years do not show any significant correlation. Energy environmental efficiency is greatly influenced by geographical factors, and each country must develop relevant strategies based on its own specific environmental conditions to improve energy environmental efficiency. From the management strategy point of view, each country should develop energy strategies based on differences in geographical and environmental conditions, like economic, culture, technology, environment, nationality etc., in order to increase energy environmental efficiency by improving energy technology and thus encourage using RE.

References

Amirteimoori, A. and S. Kordrostami (2012), "Production Planning in Data Envelopment Analysis," International Journal of Production Economics, Vol. 1 (140), pp. 212–228.

Banker, R.D., A. Charnes and W.W. Cooper (1984), "Some Models for Estimating Technical and Scale Inefficiencies in Data Envelopment Analysis," Management Science, Vol. 30(9), pp. 1078–1092.

Battese, G.E. and D.S.P. Rao (2002), "Technology Gap, Efficiency and a Stochastic Metafrontier Function," International Journal of Business and Economics, Vol. 1, pp. 87–93.

Battese, G.E., D.S.P. Rao and C.J. O'Donnell (2004), "A Metafrontier Production Function for Estimation of Technical Efficiencies and Technology Gap for Firms Operating Under Different Technologies," Journal of Productivity Analysis, Vol. 21, pp. 91–103.

Bogetoft, P., D.L. Christensen, I. Damgard, M. Geisler, T.P. Jakobsen, M. Krøigaard, J.D. Nielsen, J.B. Nielsen, K. Nielsen, J. Pagter, M.I. Schwartzbach and T. Toft (2008), "Multiparty Computation Goes Live," Financial Cryptography and Data Security. Springer Berlin Heidelberg, pp. 325–343.

Chang, H., H.L. Choy, W.W. Cooper and T.W. Ruefli (2009), "Using Malmquist Indexes to Measure Changes in the Productivity and Efficiency of US Accounting Firms Before and After the Sarbanes," Omega, Vol. 37(5), pp. 951–960.

Charnes A., W.W. Cooper and E. Rhodes (1978), "Measuring the Efficiency of Decision Making Units," European Journal of Operational Research, Vol. 2(6), pp. 429–444.

Chen, C.M. (2009), "Network-DEA, A Model with New Efficiency Measures to Incorporate the Dynamic Effect in Production Networks," European Journal of Operational Research, Vol. 194 (3), pp. 687–99.

Dritsaki, C. and M. Dritsaki (2014), "Causal Relationship between Energy Consumption, Economic Growth and CO2 Emissions: A Dynamic Panel Data Approach," International Journal of Energy Economics and Policy, Vol. 4(2), pp. 125–136.

Egilmez, G.P. and Y.S. Park (2014), "Transportation Related Carbon, Energy and Water Footprint Analysis of U.S. Manufacturing: An Eco-efficiency Assessment," Transportation Research: Part D: Transport and Environment, Vol. 32, pp. 143–159.

Fagiani, R., B. Julian and H. Rudi (2013), "Risk-based assessment of the cost-efficiency and the effectivity of renewable energy support schemes: Certificate markets versus feed-in tariffs," Energy Policy, Vol. 55, pp. 648–661.

Farrell, M.J. (1957), "The Measurement of Productive Efficiency," Journal of the Royal Statistical Society, Vol. 120 (3), pp. 253–281.

Färe, R. and S. Grosskopf (1996), "Productivity and intermediate products: A frontier approach," Economics Letters, Vol. 50(1), pp. 65–70.

Färe, R., S. Grosskopf, M. Norris and Z. Zhang (1994), "Productivity Growth, Technical Progress, and Efficiency Change in Industrialized Countries," The American Economic Review, Vol. 84 (1), pp. 66–83.

Filippini, M. and H. Wetzel (2014), "The Impact of Ownership Unbundling on Cost Efficiency: Empirical Evidence from the New Zealand Electricity Distribution Sector," Energy Econ., Vol. 45, pp. 412–418.

Galán J.E. and M.G. Pollitt (2014), "Inefficiency Persistence and Heterogeneity in Colombian Electricity Utilities," Energy Econ., Vol. 46, pp. 31–44.

Goto, M., A. Otsuka and T. Sueyoshi (2014), "DEA (Data Envelopment Analysis) Assessment of Operational and Environmental Efficiencies on Japanese Regional Industries," Energy, Vol. 66, pp. 535–549.

Hong, L., N. Zhou, D. Fridley and C. Raczkowski (2013), "Assessment of China's renewable energy contribution during the 12th Five Year Plan," Energy Policy, Vol. 62, pp. 1533–1543.

Kao, C. (2014), "Network Data Envelopment Analysis: A Review," European Journal of Operational Research, Vol. 239(1), pp. 1–16.

Klopp, G.A. (1985), "The Analysis of the Efficiency of Productive Systems with Multiple Inputs and Outputs," University of Illinois at Chicago, PhD, Doctor of Philosophy, Engineering, Industrial.

Kuo, H.-F., H.-L. Chen and K.-W. Tsou (2014), "Analysis of Farming Environmental Efficiency Using a DEA Model with Undesirable Outputs," APCBEE Procedia, Vol. 10, pp. 154–158.

Menegaki, A.N. and S. Gurluk (2013), "Greece & Turkey; Assessment and Comparison of Their Renewable Energy Performance," International Journal of Energy Economics and Policy, Vol. 3(4), pp. 367–383.

Meng, F.Y., P. Zhou, D.Q. Zhou and Y. Bai (2014), "Inefficiency and Congestion Assessment of Mix Energy Consumption in 16 APEC Countries by using DEA Window Analysis," Energy Procedia, Vol. 61, pp. 2518–2523.

Nemoto, J. and M. Goto (1999), "Dynamic Data Envelopment Analysis: Modeling Intertemporal Behavior of a Firm in the Presence of Productive Inefficiencies," Economics Letters, Vol. 64, pp. 51–56.

Nemoto, J. and M. Goto (2003), "Measurement of Dynamic Efficiency in Production: An Application of Data Envelopment Analysis to Japanese Electric Utilities," Journal of Productivity Analysis, Vol. 19(2), pp. 191–210.

O'Donnell, C.J., D.S. Rao and E. Battese (2008), "Metafrontier Frameworks for the Study of Firm-Level Efficiencies and Technology Ratios," Empirical Economics, Vol. 34, pp. 231–255.

Park, K.S. and K. Park (2009), "Measurement of Multiperiod Aggregative Efficiency," European Journal of Operational Research, Vol. 193(2), pp. 567–580.

Ruttan, V.W., H.P. Binswanger, W.W. Hayami and Weber (1978), "Factor Productivity and Growth: A Historical Interpretation, in Induced Innovation: Technology, Institution and Developments," Baltimore: John Hopkins University Press.

Shabani, A., R.F. Saen and S.M.R. Torabipour (2014), "A New Data Envelopment Analysis (DEA) Model to Select Eco-efficient Technologies in the Presence of Undesirable Outputs," Clean Technologies and Environmental Policy, Vol. 16(3), pp. 513–525.

Shrivastava, N., S. Sharma and K. Chauhan (2012), "Efficiency Assessment and Benchmarking of Thermal Power Plants in India," Energy Policy, Vol. 40, pp. 159–176.

Sueyoshi, T. and D. Wang (2014), "Radial and Non-radial Approaches for Environmental Assessment by Data Envelopment Analysis: Corporate Sustainability and Effective Investment for Technology Innovation," Energy Economics, Vol. 45, pp. 537–551.

Sueyoshi, T. and M. Goto (2011), "DEA Approach for Unified Efficiency Measurement: Assessment of Japanese Fossil Fuel Power Generation," Energy Economics, Vol. 33, pp. 292–303.

Sueyoshi, T. and M. Goto (2012), "Efficiency-Based Rank Assessment for Electric Power Industry: A Combined Use of Data Envelopment Analysis (DEA) and DEA-Discriminant Analysis (DA)," Energy Economics, Vol. 34, pp. 634–644.

Sueyoshi, T. and M. Goto (2013), "A Comparative Study among Fossil Fuel Power Plants in PJM and California ISO by DEA Environmental Assessment," Energy Economics, Vol. 40, pp. 130–45.

Sueyoshi, T. and M. Goto (2015), "Environmental Assessment on Coal-Fired Power Plants in U.S. North-east Region by DEA Non-Radial Measurement," Energy Economics, Vol. 50, pp. 125–139.

Sueyoshi, T. and K. Sekitani (2005), "Returns to Scale in Dynamic DEA," European Journal of Operational Research, Vol. 161(2), pp. 536–44.

Thanassoulis, E., M. Portela and O. Despic (2008), "The Mathematical Programming Approach to Efficiency Analysis," In: H. Fried, K. Lovell and S. Schmidt (Eds.), Measurement of Productive Efficiency and Productivity Growth, pp. 251–420, Oxford University Press.

Tone, K. and M. Tsutsui (2010), "Dynamic DEA: A Slacks-based Measure Approach," Omega, Vol. 38, pp. 145–156.

Tone K. and M. Tsutsui (2014), "Dynamic DEA with Network Structure: A Slacks-Based Measure Approach," Omega, Vol. 42, No. 1, pp. 124–131.

Wang, D., S. Li and T. Sueyoshi (2014), "DEA Environmental Assessment on U.S. Industrial Sectors: Investment for Improvement in Operational and Environmental Performance to Attain Corporate Sustainability," Energy Economics, Vol. 45, pp. 254–67.

Wang, Z. and C. Feng (2015), "A Performance Evaluation of the Energy, Environmental, and Economic Efficiency and Productivity in China: An Application of Global Data Envelopment Analysis," Applied Energy, Vol. 147, pp. 617–626.

Woo, C., Y. Chung, D. Chun, H. Seo and S. Hong (2015), "The Static and Dynamic Environmental Efficiency of Renewable Energy: A Malmquist Index Analysis of OECD Countries," Renewable and Sustainable Energy Reviews, Vol. 47, pp. 367–376.

Xie B.C., L.F. Shang, S.B. Yang and B.-W. Yi (2014), "Dynamic Environmental Efficiency Evaluation of Electric Power Industries: Evidence from OECD (Organization for Economic Cooperation and Development) and BRIC (Brazil, Russia, India and China) Countries," Energy, Vol. 74(1), pp. 147–157.

Yago, L.T., V.R. Ian, S. Chenel, M.N. Desirée, M.T. Moreira and G. Feijoo (2015), "Eco-efficiency Analysis of Spanish WWTPs Using the LCA + DEA Method," Water Research, Vol. 68, pp. 651–666.

Yang, L., H. Ouyang, K. Fang, L. Ye and J. Zhang (2015), "Evaluation of Regional Environmental Efficiencies in China Based on Super-Efficiency-DEA," Ecological Indicators, Vol. 51, pp. 13–19.

Part III
Studies in Transitional Green Growth

Chapter 12
Factor Price Distortion, Technological Innovation Pattern and the Biased Technological Progress of Industry in China: An Empirical Analysis Based on Mediating Effect Model

Xuejie Bai and Shuang Li

1 Introduction

Structural contradictions, including the imbalance between supply and demand as well as the mismatch of production factors, occur during China's current economic development. In order to mitigate these problems, Chinese government implemented a "Supply-side Structural Reform" strategy, and unlike the previous reform strategies, the supply-side structural reform stresses the decisive role of market in resources allocation and the function of technological innovation to optimize factor allocation. In the economic field, the factor price distortion is common due to the imperfect market mechanism. Factor price does not always equal to the marginal output: in terms of labor price, the economic blue book "Analysis on the Prospect of China's Economy (2014)" states that China's per capita GDP has increased by 31.1 times from 1985 to 2012, while the average wage of workers has increased by only 25.85 times, which is far behind the growth rate of per capita GDP. The proportion of laborers' remuneration in GDP continues to decline. In terms of capital price, in order to support the development of capital-intensive industries, the government has adopted financial restraint policies on long term basis to reduce capital price, so as to lower the capital threshold for enterprises[1] (Chen and Lin 2012), which is against

---

[1]When comparing with capital, labor and other factors, land resources factor has its special features and it is difficult to acquire data, therefore, this article discusses the distortions of capital and labor only.

X. Bai
School of Economics and Social Development, Nankai University,
Tianjin 300071, China

S. Li (✉)
School of Business, Zhengzhou University, Zhengzhou 450001, China
e-mail: 812983664@qq.com

© Springer Nature Singapore Pte Ltd. 2018
R. Pang et al. (eds.), *Energy, Environment and Transitional Green Growth in China*, https://doi.org/10.1007/978-981-10-7919-1_12

China's comparative advantages. Changes in the relative prices of factors will in turn affect the innovation factor allocation of enterprises at micro-level, demonstrating the non-neutral characteristics of technological progress. Meanwhile, China's current technological innovation pattern is steered to technology introduction seriously. With the deepening of economic development, this pattern, which was vitally important to China's technological progress, is suffering from bottleneck effect. Therefore, China's supply-side structural reform is confronted with two challenges, namely, the defective factor price mechanism and the particularly technology-introduction-biased technological innovation pattern. In the following parts, this paper will study the effects of factor price distortion and technological innovation pattern on the biases of technological progress in China's industry, and the mediating role of technological innovation pattern under this influencing mechanism, so as to find a more reasonable direction and path of technological progress for Chinese industries.

2 Literature Review

Biased technological progress is one of the prevailing economic phenomena in any countries and is considered to be one of the causes of wage disparities (Zhang et al. 2012). As early as the 1930s, Hicks (1932) discovered the non-neutral characteristics of technological progress, pointing out that "the change in the relative price of a factor is the driving force behind the technological invention and it promotes the specific technological invention". David and Klundert (1965) firstly used Constant Elasticity of Substitution (CES) production function to predict the direction of technological progress in America between 1899 and 1960, and the results showed that technological progress was generally biased towards capital. Acemoglu (2002) applied technological progress to any factor. If the technological progress is more conducive to improving the marginal output of factor "S", then it is called the "S-biased technology progress". In recent years, scholars have been successively using standardized systems approach (Klump et al. 2007, 2008), TFP index decomposition method (Barros and Weber 2009) and other new methods to estimate the technological progress bias in the United States, Japan, Europe and other developed countries and regions. The technological progresses in these places were found to be biased towards capital. Cruz (2015) analyzed the implications of this non-constant sectoral biased technical change for structural change and developed a multi-sectoral growth model where TFP growth rates across sectors are non-constant. Khaled (2017) used both additional theoretical information and appropriate statistical techniques to alleviate problems of estimation and inference with small samples. In china, Dai and Xu (2010), Deng (2014), Chen and Wang (2015) et al. measured and analyzed the provincial technological progress bias of industries and that of industries within manufacturing sector in China with standardized system method; Wang and Hu (2015), Wang and Qi (2015) studied the technological progress bias in Chinese industries with TFP index decomposition method. In conclusion, the researches of overseas scholars are mostly limited to the technological progress bias in developed countries, which is not in line with developing countries where factor prices are more distorted and the market mechanism is less mature. Chinese scholars have measured the technological progress bias in China empirically, but they lack relevant theoretical analysis. As pointed out by Hicks, changes in relative factor price are the driving force of technological progress. It is prevalent that it is difficult for factor prices to accurately reflect the number of factor endowments that have been distorted and their distortion degree; therefore, though there is certain connection between factor price distortion and technological progress bias, this connection is rarely established by past studies.

In the past, researches on factor price distortion were limited to the estimation of distortion degrees and the effects of distortions on R&D expenditure, export behavior and so on. When measuring and calculating the degree of factor distortion, Zhang et al. (2011), Yang et al. (2015) estimated the degrees of distortions of provincial factor prices indirectly in China based on the "China Marketization Process Index Report", Shi and Xian (2012), Li and Ji (2014), Huang and Zhang (2014) and others used CD production functions to measure the factor price distortions in different provinces (or the industries). When studying the effects of factor price distortion on R&D expenditure of enterprises, Zhang et al. (2011), Huang and Zhang (2014), Zheng and Liu (2013) have come to the conclusion that factor price distortion will inhibit the independent innovation of enterprises; and factor price distortion is often inversely related to R&D expenditure of enterprises. These researches indicate that factor price distortion will further affect the technological innovation pattern of a country, and the technological innovation pattern may be the way through which factor price distortion affects technological progress bias. Based on the perspective of industry factor intensity, this paper aims to explore the exact intrinsic links among the factor price distortion, technological innovation pattern and technological progress bias of subdivision industries in China. This paper provides the objective fact-based reasons for optimizing the direction of China's industrial technological progress. The definition of technological innovation pattern refers to the proportion of technology introduction to its independent research in a country's technological innovation system. Former scholars' researches mainly focused on the comparison of the effects of technology introduction and independent research on technological progress and economic development. According to Lin et al. (1999), Lin and Zhang (2006), Lin and Su (2012), the new structural economists believe that technology introduction has cost advantage over independent research; therefore, it is possible for developing countries, who are usually short of funds, to catch up by increasing technology introduction to make the most of the "backward advantage". On the other hand, researchers like Cooper (1994), Kim and Inkpen (2005) claim that most of the technologies are extremely sensitive to the environment. Only by possessing the appropriate attracting capability and increasing the resource investment in both materials and personnel can the enterprises in developing countries realize the value of these advanced technologies. Yang (2004) points out that, developing countries can introduce technology, but cannot easily imitate the advanced institutions of developed countries.

Disconnection between technology and institution tends to undermine the long-term economic development and create the so-called "backward disadvantage". Thus, it can be seen that, there is no consensus about technological innovation pattern choices in academic society, and different technological innovation pattern can lead to extremely diversified allocation results of different factor resources. In this way, the technological innovation pattern will affect its technological progress direction through factor resources allocation. This paper will explore these effects with mediating effect model.

To sum up, it has become a consensus among scholars that during the current stage of China's industrial development, technological progress is biased towards capital. However, previous scholars have only used provincial data to study the degree to what extent Chinese industry factor prices are distorted and technological progresses are biased, but barely studied the differences between factor price distortions and technological progress biases in different industries and their relevant reasons. More importantly, factor price distortion, an institutional derivative during China's economic transition period, has profound impacts on many economic issues in contemporary China, and technological progress bias is one of them. However, previous researches often split these two elements, possibly resulting from the failure to establish an effective transmission mechanism between them. Based on the analysis made earlier in this paper, technological innovation pattern may be an important mediator variable between the two. Therefore, these are the major advances achieved by this paper: (1) Use the standardized system method and the production function method to calculate the degrees of technological progress biases and factor distortions of different sectors in China's industries. (2) Use the mediating effect model to estimate the direct effects of factor price distortion on China's industrial technological progress bias and the effects of technological innovation pattern. The latter is an important innovative indicator and works as a mediator between the two. (3) Establish the complete relation system between factor price distortion and technological progress bias, so as to provide an objective reference for optimizing the direction of China's industrial technology progress and realizing the development of mode transformation.

3 Mechanism Analysis of How Factor Price Distortion Affects Industrial Technological Progress Direction

The effects of factor price distortion on China's industrial technological progress bias are realized through both direct and indirect ways. Specifically, the direct effect mechanism means that the relative distortion degrees of capital and labor prices determine the bias of technological progress. And the indirect effect mechanism of factor price distortion on technological progress bias means that factor price distortion could influence the technological progress bias through the technological innovation pattern.

3.1 Direct Effect Mechanism of Factor Price Distortion on Technological Progress Bias

3.1.1 Relative Distortion Degrees of Capital and Labor Prices Determine the Bias of Technological Progress

When the capital and labor prices are negatively distorted, and if the degree of distortion in capital price is higher than that of labor price, enterprises can replace the labor force with capital to improve profit margins in their production processes. Manufacturers who pursue maximized profit are bound to choose the capital biased technology, and vice versa. When the capital and labor price are simultaneously positively distorted, and if the degree of distortion in capital price is higher than that of labor price, enterprises can replace the capital with labor force to improve profit margins in their production processes. The manufacturers who pursue maximized profit are bound to choose the labor force biased technology, and vice versa; when the capital price is negatively distorted and the labor price is positively distorted, enterprises will naturally choose the capital biased technological progress, and vice versa. We can see that because the enterprises are the main bodies of factors allocation choices, the direct effects of factor price distortion on technological progress bias are still the choices of enterprises, which are made on the basis of the price level after factor distortion so as to make the most of advantages and avoid disadvantages. Since it is the ideal state that the prices of production factors fully reflect the levels of supply and demand and the marginal output capacity, it is inevitable to have technological progress biases.

3.1.2 Industrial Difference of Factor Price Distortion—Based on the Law of Diminishing Factor Marginal Returns

If all industries are divided into capital-intensive ones and labor-intensive ones on the basis of their factor intensities, and the law of diminishing factor marginal returns suggests that the capital-intensive industries tend to have higher capital intensity (or abundance) than labor-intensive industries; therefore, their marginal capital output is usually lower than that of labor-intensive industries, and their marginal labor output is usually higher than that of labor-intensive industries. Then, when the capital price is negatively distorted, the lower marginal capital output makes the gap between capital price and marginal output in capital-intensive industries smaller than that of labor-intensive industries, and thus the capital price in capital-intensive industries less negatively distorted than that of labor-intensive industries; when labor prices are negatively distorted, higher marginal labor output leads to a greater degree of distortion in the labor price of capital-intensive industries than that of labor-intensive industries. Similarly, when capital prices are positively distorted, the capital price surpasses marginal output is much greater than that of labor-intensive industries, and thus leads to higher degree of positive distortion in capital price of capital-intensive industries than that of labor-intensive industries; When labor prices are positively distorted, higher marginal labor output makes the labor prices of capital-intensive industries less positively distorted than that of labor-intensive industries. As to whether the industry's technological progress is generally biased towards capital or labor, the determinative factors are the type and relative size of factor price distortions in capital-intensive industries and labor-intensive industries.

3.2   Indirect Effect Mechanism of Factor Price Distortion on Technological Progress Bias

3.2.1   The More Factor Price Is Distorted, the More Technological Innovation Pattern Is Biased Towards Technology Introduction

The indirect effects of factor price distortion on technological progress bias mainly work through the technological innovation pattern. Here we define technological innovation pattern as the proportional relationship between independent R&D and technology introduction. When factor prices are negatively distorted, enterprises—the main bodies at the micro-level that pursue profit maximization—will use cheap capital and unskilled labor factors to compensate for the lack of technology with low-cost advantage, or introduce materialized progress pattern which uses capital intensively, that is, introduce advanced foreign machinery and production equipment; however, these measures will make the enterprises lose the impetus of independent research and development. Industries with highly distorted factors are more likely to have low initiatives to undertake independent research and development within the enterprises. Secondly, the underestimation of labor price will directly lower the average living standards of social residents and inhibit average families' demands for developing education of future generations, which are not conducive to the demands for high-tech commodities, nor the cultivation of human capital and scientific and technological innovation ability. In the long term, these consequences go against the R&D enthusiasm of enterprises and slow the supply of high-tech talents. Therefore, negative distortion of both capital price and labor price can lead to the preference for the pattern of technology introduction. In addition, although both independent R&D and technology introduction require a lot of capital investment, compared to the high risk of independent R&D and the "innovation rent" of possible research findings, the costs and benefits of technology introduction are more certain. In China where the protection system for intellectual property is not perfect and the risk for independent research and development is extremely high, enterprises are more willing to introduce mature technologies from other countries rather than enhance the production efficiency by doing independent research and development. Relevant data show that, since reform and opening up, China's foreign technology dependence has been maintaining at a rate greater than

50%. Although the percentage has declined in recent years, it is still far higher than the average level of developed countries (10% or less). On the other hand, when there is a positive distortion in factor prices, market prices of capital and labor are both expensive, which will encourage enterprises to take the initiative to use advanced technology to maximize the use of capital and labor, and to improve labor productivity. However, the scarcity of capital may increase the shortage of funds when enterprises import foreign technologies, forcing them to make great efforts to carry out independent R&D activities, which alleviates their dependence on foreign technology objectively. At the same time, the positive distortions of labor price mean the substantial improvement of wages, which contributes to the cultivation of skilled labor force and thus increases the demand for high-tech products. In the long run, it would help to enhance the enthusiasm and innovation level of independent research and development.

3.2.2 When the Factor Price Is Distorted, the Higher the Proportion of Technology Introduction, More Capital-Biased the Technological Progress Is—Based on "Transnational Technology Diffusion Theory"

According to the theory of transnational technology diffusion, the technological progress direction of countries that import technologies will be deeply affected by the technology exporting countries. A large number of empirical studies have shown that the direction of technological progress in developed countries is generally biased towards capital, in which case developing countries introduce technologies in large-scale will inevitably have capital-biased technological progress (Acemoglu and Zilibotti 2001; Gancia and Zilibotti 2009). It can be seen that when there are negative distortions of both capital and labor prices, the greater the degree of distortions, the higher the proportion of technology introduction, so that the technological progress of the country that imports technology is affected by the country that exports technology to a greater degree. This finally leads to more obvious capital bias in the technological progress of the country that imports technologies. That is the indirect transmission mechanism in which factor price distortion affects technological progress bias. On the contrary, the positive distortion of factor price will limit the ability of enterprises to purchase advanced technology and equipment, meanwhile enhance the enthusiasm of independent research and development, thereby weaken the capital bias characteristic of technological progress. In other words, the magnitude of indirect impacts of factor price distortion on technological progress bias through technological innovation pattern is inversely proportional to the actual price level.

3.2.3 Differences Among Industries: The Indirect Effects of Factor Price Distortion on Technological Progress Bias on Capital-Intensive Industries Are Bigger Than that of Labor-Intensive Industries

In terms of industry characteristics, the introduction of both advanced production equipment and technical patents require significant financial support, and labor-intensive industries are usually more financially limited than capital-intensive industries. Therefore, this paper argues that, in terms of feasibility, capital-intensive industries are more equipped with financial resources to import technology in large scale. Therefore, they tend to adopt importing foreign technology as their technological innovation pattern. Thus, the indirect effects of factor price distortion on technological progress bias may be more pronounced in capital-intensive industries. In summary, the factor price distortion affects the technological progress bias of Chinese industry in both direct and indirect ways, and the distortion of capital price and the distortion of labor price have different effects on technological progress bias. The magnitude of direct effects and indirect effects varies among industries different in factor intensities.

4 Empirical Methods and Variable Description

The mechanism analysis in this paper will focus on the dual effect of factor price distortion on technological progress bias. And, the empirical analysis part will use the mediating effect model to test this dual effect.

4.1 Calculation Method of Industrial Technological Progress Bias

In present academia, there are two major methods to measure technological progress bias: one is the "TFP index decomposition method" (Färe et al. 1997), which further decomposes the pure technological progress in TFP into three parts: the scale technological progress, input-biased technological progress and output-biased technological progress, so as to determine the contribution rate of input factors to technological progress. The advantage of this approach is that there is no need to set a specific form for the production function; however, it is impossible to identify the exact factor towards which the technological progress is biased and to what extend it is biased. The other method is called the "standardized system method", which sets production function into standardized CES function, and calculates the technological progress bias index by combining the production function and the demand function; however, systematic bias in each equation is inevitable. In order to overcome this shortcoming, Lu (2013) et al. have modified standardized system method with mathematical derivation such as Taylor expansion, and considerably reduced the risks of systematic bias. With this method this paper will estimate the technological progress bias indexes in different industries. And the method works like this.

Set the standardized CES production function as follows:

$$Y_{it} = \left[\alpha(A_{it} * K_{it})^{\frac{\sigma-1}{\sigma}} + (1 - \alpha)(B_{it} * L_{it})^{\frac{\sigma-1}{\sigma}}\right]^{\frac{\sigma}{\sigma-1}} \tag{1}$$

in which Y_{it}, K_{it}, and L_{it} represent the industrial added value, capital stock and labor force in industry i and during the period of t; A_{it} and B_{it} are capital efficiency and labor efficiency respectively. It is assumed that factor-enhanced technological progress is growing exponentially, and γK_{it}, γL_{it} are the growth rates of A_{it} and B_{it}, then

$$A_{it} = \frac{Y_{it}}{K_{it}} \left(\frac{r_{it}K_{it}/Y_{it}}{\propto}\right)^{\frac{\sigma}{\sigma-1}} = A_{i0} * e^{\gamma_{K_{it}}} = Y_{i0}/K_{i0} * e^{\gamma_{K_{it}}} \tag{2}$$

$$B_{it} = \frac{Y_{it}}{L_{it}} \left(\frac{1 - r_{it}K_{it}/Y_{it}}{1-\propto}\right)^{\frac{\sigma}{\sigma-1}} = B_{i0} * e^{\gamma_{L_{it}}} = Y_{i0}/L_{i0} * e^{\gamma_{L_{it}}} \tag{3}$$

put (2), (3) into (1) to get the derivation and simplify it[2], and change ratio of the capital-labor output, which is equal to technological progress bias index,

$$D_{it} = \frac{d(MP_{K_{it}}/MP_{L_{it}})}{dt} = \frac{\sigma - 1}{\sigma} \left(\gamma_{K_{it}} - \gamma_{L_{it}}\right) \tag{4}$$

It can be seen that, in order to calculate D_{it}, it is necessary to calculate the factor replacement elasticity σ and growth rates of factor efficiency $\gamma_{K_{it}}$, $\gamma_{L_{it}}$. When the factor replacement elasticity is less than 1 and the growth rate of capital efficiency is less than the growth rate of labor efficiency, the value of D_{it} is greater than 0. It means that the direction of technological progress is capital-biased. And the greater the value of D_{it}, the more obvious of the bias. And then we use Kmenta approximation method (León-Ledesma et al. 2010) to estimate the factor replacement elasticity σ. The basic principle of this method is to develop the CES production function in Taylor expansion on the datum point (Y_{i0}, K_{i0}, L_{i0}), so as to obtain an equation that can be directly measured:

---

[2]Due to limited space, the detailed derivation process has been omitted.

$$\ln \frac{Y_{it}/Y_{i0}}{L_{it}/L_{i0}} = \propto$$

$$\ln \frac{K_{it}/K_{i0}}{L_{it}/L_{i0}} + \underbrace{\frac{\alpha(1-\alpha)(\sigma-1)}{2\sigma}}_{a} \left(\ln \frac{K_{it}/K_{i0}}{L_{it}/L_{i0}} \right)^2 + \underbrace{\lfloor \alpha\gamma_K + (1-\alpha)\gamma_L \rfloor}_{b} t \quad (5)$$

$$+ \underbrace{\frac{\alpha(1-\alpha)(\sigma-1)}{2\sigma} (\gamma_K - \gamma_L)^2 t^2}_{c}$$

Through the regression analysis of (5), we can get the estimated values of the coefficient a, b, c, and solve the factor replacement efficiency γ_K, γ_L; then use (2), (3) and (4) to find the factor efficiency growth rate and technological progress bias index of each industry in each year. Compared with similar researches, the improvement in this paper mainly lies in considering the parameters in production function as representing the relative importance of capital and labor in production process. It varies with the factor intensities in different industries. The relative importance of capital and labor will differ a lot in capital-intensive industries and labor-intensive industries. Therefore, based on the generally estimated parameters, this paper classifies all the industries into capital-intensive ones and labor-intensive ones according to the level of per capita capital stock (industries whose per capita capital is higher than the average has been classified as capital-intensive industries, otherwise labor-intensive industries[3]). Furthermore, this paper will also measure the parameters in capital-intensive industries and labor-intensive industries, so as to accurately depict the technological progress bias indexes in different industries.

---

[3]Capital-intensive industries include (according to per capita capital in descending order): the production and supply of electricity, steam hot and water; petroleum and natural gas exploitation; petroleum refining and coking; coal gas production and supply; tap water production and supply; chemical fiber manufacturing; tobacco processing industry; ferrous metal smelting and rolling processing; non-ferrous metal smelting and rolling processing; chemical raw materials and products manufacturing; food manufacturing; paper and paper products; beverage manufacturing; ferrous metal mining; transportation equipment manufacturing; non-metallic mineral products; non-ferrous metal mining industry; pharmaceutical manufacturing; labor-intensive industries include (according to per capita capital in ascending order): leather, fur, down and relative products; clothing and other fiber products manufacturing; cultural, educational and sporting goods manufacturing; furniture manufacturing; instrument, meter, cultural and office machinery; wood processing and bamboo, rattan, palm products; general equipment manufacturing industry; metal products industry; electrical machinery and equipment manufacturing; special equipment manu-facturing; plastic products industry; textile industry; food processing industry; rubber products industry; electronic and communication equipment manufacturing; record media reproduction of printing industry; non-metallic mining industry; coal mining industry.

4.2 Calculation Method of Factor Price Distortion Degree

This paper draws on the practice of most scholars in the past, using the production function method to measure the degree of factor price distortion. The basic idea is that: as the factor price distortion degree refers to the extent to which the market price of the factors deviates from their marginal output (i.e., the real price), it is necessary to assume the specific form of production function and estimate its coefficients to obtain the marginal output of the factors. And then this paper will compare the real price with the marginal output of the factors. If the ratio is less than 1, the real results of the factor is less than the due return of the factor, which means the factor price is negatively distorted; conversely, if the factor price is positively distorted, the closer the ratio is to 1, the lower the degree of distortion. When choosing function form, this paper abandons the most commonly used CD production function in previous studies, and uses the fixed substitution effect (CES) production function for mainly two reasons. Firstly, in the process of estimating the technological progress bias, this paper uses the CES production function to deduce the standardized system of technological progress bias. In order to maintain the consistency of the empirical methods, we choose to use CES function to estimate the degree of distortion. Secondly, as the general form of the CD production function,[4] the CES production function is more in line with the economic reality; therefore, the estimation is no less accurate than that of CD production function.[5]

The specific steps are as follows: First, let the production function be

$Y = A\left[\alpha K^{\frac{\sigma-1}{\sigma}} + (1-\alpha)L^{\frac{\sigma-1}{\sigma}}\right]^{\frac{\sigma}{\sigma-1}}$, α be the output elasticity of the capital, and σ be

the factor replacement elasticity between K and L. Take the partial derivatives of K and L at two sides of the equation, and the marginal outputs of capital and labor are

$MP_K = \dfrac{\alpha Y}{\left[\alpha + (1-\alpha)\left(\frac{L}{K}\right)^{\frac{\sigma-1}{\sigma}}\right]K}$, $MP_L = \dfrac{(1-\alpha)Y}{\left[\alpha\left(\frac{K}{L}\right)^{\frac{\sigma-1}{\sigma}} + (1-\alpha)\right]L}$ respectively. Then, use the

Kmenta approximation to estimate the CES production function[6] and substitute the estimation of α, σ into the marginal output expression, so the marginal outputs of capital and labor can be obtained. Finally, the marginal outputs values of the factor are substituted into the expressions of factor price distortion $distK = r/MP_K$ and $distL = w/MP_L$, and we get the price distortion degrees of capital and labor, so as to estimate the general distortion degrees in different industries $dist = (distK)^{\alpha}(distL)^{1-\alpha}$. In order to examine the effects of factor intensity on

---

[4]It can be proved that, CD production function is the special form of CES production function when $\rho \to -\infty$ or $\rho \to 0$ and its factor replacement elasticity is kept at 1.

[5]In order to testify the robustness of estimated results derived by CES function, this paper adopts CD production function to predict α, σ simultaneously, and estimations derived from both production functions have little difference.

[6]Due to space limitation, the specific steps of the Kmenta approximation are omitted. See above for the derivation of technological progress bias, or refer to Wang et al. (2006).

factor price distortion, the degrees of distortion of factor prices in capital-intensive industries and labor-intensive industries are measured separately after estimating the general industrial degree of factor price distortion.

4.3   Design of Regression Model—Mediating Effect Model

In the regression analysis process, if the relationship between the dependent variable Y and the independent variable X meet the following requirements: X not only affects the Y directly, but also affects Y indirectly through the mediator variable M, then it is suitable to use the mediating effect model to estimate variable relationship. According to the mechanism analysis which has been done previously, factor price distortion affects the technological progress bias of Chinese industries through the dual mechanism with both direct and indirect effects. Therefore, this paper constructs the following mediating effect model to analyze the relationship between the two:

$$D_{it} = a_0 + a_1 dist_{it} + a_2 C_{1it} + \varepsilon_{1it} \tag{6}$$

$$P_{it} = b_0 + b_1 dist_{it} + b_2 C_{2it} + \varepsilon_{2it} \tag{7}$$

$$D_{it} = c_0 + c_1 dist_{it} + c_2 P_{it} + c_3 C_{1it} + \varepsilon_{3it} \tag{8}$$

P_{it} is the mediator variable—the technological innovation pattern; ε_{it} is the random error term, and C_{it} is the control variable. The coefficient a_1 in Eq. (6) measures the total effects of factor price distortion on China's industrial technological progress bias. b_1 in Eq. (7) measures the influence of factor price distortion on technological innovation pattern. c_1 in Eq. (8) represents the direct effects of factor price distortion on technological progress bias. Substituting Eq. (7) into Eqs. (8), and (9) can be got:

$$D_{it} = (c_0 + c_2 b_0) + (c_1 + c_2 b_1) dist_{it} + c_3 C_{1it} + c_2 b_2 C_{2it} + \varepsilon_{1it} \tag{9}$$

Among them, the coefficient c_2, and b_1 represent the indirect effects of factor price distortion on technological progress bias. It can be seen that the direct effects, indirect effects and total effects of factor price distortion on technological progress bias can be obtained by estimating Eqs. (6–8). This model involves five control variables, the control variables of Eq. (6) include the factor endowment structure and the proportion of state-owned economy. The control variables in Eq. (7) include industrial R&D intensity, R&D personnel and governmental R&D support. The five control variables are described separately as follows:

Factor Endowment Structure According to the basic principles of economics, while other conditions remain unchanged, the value of a factor is in direct proportion to its scarcity; combined with the theory of comparative advantage, a country's technological progress direction is closely related to the country's factor endowment structure, and its optimal direction of technological progress should be biased towards the country's relatively abundant factor resources. Therefore, this paper constructs the proxy variable of the factor endowment structure—per capita capital stock to control the influence of factor scarcity levels on the technological progress bias.

The Proportion of State-owned Economy As a result of the long-term preferential policies government issued to China's state-owned economy in forms of financial subsidies and tax relief, and the fact that bank loans are also more inclined to large-scale, low-risk state-owned enterprises, the cost of capital use of state-owned enterprises is generally lower than that of other types of enterprises. According to Shi and Zhao (2007), the capital cost of the state-owned economy is about 15–20% lower than that of the non-state economy, which makes the state-owned enterprises more inclined to adopt capital-biased technologies. Therefore, this paper argues that the higher the proportion of state-owned economy in the industry, the greater the distortion degree of capital bias of its technological progress.

R&D Intensity and Personnel These two indicators represent the material capital and human resource input of the technological innovation of an industry, which reflect the strength and enthusiasm of technological innovation activities in the industry. In general, the higher the R&D intensity and the number of R&D personnel, the more the industry is inclined to achieve technological progress through independent R&D rather than technology introduction. Therefore, this paper argues that the higher the R&D intensity and the number of R&D personnel, the more biased this industry is towards independent innovation.

Governmental R&D Support This paper uses the proportion of government funds in industrial R&D internal expenditure to measure the degree of governmental R&D support. It is an important means of government incentives. This approach will influence the technological innovation of enterprises at the micro level and the industrial technological progress pattern as a whole. The more the government supports, the more it is supportive to independent R&D behavior, and then the proportion of technology introduction will be reduced. However, according to the former analysis of scholars, the incentive function of government subsidies on companies' technological innovation activities will be greatly reduced by the existence of "crowding out effect" (Busom 2000). Therefore, this paper argues that the impact of governmental R&D support on technological innovation pattern may not be significant.

4.4 Description of Variables and Data

This paper takes the classified industries in China as research objects. According to the latest revision of the "Classification of National Economy Sectors" in 2011, there are 41 secondary industries in China's industry, excluding mining assistance industry, other mining industry, other manufacturing, comprehensive utilization of waste resources and metal products, machinery and equipment repair industry because of the serious lack of data. The research objects of this paper contain a total of 36 secondary industries in China. According to the data availability of the important indicators involved in this study, the survey period was determined as the period from 1996 to 2013, and the data were from the *China Statistical Yearbook*, *China Industrial Statistical Yearbook*, *China Statistical Yearbook on Science and Technology* and *China Labor Statistical Yearbook* in corresponding years. The descriptions of variables involved in the empirical model in this paper are as follows (Table 1).

5 Analysis of Measured Results of China's Industrial Technological Progress Bias and Factor Price Distortion

In this section, we will confirm the outputs of the used empirical model. And then we will give their economic meaning.

5.1 China's Current Industrial Technological Progress Is Generally Biased Towards Capital

As the industry panel data is prone to be bothered by inter-group heteroskedasticity and intra-sequence sequence autocorrelation problems[7], we use the feasible generalized least squares (FGLS) method to estimate the production function. 1996 is set as the base period, and $Y0$, $K0$, $L0$ are industrial added value, capital stock and labor force in 1996. Respectively we put them into Eq. (4) and estimate with FGLS, and the four coefficients have all passed the significance test. The parameter estimation results are shown as follows:

$$\begin{cases} \alpha = 0.84 \\ a = \frac{\alpha(1-\alpha)(\sigma-1)}{2\sigma} = -0.09 \\ b = \alpha\gamma_K + (1-\alpha)\gamma_L = 0.11 \\ c = \frac{\alpha(1-\alpha)(\sigma-1)}{2\sigma}(\gamma_K - \gamma_L)^2 = -0.0008 \end{cases} \Rightarrow \begin{cases} \sigma = 0.44 \\ \gamma_K = 0.09 \\ \gamma_L = 0.19 \end{cases} \tag{10}$$

The results of, $\sigma, \gamma_K, \gamma_L$ are substituted into Eq. (4), and it can be achieved that the general technological progress bias index of China's industry is 0.13, which indicates that the technological progress of China's industry in the period from

---

[7]The modified heteroscedasticity Wald test and Wooldridge test were used to test the panel data. It was found that there were intergroup heteroskedasticity and first order autocorrelation.

Table 1 Definitions and descriptions of the variables

Variables	Symbol	Unit	Description
Total output value	Y	100 million yuan	Represented with the "industrial added value[a]", and adjusted to the price in 1996 according to the producer price index of industrial producers
Capital stock	K	100 million yuan	Estimated by perpetual inventory method[b] $K_{it} = K_{i(t-1)}(1 - \delta_{it}) + I_{it}$, and adjusted to the price in 1996 based on the fixed asset investment price index
Labor force	L	10 thousand people	Represented with "average number of employees"
Capital price	r	100 million yuan	r = capital income/capital stock, where capital income = industrial added value— total remuneration of laborers = Y − wL
Labor price	w	yuan	Represented with "average wage of employees", and adjusted to the price in 1996 according to the consumer price index
Technological innovation pattern	P	%	Represented with the ratio of the technology introduction funds of industry "i" in the year t to the internal expenditure of R&D
Factor endowment Structure	R	yuan	Represented with the relative scarcities of capital and labor, expressed with the per capita capital stock of industry "i" in year "t"
The proportion of state—owned economy	S	%	Represented with the proportion of the output value of state-owned and state-holding enterprises in the total output value of the industry
R&D intensity	F	%	Represented with the ratio of R&D internal expenditure to the total industrial output value of industry "i" in year "t − 1"[c]
R&D personnel	H	%	Represented with the ratio of R&D personnel to the total number of employees of industry "i" in year "t − 1"
Governmental R&D support	G	%	Represented with the ratio of governmental funds in the total R&D internal expenditure of industry "i" in year "t − 1"

Source Organized by the authors

[a]Since the statistical yearbooks after 2008 don't include statistical industrial added value any longer, this paper estimates industrial added value after 2008 on the basis of ratios of the industrial output value to industrial added value from 1996 to 2007

[b]Depreciation rate δ_t = depreciation in this year$_t$/original value of fixed assets$_{t-1}$ = (cumulative depreciation$_t$ − accumulated depreciation$_{t-1}$) /original value of fixed assets$_{t-1}$ = [(original value of fixed as se ts$_t$-net value of fixed as set s$_t$) − (original value of fixed assets$_{t-1}$-net value of fixed assets$_{t-1}$)] /original value of fixed assets$_{t-1}$; investment volume I_{it} is represent with newly increased fixed assets, newly increased fixed as set s$_t$ = original value of fixed as set s$_t$-original value of fixed assets$_{t-1}$; the capital stock of the base period is represented with the original value of fixed assets in 1986

[c]Taking into account the hysteretic nature of the effects of R&D activities on technological progress bias, the data of R&D intensity, R&D personnel and governmental R&D support are collected from the later year

1996 to 2013 was generally capital-oriented. Various industries tend to achieve technological progress by increasing capital input rather than labor input. Technological progress has made the marginal output ratio of capital to labor increases 13% annually.

From the point of the changing trend, the capital-biased feature of China's industrial technological progress has boosted at the turn of the century, but it has been eased after 2007 (as shown in Fig. 1). The reason is that between the period of the establishment of the PRC in 1949 and the implement of the reform and opening up policy in 1978, China's economy had long been underdeveloped and closed. The domestic capital was deficient, and the technology was far from being advanced. It was difficult for foreign capital and advanced technology to enter the country. Industrial technological progress depended more on abundant labor resources. As the production factor market was extremely closed, labor prices had long been low and stable. After the reform and opening up, especially after the opening of economic system after joining the WTO in 2001, the introduction of foreign trade and technology continued to grow. The technological progress pattern of China's industry has been increasingly affected by developed countries. Technological progress pattern, with technology introduction as its main body, has significant impact on the technological progress pattern bias of Chinese industry, especially in capital-intensive industries. However, after the global financial crisis in 2007, China's industries are facing fierce transition pressure. When the market is not optimistic, enterprises usually invest cautiously; therefore, capital bias tends becomes stable.

5.2 Factor Prices in China's Industries Is Seriously Negatively Distorted and Have not Been Mitigated yet

From Table 2, we can see that the estimated results of α and σ are 0.84 and 0.44, respectively. Both of them have passed the significant test. By substituting them into the expression of factor distortion degree, the price distortion degrees of capital, labor and the overall price distortion degree can be achieved. Figure 2 depicts the average value and changing trends of the factor price distortion of capital, labor force, and the two factors combined in capital-intensive and labor-intensive industries from 1996 to 2013. It can be seen that the values of distK, distL and dist

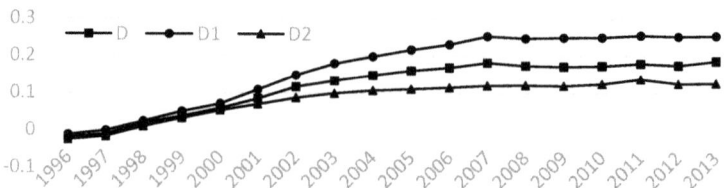

Fig. 1 The changing trend of China's industrial technological progress bias, 1996–2013. *Source* The author compiles the results according to the STATA software output

Table 2   The summary of estimated results of technological progress biases

Industry type		All the Industries	Capital—intensive industries	Labor—intensive industries
parameters being estimated	α	$0.84^{***}(13.08)$	$0.87^{***}(13.42)$	$0.60^{***}(2.51)$
	a	$-0.09^{*}(-2.13)$	$-0.12^{***}(-2.92)$	$-0.22^{*}(-1.8)$
	b	$0.11^{***}(7.85)$	$0.11^{***}(8.03)$	$0.14^{***}(5.27)$
	c	$-0.0008^{*}(-2.13)$	$-0.0008^{*}(-2.08)$	$-0.0006^{**}(-2.4)$
σ		0.44	0.31	0.35
γ_K		0.09	0.10	0.12
γ_L		0.19	0.18	0.17
D		0.13	0.18	0.10

Note Numbers in the brackets are the t values correspond to the estimated results of the parameters, *, **, and *** mean the results are significant at the test levels of 10, 5 and 1%, the same below
Source The author summarizes the results according to the STATA software output

in all years lie between 0.4 and 1, indicating that China's industrial capital and labor factor prices are negatively distorted, and the overall degree of distortion is negative. The prices of factors in all industries are generally underestimated.

In the case of changing trends, the negative distortions of capital prices were mitigated between 1999 and 2013, but the negative distortions of labor prices were deteriorating, leading to no significant improvement in overall distortion degrees. The degree of distortion in the price of production factors is the deviation to its relative marginal output ability. In recent years, due to the continuous upgrading of production technology and equipment as well as the extensive use of modern technology and management methods, the labor marginal output has been greatly improved. This leads to the growth of labor marginal output ability is much faster than that of wage rising. The results also show that in China's labor market, the labor suppliers are at disadvantaged status. They lack sufficient price negotiation ability, and the improvement of labor productivity cannot necessarily bring increase on the level of wage. In contrast, the pursuit of profits embedded in capital makes leads it to flow freely. So, its marketization level is also relatively high. Meanwhile, the negative distortion of labor price is more serious and has not been fundamentally reversed. It can be seen that, after the reform and opening up, the market-oriented reform of factors has played a positive role in capital market, but it has achieved little effects in labor market. The problem of factor price distortion of Chinese industries has not been fundamentally solved yet.

5.3   China's Capital-Intensive Industrial Technological Progress Is Strongly Biased Towards Capital

In its current technological progress pattern, China's industrial technological progress is generally biased towards capital. The technological progress in capital-intensive industries is more biased towards capital than that of labor-intensive industries[8]. As shown in Table 2, the technology-oriented bias indexes for capital-intensive and labor-intensive industries were 0.18 and 0.10. This is because the technological bias of capital-intensive industries is affected not only by the direct effects of factor price distortion as in labor-intensive industries. Capital-intensive industries have more sufficient capital, coupled with the relatively low cost of capital because of the negatively distorted capital price. These industries are stimulated to enlarge their capital use and tend to adopt the technological innovation pattern in which imports of machinery, equipment and mature technology are preferred. This pattern will strengthen the deepening of industry's capital. In other words, the indirect effects of factor price distortion on technological innovation bias through technological innovation are more pronounced in capital-intensive industries than those in labor-intensive industries. Capital-intensive industries, with their advantage of relatively abundant and low-price capital, have passively encouraged the advancement of technological innovative pattern. Capital has not been invested into the field of independent innovation. The result is that the materialized technological level in our capital-intensive industries is not lower than but even higher than that of their counterparts in some developed countries. However, the product innovation capability driven by technology and expertise is very low, which is the fundamental problem for capital-intensive industries during industrial transition development.

5.4 Factor Intensity of an Industry Determines the Price Distortion Degrees of Different Factors

Empirical studies show that the degree of labor price distortion in China's capital-intensive industries is greater than that in labor-intensive industries. The degree of capital price distortion in China's labor-intensive industries is greater than that in capital-intensive industries (see Fig. 2). The reason is that the factor endowment structure of each industry differs: according to the law of diminishing marginal output, the capital of labor-intensive industries is scarce, and the marginal output level of the unit capital is generally higher than that in capital-intensive industries where capital factor is abundant, resulting in greater gap between capital price and capital marginal output. While in capital-intensive industries, it is just the opposite. Higher per capita capital stock allows companies to have more adequate funds for personnel training, purchase of machinery and equipment, carrying out technology R&D research and so on. It is conducive to promoting its labor

---

[8]According to the measured results of factor price distortion, the distortion degrees in capital-intensive industries are lower than that in labor-intensive industries, but the gap is very narrow. So the direct effects on the technological progress bias in these two types of industries should not differ tremendously. The empirical results hereinafter validate this hypothesis.

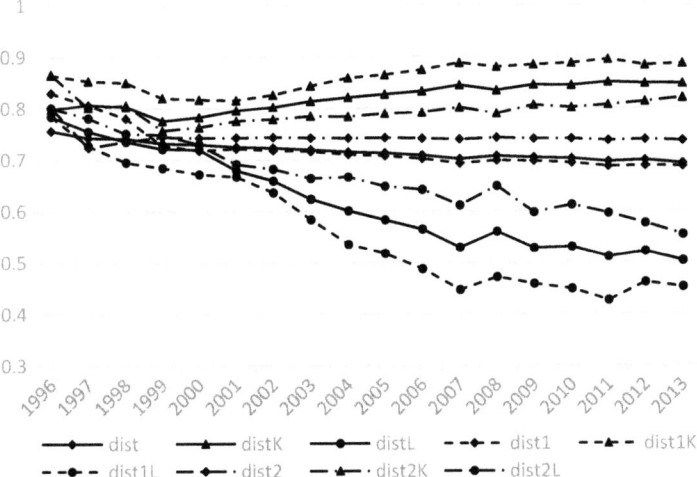

Fig. 2 The changing trends of the degrees of factor price distortion in China's industries from 1996 to 2013. *Source* The author compiles the results according to the STATA software output

productivity and labor marginal output. As the wage level is sticky, it is bound to aggravate the degree of labor price negative distortion. In addition, in recent years, the change of China's labor market structure and the increasingly strong protection for the rights and interests of migrant workers and grassroots workers have alleviated the degree of labor price distortion in labor-intensive industries where grass-roots labor force is abundant. It makes the labor price less distorted in labor-intensive industries than that of capital-intensive industries.

6   Empirical Analysis of Mediating Effect Model

In this section, we will show the estimated results of the metering model and. And then we will analyze their economic implications on this basis.

6.1   Estimate of the Benchmark Model

In order to investigate the effects of factor price distortion on the bias of technological progress, this paper first estimates the benchmark model of Eqs. (6–8). Through the F-test and Hausman test, we can see that the individual effect of the panel data is significant, and the error term and the explanatory variables are correlated. Therefore, fixed effect model is chosen to estimate the benchmark model

Table 3 Estimated results of benchmark model parameters

Model Variable	(6)		(7)		(8)	
dist	−0.36***	−0.29**	−1.98***	−2.30***	−0.32***	−0.26***
	(−5.48)	(−2.35)	(−3.61)	(−4.76)	(−10.75)	(−8.02)
P					0.0002	0.0006
					(0.68)	(1.35)
R		0.0070*				0.0081**
		(1.95)				(2.19)
S		0.03***				0.11**
		(6.10)				(2.23)
F				−9.57***		
				(−8.61)		
H				−2.63***		
				(−4.01)		
G				−0.33		
				(−1.15)		
Individual	Controlled	Controlled	Controlled	Controlled	Controlled	Controlled
Year	Controlled	Controlled	Controlled	Controlled	Controlled	Controlled
Number of observations	648	648	648	648	648	648
R^2	0.65	0.66	0.68	0.71	0.71	0.74
Hausman examination	189.52	201.45	225.71	263.15	267.94	288.42
	[0.0000]	[0.0000]	[0.0000]	[0.0000]	[0.0000]	[0.0000]

Note Numbers in the brackets are the t values correspond to the estimated results of the parameters, *, **, and *** mean the results are significant at the test levels of 10, 5 and 1%
Source The author summarizes the results according to the STATA software output

of (6–8). Table 3 shows the estimated results of the fixed effect model before and after the introduction of control variables[9]. It can be found through comparison that the coefficient estimation and the significance of the model core variables have not changed significantly before and after the introduction of the control variables. This indicates that the model set is very robust. In terms of coefficient significance, the regression coefficient estimations of the factor price distortion on the basis of technological progress and technological innovation pattern have all passed the significance test at the significance level of 1%, but in Eq. (8), the coefficient value of the technological innovation pattern is not significant, which may be caused by the endogenous problems of the variables.

---

[9]Due to space limitation, this paper omits the estimated results of the control variables which were introduced gradually, and only lists the estimated results of the model after introducing all the control variables. Readers interested in the estimated results in the process of estimations can contact the author.

The higher the proportion of capital in the factor endowment structure that equals to higher per capita capital within the industry, the more capital-biased its technological progress is, but the coefficiency is less than 1%. This indicates that the impacts of resource endowment on technological progress are extremely weak, which is consistent with the previous conclusions. The proportion of state-owned economy is proportional to the capital bias of technological progress, indicating that the higher the proportion of state-owned economy, the more capital-oriented its technological progress is. This is mainly because of the governmental support to state-owned economy in forms of financial subsidies, tax relief and other aspects of preferential treatment. In addition, banks and other financial institutions adopt discriminatory loan policies towards non-state economy. These lead to a significant cost advantage of using capital factors in state-owned economy and a technological advance biased more towards capital. In addition, the results from the sixth to eighth lines show that industries with limited R&D funds and lack of staff are more inclined to introduce foreign technologies, because independent R&D is a highly risky activity with huge investment and long cycle. It has extremely high demand for R&D funds and personnel. So, when the R&D funds and personnel are relatively insufficient, companies tend to give up independent R&D and invest their limited funds to technology introduction which is of low risk and quick returns. Government R&D subsidies did not have a significant impact on the choice of industrial technological innovation pattern. The results can be explained by the "crowding out" effect of governmental subsidies on enterprises' R&D investment. Enterprises having access to governmental R&D subsidies often reduce their own R&D investment, and thus the funds which have been used to do technological innovation has not increased actually, so that the impact of governmental subsidies on the technological innovation pattern of enterprises is invalid.

6.2   Endogenous Problems and the Regression of Instrumental Variable 2SLS

It is known that technological progress bias may be counteractive to factor price distortion through the relative price of the factor price, and it causes endogenous problems because of two-way causal relationship. Instrumental variables are introduced to solve this problem. First, Hausman endogeneity test has been applied to test the existence of endogeneity. The test results show that the value of "p" is 0, thus this result rejects the original hypothesis of "the exogenous explanatory variables"; therefore, it is necessary to introduce instrumental variables. Accordingly, we learn from the experience with factor price distortion regression model gained by previous scholars, and construct $\left(Dist_{it} - \overline{Dist_{it}}\right)^3$ as the instrumental variable of $Dist_{it}$ (Lewbel 1997; Chen and Wang 2013). The advantage of this instrumental variable is that it can satisfy the basic requirements associated with the endogenous explanatory variables and are not related to the residuals in the model simultaneously without increasing the number of model variables. First, the Sargan over-identification tests have been carried out for the models (1)–(3). All the corresponding "p" values were greater than 0.1, indicating that the residuals were not related to the explanatory variables. Second, from the estimated results of under-identification tests, all the values of p estimated by Anderson canon. corr. LM was 0.0000, indicating that the original hypothesis that "instrumental variable is unrecognizable" should be rejected. Finally, from the results of weak instrumental variable test, the statistics of the Cragg-Donald Wald F were much larger than 16.38, which is the critical value of the stock-Yogo test at the 10% level. So, the original hypothesis of the "weak instrumental variable" can be rejected. In summary, the instrumental variables constructed in this paper are reasonable.

Table 4 Estimated parameters results of model 2SLS

Model Variable	(6)		(7)		(8)	
dist	−0.16***	−0.18**	−1.98***	−1.98***	−0.13***	−0.16***
	(−6.59)	(−8.21)	(−3.61)	(−3.95)	(−8.74)	(−8.04)
P					0.0235	0.0210
					(3.16)	(1.82)
R			0.0085*			0.01**
			(11.75)			(2.42)
S			0.07***			0.12***
			(12.16)			(6.85)
F				−13.48**		
				(−2.33)		
H				−1.9***		
				(−1.99)		
G				−0.16		
				(−1.22)		
Individual	Controlled	Controlled	Controlled	Controlled	Controlled	Controlled
Year	Controlled	Controlled	Controlled	Controlled	Controlled	Controlled
Number of observations	648	648	648	648	648	648
Sargan statistic	0.38	0.41	0.65	0.58	0.29	0.34
	[0.5869]	[0.5856]	[0.7459]	[0.7603]	[0.6025]	[0.5748]
Anderson canon. corr. LM statistic	189.20 [0.0000]	196.15 [0.0000]	148.28 [0.0000]	155.69 [0.0000]	167.21 [0.0000]	159.83 [0.0000]
Cragg-Donald Wald F statistic	166.75 {16.38}	208.52 {16.38}	211.45 {16.38}	207.71 {16.38}	157.26 {16.38}	161.45 {16.38}

Note Numbers in the brackets are the t values correspond to the estimated results of the parameters, *, **, and *** mean the results are significant at the test levels of 10, 5 and 1%
Note { } are the corresponding Stock-Yogo test thresholds of Cragg-Donald Wald F statistics (at 10% significance level), the same below
Source The author summarizes the results according to the STATA software output

The economic implications of the estimated results of each parameter will be analyzed by the regression results of the instrumental variable 2SLS after the introduction of the control variables. As shown in Table 4, the regression coefficients of the factor price distortion to the technological progress bias and the technological innovation pattern are estimated to be -0.18 and -1.98 respectively. Both of them have passed significant test at the test level of 1%. This shows that the factor price distortion has significant impact on the direction of technological progress and technological innovation pattern. The closer the factor distortion coefficient is to 1, which equals lower level of distortion in factor prices, the less capital-biased the direction of technological progress is, and the less the technological innovation depends on external resources. The general effect of factor price distortion on industrial technological progress bias is $a_1 = -0.18$, which means when the negative distortion level of factor price increases by one unit. The bias of industrial technological progress towards capital increases by 0.18 unit. The direct effect of factor price distortion on industrial technological progress bias i $c_1 = -0.16$, and it has statistical significance at the test level of 1%. It means that when the actual price of the factor is lower than its marginal output by one unit, the bias of industrial technological progress towards capital increases by 0.16 unit. According to the above derivation, the indirect effect is $b_1 c_2 = -1.98 \times 0.0210 = -0.0416$. It means that when the factor price is distorted for one more unit, the bias of industrial technological progress towards capital works through technological innovation pattern increases by 0.16 unit. It can be seen that the indirect effects of factor price distortion on technological progress bias through technological innovation pattern do play an important role in the relationship between factor price distortion and technological progress bias.

6.3 Examination of the Mediating Effect

In order to fully demonstrate that the indirect effects of factor price distortion do exist and they work on industrial technological progress bias through technological innovation pattern, the significance of mediator variable "P" needs to be examined. This paper uses the method introduced by Wen and Ye (2014) to test the mediating effect. In the first step, we can see from Table 3 that: (1) The coefficient a1 of the Eq. (1) is significantly not 0, which indicates that the point should be made according to mediating effect. In the second step, with the information gained from Table 3, the coefficient b_1 of Eq. (2) and the coefficient c_2 of Eq. (3) are both significant at the test level of 1%, which means there are indirect effects between models. In the fourth step, the estimation of coefficient c_1 in Table 3 is significant at the test level of 1%, which means that there are indirect effects between models and direct effects. In the fifth step, by comparing the signs of $c_2 b_1$ and c_1, we can know that the signs of the two are the same. This indicates that the model has partial mediating effect, and the proportion of the mediating effect accounting for the total effect is $c_2 b_1 / a_1 = -0.0416/0.18 = 0.23$. To sum up, the technological innovation pattern does play an important mediating role between the negative price distortion and the technological progress bias. This mediating effect accounts for 23% of the total effects of the factor price negative distortion on the basis of technological progress.

6.4   Analysis of Estimated Results Based on Characteristics of Industries

Through the previous measure and estimation of the degrees of distortion in factor price and the biases of technological progress, we can find that there are some differences between factor price distortion and technological progress biases in industries with difficult factor intensities. In order to verify whether there is a causal relationship among these differences, the panel data of capital-intensive industries and labor-intensive industries are respectively regressed with mediating effect model containing instrumental variables, and their coefficients will be compared in this paper.

As shown in Table 5, the direct effects of factor price distortion on technological progress bias in capital-intensive industries and labor-intensive industries are almost identical and are consistent with the industry-wide estimations, which are −0.15 and −0.12 respectively. The effects of factor price distortions on technological innovation pattern of the two types of industries are −1.98 and −2.01 respectively. The results are consistent with the whole industry as well; however, the coefficients of the effects of technological innovation pattern on technological progress bias are quite different between the two types of industries. The coefficient value of capital-intensive industry is 0.0696 and that of labor-intensive industry is only 0.0136. Thus, the indirect effects of factor price distortion in the two types of industries on technological progress bias are −0.1378 and −0.0273 respectively. This difference leads to a significant gap between the effects of factor price distortion on technological progress bias in capital-intensive industries and labor-intensive industries. The effects of the former are significantly greater than that of the latter. It can be seen from Table 2 that when the factor distortion degree in capital-intensive industries increases by one unit, the bias of industrial technological progress towards capital increases by 0.13 unit. While when the factor distortion degree in labor-intensive industries increases by one unit, the bias of industrial technological progress towards capital increases by 0.10 unit. In summary, the direct effects of factor price distortion on technological progress bias will not differ in industries with different factor intensities, but the indirect effects of factor price distortion on technological progress bias are clearly influenced by industry capital intensity. Capital-intensive industries tend to prefer technology introduction, making its technological progress direction more biased towards the capital.

Table 5 Comparison of estimated results between capital-intensive industries and labor-intensive industries

Model Variable	Capital-intensive industries			Labor-intensive industries		
	(6)	(7)	(8)	(6)	(7)	(8)
dist	−0.16***	−1.98***	−0.15***	−0.13***	−2.01**	−0.12***
	(−5.16)	(−7.33)	(−11.27)	(−5.15)	(−2.24)	(−6.65)
P			0.07***			0.014**
			(2.79)			(2.11)
R	0.0076***		0.0090**	0.0080***		0.01**
	(3.66)		(2.13)	(10.76)		(2.22)
S	0.04**		0.03***	0.06***		0.05**
	(2.08)		(7.57)	(7.81)		(2.35)
F		−9.82***			−6.98**	
		(−3.48)			(−2.41)	
H		−1.97*			−2.34*	
		(−1.90)			(−1.85)	
G		−0.12			−0.15	
		(−1.14)			(−0.98)	
Individual	Controlled	Controlled	Controlled	Controlled	Controlled	Controlled
Year	Controlled	Controlled	Controlled	Controlled	Controlled	Controlled
Number of observations	324	324	324	324	324	324
Sargan statistics	0.50 [0.3691]	0.48 [0.3905]	0.36 [0.5996]	0.35 [0.5763]	0.69 [0.2991]	0.70 [0.2795]
Anderson canon. corr. LM statistic	306.28 [0.0000]	285.25 [0.0000]	256.32 [0.0000]	228.41 [0.0000]	201.48 [0.0000]	196.03 [0.0000]
Cragg-Donald Wald F statistic	148.12 {16.38}	156.23 {16.38}	314.25 {16.38}	296.57 {16.38}	259.68 {16.38}	248.17 {16.38}

Note Numbers in the brackets are the t values correspond to the estimated results of the parameters, *, **, and *** mean the results are significant at the test levels of 10, 5 and 1%
Source The author summarizes the results according to the STATA software output

7 Conclusion and Perspective

This paper can be summarized as follows through the mechanism analysis and empirical test of China's industrial factor price distortion degrees, technological progress bias indexes and the relationship between them:

First, the market-oriented reform of China's industrial factor prices requires long-term hard work. The empirical results of this paper show that the distortions of factor price in Chinese industries during recent years have not been effectively mitigated as expected, especially the deteriorated distortion of labor prices.

Through careful analysis it can be found that the emergence of this phenomenon has its profound institutional roots. With the establishment of the domestic capital market, the deepening market-oriented reform of interest rates and the influx of foreign capital, the marketization level of capital pricing is increasingly improving. While governmental interventions of capital prices are decreasing, so that the underestimation problem of capital price has been relieved to some extent. But in labor market, with the continuous improvement of technological level, China's industrial labor productivity is rising continuously as well. But because of the structure which mismatches the labor force supply and demand and the lack of trade unions, the vast number of workers are at disadvantages and cannot effectively protect their own rights and interests, leading to the widening gap between actual wage level and the marginal labor output, and the deterioration of labor price distortion. Thus, the market-oriented reform of the factors is not only to reduce the administrative intervention of the factor market. The government should also be committed to the adjustment of personnel training structure, the maintenance of market order, the protection of the legitimate rights and interests of workers, and the feasibility of technological progress and economic growth to benefit the public. Only in this way can the goals of boosting domestic demand and changing the mode of economic development can be achieved.

Second, the degree of factor price distortion and technological progress bias indexes are affected by industrial factor intensity. Based on the law of diminishing factor marginal returns and the differences of factor intensities in different industries, there are differences between the capital and labor marginal outputs of the capital-intensive industries and the labor-intensive industries. This results in greater distorting degree of labor price in capital-intensive industries than that in labor-intensive industries, which leads to the differences of factor price distortion degree in two kinds of industries. Thus, even if the direct effect coefficients of factor price distortion on technological progress bias in the two types of industries are almost equal, the actual sizes of the direct effect are significantly different. In terms of the differences of technological progress bias, since the capital-intensive industries are generally more abundant in capital than labor-intensive industries, there are significant differences in financial resources and initiatives to introduce technologies between the two types of industries. Therefore, the indirect effects of factor price distortion on technological progress bias in capital-intensive industries are markedly greater than that in labor-intensive industries. To sum up, the industrial factor intensity characteristics have significant impacts on factor price distortion degree and technological progress bias.

As concluded above, we can expect that guided by the innovation-driven development strategy, China's industrial technological progress pattern is expected to be upgraded to labor-biased pattern in the future. First of all, in the empirical part of this paper, it has been verified that the technological innovation pattern is playing an important mediating and conducting role when factor price distortion affects industrial technological progress bias. The implementation of innovation-driven development strategy and the deepening of the supply-side structural reform come down to change the previous factor-driven growth mode, to change the technological innovation pattern, to reduce the dependence on other countries, so as to achieve technological progress. Therefore, it is foreseeable that in the future, with the improvement of independent innovation capability, the distance between China's industrial technological level and international forefront technological level will be shortened. The introduction of foreign technology will shrink, and the technological innovation pattern will be changed fundamentally. The original conducting chain will be broken, the capital-biased progress made by technology introduction will be naturally weakened. Secondly, according to Li Yining's discussion on the "old and new demographic dividend" (2013), a country can adapt to its human resource advantages at all stages of economic development. When the country approaches or becomes a middle-income country, the advantage of cheap labor and the "old demographic dividend" will disappear, then the country should strive to create skilled labor force advantage by increasing personnel investment, expanding vocational and technical training, strengthening professional ethics education and so on, to cultivate a" new demographic dividend". It can be inferred that the technological progress bias generally follows the evolutionary trend of "non-skilled-labor-biased type → capital-biased type → skilled-labor-biased type". Then, with the improvement of independent innovation ability and the formation of "new population dividend", Chinese direction of technological progress in industry is expected to be upgraded to skilled-labor-biased technological progress under the condition that the labor supply structure is continuously optimize, and the factor market reform continues to be deepened. Thus, it contributes to the realization of inclusive economic development in line with its own factor endowment structure.

This paper only explores the one-way influence of factor price distortion on the bias of industrial technological progress, and does not analyze the counteraction of factor price distortion on industrial technological progress. In addition, the impact of factor price distortion on industrial technological progress can be seen not only in the technological progress bias at the industry level, it can also be found in several aspects concerned with innovation activities and performances at micro-level, including its effects on enterprises R&D expenditure, technological innovation efficiency and so on, which could be further explored in future researches.

References

Acemoglu, D (2002). "Directed Technical Change". The Review of Economic Studies, 69(4): 781–809.
Acemoglu, D. and Zilibotti (2001). "Productivity Differences". Quarterly Journal of Economics, (116):563–606.
Barros, C.P. and Weber, W.L (2009). "Productivity Growth and Biased Technological Change in UK Airports". Transportation Research Part E Logistics & Transportation Review, 45(4): 642–653.
Busom, I (2000). "An empirical evaluation of the effects of R&D subsidies". Economics of innovation and new technology, 9(2):111–148.

Chen, B. and Lin, Y (2012). "Financial Restraint, Industrial Structure and Income Distribution". The Journal of World Economy, (1):3–23.

Chen, H., and Wang, Y (2015). "Research on the Revolution Characteristics and Differences of Technical Progress in China's Manufacturing Industry". Studies in Science of Science, 33 (6):859–867.

Chen, Y., and Wang, E (2013). "Factor Market Distortion, Dual Inhibition and Total Factor Productivity of Producer Services Industry of China: An Empirical Research Based on Mediating Effect Model". Nankai Economic Studies, (5):71–82.

Cooper, C (1994). "Relevance of innovation studies to developing countries". Technology and Innovation in the International Economy, Edward Elgar, 1–40.

Cruz E. Structural Change and Non-Constant Biased Technical Change[C]// Universitat de Barcelona, Facultat d'Economia i Empresa, UB Economics, 2015.

Dai, T. and Xu, X (2010). "The Direction of China's Technological Progress". The Journal of World Economy, (11):54–70.

David, P.A. and Klundert, T (1965). "Biased Efficiency Growth and Capital-Labor Substitution in the U.S. 1899–1960". The American Economic Review, (55):357–394.

Deng, M (2014). "Age Structure of Population and China's Provincial Technical Progress". Economic Research Journal, (3):130–143.

Färe Grifell-Tatje, E. and Grosskopf, S (1997). "Biased Technical Change and Malmquist Productivity Index". The Scandinavian Journal of Economics, 99(1):199–127.

Gancia, G. and Zilibotti (2009). "Technological Change and the Wealth of Nation". Annual Review of Economics, (1).

Hicks, J. R (1932). Marginal Productivity and the Principle of Variation. Economica, (35):79–88.

Huang, P. and Zhang, Y (2014). "The Effect of Factor Price Distortion on Firms R&D Activities in China: A Probit-Model Examination of Film-Level Data". Shanghai Journal of Economics, (7):31–41.

Kim, C.S and Inkpen, A.C (2005). "Cross-border R&D alliances, absorptive capacity and technology learning". Journal of International Management, 11(3):313–329.

Khaled M. Estimating Bias of Technical Progress with a Small Data Set[J]. Working Paper, 2017.

Klump, R., McAdam, P. and Willman, A (2007). "Factor substitution and factor augmenting technical progress in the United States: A normalized supply side system approach". The Review of Economics and Statistics, 89(1):183–192.

Klump, R., McAdam, P. and Willman, A (2008). "Unwrapping some euro area growth puzzles: Factor substitution, productivity and unemployment". Journal of Macroeconomics, 30(2):645–666.

León-Ledesma, M.A., McAdam, P and Willman, A (2010). "Identifying the Elasticity of Substitution with Biased Technical Change". The American Economic Review, 100(4):1330–1357.

Lewbel, A (1997). "Constructing Instruments for Regressions with Measurement Error when No Additional Data are Available, with an Application to Patents and R&D". Econometrica: Journal of the Econometric Society, (65):1201–1213.

Li, Y (2014). "Does Factor Price Distortion Barrage China's Independent Innovation?". World Economy Study, (1):10–15.

Lin, Y., Cai, F. and Li, Z (1999). "Competitive Advantage and Development Strategy – the Reinterpretation of the Successes of Japan and 'Four Asian Small Dragons'". Social Sciences in China. 5(14):4–20.

Lin, Y. and Su, J (2012). New Structural Economics: A Framework for Rethinking, Development and Policy, Beijing, Peking University Press.

Lin, Y. and Zhang, P (2006). "Appropriate Technology, Technological Selection and Economic Growth in Developing Countries". China Economic Quarterly, 3(985):985–1006.

Lu, X (2013). "The Identification of Factor-biased Technical Change". The Journal of Quantitative & Technical Economics, (8):20–34.

Shi, B. and Xian, G (2012). "Factor Price Distortion and Export Behavior of China's Industry Firms". China Industrial Economics, (2):47–56.

Shi, J. and Zhao, Z (2007). "Restrictions of Ownership and Factors Price Distortion: An Empirical Study Using the Industrial Data in China". Statistical Research, 24(6): 42–47.

Wang, B., and Qi, S (2015). "Does the Bias of China's Industrial Technical Change Energy-saving". China Population, Resources and Environment, 25(7):24–31.

Wang, J. and Hu, Y (2015). "Measure and Analysis of Skill-based Technological Progress in China's Manufacturing Industry". The Journal of Quantitative & Technical Economics, (1):82–96.

Wen, Z. and Ye, B (2014). "Analyses of Mediating Effects: The Development of Methods and Models". Advances in Psychological Science, 22(5):731–745.

Yang, X (2004). "Backward Disadvantage". New Finance and Economics, (8): 120–122.

Yang, Y., Wei, J. and Luo, L (2015). "Who is Using Governmental Subsidies to Innovate? –The Joint Regulatory Effect of Ownership and Factor Market Distortions". Management World, (1):75–98.

Zhang, J., Zhou, X. and Li, Y (2011). "Does Factor Market Distortion Barrage Chinese Firms' R&D?". Economic Research Journal, (8):78–91.

Zhang, L., Li, J. and Xu, X (2012). "International Trade, Biased Technology Progress and Factor Income Distribution". Economic Research Journal, 11(1):409–428.

Zheng, Z. and Liu, Y (2013). "The Empirical Analysis of the R&D Expenditure Effect of Factor Price Distortion –Based on Large and Medium-sized Industrial Enterprises Panel Data". Social Scientist, (7):63–66.

Chapter 13
Environmental Innovation and Green Transformation of Economic Growth Pattern: Evidence from China

Xie Rong-hui

1 Introduction

Since the reform and opening-up policy implemented at the end of 1970s, China has achieved remarkable economic growth rates. However, the traditional comparative advantages, such as the Demographic Dividend, are disappearing, which causes a slowdown of Chinese economy. Especially after the global financial crisis breaking out in 2008, many internal structural flaws in the economic growth are exposed. On one hand, China only embedded mostly on the low-end sector of the global value chain, and locked at the lower process level, and lower value added activities. On the other hand, China's growth model has turned out to be unsustainable and extensive, which favors exports and investment over domestic consumption, and the economic growth over the environment quality. As a result, such growth pattern leads to great amount of energy consumption and pollution emissions. Undoubtedly, Chinese economy is stepping to a critical stage of structural transforming and upgrading.

Some scholars and policy makers point out that innovation and technological progress are the essential impetus of economic transformation (Tong 2013; Peng et al. 2014). However, in the book, *The Limits to Growth* published in 1972, the Club of Rome claims that many traditional technologies innovated after the Industrial Revolution accelerate the damage to the environment. Therefore, we mainly focus on the environmental technologies. Moreover, we will employ a province-level panel dataset for the 2000–2012 period to find out empirical evidence on the relationship between environmental innovations and the green transformation of Chinese economy, and compare the promoting effect driven by environmental innovations with traditional innovations.

X. Rong-hui (✉)
School of Economics & Management, Nanjing University of Science & Technology, Nanjing, China
e-mail: sparking_rh@126.com

© Springer Nature Singapore Pte Ltd. 2018
R. Pang et al. (eds.), *Energy, Environment and Transitional Green Growth in China*, https://doi.org/10.1007/978-981-10-7919-1_13

277

The remainder of this paper is structured as follows. Section 2 reviews the relevant literature. Section 3 describes the specifications of empirical model and variables. Section 4 presents our empirical results and robustness analysis. The last section is our conclusions.

2 Literature Review

Since the phrase of green transformation was first proposed by OECD in one of their working papers (Harrison 1995), it has stimulated a large body of academic research. A large body of literature gives a definition as the transformation from the extensive growth model depended heavily on material inputs to the intensive model with dependence on innovation and technological progress, from the heavy dependence on emissions and environmental damage to green development, from the unsustainable pattern to a sustainable pattern (Research Group of Institute of Industrial Economics CASS 2011; Chen and Golley 2014). Peng and Li (2015) claim that the core connotation of green transformation focuses on the process from the high carbon and high pollution emissions to cleaner production and pollution abatement. Based on those studies, we can conclude that the common point about the green transformation emphasizes the "win-win" situation between economic growth and the environmental quality. But how can we achieve this "win-win" situation? Lin (2004) points out that the transformation of economic growth model has been mainly driven by innovation and technological progress. This view of point has been supported widely (Liu 2006; Lin and Zhang 2009; He and Zhang 2015).

Cai and Guo (1996), however, claim that with regard to environment, technological innovation can be divided into two different types: one is the environmentally-friendly type, while the other is the environmentally-harmful type. By reading the environment history since the Industrial Revolution, we can conclude that the traditional technological innovation is the main cause of environmental pollution to a great extent, and creates a "Gray" Civilization (Clapp 1994). On the other word, the traditional technological innovation is mainly environmentally harmful. The major objectives of traditional innovation are to expand the scale of production, to enhance productivity and eventually gain extra profit, but fail to consider the impact on environment. As a result, tradition technological progress leads to large amount of consumption of fossil energy and serious environmental damage. Nowadays, more and more policy makers and scholars realize that it is time to create a "Green" Civilization instead of the "Gray" one. Further, it is the environmental innovation that plays the critical role, rather than the traditional innovation. Braun and Wield (1994) propose the concept of "clean technology" for the first time[1]. OECD (2009) provides a standardized statement about the definition of green innovation as "the implementation of a new or significantly improved product (good or service), or process, a new marketing method, or a new organizational method in business practices, workplace organization or external relations that results in a reduction of environmental impact, no matter whether that effect is intended or not". We can summarize two unique features of green innovation: fewer adverse effects on the environment and more efficient use of resources (Hojnik and Ruzzier 2015). However, environmental effect is not the primary reason for green innovation, but to potentially affect the entire trajectory and paradigm of corporate innovation (Aghion et al. 2015; Amore and Bennedsen 2016), then further the transformation of economic growth pattern (Lan and Han 2012).

However, as we summarize from the existing literature that a majority of previous studies emphasize the environmental goals of green innovation, only several focus on its effect on the transformation of economic growth pattern. Furthermore, these several studies mainly adopt methodology of descriptive statistical analysis (Research Group of Institute of Industrial Economics CASS 2011; Guo et al. 2013), while lack of empirical evidence. Finally, most previous literature focuses on highly developed economies, but lacks of research on developing countries, such as China. But in practice, China is experiencing its critical stage of economic transformation and upgrading, as well as suffering serious environmental damages. Therefore, it is of fundamental importance to analyze how environmental innovation affects economic green transformation. Our study attempts to fill these gaps.

3 Empirical Model and Variables

3.1 Specifications of Empirical Model

We begin our empirical analysis by defining an equation which relates an indicator of green transformation of economic growth pattern to an indicator of environmental innovation, and to an indicator of traditional innovation. The empirical model is specified as following dynamic panel data model:

$$GT_{i,t} = \alpha_0 + \alpha_1 GT_{i,t-1} + \alpha_2 ERD_{i,t} + \alpha_3 NERD_{i,t} + \alpha_4 Z_{i,t} + \varepsilon_{i,t} \tag{1}$$

where $GT_{i,t}$ is the dependent variable, an indicator of green transformation for industry i in period t. $GT_{i,t-1}$ is the lagged dependent variable as one of independent variables. $ERD_{i,t}$ indicates the environmental R&D, while $NERD_{i,t}$ indicates the traditional R&D. $Z_{i,t}$ denotes a vector of control variables. The subscripts i and t denote industry and year. $\varepsilon_{i,t}$ is the disturbance term.

---

[1]The terms of eco-innovation, green innovation, and environmental innovation in this paper are used interchangeably, while terms of clean technology, green technology and environmental technology are interchangeable as well.

When there exists an endogenous problem, the OLS estimate or the fixed effects estimate will yield biased and inefficient estimators. In order to overcome potential endogeneity, we adopt the system GMM approach initiated by Arellano and Bover (1995) and fully developed by Blundell and Bond (1998). The system GMM can control the issue of endogeneity by using lagged levels of the endogenous variables as instruments. Normally, the valid instruments for endogenous variables are two lags and above (Roodman 2009).

In order to obtain robust results, two standard statistical tests must be proceeded after system GMM estimation. One is the Arellano-Bond (AR) test. This test checks whether there is serial autocorrelation in the residuals of the specification which leads to inconsistent estimators. In order for estimators to be consistent, the first order autocorrelation of the residuals (AR(1) test) needs to be rejected; and the second order autocorrelation (AR(2) test) needs to be accepted (Iwamoto and Nabeshima 2012). The other is the Sargan test of overidentification to check out if the applied instruments are jointly valid.

3.2   Variables and Data Sources

3.2.1   The Indicator of Green Transformation of Economic Growth Pattern

The essence of economic transformation is to increase the contribution of productivity growth to economic growth (Wu 2008; Chen 2012; Li et al. 2013). In order to take the environmental impact into account, we employ the environmental TFP to construct the indicator of green transformation. Specifically, we regard the contribution of environmental TFP to total industrial output value (TIV) growth calculated by dividing the environmental TFP growth rate by the TIV growth rate as the indicator of green transformation (GT). Moreover, this paper uses a slacks-based measure (SBM) and Luenberger Productivity Index, accounting for energy consumption and undesirable outputs, to evaluate the industrial environmental productivity growth rates of China's 30 provinces. There includes two outputs corresponding to a desirable output (given by total industrial output value) and an undesirable output (given by CO_2 emissions), and three inputs corresponding to capital, labor and energy consumption.[2]

3.2.2   Environmental R&D and Traditional R&D

Owing to limitation of data, we employ the method developed by Hamamoto (2006) to calculate the values of environmental R&D and traditional R&D. We first

---

[2]Details for calculating techniques of environmental TFP growth rates are provided in Xie et al. (2017).

develop the following log-log form fixed effects panel data model (results of estimation see Appendix A.) and the estimated coefficient can be interpreted as the elasticity with respect to R&D:

$$\ln RD_{i,t} = \beta_1 \ln REG_{i,t-1} + \beta_2 H_{i,t-1} + v_i + t + \varepsilon_{i,t} \tag{2}$$

where $RD_{i,t}$ denotes the total R&D expenditure. $REG_{i,t-1}$ is a proxy for regulatory stringency. REG is constructed by the data of emissions of waste water, sulfur dioxide, smoke and dust, and solid waste to measure the level of pollution abatement [details see Yuan and Xie (2014)]. When an environmental regulation is implemented, firms need time to reset the strategies and to carry out R&D activities. Therefore, following Jaffe and Palmer (1997), we allow one-year lag in the variable of regulation stringency. $H_{i,t-1}$ indicates a vector of control variables, including a scaling variable (*SCALE*), foreign direct investment (FDI), an indicator of human capital (HC), export intensity (EXP), and an indicator of marketization level (*MARKET*). All of the control variables are lagged one year to avoid two-way causation with R&D expenditures (Rubashkina et al. 2015). v_i captures unobservable industry characteristics, t is a trend variable, and $\varepsilon_{i,t}$ is a residual error term.

The coefficient of $REG_{i,t-1}$ represents the elasticity of R&D expenditures with respect to environmental regulation. Following Hamamoto (2006) we regard the increased R&D induced by environmental regulation as the environmental R&D, while the remainder as the traditional R&D. Therefore, the environmental R&D (*ERD_{i,t}*) and the traditional R&D (*NERD_{i,t}*) can be calculated by Eqs. (3) and (4).[3]

$$ERD_{i,t} = \hat{\beta}_1 \times \left[\frac{\Delta REG_{i(t,t-1)}}{REG_{i,t-1}} \right] \times RD_{i,t} \tag{3}$$

$$NERD_{i,t} = RD_{i,t} - ERD_{i,t} \tag{4}$$

3.2.3 Control Variables

Three control variables of interest for our investigation are included. Firstly, the structure of factor endowments (CAL) is one of the most essential factors impacting economic transformation. We use the capital-labor ratio as a proxy. Secondly, an indicator of marketization level (*MARKET*) is defined by the output shares of non-state-owned enterprises. Finally, an indicator of human capital (*HC*) is included, using education level of employees as a proxy.

Table 1 summarizes the descriptive statistics of key variables. The province-level panel data during the period 2000–2012 is obtained from the database of the National Bureau of Statistics of China.

---

[3]When the values of $ERD_{i,t}$ appear to be negative, they will be treated as zero to avoid the case that predicted values of traditional R&D exceed the actual values of total R&D expenditures.

Table 1 Descriptive statistics of key variables

Variable	Obs	Mean	S.D.	Minimum	Maximum
GT	390	0.1791	0.4949	−5.1246	3.9024
RD	390	134.3185	203.6111	0.8306	1287.862
REG	390	0.6395	0.3705	0.0522	2.2882
CAL	390	19.4338	11.5112	6.1925	82.2344
MARKET	390	0.4973	0.2140	0.0615	0.8949
HC	390	8.7417	1.1843	6.1120	13.31

4 Empirical Results and Discussions

4.1 Effect on the Green Transformation of Economic Growth Pattern

In this section, we employ the system GMM approach to examine the relationship between environmental innovation and the green transformation of economic growth pattern, and further to make comparative analysis with traditional innovation. The results of two statistical tests for the system GMM estimation are reported in Table 2. The AR test rejects the null hypothesis of the first order autocorrelation with the p-value of the AR(1) test being 0.0620, but accepts the null hypothesis of the second order autocorrelation with the p-value of the AR(2) test being 0.1530. Meanwhile, the Sargan test of over identification shows the applied instruments are jointly valid as the null hypothesis is not rejected with the p-value being 1.0000. It implies that the estimations in Table 2 are robust.

Results in Table 2 show that the coefficient of $ERD_{i,t}$ equals to 0.0162 and highly significant at the 1% level, which confirms that $ERD_{i,t}$ appears to be

Table 2 Results of effects of environmental innovation on the green transformation

Variables	System GMM model
$GT_{i,t-1}$	$-0.3202^{***}(0.0182)$
$ERD_{i,t}$	$0.0162^{***}(0.0014)$
$NERD_{i,t}$	$-0.0003^{**}(0.0001)$
$CAL_{i,t}$	$-0.0049^{***}(0.0007)$
$HC_{i,t}$	$0.1314^{***}(0.0161)$
$MARKET_{i,t}$	$-0.0438(0.1234)$
Constant	$-0.7871^{***}(0.2047)$
AR(1) test	$-1.8662^{*}(p = 0.0620)$
AR(2) test	$-1.4292(p = 0.1530)$
Sargan test	$22.6793(p = 1.0000)$
Obs	359

Notes to the table (a) Figures in parentheses are standard error. (b) ***, **, * indicate that the levels of significance are 1%, 5% and 10%, respectively

positively related to $GT_{i,t}$. However, traditional innovation has a negative effect on green transformation with coefficient being −0.0003 and significant at the 5% level. The empirical results provide evidence that environmental innovation is an essential impetus to promote economic green transformation, but traditional innovation impedes the process of green transformation. It is mainly because the traditional innovation mainly aims at enhancing the efficiency and productivity, and expanding the scale of production, however, is not able to take the environmental objectives into account. The traditional technological progress leads to a rapid increase in energy consumption, and consequently a sharp increase in pollutant emissions.

Crucially, environmental technologies include not only the end-of-pipe technologies, but also cleaner production technologies, new energy technologies and recycling technologies. Generally, there are two ways for environmental innovation to affect firms to upgrade and go "green". First of all, firms can remain their original types and structures of products, while only upgrade their traditional and pollution-intensive technologies to environmental technologies. By this means, firms will achieve cleaner production and enhanced productivity simultaneously. Secondly, firms could implement environmental innovation and switch to a new line, even a new area of product, and eventually upgrade to high value-added sectors of the global value chain. The most typical example is the new-energy automobile industry. On the foundation of the original technologies and patents, firms of traditional automobile industry could research and develop environmental and new-energy techniques, innovate and improve their manufacturing process, and finally embed the product chains or industry chains of the new-energy automobile. Therefore, the traditional industries could effectively transform to the clean and high-end field.

In addition, the structure of factor endowments (*CAL*) is negatively related to green transformation with the coefficient of −0.0049. Zhang (2002) claims that China's lasting industrialization programs initiated on the outset of reform lead to a rising of capital-output ratio and excess production capacity. The over-investment and capital deepening further hamper the productivity and hinder the dynamic transformation of an economy (Young 1994; Kim and Lau 1994). The coefficient of human capital (*HC*) is 0.1314 and highly significant at the 1% level, implying that it is necessary to increase investments in human capital in order to promote China's economic green transformation. While the coefficient of the marketization level (MARKET) is far from significant, indicating that China's current level of marketization has little effect on economic green transformation.

4.2 Robustness Analysis

In order to examine if the estimated results above are robust, we further make a robustness test for the empirical model of Eq. (1). As the *China Environment Year Book* reports the data of environmental scientific research project funds (*ENVRD$_{i,t}$*),

Table 3 Results of the robustness analysis

Variables	System GMM model
$GT_{i,t-1}$	$-0.3679^{***}(0.0172)$
$ENVRD_{i,t}$	$0.0001^{***}(3.20*10^{-6})$
$CAL_{i,t}$	$-0.0174^{***}(0.0007)$
$HC_{i,t}$	$0.1549^{***}(0.0046)$
$MARKET_{i,t}$	$-0.6343^{***}(0.0396)$
Constant	$-0.5458^{***}(0.0563)$
AR(1) test	$-1.9417^{*}(p = 0.0522)$
AR(2) test	$-1.1079(p = 0.2679)$
Sargan test	Chi2(57) = 26.2967(p = 0.9998)
Obs	300

Notes to the table (a) Figures in parentheses are standard error. (b) ***, **, * indicate that the levels of significance are 1%, 5% and 10%, respectively

we will choose this indicator to substitute the variable of $ERD_{i,t}$ in Eq. (1), and further re-examine the relationship between $ENVRD_{i,t}$ and $GT_{i,t}$ by employing the system GMM approach. The results are presented in Table 3.

First of all, the results in Table 3 are robust as they meet two standard conditions for the system GMM estimation. Moreover, the coefficient of $ENVRD_{i,t}$ is positive (0.0001) and highly significant at the 1% level, which is consistent with the results in Table 2. Therefore, our estimated results in Table 2 have been confirmed to be robust.

5 Conclusions

As the economic growth rate of China is slowing down after 2008, many serious issues of the economy have been exposed gradually. Most obviously, the growth model has turned out to be unsustainable and extensive, and lead to increasingly severe environmental pollution. Therefore, China's economy is urgent to transform and upgrade to a more advanced, cleaner growth pattern. The State Council of China has issued the "China manufacturing 2025" strategy in 2016. This strategy sets the "innovation driven" and "green development" as the basic principles of China's manufacturing in the future for the first time. Therefore, it is of great importance to focus on environmental innovation and its effect on the green transformation of China's economic growth pattern. Based on this background, this paper chooses the perspective of environmental innovation, and then examines the relationship between environmental innovation and green transformation of Chinese economic growth pattern. By employing a panel dataset of China's 30 provinces during 2000–2012 and the system GMM approach, we draw some interesting conclusions. The environmental innovation has a positive effect on economic green transformation, but traditional innovation impedes the process of green transformation. It is because environmental innovation includes not only innovation of end-of-pipe techniques, but also of cleaner production, new-energy and recycling techniques. Therefore, it is able to achieve cleaner production and enhanced productivity at the same time. However, traditional innovation mainly aims at expanding the scale of production, while fails to consider the environmental impact.

What calls for special attention is that environmental innovation has significant positive externality which would leads to market failure (Li 2005). If there lacks of exogenous rigid constrains, firms who pursue the maximization of profit will not engage in environmental R&D activities initiatively. Therefore, it is necessary for Chinese government to make reasonable and stringent environmental policies to regulate firms' behavior, as well as to incentive them innovate environmental technologies. Moreover, China should establish a system of rewards and punishments to stimulate environmental innovation and offer certain support for the leading firms who have advantages in environmental R&D activities.

Acknowledgements I would like to thank all professors working for the 2016 Asia-Pacific Productivity Conference, and the editors and reviewers. This work is funded by the Major Project of National Social Science Fund of China (15ZDA053) and the Project of Natural Science Fund of Jiangsu Province (BK20171422).

Appendix A. The Estimated Results of Eq. (2)

See Table 4.

Table 4 The estimated results of Eq. (2)

Variables	Fixed-effect panel data model
$lnREG_{i,t-1}$	$0.2310^{***}(3.14)$
$lnSCALE_{i,t-1}$	$1.5594^{***}(6.59)$
$lnHC_{i,t-1}$	$5.1965^{***}(12.02)$
$lnEXP_{i,t-1}$	$0.3559^{***}(4.99)$
$lnFDI_{i,t-1}$	$-0.3806^{***}(-5.35)$
$lnMARKET_{i,t-1}$	$0.9726^{***}(10.00)$
Constant	$-4.3008^{***}(-4.22)$
Time fixed-effect test	Fixed
Individual fixed-effect test	Random
Hausman test	Chi-Sq. = 2.28(P = 0.9429)
Adjusted R^2	0.7831
F-statistics	1217.07^{***}

Notes to the table (a) Figures in parentheses are t-values. (b) ***, **, * indicate that the levels of significance are 1%, 5% and 10%, respectively

References

Aghion P., Dechezlepretre A., Hemous D., Martin R., Van Reenen J. Carbon taxes, path dependency and directed technical change: Evidence from the auto industry [J]. Journal of Political Economy, 2015, 124(1): 1–51.

Amore M. D., Bennedsen M. Corporate governance and green innovation [J]. Journal of Environmental Economics & Management, 2016(75):54–72.

Arellano M., Bover O. Another look at the instrumental variable estimation of error-components models [J]. Journal of Econometrics, 1995, 68(1): 29–51.

Blundell R., Bond S. Initial conditions and moment restrictions in dynamic panel data model [J]. Journal of Econometrics, 1998, 87(1): 115–143.

Braun E, Wield D. Regulation as a means for the social-control of technology [J]. Technology Analysis & Strategic Management, 1994, 6(3): 259–272.

Cai Ning, Guo Bing. From the Environmental resource scarcity to sustainable development: The changes and development of the theory of western environmental economics [J]. Economic Science, 1996(6): 59–66.

Chen Shiyi. Evaluation of Low Carbon Transformation Process for Chinese Provinces [J]. Economic Research Journal, 2012(8): 32–44.

Chen, S., Golley, J., 2014. 'green' productivity growth in China's industrial economy. Energy Econ. 44, 89–98.

Clapp B. W. An environmental history of Britain since the Industrial Revolution [M]. New York: Longman, 1994.

Guo Pibin, Zhou Xijun, Li Dan, Wang Ting. Predicament and its solution in the transformation of coal resource based economy: A perspective of energy technology innovation [J]. China Soft Science, 2013(7):39–46.

Hamamoto M. Environmental regulation and the productivity of Japanese manufacturing industries [J]. Resource and Energy Economics, 2006, 28(4): 299–312.

Harrison D. Climate Change: Economic Instruments and Income Distribution [R]. Organisation for Economic Co-operation and Development (OECD), Paris, 1995.

He Xiaogang, Zhang Ning. The motivation of transformation of economic growth in China: Technology, efficiency or factor costs? [J]. The Journal of World Economy, 2015(1): 25–52.

Hojnik J, Ruzzier M. What drives eco-innovation? A review of an emerging literature [J]. Environmental Innovation and Societal Transitions, 2015(19): 31–41.

Iwamoto M., Nabeshima K. Can FDI promote export diversification and sophistication of host countries? Dynamic panel system GMM analysis [R]. IDE Discussion Paper No. 347, 2012.

Jaffe A.B., Palmer K. Environmental regulation and innovation: a panel data study [J]. Review of Economics and Statistics, 1997, 79 (4): 610–619.

Kim J., Lau L. J. The sources of growth of the East Asian newly industrialized countries [J]. Journal of the Japanese and International Economies, 1994, 8(3): 235–271.

Lan Qingxin, Han Jing. Research on the green transformation strategy of Chines industry [J]. Reform of Economic System, 2012, (1):24–28.

Li Ping. Study on the subject system of green technology innovation [J]. Studies in Science and Science, 2005, 23(3): 414–417.

Li Bin, Peng Xing, OuYang Mingke. Environmental Regulation,Green Total Factor Productivity and the Transformation of China's Industrial Development Mode [J]. China Industrial Economics, 2013(04): 56–68.

Lin Yong, Zhang Zongyi. The influential factors & periodic characteristics of technical progress during the economic transition period of China [J]. The Journal of Quantitative & Technical Economics, 2009(7): 73–85.

Lin Justin Yifu, 2004, Is China's growth real and sustainable? [J]. Asian Perspective, 28(3): 14–29.

Liu Wei. Historical change of the reform and fundamental transition of the economic growth mode of China [J]. Economic Research Journal, 2006(1): 4–10.

OECD. Sustainable manufacturing and eco-innovation: Towards a green economy [R]. Policy Brief Working Paper, 2009.

Peng Yizhong, Tong Jian, Wu Min. What exactly promotes the transformation of China's economic growth pattern? [J] The Journal of Quantitative & Technical Economics, 2014(6): 20–35.

Peng Xi, Li Bin. Trade Openness, FDI and Green Transformation of Chinese Industry: An Empirical Analysis Based on Dynamic Threshold Model Using Panel Data [J]. Journal of International Trade, 2015(1): 166–176.

Research Group of Institute of Industrial Economics CASS. A Study on the Green Transformation of Chinese Industry [J]. China Industrial Economics, 2011(4): 5–14.

Roodman D. How to do xtabond2: An introduction to difference and system GMM in stata [J]. Stata Journal, 2009, 9(1): 86–136.

Rubashkina Y., Galeotti M., Verdolini E. Environmental regulation and competitiveness: empirical evidence on the Porter Hypothesis from European manufacturing sectors [J]. Energy Policy, 2015(83): 288–300.

Tong Yilun. Technical progress: A process of social transformation in Chinese transition period [J]. South China Journal of Economics, 2013(9): 1–7.

Wu Y. R. The role of productivity in China's growth: New estimates [J]. China Economic Quarterly, 2008, 7(3): 827–842.

Xie R. H., Yuan Y. J., Huang J. J. Different types of environmental regulations and heterogeneous influence on "green" productivity: Evidence from China [J]. Ecological Economics, 2017(132): 104–112.

Young A. Lessons from the East Asian NICs: A contrarian view [R]. NBER Working paper No. 4482, 1994.

Yuan Yijun, Xie Ronghui. Research on the Effect of Environmental Regulation to Industrial Restructuring—Empirical Test Based on Provincial Panel-Data of China [J]. China Industrial Economics, 2014(08): 57–69.

Zhang Jun. Capital formation, industrialization and economic growth: Understanding China's economic reform [J]. 2002(6):3–13.

Chapter 14
Study of Regional Efficiency in China: Perspectives of FDI and Green Development

Yang Li, Chao-Ling Guo, Xiaoying Guo and Yu-Hsuan Liao

1 Introduction

Since the launch of the economic reform in 1978, China has, on average, experienced a 10% economic growth rate, which attracts many scholars' attention (Sun et al. 2002; Hsiao and Shen 2003; Wijeweera et al. 2010). Many studies found that foreign direct investment (FDI) has contributed positively to China's economic growth. However, pollution haven hypothesis suggests that FDI might result in environmental deterioration. The Blacksmiths Institute (2007) indicated that two of the top ten polluted cities of the world are located in China. This may imply that in order to pursue economic development, China, like other transitional and less developing countries, has excessively exploited its natural resources, which has resulted in environmental disasters. In addition, the United Nations Commission on Sustainable Development suggests that sustainable development should consist of four dimensions: economic, environmental, social, and institutional. Because regions in a country should establish a similar institutional framework, we evaluate

Xiaoying Guo thanks the Ministry of Education in China (14JZD020) for financial support.

Y. Li (✉)
Newhuadu Business School, Minjiang University, Fuzhou, China
e-mail: isu.yangli@nbs.edu.cn

C.-L. Guo
Department of Accounting, Soochow University, Suzhou, Taiwan

X. Guo
International Economics and Trade, Tianjin University of Commerce, Tianjin, China

Y.-H. Liao
Institute of Business and Management, National University of Kaohsiung,
Kaohsiung, Taiwan

289

the regional sustainable development of China from the perspectives of economic, environmental, and social dimensions.

In the initial stage of its reforms, China faced serious insufficiency of capital and exhibited technology lags. In an effort to accelerate the pace of industrialization based on FDI, China opened up 14 coastal cities and established four special economic zones and three major economic regions in order to promote national efficiency and productivity (Li and Chen 2010). According to the 2010 World Investment Report published by United Nations Conference on Trade and Development (UNCTAD), FDI inflow into China hit US$95 billion in 2009, making China the second largest host of FDI in the world only behind the U.S.

Sun et al. (2002) and Hsiao and Shen (2003) found that FDI has contributed positively to China's economic growth. Although FDI may benefit the host country's economic development, the pollution haven hypothesis suggests that foreign investment might result in environmental deterioration, especially in transitional and less developing countries. Developing countries in general have laxer environmental regulations, which attract pollution intensive foreign capital seeking a "pollution haven" to avoid paying costly expenditures domestically (He 2006). Lucas et al. (1992) and Birdsall and Wheeler (1993) indicated that the pollution intensity in developing countries reach its peak when OECD countries formulate strict environmental regulations, which is consistent with the pollution haven hypothesis. A report by the Blacksmiths Institute (2007) showed that Linfen of Shanxi and Tianying of Anhui in China are two of the top ten polluted cities in the world. Hence, a fairly evaluation of China's regional developments should not only include FDI, but also incorporate the environmental dimension.

China's FDI policy has a strong effect on the location choice of FDI, as the policy is mainly concentrated in the eastern coastal regions. As a result, the eastern coastal area regions has been the top choice for FDI after the reforms and opening up policy. According to the department of Foreign Investment Administration, Ministry of Commerce of the People's Republic of China, the 11 eastern coast provinces received 80% of total FDI inflow, whereas 12 provinces in the western regions only accounted for less than 5%. As time goes by, due to the imbalanced regional economic developments, the gaps in incomes and unemployment rates widened among different areas. In addition, as economic development grows, the price level starts to increase the living standards of people in lower-developed areas, making it more serious than those in higher-developed areas (Groot et al. 2004). Facing such unbalanced development, Chinese authorities have devoted a lot of money and effort to promote the western regions to foreign investors. Furthermore, China established the State Council Leading Group on Western Development to implement the Great Western Development.

Previous literature only focused on economic and/or environmental dimensions to evaluate regional development in China, but the United Nations Commission on Sustainable Development indicates that sustainable development should include economic, environmental, social, and institutional dimensions. Because regions in a country should establish a similar institutional framework, this study analyzes regional sustainable development of China from the perspectives of economic, environmental, and social dimensions. In addition, Crespo and Fontoura (2007) claimed that the FDI spillover effect is usually determined by the absorptive capacity of local corporations and the technology gap between local and foreign firms. Buckley et al. (2002) argued that FDI from oversea Chinese regions (Hong Kong, Macau, and Taiwan) are mainly motivated by resource seeking, while non-overseas Chinese regions are more market-oriented. Hence, we also investigate the effect of the origins of FDI on regional sustainable development in China.

This study is organized as follows. Sections 2 and 3 provide the research hypotheses and methodology, respectively. Section 4 consists of data sources, variable description, empirical results, and discussions. Section 5 concludes this study.

2   Hypotheses

FDI not only brings capital and promotes employment directly to host countries, but also indirectly creates productivity spillovers, which embody the fact that MNEs (multinational enterprises) own technology and are interpreted in a broad sense to include products, processes, distribution technology, and as management and marketing skills, which can be transferred to domestic firms and thereby raise their productivity level. Many countries, especially transition economies and developing countries, adopt preferential policies in order to attract foreign investors and thus gain spillover effects of FDI (Blomström and Kokko 1996; Sinani and Meyer 2004).

Spillovers may occur in several ways. First, demonstration effects allow local firms to learn by observing multinational enterprises (MNCs) operating at a higher level of technology. Second, local employees trained by MNCs may move to jobs in domestic firms, taking with them their upgraded human capital. Third, spillovers from backward and forward linkages occur through business transactions between foreign affiliates and both domestic suppliers and their customers (Sinani and Meyer 2004). However, some studies show that FDI may not contribute positively to host countries due to market-stealing and skill-stealing effects (Haddad and Harrison 1993; Aitken and Harrison 1999). The market-stealing effect means that FDI may draw demand away from local firms and force them to cut production. The skill-stealing effect means that FDI might attract the best workers away from local firms, leaving them with less-skilled workers.

The spillover, however, is not automatic and requires the recipient enterprise to have the capacity to absorb and adopt such technology (what technology? This is the first mention). Crespo and Fontoura (2007) stated that the spillover effect of FDI is usually determined by the absorptive capacity of the local firms and the technology gap between local companies and multinational enterprises. Lapan and Bardhan (1973) pointed out that an enterprise needs to have a certain level of absorptive capacity in order to benefit from the technologies developed by other enterprises. The contribution of the spillover effect on the technology or productivity of enterprises in the host country depends on the technological absorptive capacity of local enterprises. When the absorptive capacity of the host country is strong, it can benefit more from the spillover effect or make the spillover effect more pronounced (Hsu and Chuang 2014; Sánchez-Selleroet et al. 2014; Zhang et al. 2010).

Since the beginning of its reforms China has attracted FDI in order to speed up industrialization and upgrade its industries. Many studies found that FDI is positively related to the economic growth of China (Chen et al. 1995; Wei and Liu 2001; Sun et al. 2002; Hsiao and Shen 2003; Blonigen 2005). Although FDI has contributed significantly to China's economic growth, a series of reforms and preferential policies have strong area tendency, resulting in unharmonious regional development. The economic development of China started from south to north and then from east to west. The earlier-developed regions enjoyed higher economic growths and have experienced better infrastructures and absorptive capacities. Hence, the spillover effects are uneven across regions of China.

The countries investing in China can be generally divided into two groups: the overseas Chinese regions (Hong Kong, Macau, and Taiwan) and the non-overseas Chinese regions (Buckley et al. 2002, 2007; Wang et al. 2009). Both types of FDI have different objectives and characteristics, as well as productivity advantages. Buckley et al. (2002) argued that the overseas Chinese regions (Hong Kong, Macau, and Taiwan) are mainly motivated by resource seeking, while the non-overseas Chinese regions are more market-oriented. FDI from the overseas Chinese regions do not view China as the main market and consider it as a production base to export products to overseas customers (Buckley et al. 2002; Sun et al. 2002; Wang et al. 2009). They are mainly labor-intensive and export-oriented (Buckley et al. 2007).

The main advantages of FDI from the non-overseas Chinese regions are intangible assets, such as advanced technology, branding, marketing network, management capability, etc. (Buckley et al. 2002; Buckley et al. 2007; Lin et al. 2009; Wang et al. 2009). Their investment motive is to access the market in China, so as to pursue market growth in the long term, and mainly invest in advanced and complex technology and capital-intensive industries.

All of this evidence imply that different origins of FDI may carry distinctive spillover effects to the local companies and thus have different impacts on various regional developments of China. Therefore, we present the first hypothesis.

H1 In China, the optimal demands for the origins of FDI defer in regions.

The economic development of a nation is sustained by mass consumption of natural resources, particularly the utilization of energy (Lu and Ma 2004). For regional development, energy is not only an important resource, but also a necessary investment (Lee and Chang 2007). Ang (2008) indicated that the economic development of a country is positively related to energy consumption.

Although energy consumption helps the development of a country, it also endangers environmental quality. The pollution haven hypothesis argues that foreign investment transfers polluted industries to recipient countries and deteriorates their environment. Lucas et al. (1992) and Birdsall and Wheeler (1993) found that the pollution intensity in developing countries reach its peak when Organization for

Economic Co-operation (OECD) countries formulate strict environmental regulations, which consistent with the pollution haven hypothesis. He (2006) studied the industrial SO_2 emissions of China's 29 provinces and indicated that when FDI stock increases 1%, industrial SO_2 emissions rise 0.098%.

Zeng and Zhao (2009) suggested that if environmental regulation is more stringent in the receiving country of FDI, the pollution haven may not occur. Grossman and Krueger (1995) analyzed the relationships between air quality and economic growth for 58 countries and found that the increasing emissions of sulfur dioxide accompany the economic growth of low-income level countries, while reductions of pollutants accompany economic growth of high-income level countries. Selden and Song (1994) noted that the relation between pollutant emissions per capita and per capita GDP exhibits an inverted-U shape. Groot et al. (2004) investigated 30 provinces of China for period 1982–1997 and categorized pollutants into three groups: waste water, waste gas, and solid waste. Their empirical results indicated that regional developments are imbalanced and that the relationships between pollutants and the level of income are distinctive. Due to the imbalanced development in China, energy consumption also varies across regions (Chontanawat et al. 2008). Hence, this study proposes the second hypothesis as follows.

H2 The optimal energy consumptions vary in different regions of China.

3 Methodology

Data Envelope Analysis (DEA) is essentially a linear programming technique that converts multi-outputs and multi-inputs into a scale measure of efficiency. It was initially proposed by Charnes et al. in 1978, based on the concept of technical efficiency (TE) by Farrell (1957). The efficiency of a decision making unit (DMU) is calculated by transforming inputs into outputs in relation to its peer group. However, conventional DEA treats production as a "black box" that transforms inputs into outputs (Färe and Grosskopf 2000). One way to open this black box is to divide the production process into sub-processes—for instance, some intermediate products are both the outputs of one sub-process and the inputs of another sub-process. Färe and Grosskopf (1996, 2000) and Färe et al. (2007) proposed several network models to decompose production processes. Although there exists some mathematical relationship between sub-processes, they only offer overall efficiency while lacking the efficiencies of the sub-processes. Fukuyama and Webber (2010) used a slacks-based inefficiency measure of a two-stage network model to estimate the performance of Japanese banks.

Seiford and Zhu (1999) decomposed the bank production process into two stages: profitability and marketability. The first stage measures a bank's ability to generate revenue and profitability from labor, assets, and capital stock, while the second stage evaluates a bank's performance in the stock market in terms of the revenue and profitability it generates. Decomposition of the production process is useful for identifying the sources of inefficiencies, but the efficiencies of the first stage, the second stage, and the whole production process are evaluated by three independent DEA models. In other words, this approach treats the whole production process and the sub-processes as independent, while not dealing with the potential conflicts between the two stages arising from intermediate measures, which are the first-stage inputs and the second-stage outputs (Chen et al. 2010).

Kao and Hwang (2008) proposed a relational two-stage DEA model to take the serial relation of two sub-processes into account when calculating efficiencies. Assume that there are H DMUs, where DMU h employs N inputs $\underset{\sim h}{x} = (x_{1h}, \ldots, x_{Nh})$ to produce D outputs $\underset{\sim h}{q} = (q_{1h}, \ldots, q_{Dh})$ in the first stage. These D outputs become inputs in the second stage to generate M outputs $\underset{\sim h}{y} = (y_{1h}, \ldots, y_{Mh})$. Define the efficiencies of the first-stage θ_h^1 and those of the second-stage θ_h^2 to be:

$$\theta_h^1 = \frac{\sum_{d=1}^{D} \phi_d q_{dh}}{\sum_{n=1}^{N} v_n x_{nh}} \tag{1}$$

$$\theta_h^2 = \frac{\sum_{n=1}^{M} u_m y_{mh}}{\sum_{d=1}^{D} \tilde{\phi}_d q_{dh}}, \tag{2}$$

where v_n, u_m, ϕ_d, and $\tilde{\phi}_d$ are unknown non-negative weights. Kao and Hwang (2008) set both ϕ_d and $\tilde{\phi}_d$ to be equal. The output-oriented overall efficiency θ_h, defined as the product of θ_h^1 and θ_h^2, can then be solved by the following model:

$$\underset{\substack{u_1, \ldots, u_M, v_1, \ldots, v_N \\ \phi_1, \ldots, \phi_D}}{\text{Min}} \quad \sum_{n=1}^{N} v_n x_{nh} \tag{3}$$

$$\text{s.t.} \quad \sum_{n=1}^{M} u_m y_{mh} = 1$$

$$\sum_{d=1}^{D} \phi_d q_{dj} - \sum_{n=1}^{N} v_n x_{nj} \leq 0, \quad j = 1, 2, \ldots, H$$

$$\sum_{n=1}^{M} u_m y_{mj} - \sum_{d=1}^{D} \phi_d q_{dj} \leq 0, \quad j = 1, 2, \ldots, H$$

$$\phi_d \geq 0, d = 1, \ldots, D; \quad v_n \geq 0, n = 1, \ldots, N; u_m \geq 0, m = 1, \ldots, M$$

The optimal weights $(u_1^*, \ldots, u_M^*, v_1^*, \ldots, v_N^*, \phi_1^*, \ldots, \phi_D^*)$ obtained from Eq. (3) can be used to construct the efficiencies θ_h^1 and θ_h^2 through Eqs. (1) and (2), respectively. The reciprocal of the optimal objective value is the overall efficiency θ_h, which is the product of θ_h^1 and θ_h^2 i.e., $\theta_h = \theta_h^1 \times \theta_h^2$.

The dual form of model (3) is:

$$\underset{\substack{\alpha_h, \lambda_1, \ldots, \lambda_H \\ \pi_1, \ldots, \pi_H}}{\text{Max}} \quad \alpha_h \tag{4}$$

$$\text{s.t.} \sum_{j=1}^{H} \lambda_j x_{nj} \leq x_{nh}, \quad n = 1, 2, \ldots, N,$$

$$\sum_{j=1}^{H} \pi_j y_{mj} \geq \alpha_h y_{mh}, \quad m = 1, 2, \ldots, M,$$

$$\sum_{j=1}^{H} (\lambda_j - \pi_j) q_{dj} \geq 0, \quad d = 1, 2, \ldots, D,$$

$$\lambda_j, \pi_j \geq 0, \quad j = 1, 2, \ldots, H; \alpha_h \text{ is free.}$$

Here, the optimal solution α_h^* is the reciprocal of the overall efficiency θ_h, i.e., $\theta_h = 1/\alpha_h^*$. Note that if $\lambda_j = \pi_j$ for all j, then model (4) is identical to the CCR model.

Chen et al. (2010) showed that the above relational two-stage DEA model cannot project inefficient DMUs onto the DEA frontier. They thus created a set of new intermediate measures $\underset{\sim h}{\hat{q}} = (\hat{q}_{1h}, \cdots, \hat{q}_{Dh})$ for DMU h to be determined in order to constitute an efficient projection point under model (4). The constraint $\sum_{j=1}^{H} (\lambda_j - \pi_j) q_{dj} \geq 0$ is then separated into two new constraints:

$$\sum_{j=1}^{H} \lambda_j q_{dj} \geq \hat{q}_{dh}, d = 1, 2, \ldots, D, \tag{5}$$

$$\sum_{j=1}^{H} \pi_j q_{dj} \leq \hat{q}_{dh}, d = 1, 2, \ldots, D. \tag{6}$$

Equations (5) and (6) treat $\hat{q}_{dh}$ as outputs and inputs, respectively. Model (4) becomes:

$$\underset{\substack{\alpha_h, \lambda_1, \ldots, \lambda_H \\ \pi_1, \ldots, \pi_H, \hat{q}_{1h}, \ldots, \hat{q}_{Dh}}}{\text{Max}} \quad \alpha_h \tag{7}$$

$$\text{s.t.} \sum_{j=1}^{H} \lambda_j x_{nj} \le x_{nh}, \quad n = 1, 2, \ldots, N,$$

$$\sum_{j=1}^{H} \pi_j y_{mj} \ge \alpha_h y_{mh}, \quad m = 1, 2, \ldots, M,$$

$$\sum_{j=1}^{H} \lambda_j q_{dj} \ge \hat{q}_{dh}, \quad d = 1, 2, \ldots, D,$$

$$\sum_{j=1}^{H} \pi_j q_{dj} \le \hat{q}_{dh}, \quad d = 1, 2, \ldots, D,$$

$$\lambda_j, \pi_j \ge 0, \quad j = 1, 2, \ldots, H; \quad \hat{q}_{dh} \ge 0, d = 1, \ldots, D; \alpha_h \text{ is free.}$$

Note that model (4) and model (7) generate the same efficiency score (Chen et al. 2010). However, model (7) not only measures the overall efficiency by taking into account the serial relation of two sub-processes, but also provides the optimal intermediate measures $\underset{\sim h}{q} = (\hat{q}_{1h}, \ldots, \hat{q}_{Dh})$. In addition, these optimal intermediate measures offer guidelines to DMUs in how to adjust intermediate measures in order to reach the efficiency frontier.

Outputs sometimes can be classified into several groups according to their characteristics. For instance, GDP is a desirable output, while waste or emissions are ecologically undesirable. Different types of outputs should generally have different rates of adjustment to the frontier. Suppose that there are two types of desirable outputs, $\underset{\sim}{y} = (y_1, \ldots, y_M)$ and $\underset{\sim}{z} = (z_1, \ldots, z_E)$, and one type of undesirable outputs $\underset{\sim}{b} = (b_1, \ldots, b_R)$. Assume that all three types of outputs are equally important. Equation (7) can then be extended as:

$$\underset{\substack{\alpha_h, \beta_h, \gamma_h, \lambda_1, \ldots, \lambda_H \\ \pi_1, \ldots, \pi_H, \hat{q}_{1h}, \ldots, \hat{q}_{Dh}}}{\text{Max}} \quad \alpha_h - \beta_h + \gamma_h \tag{8}$$

$$s.t. \sum_{j=1}^{H} \lambda_j x_{nj} \le x_{nh}, \quad n = 1, 2, \ldots, N,$$

$$\sum_{j=1}^{H} \pi_j y_{mj} \ge \alpha_h y_{mh}, \quad m = 1, 2, \ldots, M,$$

$$\sum_{j=1}^{H} \pi_j b_{rj} = \beta_h b_{rh}, \quad r = 1, 2, \ldots, R,$$

$$\sum_{j=1}^{H} \pi_j z_{ej} \ge \gamma_h z_{kh}, \quad e = 1, 2, \ldots, E,$$

$$\sum_{j=1}^{H} \lambda_j q_{dj} \geq \hat{q}_{dh}, \quad d = 1, 2, \ldots, D$$

$$\sum_{j=1}^{H} \pi_j q_{dj} \geq \hat{q}_{dh}, \quad d = 1, 2, \ldots, D$$

$$\lambda_j, \pi_j \geq 0, \quad j = 1, 2, \ldots, H; \quad \hat{q}_{dh} \geq 0, d = 1, 2, \ldots, D.$$

As suggested by Färe and Grosskopf (1996) and Chung et al. (1997), we impose weak disposability in the undesirable outputs, represented by the equality sign in the undesirable output constraints. The other outputs and inputs satisfy strong disposability, characterized by an inequality sign in constraints.

4   Empirical Analysis

4.1   Data Sources and Input-Output Variables

The dataset, obtained from China Statistics Yearbook, consists of 30 regions (13 from eastern, 6 from middle, and 11 from eastern) in China for the period 2006–2009. We exclude Tibet, because of missing data. Since we have a four-year period of panel data, all nominal variables are deflated by the GDP deflator with 2005 as the base year.

This study decomposes the production process of China's provinces into two sequent sub-processes. The first sub-process measures the performance for how provinces magnetize production factors such as labor and capital, named the attractiveness stage, while the second sub-process evaluates the efficiency of development, consisting of economic, environmental, and social dimensions, named the sustainable development stage. Infrastructures are key factors to promote economic development. Regions with well-established infrastructures not only stimulate productivity, but also magnetize investment effectively. Li and Chen (2010) found that infrastructures offer a positive contribution to the efficiencies of the Pearl River, the Yangtze River Delta, and BoHai Rim regions. In addition, Zhan (1993) and Zhang and Felmingham (2002) argued that well-established infrastructures attract FDI. Hence, this study consists of three infrastructure variables as inputs in the first stage: local government expenditures in education, science and technology, medical and health care, and transportation (*GOV*); water supply (*Water*); and area of paved roads (*Road*).

Intermediate measures are the outputs in the first stage and the inputs in the second stage. We have five intermediate measures: number of employees (*Labor*), energy consumption (*Energy*), capital stock (*Capital*), FDI stock from Hong Kong, Macao, and Taiwan (*HMT*), and Other FDI stock (*OF*). The stocks of capital and two types of FDI are estimated by the following steps. First, we assume that the capital stock at time *t* is:

$$K_t = (1 - \gamma)K_{t-1} + I_t, \tag{9}$$

where K_t and I_t are the capital stock and gross capital formation at time t, respectively, and γ is the depreciation rate and assumed to be 5%. Second, the method proposed by Wu (2000) suggests the following formula to calculate the stock of the first period (K_1):

$$K_1 = \int_{-\infty}^{1} I_t \mathrm{d}t = \frac{I_0 e^{\theta}}{\theta}, \tag{10}$$

where $I_t = I_0 e^{\theta t}$. Finally, we estimate I_0 and θ by OLS (Wu 2000):

$$\ln I_t = \ln I_0 + \theta t + \varepsilon_t, \tag{11}$$

in order to obtain the estimate of K_1. Because of data limitations, we assume that the first period of capital stock is in 1982 and both types of FDI are in 1992.

We consider three types of outputs in the second stage: economic, environmental, and social dimensions. The economic dimension consists of GDP per capital (*GDPP*) and patents filed (*Patent*). All variables in the environmental dimension are undesirable, containing SO_2 emissions (*SO2*) and soot emissions (*Soot*). The social dimension includes employment rate (*EMP*), daily disposal capacity of sewage (*DDCS*), and the percentage of persons who graduated from a senior high school or higher level over the total population (*ECU*). The definition and descriptive statistics of all variables are presented in Tables 1 and 2, respectively.

4.2 Empirical Results

This study employs the mathematical programming software LINGO 11.0 to calculate the technical efficiencies of all three output dimensions and the optimal intermediate measures. Due to the imbalanced regional developments, the incomes and unemployment rates in the regions reveal considerable variations. In addition, China's FDI policy is mainly concentrated in the eastern coastal areas, which has attracted over 80% of total FDI inflow. Therefore, efficiencies and optimal intermediate measures among the eastern, middle, and western regions may have structural variations. Moreover, the global financial tsunami in 2008 severely impacted Chana as well as the rest of the world. Hence, there may exist structural changes after the financial tsunami in 2008.

Table 3 shows that the mean efficiencies of the economic dimension in the eastern region are higher than those in the western and middle regions over the study period. Both the environmental and the social dimensions exhibit the same

Table 1 Definitions of variables

Variable	Definition
Inputs	
GOV	Education, science and technology, medical and health care, and transportation expenditures over total expenditures (%)
Water	Water supply (million tons)
Road	Area of paved roads (million square meters)
Intermediates	
Labor	Number of employees (10,000 persons)
Capital	Capital stock funds (100 million yuan)
Energy	Energy consumption (million standard coal equivalent)
HMT	FDI stock from Hong Kong, Macao, and Taiwan (100 million yuan)
NHMT	Other FDI stock (100 million yuan)
Outputs	
GDPP	GDP per capita (yuan)
Patent	Number of patents filed (number)
SO2	SO_2 emissions (10,000 tons)
Soot	Soot emissions (10,000 tons)
EMP	Employment rate (%)
DDCS	Daily disposal capacity of sewage (per 10,000 cubic meters)
EDU	Percentage of persons who graduated from a senior high school or higher level over the total population (%)

pattern as the economic dimension. In addition, the western region outperforms the middle region in all dimensions over the study period. Although we find that the eastern region has the highest efficiency and the middle region has the lowest value, we cannot assert in these mean efficiencies that there do exist significant differences until some appropriate statistical methods are performed to test them. Hence, we employ a non-parametric test to examine whether or not the mean efficiencies are significantly different among these regions.

The results of the Kruskal Wallis test shown in Table 4 indicate that all dimensions are significant at the 5% level, except for the environmental dimension during the period 2008–2009 with a p-value of 0.129. These empirical results suggest that the mean efficiencies of different regions are notably different. Nevertheless, the factor region consists of three categories. The conclusion inferred from the Kruskal Wallis test can only be that these three mean efficiencies are not all equal. We thus go a step further and determine where the differences are among the mean efficiencies.

Table 5 contains pairwise comparisons among the eastern, middle, and western regions based on the Mann-Whitney U test (Wackerly et al. 2008). Results show that the mean efficiency of the eastern region is significantly larger than those of the middle and western regions at the 10% level of significance. Furthermore, the western region outperforms the middle region only in the economic dimension at

Table 2 Descriptive statistics

Variable	Mean	Std. Dev.	Minimum	Maximum
Inputs				
GOV	0.270	0.047	0.167	0.406
Water	169,866.04	164,144.38	15,641.00	993,218.00
Road	12,392.68	11,039.44	580.00	55,756.00
Intermediates				
Labor	403.60	232.71	43.20	1055.00
Capital	21,992.62	15,637.84	2413.63	76,832.23
Energy	10,511.19	6596.86	900.77	30,828.21
HMT	1001.41	1606.15	14.19	9588.18
NHMT	1394.02	1771.81	28.37	8299.53
Outputs				
GDPP	21,257.79	13,097.29	5,582.14	67,013.66
Patent	21,264.67	31,189.05	325.00	174,329.00
SO2	68.58	40.35	2.10	168.70
Soot	24.25	17.17	0.80	84.50
EMP	0.96	0.01	0.95	0.99
DDCS	361.89	310.46	13.50	1432.20
EDU	0.25	0.10	0.12	0.57

Note All nominal variables are deflated by the GDP deflator with 2005 as the base year

Table 3 Mean efficiencies of different regions for various periods

	Periods	East	Middle	West
Econ. Dim.	2006–07	0.80642	0.30015	0.49593
	2008–09	0.76428	0.29659	0.50342
Environ. Dim.	2006–07	0.80669	0.58075	0.65442
	2008–09	0.77589	0.60014	0.66451
Social Dim.	2006–07	0.94638	0.74939	0.80357
	2008–09	0.90094	0.72050	0.76566

Table 4 Kruskal Wallis tests of mean efficiencies for various regions

	Econ. Dim.		Environ. Dim.		Social Dim.	
	χ^2 [d.f]	*p*-value	χ^2 [d.f]	*p*-value	χ^2 [d.f]	*p*-value
2006–07	25.909^{***} [2]	< 0.001	8.192^{**} [2]	0.017	10.338^{***} [2]	0.006
2008–09	22.424^{***} [2]	< 0.001	4.090 [2]	0.129	8.277^{**} [2]	0.016

Note [*], [**], and [***] represent the 10, 5, and 1% levels of significance, respectively

Table 5 Mann-Whitney U tests of mean efficiencies for various regions

	East versus Middle		East versus West		Middle versus West	
	Z	p-value	Z	p-value	Z	p-value
Econ. Dim.						
2006–07	−4.537***	<0.001	−3.529***	<0.001	−2.595***	0.009
2008–09	−4.244***	<0.001	−3.143***	0.002	−2.451**	0.014
Environ. Dim.						
2006–07	−2.723***	0.006	−2.097***	0.036	−0.578***	0.563
Social Dim.						
2006–07	−3.355***	0.001	−1.918*	0.055	−0.958	0.338
2008–09	−2.579***	0.010	−2.205**	0.027	−0.727	0.467

Notes (1) *, **, and *** represent the 10, 5, and 1% levels of significance, respectively
(2) Since the Kruskal Walli Test for the period 2008–2009 is insignificant at the 10% level of significance, it is not necessary to perform the Mann-Whitney U test

the 5% level of significance, while the other two dimensions are insignificant at the 33% level of significance.

Table 6 presents the optimal intermediates. The results show that for all intermediates, the eastern region has the highest optimal estimates among the three regions and that the middle region has the second highest optimal values. Moreover, all optimal intermediates have increased after the financial tsunami except for labor in the eastern region. We further use non-parametric tests to investigate whether these optimal intermediates do exhibit significant differences among the three regions.

The Kruskal Wallis test results shown in the top part of Table 7 indicate that all optimal intermediates are significant at the 1% level, suggesting that the optimal intermediates of different regions are remarkably distinctive. Furthermore, the Mann-Whitney U test results at the bottom part of Table 7 suggest that during the study period, all optimal intermediates in the western region are significantly lower

Table 6 Mean of optimal intermediates for various regions

	Period	East	Middle	West
Labor	2006–07	504.4943	469.9397	240.1388
	2008–09	501.0712	494.1548	243.0013
Energy	2006–07	10,610.6086	9,489.1526	5,846.4162
	2008–09	11,129.2505	9,950.8114	6,340.7490
Capital	2006–07	25,939.0545	22,091.3891	11,181.0264
	2008–09	34,530.8578	27,961.2297	14,704.3836
HMT	2006–07	1,736.9962	1,176.1267	500.2681
	2008–09	1,795.4678	1,423.8260	569.7545
NHMT	2006–07	2,725.9184	2,285.7091	963.4675
	2008–09	3,634.1349	2,552.9975	1,218.7948

Table 7 Non-parametric tests of optimal intermediates for various regions

Kruskal Wallis test

	2006–07		2008–09	
	χ^2 [d.f]	p-value	χ^2 [d.f]	p-value
Labor	20.775[***] [2]	<0.001	21.386[***] [2]	<0.001
Energy	14.246[***] [2]	0.001	11.811[***] [2]	0.003
Capital	2.191[***] [2]	<0.001	21.634[***] [2]	<0.001
HMT	19.257[***] [2]	<0.001	21.901[***] [2]	<0.001
NHMT	19.927[***] [2]	<0.001	22.208[***] [2]	<0.001

Mann-Whitney U test

	East versus Middle		East versus West		Middle versus West	
	Z	p-value	Z	p-value	Z	p-value
Labor						
2006–07	−0.597	0.551	−3.952[***]	<0.001	−3.820[***]	<0.001
2008–09	−0.157	0.875	−3.890[***]	<0.001	−4.072[***]	<0.001
Energy						
2006–07	−0.471	0.638	−3.249[***]	0.001	−3.207[***]	0.001
2008–09	−0.220	0.826	−2.959[***]	0.003	−2.919[***]	0.004
Capital						
2006–07	−0.628	0.530	−3.952[***]	<0.001	−3.928[***]	<0.001
2008–09	−0.722	0.470	−3.993[***]	<0.001	−3.964[***]	<0.001
HMT						
2006–07	−0.722	0.470	−3.952[***]	<0.001	−3.388[***]	0.001
2008–09	−0.188	0.851	−4.304[***]	<0.001	−3.496[***]	<0.001
NHMT						
2006–07	−0.220	0.826	−3.952[***]	<0.001	−3.604[***]	<0.001
2008–09	−0.911	0.362	−4.407[***]	<0.001	−3.279[***]	0.001

Note [*], [**], and [***] represent the 10, 5, and 1% levels of significance, respectively

than those in the eastern and the middle regions at the 1% level, while they are insignificant between the eastern and the middle regions at the 47% level.

4.3 Discussion

In the beginning of its reforms, China proposed numerous policies to attract FDI in order to overcome insufficiency of capital and lags of technology. Many studies found that FDI contributed positively to China's economic growth, while some researchers proposed the pollution haven hypothesis, arguing that foreign investment might result in environmental deterioration. Hence, this study evaluates regional sustainable development of China from the perspectives of economic, environmental, and social dimensions.

The main objective of this study is to investigate how different origins of FDI influence the development of various regions in China. Table 8 shows that for all regions during the study period, the optimal values of capital from the overseas Chinese regions (Hong Kong, Macau, and Taiwan) are significantly lower than those from the non-overseas Chinese regions at the 5% level. In addition, the Kruskal Wallis test results exhibited at the top part of Table 7 disclose that during the study period, the optimal values of both types of FDI (*HMT* and *NHMT*) are notably different among three regions. These results support Hypothesis 1: *In China, the optimal demands for the origins of FDI defer in regions.*

Table 6 reveals not only that the optimal values of FDI from the overseas Chinese regions are lower than those from the non-overseas Chinese regions, but also that their gaps are wider after the global financial tsunami of 2008, especially in the eastern region. More precisely, the optimal values of *HMT* in the eastern region are almost the same between before and after the financial tsunami, while they increase about 32% for *NHMT*; for the middle and western regions, they are 21 and 13.8% respectively for *HMT*, and 11.69 and 26.48% respectively for *NHMT*. This suggests that the contribution of FDI from the non-overseas Chinese regions is higher than that from the overseas Chinese regions, especially in the east region after the financial tsunami in 2008. Furthermore, the adjustments of intermediates (optimal intermediates minus actual ones) shown in Table 9 reveal that all FDI should increase except FDI from the overseas Chinese regions in the east region after the financial tsunami in 2008. Hence, we may conclude that the eastern region

Table 8 Mann-Whitney U tests of optimal values for origins of FDI

	2006–07		2008–09	
	Z	p-value	Z	p-value
East	-2.855^{***}	0.004	-4.278^{***}	<0.001
Middle	-2.944^{***}	0.003	-2.309^{**}	0.021
West	-2.418^{**}	0.016	-2.723^{***}	0.006

Table 9 Adjustments of intermediates (optimal intermediates minus actual ones)

	Period	East	Middle	West
Labor	2006–07	−0.5326	31.5980	−1.5612
	2008–09	−30.0750	45.3548	−8.2941
Energy	2006–07	−1,745.8844	−1,126.5050	−724.2719
	2008–09	−2,405.0351	−2,206.5532	−1,402.4951
Capital	2006–07	−92.1423	4,193.7757	1,238.3056
	2008–09	−18.5381	1,788.3932	321.0125
HMT	2006–07	128.8827	695.8213	329.7275
	2008–09	−311.7412	744.5846	301.3701
NHMT	2006-07	327.4543	1,738.8292	750.3150
	2008-09	629.2893	1,820.6963	911.6569

should invite only FDI from non-overseas Chinese regions and that the better place of FDI from overseas Chinese regions is in the middle region.

The Kruskal Wallis test results presented at the top of Table 7 suggest that the optimal energy consumptions are significant at the 0.1% level; in other words, the optimal energy consumptions of different regions are truly diverse, supporting Hypothesis 2: *The optimal energy consumptions are different in various regions.* In addition, the Mann-Whitney U test results revealed at the bottom part of Table 7 suggest that the optimal energy consumption in the western region is significantly lower than those in the eastern and the middle regions at the 1% level, while they are insignificant between the eastern and the middle regions at the 63% level. Table 8 displays that the adjustments of energy consumptions are all negative, indicating that China should reduce energy consumption nationwide, especially in the eastern and middle regions.

The optimal intermediates have increased after the financial crisis in China except for labor in the eastern region. In addition, the optimal value of labor in the western region is almost the same between before and after the financial tsunami of 2008, and the optimal capital (local capital and both types of FDI) increases considerable from 2006–07 to 2008–09. These may suggest that the economic development of China should move forward more into capital intensive methods, especially in the eastern region.

5 Conclusions

Since the beginning of its reform, China has adopted a series of policies to attract FDI in order to accelerate industrialization. Although FDI has contributed significantly to the country's economic development, a series of reforms and preferential policies have tended towards certain areas, resulting in unbalanced regional development. Moreover, the pollution haven hypothesis argues that foreign investment might result in environmental deterioration of the recipient countries, especially in transitional and less developing countries. Therefore, this study has analyzed regional sustainable development of China from the perspectives of economic, environmental, and social dimensions.

The dataset, obtained from China Statistics Yearbook, consists of 30 regions of China for the period 2006–2009. Empirical results indicate that the optimal values for origins of FDI are different in these various regions. Similar phenomena also exist in the optimal energy consumptions. Other findings include that: (1) the eastern region should focus only on FDI from non-overseas Chinese regions; and (2) FDI from overseas Chinese regions is better invested in the middle region; (3) China should decrease energy consumptions nationwide, especially in the eastern and middle regions; and (4) the economic development of China should be moving forward to being more capital intensive, especially in the eastern region.

References

Aitken, B. J. and Harrison, A. E. (1999), "Do Domestic Firms Benefit from Direct Foreign Investment? Evidence from Venezuela," The American Economic Review, 89: 605–618.

Ang, J. B. (2008), "Economic Development, Pollutant Emissions and Energy Consumption in Malaysia," Journal of Policy Modeling, 30: 271–278.

Birdsall, N. and Wheeler, D. (1993), "Trade Policy and Industrial Pollution in Latin America: Where are the Pollution Havens?" Journal of Environment and Development, 2: 137–149.

Blacksmith Institution (2007), Blacksmith Institution Annual Report, Blacksmith Institute Press.

Blonigen, B. A. (2005), "A Review of the Empirical Literature on FDI Determinants," Atlantic Economic Journal, 33: 383–403.

Blomström, M. and Kokko, A. (1996), "Multinational Corporations and Spillovers," Journal of Economic Surveys, 12: 1–31.

Buckley, P. J. Clegg, J. and Wang, C. (2002), "The Impact of Inward FDI on the Performance of Chinese Manufacturing Firms," Journal of International Business Studies, 33: 637–655.

Buckley, P. J., Wang, C., and Clegg, J. (2007), "The Impact of Foreign Ownership, Local Ownership and Industry Characteristics on Spillover Benefits from Foreign Direct Investment in China," International business review, 16(2): 142–158.

Charnes, A., Cooper, W. W. and Rhodes, E. (1978), "Measuring the Efficiency of Decision Making Units," European Journal of Operational Research, 2: 429–444.

Chen, C., Chang, L. and Zhang, Y. (1995), "The Role of Foreign Direct Investment in China's post-1987 Economic Development," World Development, 23: 691–703.

Chen, Y., Cook, W. D. and Zhu, J. (2010), "Deriving the DEA Frontier for Two-stage Processes," European Journal of Operational Research, 202: 138–142.

Chontanawat, J., Hunt, L. C. and Pierse, R. (2008), "Does Energy Consumption Cause Economic Growth? Evidence from A Systematic Study of over 100 countries," Journal of Policy Modeling, 30: 209–220.

Chung, Y. H., Färe, R. and Grosskopf, S. (1997), "Productivity and Undesirable Outputs: A Directional Distance Function Approach," Journal of Environmental Management, 51: 229–240.

Crespo, N. and Fontoura, M. P. (2007), "Determinant Factors of FDI Spillovers - What Do We Really Know?," World Development, 35: 410–425.

Färe, R. and Grosskopf, S. (1996), "Productivity and Intermediate Products: A Frontier Approach," Economics Letters, 50: 65–70.

Färe, R., Grosskopf, S., 2000. Network DEA. Socio-Economic Planning Sciences 34, 35–49.

Färe, R., Grosskopf, S. and Whittaker, G. (2007), "Network DEA," in: Zhu, J., Cook, W.D. (Eds.), Modeling data irregularities and structural complexities in DEA, Springer: New York, 209–240.

Farrell, M. J. (1957), "The Measurement of Productive Efficiency," Journal of the Royal Statistical Society Series A (General), 120: 253–290.

Fukuyama, H., Weber, W.L. (2010), "A Slacks-based Inefficiency Measure for a Two-stage System with Bad Outputs," Omega, 38: 398–409.

Groot, H. L. F. de, Withagen, C. A. and Zhou, M. (2004), "Dynamics of China's Regional Development and Pollution: An Investigation into the Environmental Kuznets Curve," Environment and Development Economics, 9: 507–537.

Grossman, G. M. and Krueger, A. B. (1995), "Economic Growth and the Environment," Quarterly Journal of Economics, 110: 353–377.

Haddad, M. and Harrison, A. (1993), "Are there Positive Spillovers from Direct Foreign Investment? Evidence from Panel Data from Morocco," Journal of Development Economics, 42: 51–74.

He, J. (2006), "Pollution Haven Hypothesis and Environmental Impacts of Foreign Direct Investment: The Case of Industrial Emission of Sulfur Dioxide (SO2) in Chinese Provinces," Ecological Economics, 60: 228–245.

Hsiao, C. and Shen, Y. (2003), "Foreign Direct Investment and Economic Growth: The Importance of Institutions and Urbanization," Economic Development and Cultural Change, 51: 883.

Hsu, J., and Chuang, Y. P. (2014), "International Technology Spillovers and Innovation: Evidence from Taiwanese High-tech Firms," The Journal of International Trade and Economic Development, 23(3): 387–401.

Kao, C. and Hwang, S. N. (2008), "Efficiency Decomposition in Two-stage Data Envelopment Analysis: An Application to Non-life Insurance Companies in Taiwan," European Journal of Operational Research, 185: 418–429.

Lapan, H. and Bardhan, P. (1973), "Localized Technical Progress and Transfer of Technology and Economic Development," Journal of Economic Theory, 6(6): 585–595.

Lee, C. C. and Chang, C. P. (2007), "Energy Consumption and GDP Revisited: A Panel Analysis of Developed and Developing Countries," Energy Economics, 29: 1206–1223.

Li, Y. and Chen, S. Y. (2010), "The Impact of FDI on the Productivity of Chinese Economic Regions," Asia-Pacific Journal of Accounting &Economics, 17: 299–312.

Lin, P., Z. Liu and Y. Zhang (2009), "Do Chinese Domestic Firms Benefit from FDI Inflow? Evidence of Horizontal and Vertical Spillovers," China Economic Review, 20(4): 677–691.

Lu, W. and Ma, Y. (2004), "Image of Energy Consumption of Well off Society in China," Energy Conversion and Management, 45: 1357–1367.

Lucas, R. E. B., Wheeler, D. and Hettige, H. (1992), "Economic Development, Environmental Regulation and the International Migration of Toxic Industrial Pollution: 1960-1988," in: Low P. (Ed.) International Trade and the Environment, World Bank discussion paper, 159: 67–87.

Sánchez-Sellero, P., Rosell-Martínez, J., and García-Vázquez, J. M. (2014), "Spillovers from Foreign Direct Investment in Spanish Manufacturing Firms," Review of International Economics, 22(2): 342–351.

Seiford, L. M. and Zhu, J. (1999) 'Profitability and Marketability of the Top 55 U.S. Commercial Banks', Management Science 45: 1270–1288.

Selden, T. and Song, D. (1994), "Environmental Quality and Development: Is there A Kuznets Curve for Air Pollution Emissions?" Journal of Environmental Economics and management, 27: 147–162.

Sinani, E. and Meyer, K.E. (2004), "Spillovers of Technology Transfer from FDI: The Case of Estonia," Journal of Comparative Economics, 32: 445–466.

Sun, Q., Tong, W. and Yu, Q. (2002), "Determinants of Foreign Direct Investment across China," Journal of International Money and Finance, 21: 79–113.

Wackerly, D. D., Mendenhall III, W. and Scheaffer, R. L. (2008), Mathematical Statistics with Applications, Seventh Edition (CA: Thomson Learning).

Wang, C., J. Clegg and M. Kafouros (2009), "Country-of-origin effects of foreign direct investment," Management International Review, 49(2): 179–198.

Wei, Y. and Liu, X. (2001), Foreign Direct Investment in China: Determinants and Impact, Edward Elgar: Cheltenham.

Wijeweera, A., Villano, R. and Dollery, B. (2010), "Economic Growth and FDI Inflows, A Stochastic Frontier Analysis," The Journal of Developing Areas, 43: 143–158.

Wu, Y. (2000), "Measuring the Performance of Foreign Direct Investment: A Case Study of China," Economics Letters, 66: 143–150.

Zhan, X. J. (1993), "The Role of Foreign Direct Investment in Market-oriented Reforms and Economic Development: The Case of China," Transnational Corporations, 2: 121–148.

Zhang, Q. and Felmingham, B. (2002), "The Role of FDI, Exports and Spillover Effects in the Regional Development of China," Journal of Development Studies, 38: 157–178.

Zhang, Y., Li, H., Li, Y., and Zhou, L. A. (2010), "FDI Spillovers in an Emerging Market: The Role of Foreign Firms' Country Origin Diversity and Domestic Firms' Absorptive Capacity," Strategic Management Journal, 31(9): 969–989.

Zeng, D. Z. and Zhao, L. (2009), "Pollution Havens and Industrial Agglomeration," Journal of Environmental Economics, and Management, 58: 141–153.

Chapter 15
Emissions Cost and Value-Added Benefit of Exports in China: An Analysis Based on a Global Input-Output Model

Wencheng Zhang and Rui Wei

1 Introduction

China's exports have shifted to a fast lane since China's accession to the World Trade of Organization (WTO) in 2001 (Fig. 1), and its export share in the world increased from 4% in 2000 to 14% in 2009. As a result, China became the largest exporter of commodities in the world in 2009. In fact, exports have long been a powerful engine of China's economic growth since China adopted the reform and opening-up policy in 1978 (Chen and Feng 2000; Yu 1998). Large numbers of jobs are created in China by the export production particularly via transferring China's huge rural surplus labor to manufacturing sectors (Arto et al. 2014; Chen et al. 2012; Feenstra and Hong 2010).

Exports induce domestic production in China which generates various air pollutants as its by-product. While the production of exports creates substantial economic benefit for China, it may also generate a great deal of emissions. Many studies have examined emissions embodied in trade of China using input-output models. Earlier studies estimated greenhouse gas (GHG) emissions embodied in China's exports and imports based on single region input-output (SRIO) models (e.g., Chen and Zhang 2010; Li and Hewitt 2008; Lin and Sun 2010; Pan et al. 2008; Shui and Harriss 2006; Weber et al. 2008), in which national input-output tables of China or one of its trade partner was used. One of the major disadvantages for SRIO models is estimation bias of emissions embodied in imports due to missing information on production technology of imported goods. As availability of

W. Zhang (✉)
Nankai Institute of International Economics, Nankai University,
Tianjin 300071, China
e-mail: wenchengzhang86@163.com

R. Wei
Academy of Mathematics and Systems Science,
Chinese Academy of Sciences, Beijing 100190, China

© Springer Nature Singapore Pte Ltd. 2018
R. Pang et al. (eds.), *Energy, Environment and Transitional Green Growth in China*, https://doi.org/10.1007/978-981-10-7919-1_15

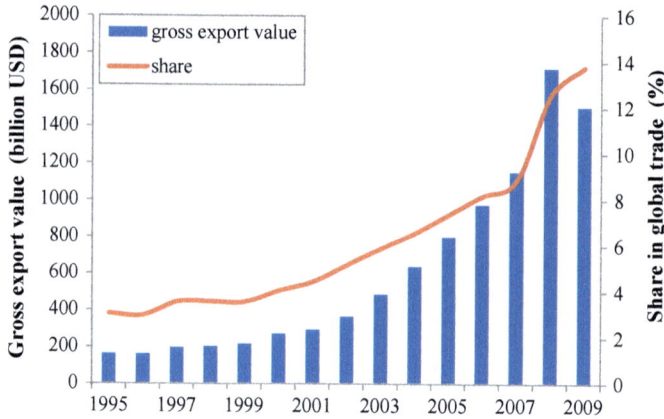

Fig. 1 China's exports and its share in the global trade during 1995–2009. *Note* Export data was expressed in constant 2002 US dollars

input-output data improved, more and more studies used Multi-Regional Input-Output (MRIO) models to examine emissions embodied in trade of China. On the one hand, national input-output tables and emissions data of both China and its major trade partners are widely used to reduce estimation bias of emissions embodied in imports of China (e.g., Guo et al. 2010; Li et al. 2014; Liu et al. 2010; Peters and Hertwich 2008; Tan et al. 2013). These models are also known as the emissions embodied in bilateral trade (EEBT) models. On the other hand, thanks to the development of international input-output databases (see Tukker and Dietzenbacher 2013 for an overview), full MRIO models including many countries and regions and covering the global economy were used to quantifying emissions embodied in trade and consumption of China (e.g., Arto et al. 2014; Davis and Caldeira 2010; Liu and Wang 2015; Peng et al. 2016; Peters et al. 2011; Su and Ang 2014; Wiebe et al. 2012).[1] MRIO analysis has been considered as a powerful method to assess environmental impacts of trade and consumption (Wiedmann et al. 2007; Wiedmann 2009). Besides the estimation of emissions embodied China's trade, some studies also explored factors determining the changes of embodied emissions in China using structural decomposition analysis (SDA), a widely used technique in the input-output literature (e.g., Su and Thomson. 2016; Xu et al. 2011; Yan and Yang 2010; Zhang 2012).

Although both economic benefit and environmental cost are two important factors for the sustainable growth of exports, few studies focused on analyzing exports of China from both economic and environmental perspectives. Arto et al. (2014), as an exception, analyzed both employment and GHG emissions generated

---

[1]Peters (2008) and Kanemoto et al. (2012) have discussed in detail the differences between an EEBT model and a full MRIO model applied to estimate emissions embodied in trade and consumption of a country.

in the production of exports in China based on a MRIO model. The present study examined environmental burden of exports in China combining the analysis on economic benefit in a consistent framework. In this paper, we use value-added exports as an indicator for measuring economic benefit of exports which is coined in the literature on value-added accounting of international trade (Daudin et al. 2011; Johnson and Noguera 2012; Koopman et al. 2014). While employment created by exports may be different across countries in terms of skill level and types, value-added exports in monetary unit is an arguably more comparable index among countries. In addition, we estimate emissions embodied in exports of China for 8 types of air pollutants as rough indicators (Giljum and Eisenmenger 2004; Muradian et al. 2002; Peng et al. 2016) for measuring environmental cost of exports. While most of previous studies focus on GHG emissions (e.g., Arto et al. 2014; Davis and Caldeira 2010; Peters et al. 2011; Su and Ang 2014; Wiebe et al. 2012)[2], the air pollutants analyzed in this paper include 3 types of GHG emissions (CO_2, CH_4, and N_2O) and 5 types of non-GHG air pollutants (NO_X, SO_X, CO, NMVOC, and NH_3).

We carried out the analysis in three steps. First, we estimate value-added exports and emissions embodied in exports for 8 types of air pollutants during 1995–2009 using a global input-output model. We compare value-added exports and emissions embodied in exports between China and the other major exporters. Second, we calculate the pollution intensity of value-added exports of China. that is, emissions generated in China for per unit of value-added benefit. We analyzed the trend of China's pollution intensities of value-added exports and carried out cross-country comparison. Thirdly, we identified factors determining the gaps in pollution intensities of value-added exports between China and the other major exporters using SDA technique.

2 Methodology

2.1 Measurement of Emissions and Value-Added Created by Exports

Suppose there are m countries and regions in the world, the basic identity of a global MRIO model can be written as

$$\begin{pmatrix} \mathbf{x}_1 \\ \mathbf{x}_2 \\ \vdots \\ \mathbf{x}_m \end{pmatrix} = \begin{pmatrix} \mathbf{A}_{11} & \mathbf{A}_{12} & \cdots & \mathbf{A}_{1m} \\ \mathbf{A}_{21} & \mathbf{A}_{22} & \cdots & \mathbf{A}_{2m} \\ \vdots & \vdots & \ddots & \vdots \\ \mathbf{A}_{m1} & \mathbf{A}_{m2} & \cdots & \mathbf{A}_{mm} \end{pmatrix} \begin{pmatrix} \mathbf{x}_1 \\ \mathbf{x}_2 \\ \vdots \\ \mathbf{x}_m \end{pmatrix} + \begin{pmatrix} \sum_i \mathbf{y}_{1i} \\ \sum_i \mathbf{y}_{2i} \\ \vdots \\ \sum_i \mathbf{y}_{mi} \end{pmatrix} \quad (1)$$

---

[2]See Wiedmann (2009) for an overviews on earlier studies.

where $\mathbf{x}_r$ is output vector of country r, $\sum_i \mathbf{y}_{ri}$ is vector of final products produced in country r in which $\mathbf{y}_{rr}$ are products used for domestic final demand and $\sum_{i \neq r} \mathbf{y}_{ri}$ are products exported to the other countries for their final demands. $\mathbf{A}_{sr} = \mathbf{Z}_{sr}(\hat{\mathbf{x}}_r)^{-1}$ is a coefficient matrix of inter-industry requirements for intermediate products, where $\mathbf{Z}_{sr}$ is a matrix of inter-industry deliveries of intermediates from country s to country r in the input-output table. $\hat{\mathbf{x}}_r$ denotes the diagonalization of vector $\mathbf{x}_r$ and $(\hat{\mathbf{x}}_r)^{-1}$ denotes the inverse of $\hat{\mathbf{x}}_r$. Trade of final products between country s and country r is reflected in vector $\mathbf{y}_{sr}$ and $\mathbf{y}_{rs}$, while trade of intermediate products is modeled in matrix $\mathbf{A}_{sr}$ $(s \neq r)$.[3]

A key exogenous variable in a input-output model is final demand. Using the MRIO model, gross output in country r, $\mathbf{x}_r$, can be partitioned to m parts according to final demands they support. Suppose $\mathbf{x}_{rs}$ denotes output induced by final demand, $\mathbf{y}_{rs}$, then $\mathbf{x}_r = \sum_s \mathbf{x}_{rs}$. $\mathbf{x}_{rs}$ can be calculated using the following operation

$$
\begin{pmatrix}
\mathbf{x}_{11} & \mathbf{x}_{12} & \cdots & \mathbf{x}_{1m} \\
\mathbf{x}_{21} & \mathbf{x}_{22} & \cdots & \mathbf{x}_{2m} \\
\vdots & \vdots & \ddots & \vdots \\
\mathbf{x}_{m1} & \mathbf{x}_{m1} & \cdots & \mathbf{x}_{mm}
\end{pmatrix}
=
\begin{pmatrix}
\mathbf{I} - \mathbf{A}_{11} & -\mathbf{A}_{12} & \cdots & -\mathbf{A}_{1m} \\
-\mathbf{A}_{21} & \mathbf{I} - \mathbf{A}_{22} & \cdots & -\mathbf{A}_{2m} \\
\vdots & \vdots & \ddots & \vdots \\
-\mathbf{A}_{m1} & -\mathbf{A}_{m2} & \cdots & \mathbf{I} - \mathbf{A}_{mm}
\end{pmatrix}^{-1}
$$
$$
\times
\begin{pmatrix}
\mathbf{y}_{11} & \mathbf{y}_{12} & \cdots & \mathbf{y}_{1m} \\
\mathbf{y}_{21} & \mathbf{y}_{22} & \cdots & \mathbf{y}_{2m} \\
\vdots & \vdots & \ddots & \vdots \\
\mathbf{y}_{m1} & \mathbf{y}_{m1} & \cdots & \mathbf{y}_{mm}
\end{pmatrix}
\tag{2}
$$

Following previous MRIO studies (e.g., Arto et al. 2014; Peng et al. 2016; Wiebe et al. 2012), *emissions embodied in exports* (EEE) are defined as

$$
EEE_r = \mathbf{f}_r' \sum_{s \neq r} \mathbf{x}_{rs}
\tag{3}
$$

where $\mathbf{f}_r$ is *direct* emissions intensity vector of country r, whose elements are emissions per unit of output in each sector. According to Eq. (3), EEE of a country r are emissions generated within country r in the production of exports satisfying final demand outside country r, which reflects the environmental burden of export production for country r.

MRIO model is also widely used in the literature on value-added accounting of international trade (e.g., Daudin et al. 2011; Johnson and Noguera 2012; Koopman et al. 2014). Besides emissions induced by exports, we also calculate the domestic value-added created by export production, as known as *value-added exports*

---

[3]For more detailed introduction on MRIO models, see Chap. 3 in Miller and Blair (2009). For similar applications of MRIO models to trade and emissions, see, e.g., Arto et al. (2014), Davis and Caldeira (2010), Peng et al. (2016) and Wiebe et al. (2012).

(VAE) in the value-added accounting literature. The VAE of country r can be calculated by

$$VAE_r = \mathbf{v}'_r \sum_{s \neq r} \mathbf{x}_{rs} \qquad (4)$$

where $\mathbf{v}_r$ is value-added ratio vector whose elements are ratios of value-added to gross output value in each sector. Comparing Eqs. (3) and (4), we can see that definitions of VAE and EEE are consistent in terms of system boundary.

To focus on the structural and technique effect of export production, we further define the *pollution intensity of value-added exports* (PIVE) as the ratio of EEE to VAE:

$$PIVE_r = \frac{EEE_r}{VAE_r} \qquad (5)$$

PIVE equals emissions generated to earn one unit of value-added from export, which can reflect the environmental efficiency of export production.

2.2 Decomposition of Differences in PIVE Across Countries

We use SDA to compare more deeply PIVE of China to those of the other major exporting countries. To begin with, we use a different expression of EEE and VAE. For country s, $\mathbf{x}_{is}$ can be calculated by the equation below

$$
\begin{pmatrix} \mathbf{x}_{1s} \\ \mathbf{x}_{2s} \\ \vdots \\ \mathbf{x}_{ms} \end{pmatrix} =
\begin{pmatrix}
\mathbf{A}_{11} & \mathbf{A}_{12} & \cdots & \mathbf{A}_{1m} \\
\mathbf{A}_{21} & \mathbf{A}_{22} & \cdots & \mathbf{A}_{2m} \\
\vdots & \vdots & \ddots & \vdots \\
\mathbf{A}_{m1} & \mathbf{A}_{m2} & \cdots & \mathbf{A}_{mm}
\end{pmatrix}
\begin{pmatrix} \mathbf{x}_{1s} \\ \mathbf{x}_{2s} \\ \vdots \\ \mathbf{x}_{ms} \end{pmatrix} +
\begin{pmatrix} \mathbf{y}_{1s} \\ \mathbf{y}_{2s} \\ \vdots \\ \mathbf{y}_{ms} \end{pmatrix} \qquad (6)
$$

Calculating $\mathbf{x}_{is}$ by rows in Eq. (6), output of country r induced by final demand of country s can be obtained by

$$\mathbf{x}_{rs} = \mathbf{L}_{rr}\left(\sum_{i \neq r} \mathbf{A}_{ri}\mathbf{x}_{is} + \mathbf{y}_{rs} \right) = \mathbf{L}_{rr}\mathbf{e}_{rs} \qquad (7)$$

where $\mathbf{L}_{rr} \equiv (\mathbf{I} - \mathbf{A}_{rr})^{-1}$, and $\mathbf{e}_{rs} \equiv \sum_{i \neq r} \mathbf{A}_{ri}\mathbf{x}_{is} + \mathbf{y}_{rs}$. $\mathbf{e}_{rs}$ are exports of country r which satisfies the final demand of country s. Total exports of country r satisfying foreign final demands are $\mathbf{e}_r = \sum_{s \neq r} \mathbf{e}_{rs}$.[4] Therefore, EEE and VAE of country r can be rewritten as

---

[4]Note $\mathbf{e}_r$ do not equal total exports of region r because they don't include the exported products which are re-imported after processing abroad to satisfy the final demand of region r itself.

$$EEE_r = \mathbf{f}'_r \mathbf{L}_{rr} \mathbf{e}_r \tag{8}$$

$$VAE_r = \mathbf{v}'_r \mathbf{L}_{rr} \mathbf{e}_r \tag{9}$$

PIVE of country r is rewritten as

$$PIVE_r = \frac{\mathbf{f}'_r \mathbf{L}_{rr} \mathbf{e}_r}{\mathbf{v}'_r \mathbf{L}_{rr} \mathbf{e}_r} = \frac{\mathbf{f}'_r \mathbf{L}_{rr} \mathbf{e}_r / (\mathbf{i}' \mathbf{e}_r)}{\mathbf{v}'_r \mathbf{L}_{rr} \mathbf{e}_r / (\mathbf{i}' \mathbf{e}_r)} = \frac{\mathbf{f}'_r \mathbf{L}_{rr} \mathbf{s}_r}{\mathbf{v}'_r \mathbf{L}_{rr} \mathbf{s}_r} \tag{10}$$

where $\mathbf{s}_r \equiv \mathbf{e}_r / (\mathbf{i}' \mathbf{e}_r)$, and $\mathbf{i}$ is a column summation vector. $\mathbf{s}_r$ indicates the product mix of exports of country r.

To compare PIVE across countries, we define a ratio, $R_{kh} \equiv PIVE_k / PIVE_h$. The larger ratio R_{kh} indicates the wider gap in PIVE between country k and country h. Based on SDA technique, R_{kh} can be decomposed into four components,

$$R_{kh} = \underbrace{\frac{\mathbf{f}'_k \mathbf{L}_{kk} \mathbf{s}_k / \mathbf{v}'_k \mathbf{L}_{kk} \mathbf{s}_k}{\mathbf{f}'_h \mathbf{L}_{kk} \mathbf{s}_k / \mathbf{v}'_k \mathbf{L}_{kk} \mathbf{s}_k}}_{R_f} \times \underbrace{\frac{\mathbf{f}'_h \mathbf{L}_{kk} \mathbf{s}_k / \mathbf{v}'_k \mathbf{L}_{kk} \mathbf{s}_k}{\mathbf{f}'_h \mathbf{L}_{kk} \mathbf{s}_k / \mathbf{v}'_h \mathbf{L}_{kk} \mathbf{s}_k}}_{R_v} \times \underbrace{\frac{\mathbf{f}'_h \mathbf{L}_{kk} \mathbf{s}_k / \mathbf{v}'_h \mathbf{L}_{kk} \mathbf{s}_k}{\mathbf{f}'_h \mathbf{L}_{hh} \mathbf{s}_k / \mathbf{v}'_h \mathbf{L}_{hh} \mathbf{s}_k}}_{R_L} \times \underbrace{\frac{\mathbf{f}'_h \mathbf{L}_{hh} \mathbf{s}_k / \mathbf{v}'_h \mathbf{L}_{hh} \mathbf{s}_k}{\mathbf{f}'_h \mathbf{L}_{hh} \mathbf{s}_h / \mathbf{v}'_h \mathbf{L}_{hh} \mathbf{s}_h}}_{R_s} \tag{11}$$

Components R_f, R_v, R_L and R_s can be used to analyze respective contribution from differences in direct emissions intensity, value-added ratio, input structure and export structure to the gap in PIVE between country k and country h. However, Eq. (11) is one polar form of decomposition, the other polar form of decomposition is

$$R_{kh} = \underbrace{\frac{\mathbf{f}'_k \mathbf{L}_{kk} \mathbf{s}_k / \mathbf{v}'_k \mathbf{L}_{kk} \mathbf{s}_k}{\mathbf{f}'_k \mathbf{L}_{kk} \mathbf{s}_h / \mathbf{v}'_k \mathbf{L}_{kk} \mathbf{s}_h}}_{\hat{R}_s} \times \underbrace{\frac{\mathbf{f}'_k \mathbf{L}_{kk} \mathbf{s}_h / \mathbf{v}'_k \mathbf{L}_{kk} \mathbf{s}_h}{\mathbf{f}'_k \mathbf{L}_{hh} \mathbf{s}_h / \mathbf{v}'_k \mathbf{L}_{hh} \mathbf{s}_h}}_{\hat{R}_L} \times \underbrace{\frac{\mathbf{f}'_k \mathbf{L}_{hh} \mathbf{s}_h / \mathbf{v}'_k \mathbf{L}_{hh} \mathbf{s}_h}{\mathbf{f}'_k \mathbf{L}_{hh} \mathbf{s}_h / \mathbf{v}'_h \mathbf{L}_{hh} \mathbf{s}_h}}_{\hat{R}_v} \times \underbrace{\frac{\mathbf{f}'_k \mathbf{L}_{hh} \mathbf{s}_h / \mathbf{v}'_h \mathbf{L}_{hh} \mathbf{s}_h}{\mathbf{f}'_h \mathbf{L}_{hh} \mathbf{s}_h / \mathbf{v}'_h \mathbf{L}_{hh} \mathbf{s}_h}}_{\hat{R}_f} \tag{12}$$

Following Xu and Dietzenbacher (2014), the geometric average of two polar forms of decomposition is used as the approximation of each component:

$$R_{kh} = \bar{R}_f \bar{R}_v \bar{R}_L \bar{R}_s = \sqrt{R_f \hat{R}_f} \times \sqrt{R_v \hat{R}_v} \times \sqrt{R_L \hat{R}_L} \times \sqrt{R_s \hat{R}_s} \tag{13}$$

To change product to summation, take the logarithm on two sides

$$\ln R_{kh} = \ln PIVE_k - \ln PIVE_h = \ln \bar{R}_f + \ln \bar{R}_v + \ln \bar{R}_L + \ln \bar{R}_s \tag{14}$$

Equation (14) is used to analyze factors determining the gap in PIVE between China and the other countries. For example, the contribution from differences in direct emissions intensity between countries k and h is estimated by $100 \times \ln \bar{R}_f / \ln R_{kh}$.

3 Data

Both input-output data and emissions data used in this paper are from World Input-Output Database (WIOD). [5] A comprehensive introduction of WIOD on its contents, data sources and construction methods can be found in Timmer et al. (2015). WIOD offers World Input-Output Table (WIOT) series for the years 1995–2009. The WIOT covers 1435 sectors and 41 countries and regions. Emissions accounts of the WIOT include 8 types of air pollutant emissions in each sector. To compare value-added and emissions intensities in different years, we need to express the value-added in constant prices. Therefore, WIOTs in current prices are converted to tables in the price of 2002 (the middle year of the study period) using double deflation method. Value-added in each sector is obtained by subtracting total intermediate input in constant price from gross output in constant prices.

4 Main Results

4.1 Value-Added and Emissions Generated by Export Production in China

As shown in the Table 1, VAE of China increased remarkably from 140.1 billion US dollars in 1995 to 1054.8 billion dollars in 2009. The proportion of VAE in Chinese GDP rose from 16.8 to 32.3% in this period, indicating that export production is of great importance for the income creation in China. However, there were also tremendous emissions generated by export production in China. For 8 types of pollutants, EEE increased by over 100% in China during 1995–2009. In particular, EEE of CO_2 and NO_X increased by 232 and 211%, respectively. The steep increase of EEE began in the year 2001 when China joined the WTO. The proportion of EEE in total emissions from production in China also rose up greatly. For example, the proportion of CO_2 EEE in total production emissions increased from 21.8% in 1995 to 31.7% in 2009. For the other pollutants, proportions of EEE in production emissions rose up by 5–9 percentage points. In 2009, EEE accounted 22–35% of total emissions from production in China. For CO_2, CO, and NMVOC, proportions of EEE were over or close to the proportion of VAE in China's GDP. Therefore, China has borne significant environmental burden for gaining the economic benefit from exports.

The environmental burden of exports in China looks more noteworthy when compared to those of the other countries. Table 2 shows that share of China's EEE in the global EEE (summation of EEE for all economies) was significantly greater than other major exporters, such as the US, Germany, Japan, etc. For instance,

---

[5]The database can be accessed at http://www.wiod.org/new_site/data.htm.

Table 1 Domestic value-added and emissions generated by production of exports in China

	Value-added	CO_2	CH_4	N_2O	NO_X	SO_X	CO	NMVOC	NH_3
	Billion US Dollar	Mt	10^4 tonnes	10^4 tonnes	10^4 tonnes	10^4 tonnes	10^4 tonnes	10^4 tonnes	10^4 tonnes
1995	140.1	593.2	778.1	21.8	185.5	475.4	924.7	247.6	71.7
	(16.8)	(21.8)	(18.7)	(14.2)	(20.8)	(21.7)	(25.8)	(24.7)	(13.2)
1997	169.4	577.1	714.3	18.9	185.0	433.7	869.9	246.9	59.9
	(16.9)	(20.9)	(17.2)	(12.5)	(19.6)	(20.7)	(23.0)	(21.9)	(11.2)
1999	184.4	538.6	618.3	17.9	180.3	372.2	1421.3	290.6	55.0
	(16.2)	(19.1)	(14.9)	(11.1)	(17.9)	(18.9)	(23.5)	(21.4)	(9.7)
2001	240.7	592.2	708.9	18.7	190.9	382.0	789.6	240.0	56.4
	(18.0)	(20.8)	(17.1)	(11.7)	(19.7)	(20.2)	(23.1)	(20.9)	(10.0)
2003	378.7	909.8	998.6	26.3	293.5	569.2	1086.4	332.9	81.1
	(23.0)	(25.5)	(21.8)	(15.3)	(24.4)	(25.1)	(28.6)	(25.9)	(13.4)
2005	590.7	1402.6	1362.8	36.1	377.8	705.0	2511.1	646.5	116.2
	(27.9)	(29.9)	(25.5)	(19.6)	(23.5)	(23.8)	(40.5)	(36.8)	(17.7)
2007	837.9	1758.0	1556.6	42.7	464.6	859.4	2789.2	559.3	140.5
	(30.0)	(31.8)	(26.6)	(21.8)	(25.0)	(24.9)	(43.2)	(31.6)	(20.1)
2009	1054.8	1971.2	1796.3	49.6	577.5	1119.9	2013.1	579.2	166.1
	(32.3)	(31.7)	(27.4)	(23.5)	(28.0)	(27.2)	(34.5)	(30.9)	(22.0)

Note Value-added is in price of year 2002. For value-added (second column), value in the brackets is proportion of value-added exports in Chinese GDP. For emissions (3rd–10th column), value in the brackets is proportion of emissions embodied in exports in total production emissions in China

China's share of CO_2 EEE reached 24.7% in 2007, while global shares of the US and Germany was only 6.9 and 4%, respectively. Similar results can be observed for the other pollutants. Meanwhile, the share of China's VAE in the global value-added exports was 10.4%, which was 3 percentage points lower than that of the US (13.4%) and 2 percentage points higher than that of Germany. Therefore, the gaps in EEE share between China and major developed exporters are much greater than their gaps in VAE share. Table 2 shows that China generated much more emissions than developed countries given the same amount of value-added obtained from exports.

Except for CO and NMVOC, Fig. 2. Further shows that China's shares of EEE were much higher than the share of VAE in every year during 1995–2009. Before 2000, China's share of VAE increased slightly while the shares of EEE for all pollutants decreased. However, emission-intensive growth path of exports in China was observed in the period 2000–2009 when both shares of VAE and EEE increased quickly.

Table 2 Shares of value-added exports and emissions embodied in exports for 41 economies in 2007 (%)

	Value-added	CO_2	CH_4	N_2O	NO_X	SO_X	CO	NMVOC	NH_3
US	13.4	6.9	5.4	6.4	7.0	5.5	4.9	2.8	5.6
China	10.4	24.7	21.7	15.7	16.2	32.1	13.9	10.9	19.5
Germany	8.4	4.0	0.9	2.7	2.0	0.8	0.6	1.4	2.8
Japan	7.9	3.8	0.1	0.3	4.6	2.3	0.6	1.0	0.2
UK	4.6	2.0	0.6	1.0	2.5	1.6	0.2	0.6	0.7
France	4.1	1.3	1.0	2.6	1.1	0.6	0.6	0.5	3.3
Italy	3.0	1.7	0.5	0.9	1.2	0.6	0.2	0.4	1.3
Canada	2.8	2.6	3.1	2.4	2.0	3.0	0.7	1.0	2.5
Taiwan	2.7	2.4	0.1	0.2	2.3	2.9	1.2	0.7	0.1
South Korea	2.5	2.7	0.2	0.3	1.8	1.2	1.2	3.0	0.1
Mexico	2.1	1.0	0.6	0.8	1.1	0.9	0.7	0.9	0.9
Netherlands	1.9	1.3	0.7	1.5	1.1	0.5	0.1	0.1	1.5
Spain	1.6	1.2	0.6	0.8	1.2	1.1	0.2	1.1	1.8
India	1.5	3.3	5.0	3.7	2.7	3.6	2.2	3.2	4.1
Russia	1.3	7.6	14.3	1.3	5.1	0.5	3.3	3.1	0.7
Belgium	1.2	0.9	0.3	0.7	0.5	0.3	0.2	0.1	0.7
Sweden	1.2	0.4	0.1	0.3	0.7	0.3	0.0	0.1	0.3
Ireland	1.0	0.2	0.4	0.5	0.1	0.1	0.0	0.0	0.8
Austria	1.0	0.4	0.1	0.2	0.2	0.0	0.1	0.1	0.3
Poland	1.0	1.4	0.8	1.2	1.0	1.1	0.2	0.3	1.0
Australia	0.8	1.3	2.8	0.9	2.6	2.3	4.6	1.4	2.1
Brazil	0.8	0.8	6.0	7.3	2.3	1.6	1.9	2.0	6.9
Indonesia	0.7	1.4	2.2	1.8	1.2	1.5	1.5	1.8	1.8
Denmark	0.6	1.0	0.2	0.6	4.8	1.8	0.1	0.1	0.6
Turkey	0.6	0.7	0.2	0.2	0.6	0.6	0.2	0.5	0.8
Finland	0.6	0.4	0.1	0.3	0.4	0.2	0.0	0.1	0.2
Czech	0.5	0.7	0.3	0.4	0.4	0.3	0.1	0.1	0.3
Hungary	0.4	0.3	0.2	0.5	0.3	0.1	0.1	0.2	0.4
Portugal	0.3	0.3	0.2	0.2	0.3	0.3	0.0	0.2	0.2
Slovak Rep.	0.3	0.3	0.1	0.3	0.2	0.1	0.1	0.1	0.1
Greece	0.2	0.1	0.1	0.1	0.1	0.3	0.0	0.0	0.1
Romania	0.1	0.4	0.4	0.3	0.3	0.7	0.1	0.1	0.3
Slovenia	0.1	0.1	0.0	0.0	0.1	0.0	0.0	0.0	0.1
Luxembourg	0.1	0.0	0.0	0.0	0.0	0.0	0.0	0.0	0.1
Bulgaria	0.1	0.4	0.2	0.2	0.3	1.6	0.1	0.1	0.2
Lithuania	0.1	0.1	0.1	0.4	0.1	0.1	0.0	0.0	0.2
Estonia	0.1	0.1	0.0	0.1	0.0	0.1	0.0	0.0	0.1
Latvia	0.0	0.0	0.0	0.0	0.1	0.0	0.0	0.0	0.1
Cyprus	0.0	0.0	0.0	0.0	0.0	0.0	0.0	0.0	0.0

(continued)

Table 2 (continued)

	Value-added	CO_2	CH_4	N_2O	NO_X	SO_X	CO	NMVOC	NH_3
Malta	0.0	0.0	0.0	0.0	0.0	0.0	0.0	0.0	0.0
RoW	20.1	21.9	30.5	42.7	31.7	29.7	59.9	62.1	37.2
World	100	100	100	100	100	100	100	100	100

Note The share of an economy is the percentage of its value-added exports (or emissions embodied in exports) in the global value-added exports (or global emissions embodied in exports)

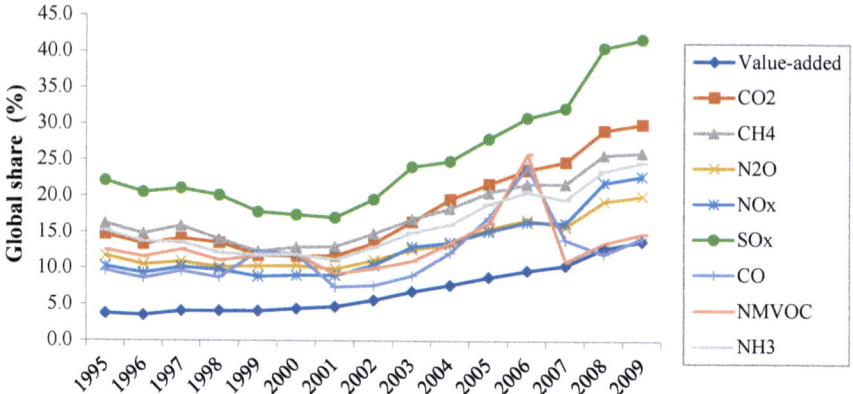

Fig. 2 Trend of China's shares of value-added and emissions embodied in exports during 1995–2009. *Note* The share of an economy is the percentage of its value-added exports (or emissions embodied in exports) in the global value-added exports (or global emissions embodied in exports)

4.2 Pollution Intensities of Value-Added Exports in China

As both the volume of EEE and their shares in total emissions from production in China increased significantly in the study period, environmental efficiency of export productions appears to be improving in China. As exhibited in Fig. 3, PIVE in China for most air pollutants decreased significantly and steadily during 1995–2009.[6] For example, the PIVE for CO_2, SO_X, and CO decreased 55.9, 68.7, and 71.1%, respectively. Therefore, given the same amount of value-added obtained from export production, emissions generated in China in the year 2009 were significantly less than those in 1995.

As a significant decrease of PIVE was achieved in China during 1995–2009, China's PIVE for all types of air pollutants is rather high compared to most countries, particularly developed countries. Figure 4 shows PIVE of CO_2 in China in 2007 is significantly higher than that in the other economies except Russia,

---

[6]Some high peaks of PIVE for CO and NMVOC have appeared in some year (1999, 2000, 2006). They are likely caused by outliers in emissions data.

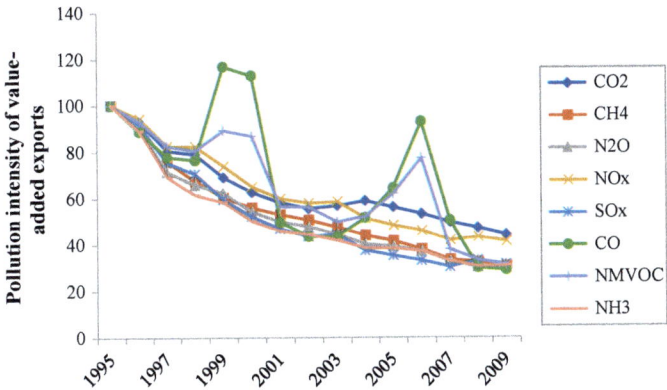

Fig. 3 Trend of pollution intensities of value-added exports in China during 1995–2009. *Note* Pollution intensities of export in 1995 are standardized to 100

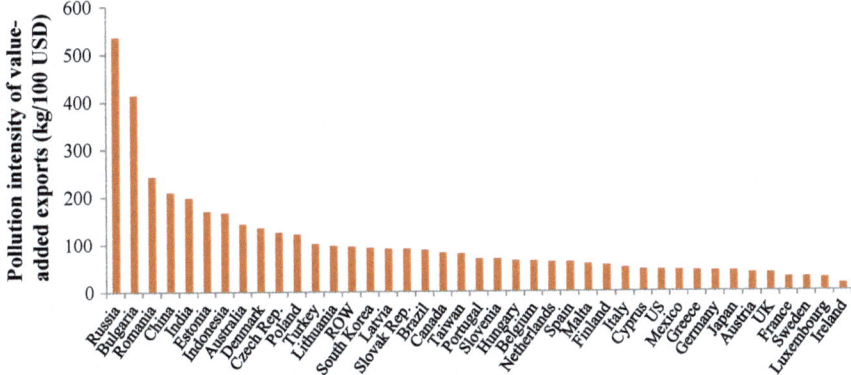

Fig. 4 Pollution intensities of value-added exports in 41 economies (for CO_2 in the year 2007)

Bulgaria and Romania. PIVE of CO_2 in China was 209.8 kg per hundred US dollars in 2007, which was six times larger than that in France, and four times larger than that in Japan. China's PIVE of the other pollutants is also greatly higher than those of South Korea and G7 countries (Table 3). Therefore, the room for improving environmental efficiency of export production in China is still very large.

4.3 Decomposition of Gaps in Pollution Intensities of Value-Added Exports Across Countries

Export has long been one of the most important engines of economic development in China, which contributes significantly to job and income creation. However, if

Table 3 Ratios of China's pollution intensity of value-added exports to those of selected economies in 2007

	CH_4	N_2O	NO_X	SO_X	CO	NMVOC	NH_3
Russia	0.2	1.4	0.4	7.4	0.5	0.4	3.6
India	0.6	0.6	0.9	1.3	0.9	0.5	0.7
Taiwan	72.9	24.4	1.8	2.9	3.0	4.2	69.3
South Korea	25.5	12.9	2.2	6.8	2.8	0.9	33.9
US	5.2	3.2	3.0	7.5	3.7	5.1	4.5
Japan	164.3	35.8	2.7	10.6	17.3	8.6	98.4
Canada	1.9	1.7	2.2	2.8	5.2	2.9	2.1
Germany	18.8	4.7	6.6	31.0	19.2	6.4	5.7
UK	15.7	7.0	2.9	9.1	24.8	8.6	12.5
France	8.9	2.4	5.6	22.0	9.1	8.9	2.4

Note Ratios in Table 2 are results of China's pollution intensity of value-added exports (PIVE) divided by the PIVE of selected economies

the PIVE is decreased, emissions cost from export can be reduced greatly while exports continue to play a major role in income creation in China. Last subsection showed that PIVE of China during 1995–2009 had declined significantly but were still much greater than those of major developed exporters. Therefore, there is still great potential for China to reduce further its PIVE. To realize such potential, we first need to know why China has higher PIVE than that of the other countries. According to Eq. (10), PIVE is determined by four factors: direct emissions intensity, value-added ratio, input structure and export structure. In this subsection, we analyze how the discrepancies in these four factors contribute to the gaps in PIVE between China and the other major economies by decomposing the PIVE ratio, R_{kl}, based on Eq. (14).

Table 4 shows PIVE of CO_2 in China was significantly greater than those of 10 selected economies.[7] Decomposition shows the gaps in PIVE are mainly caused by the differences in emissions intensity, input structure and value-added ratio between China and selected economies. However, differences in export structures narrowed the gaps in PIVE between China and selected economies except the US. For example, PIVE of China for CO_2 emissions was four times higher than the PIVE of Japan. The difference in direct emissions intensity between China and Japan contribute 63.5% to the gap in PIVE of two countries, while the difference in input structure contributes 27.4% to the gap. In addition, the difference in value-added ratios between two countries contributes 16.9% to the gap. On the contrary, the

---

[7]We select these 10 countries from two major considerations: first, they are all major exporting countries like China in the world in terms of value-added exports, and second, they have much lower PIVE than China and therefore may offer greater learning and cooperation opportunity for China to further reduce its PIVE in the future.

Table 4 Factors determining the gaps in pollution intensity of value-added exports between China and selected economies (for CO_2 in 2007)

	Gap (R_{kh}, k = China)	Contribution from the difference of (%)			
		Direct emission intensity	Value-added ratio	Input structure	Export structure
US	4.6	22.6	21.9	50.9	4.6
Germany	5.0	57.5	16.9	42.1	−16.5
Japan	5.0	63.5	16.3	27.4	−7.2
UK	5.5	48.0	18.5	35.6	−2.1
France	7.3	68.2	10.4	31.0	−9.6
Italy	4.2	73.2	3.9	33.4	−10.6
Canada	2.6	37.7	34.9	59.9	−32.6
South Korea	2.3	38.9	15.4	56.6	−10.9
Mexico	4.7	33.6	23.8	37.4	5.3
Brazil	2.4	69.8	17.4	30.6	−17.8

Note Gap in PIVE is reflected by ratios of China's pollution intensity of value-added exports (PIVE) value to the PIVE value of selected economies

difference in export structure between China and Japan contribute −7.2% to the gap, that is, narrow the gap in PIVE. In a word, Table 4 indicates that dirtier production technology (higher direct emissions intensity and dirtier input structure) in China compared to selected economies is the major cause of higher PIVE in China, whereas cleaner product mix of export in China narrows the PIVE gaps.

Contributions of the four factors to the PIVE gap are different for different country pair. For example, higher direct emissions intensity in China is the most important factor to explain the gaps in PIVE between China and Germany (or Japan/UK/France/Italy). However, more emissions-intensive input structure in China is the most important factor to explain the gap in PIVE between China and the US (or Canada/Korea). In addition, export structure in China is also more emissions intensive than that of US due to the higher share of service exports in the latter, contributing to the gap in PIVE between them. Similarly, the difference in export structure between China and Mexico also contribute positively to the gap in PIVE between two countries.

Figure 5 shows decomposition of gaps in PIVE between China and four most important exporters for the other air pollutants. Major conclusion from the results is similar to that from Table 4, that is, the higher PIVE of China compared to the other countries mainly results from dirtier production technology, while relatively cleaner export structure of China generally narrows these gaps. However, for some air pollutants, the difference in export structure also contributes positively to the gaps in PIVE between China and the US (or Japan).

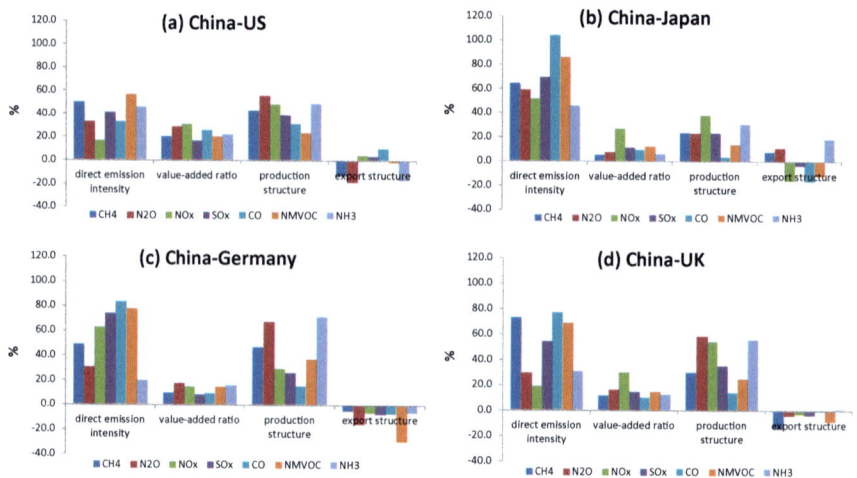

Fig. 5 Factors determining the gaps in pollution intensity of value-added exports between China and 4 major exporters (for the other pollutants in 2007)

5   Conclusion and Policy Implications

In the present paper, we estimated simultaneously value-added and 8 types of air pollutant emissions generated by China's export production. The results show that value-added exports in China increased significantly during 1995–2009. The proportion of value-added exports in Chinese GDP increased from 16.8 to 32.3% in this period. Meanwhile, substantial quantities of emissions were generated by export production in China. In the study period, CO_2 and NO_X emissions embodied in exports were tripled. For rest pollutants, emissions embodied in exports were also doubled. Sharp increase of emissions embodied in exports is observed after China joined the WTO in 2001. Proportion of emissions embodied in exports in total production emissions in China rose up greatly. In 2009, emissions embodied in exports accounted 22–35% of total production emissions in China.

We have compared the environmental burden of exports between China and the other major exporters in multiple aspects. China's share of value-added exports in the global value-added exports reached 10.4% in 2007 which was the second largest in the world. However, for most pollutants, the global share of emissions embodied in exports of China was significantly greater than shares of the other countries and much greater than the share of value-added exports. In the study period, pollution intensities of value-added exports in China declined significantly for all pollutants. But they were still much greater than those of developed countries and of some developing countries in 2009. We use structural decomposition technique to analyze the factors determining the gaps in PIVE between China and the other major exporting countries. Although there are some varieties in results for different air pollutants or different country pairs, the decomposition analysis shows that the

PIVE gaps are mainly caused by the differences in direct emissions intensity, input structure and value-added ratio between China and selected economies. On the contrary, differences in export structures generally narrowed the gaps in PIVE. In other words, the relatively higher PIVE of China mainly results from its dirtier technology reflected by the higher direct emissions intensity of production and more emissions-intensive input structure, while relatively cleaner product mix of export in China generally reduces the gaps in PIVE between China and the other major exporters.

It's of great importance for China to properly balance the economic benefit and environmental cost of export activities to realize sustainable development of trade and the whole economy. The social cost of environmental degradation has been overlooked or underestimated in China for a long time in process of pursuing the economic growth, which might have helped the boom of exports in China. In recent years, as the public pays increasing attention to environmental issues, also because of climbing pressure of carbon mitigation faced by Chinese government, exports of energy-intensive, pollution-intensive and resource-intensive goods are more strictly constrained by the Chinese government. However, the present study shows that the more prominent factor to blame is the relatively dirtier production technology in China.

Our results indicate that major effective measure for reducing emissions cost of export while make it continue to play an important role in income creation in China is to further decrease the pollution intensity of exports. To further reduce PIVE in China in the future, innovation and adoption of cleaner technology in the production of exports are critical as indicated in our decomposition analysis. Preferential policy can be arranged to promote innovation and adoption of clean technology in economic sectors. Some efforts (e.g., tax preference) have been made by Chinese government to promote the development and application of clean energy technology (in the field of new energy automobile, in particular). In addition, coal-dominated energy structure is one of the major causes for the high direct emission intensity for energy-relative emissions, such as CO_2, SO_X and NO_X, due to the fact that emissions factors of coal for these air pollutants are much greater than the other energy (Peters et al. 2006). There is still more than half of energy consumption in China coming from coal. Therefore, it's important for China to reduce emissions from export production by reducing the share of coal in the energy mix in the long run. Besides domestic efforts, our results also indicate that better results can be achieved by enlarging and deepening international cooperation. The gaps in PIVE between China and developed countries are remains significant. There are 'late-mover advantages' for China to improve its technology of production. Chinese government could stimulate international transfer of cleaner technology from developed countries to China. Facilitating and promoting international cooperation in low-carbon technology and project, like Clean Development Mechanism, can also help Chinese firms to reduce energy-related emissions.

Our decomposition also showed that difference in export structure generally reduced the gaps in PIVE. Since exports of some energy-intensive products, such as steel and metal products, are still large and the export share of service is relatively low, there is still much space for China to further clean up its export structure. Therefore, another solution for decoupling the economic benefit from environmental damage in China is to shift from exports of energy-intensive goods with relatively low value-added ratio to the exports of clean goods with high value-added ratio like high-tech products and services.

Acknowledgements We acknowledge the funding from China Postdoctoral Science Foundation project (No. 2016M591373). We would like to thank one anonymous referee whose comments and suggestions have greatly improved this paper. We also thank seminar participants for their helpful comments in the 24th International Input-Output Conference (July 2016, Seoul, Korea).

References

Arto, I., Rueda-Cantuche, J. M., Andreoni, V., Mongelli, I., Genty, A., (2014). The game of trading jobs for emissions. Energy policy 66: 517–525.

Chen, X., Cheng, L. K., Fung, K. C., Lau, L. J., Sung, Y. W., Zhu, K., Yang, C., Pei, J., Duan, Y., (2012). Domestic value added and employment generated by Chinese exports: A quantitative estimation. China Economic Review 23(4): 850–864.

Chen, B., Feng, Y., (2000). Determinants of economic growth in China: Private enterprise, education, and openness. China Economic Review 11(1): 1–15.

Chen, G. Q., Zhang, B., (2010). Greenhouse gas emissions in China 2007: inventory and input–output analysis. Energy Policy 38(10): 6180–6193.

Daudin, G., Rifflart, C., Schweisguth, D., (2011). Who produces for whom in the world economy? Canadian Journal of Economics 44(4): 1403–1437.

Davis, S. J., Caldeira, K., (2010). Consumption-based accounting of CO_2 emissions. Proceedings of the National Academy of Sciences of the United States of America 107(12): 5687–5692.

Feenstra, R. C., Hong, C., (2010). China's exports and employment. In: Feenstra, RC and Wei, SJ (ed), China's Growing Role in World Trade, University of Chicago Press, Chicago, p 167–199.

Giljum, S., Eisenmenger, N., (2004). North-South trade and the distribution of environmental goods and burdens: a biophysical perspective. The Journal of Environment & Development 13 (1): 73–100.

Guo, J., Zou, L. L., Wei, Y. M., (2010). Impact of inter-sectoral trade on national and global CO_2 emissions: an empirical analysis of China and US. Energy Policy 38(3): 1389–1397.

Johnson, R. C., Noguera, G., (2012). Accounting for intermediates: Production sharing and trade in value added. Journal of International Economics 86(2): 224–236.

Kanemoto, K., Lenzen, M., Peters, G. P., Moran, D. D., Geschke, A., (2012). Frameworks for comparing emissions associated with production, consumption, and international trade. Environmental science & technology 46(1): 172–179.

Koopman, R., Wang, Z., Wei, S. J., (2014). Tracing Value-Added and Double Counting in Gross Exports. The American Economic Review 104(2): 459–494.

Li, Y., Fu, J., Ma, Z. and Yang, B., (2014). Sources and flows of embodied CO_2 emissions in import and export trade of China. Chinese Geographical Science 24(2): 220–230.

Li, Y., Hewitt, C. N., (2008). The effect of trade between China and the UK on national and global carbon dioxide emissions. Energy Policy 36 (6): 1907–1914.

Lin, B., Sun, C., (2010). Evaluating carbon dioxide emissions in international trade of China. Energy Policy 38(1): 613–621.

Liu, X., Ishikawa, M., Wang, C., Dong, Y., Liu, W. (2010). Analyses of CO_2 emissions embodied in Japan–China trade. Energy Policy 38(3): 1510–1518.

Liu, Q., Wang, Q., (2015). Reexamine SO_2 emissions embodied in China's exports using multiregional input–output analysis. Ecological Economics 113: 39–50.

Miller, R. E., Blair, P. D. (2009). Input-output analysis: foundations and extensions. Cambridge University Press, New York.

Muradian, R., O'Connor, M., Martinez-Alier, J., (2002). Embodied pollution in trade: estimating the 'environmental load displacement' of industrialised countries. Ecological Economics 41(1): 51–67.

Pan, J., Phillips, J., Chen, Y., (2008). China's balance of emissions embodied in trade: approaches to measurement and allocating international responsibility. Oxford Review of Economic Policy 24(2): 354–376.

Peng, S., Zhang, W., Sun, C., (2016). 'Environmental load displacement' from the North to the South: A consumption-based perspective with a focus on China. Ecological Economics 128: 147–158.

Peters, G. P., (2008). From production-based to consumption-based national emission inventories. Ecological Economics 65(1): 13–23.

Peters, G. P., Hertwich, E. G., (2008), CO_2 embodied in international trade with implications for global climate policy, Environmental Science & Technology 42 (5): 1401–1407.

Peters, G.P., Weber, C., Liu, J., (2006). Construction of Chinese energy and emissions inventory. IndEcol Report 4/2006, Norwegian University of Science and Technology, Trondheim.

Peters, G. P., Minx, J. C., Weber, C. L., Edenhofer, O., (2011). Growth in emission transfers via international trade from 1990 to 2008. Proceedings of the National Academy of Sciences of the United States of America 108(21): 8903–8908.

Shui, B., Harriss, R. C., (2006). The role of CO_2 embodiment in US–China trade. Energy policy 34 (18): 4063–4068.

Su, B., Ang, B. W., (2014). Input–output analysis of CO_2 emissions embodied in trade: a multi-region model for China. Applied Energy 114: 377–384.

Su, B., Thomson, E., (2016). China's carbon emissions embodied in (normal and processing) exports and their driving forces, 2006–2012. Energy Economics 59: 414–422.

Tan, H., Sun, A., Lau, H., (2013). CO_2 embodiment in China–Australia trade: The drivers and implications. Energy Policy 61: 1212–1220.

Timmer, M. P., Dietzenbacher, E., Los, B., Stehrer, R., de Vries, G. J., (2015). An illustrated user guide to the World Input–Output Database: the case of global automotive production. Review of International Economics 23(3): 575–605.

Tukker, A., Dietzenbacher, E., (2013). Global multiregional input–output frameworks: An introduction and outlook. Economic Systems Research 25(1): 1–19.

Weber, C. L., Peters, G., Guan, D., Hubacek, K., (2008). The contribution of Chinese exports to climate change. Energy Policy 36(9): 3572–3577.

Wiebe, K. S., Bruckner, M., Giljum, S., Lutz, C., (2012). Calculating energy-related CO_2 emissions embodied in international trade using a global input–output model. Economic Systems Research 24(2): 113–139.

Wiedmann, T., Lenzen, M., Turner, K., Barrett, J., (2007). Examining the global environmental impact of regional consumption activities—Part 2: Review of input–output models for the assessment of environmental impacts embodied in trade. Ecological Economics 61(1): 15–26.

Wiedmann, T., (2009). A review of recent multi-region input–output models used for consumption-based emission and resource accounting. Ecological Economics 69(2): 211–222.

Xu, Y., Dietzenbacher, E., (2014). A structural decomposition analysis of the emissions embodied in trade. Ecological Economics 101: 10–20.

Xu, M., Li, R., Crittenden, J. C., Chen, Y., (2011). CO_2 emissions embodied in China's exports from 2002 to 2008: a structural decomposition analysis. Energy Policy 39(11): 7381–7388.

Yan, Y., Yang, L., (2010). China's foreign trade and climate change: a case study of CO_2 emissions. Energy policy 38(1): 350–356.

Yu, Q., (1998). Capital investment, international trade and economic growth in China: Evidence in the 1980–1990s. China Economic Review 9(1): 73–84.

Zhang, Y., (2012). Scale, technique and composition effects in trade-related carbon emissions in China. Environmental and Resource Economics 51(3): 371–389.

Printed by Printforce, the Netherlands